I0622748

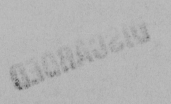

Minnesota Farmer-Laborism

The Third-Party Alternative

The University of Minnesota Press
gratefully acknowledges the support for its program
of the Andrew W. Mellon Foundation.
This book is one of those in whose financing
the Foundation's grant played a part.

Minnesota Farmer-Laborism

The Third-Party Alternative

by Millard L. Gieske

Department of Political Science
University of Minnesota

UNIVERSITY OF MINNESOTA PRESS □ MINNEAPOLIS

Library of Congress Cataloging in Publication Data

Gieske, Millard L.
    Minnesota farmer-laborism.

    Includes bibliographies and index.
    1. Democratic-Farmer-Labor Party.
2. Minnesota—Politics and government. I. Title.
JK2391.D4G53   39'.893   79-1115
ISBN 0-8166-0890-3

Preface

For the last century and three-quarters American politics has been dominated by two major parties. Each attracts a coalition of parallel and sometimes competing economic and social interests. The basic two-party appeal for popular support is wide, is directed toward the average or common American, is moderate and centrist. One party is more liberal, the other more conservative. Although their constituencies differ somewhat as to class, ethnicity, residence, religion, and region, even these factors are not hard and fast since both parties depend to a certain extent upon nearly all demographic classifications for some necessary support. Since 1860, the Democratic and Republican parties have monopolized political power, effectively excluding smaller parties from an active role in government. Conventional wisdom is that the Constitution and the single-member election district have pointed the United States in a two-party direction, at least to the point where custom has taken hold and Americans have come to prefer two parties, even those voters we label "Independents."

Occasionally, a third party will make a strong effort to dislodge a major party. Third parties tend to be more radical or extreme than centrist. They begin by appealing to individuals or interests that Republicans and Democrats are least effective in representing. Usually they advocate different ways of organizing society and owning property; they offer alternative methods of allocating social benefits and costs; or they propose redistribution of wealth, power, influence, and income. Some of the better-known attempts to achieve such ends were found in the Greenback, Populist, Progressive, Socialist, Communist, and Workers parties. A few minor parties have resisted changes advocated or accepted by the major parties; usually such parties are referred to as reactionary, or as parties of the right, like the States' Rights (1948) or American (1968) parties.

Third parties can play one of several general roles. They can choose to be small, closely knit units adhering to a strict ideological program with little hope of winning power through the electoral process. As such, they are social critics, parties without power. Some assume this role after abandoning an earlier vision to lead a revolution fueled by some mass unrest such as depression or other economic suffering. Another set of third parties see themselves as substitutes for an established major party which they expect to displace from power eventually. To them, third-party status is temporary. Highly critical of two-party programs, they usually propose sweeping reforms (or reactions), though they still avoid more stringent ideological controversy out of fear of undermining the competitive appeal they must make to two-party voters. This second group normally appears or enjoys its greatest growth during presidential election years: for example, 1880, 1892, 1912, 1924, 1948, 1968.

What conditions permit a third party, nationally or in an individual state, to effectively challenge a major party to the point of temporarily displacing it? What must a third party do, and what happens to it, when it seeks to displace a major party? Can a third party simultaneously remain strongly ideological in its demands and popularly centrist in its appeals? At what price does a third party cooperate or reach agreements with a major party?

We can gain some insight into these questions by studying Minnesota's Farmer-Labor movement, which lasted from 1918 to 1944. Farmer-Laborism had a regional and for a brief time even a national thrust; fundamentally it was midwestern, and that is where it enjoyed limited success. Its founders were anticapitalist and often socialist, though this obscures the equally important fact that campaign compromises forced it to propose reforms more often than fundamental changes in society. As some of its candidates were elected to local, state, or congressional office, it was held up as an example of what could be accomplished through the third-party route. Those who looked upon it as a cause to applaud and emulate conveniently overlooked whom Farmer-Laborism elected—usually they were moderate reformers and progressives—and why they succeeded.

Minnesota Farmer-Laborism was three things: an economic protest movement, an education association that transmitted ideas and alternative solutions to timeless social questions, and a political party. These constituent elements sometimes combined and at other times remained separate and independent. Most Farmer-Labor adherents shared the belief that the political and economic systems were unresponsive and malfunctioning and that the two major parties were either unwilling or incapable of reforming them. Their very first leaders, the architects who endowed the movement with institutional body and soul, had abandoned the Socialist party for the practical reason that socialism lacked popular appeal. That in itself was an act of compromise, a willingness to discard some of socialism's ideological baggage. A second major type of Farmer-Laborite was not socialist but was drawn to the movement by another common denominator: opposition to bigness, trusts, monopolies, the big city grain marketing system, concentrated power, railroads, millers. Farmer-Laborites believed that nothing up to their time seemed to long endure in expressing opposition to corporate interests and otherwise protecting small people, farmers, workers, individual merchants, and the general public from predatory exploitation.

Two major interests or sectors of the economy fed into Minnesota Farmer-Laborism. One was the midwest farmers' cooperative movement, including the Equity Cooperative Exchange, a farmers' grain marketing exchange created to counterbalance the power of the Minneapolis, Duluth, and Chicago commodity markets. The other major interest was the emerging organized labor movement in Minneapolis, St. Paul, and the Iron Range, particularly its liberal and sometimes socialist leaders who sought to break away from the more traditional and conservative ideas of Samuel Gompers's American Federation of Labor.

Farmer-Laborites, in other words, did not think identically, did not adhere to the same ideological principles, and they had different economic bases to which they were attached and toward which they felt a primary obligation. The movement began as a coalition, and its creators never were completely able to control or direct where it was going. Like the situation in the major parties they sought to push aside, there was a constant struggle between interests, factions, and men and women with rather divergent ideological dispositions.

The movement was split even more by the aftermath of the Russian Revolution. Some socialists wanted to continue their fellowship with the Communists; others rejected them for either practical or philosophical reasons (moderate agrarians and most of the movement's farmers were prepared to leave the new party if the Communists were permitted to stay in). From the beginning to the end of its life there was never-ending disagreement over these two attitudes toward the Communists and the American radical movement.

Farmer-Laborism was primarily a domestic economic protest movement which only incidentally, and accidentally, was forced to consider issues of foreign policy. The effect of the 1917-18 war on Farmer-Labor fortunes is, therefore, ironic. Reactionary and repressive wartime excesses turned many Scandinavian and German-Americans to the Farmer-Labor cause during its formative years. Belief in a common foreign policy—isolationism—united many otherwise cantankerous factions in the movement. It did, that is, until a divisive foreign policy problem in the 1930s once again set the Farmer-Labor left against the right over the Communist issue and over the left's urging of Farmer-Laborites to join the anti-Nazi Popular Front movement in Europe and the United States. Foreign policy also brought the party to the point of dissolution and merger in 1944.

Farmer-Laborism survived as long as it did, from 1918 to 1944, largely because in 1930 it experienced a rebirth brought on by the beginning of the Great Depression. Unemployment and farm foreclosures, low wages where work could be found, and low prices for those who stayed on their farms gave the movement new life. But even then the ideological and political gulf separating left and right was barely narrowed. Officeholding Farmer-Laborites resisted radicalization of their party and the movement, and many of them were prepared to sacrifice and destroy both rather than accommodate Communists and radicals. During this time the Democrats, usually with not much courage and even less skill, bided time while awaiting the opportunity to absorb or diminish the Farmer-Labor party. There was little wrong with the general Democratic strategy; the error was in the manner and slowness of its execution. The popular appeal of the New Deal, with the strong assist that came from Minnesota Democrats' access to national patronage, made the outcome nearly inevitable.

The author is indebted to a score or more of individuals who have generously lent assistance and encouragement in the planning, research, and production stages of this book. When necessary criticism has been offered, it has always been delivered in helpful, even genteel fashion. Special recognition must be given to Lucille Kane and many others at the Minnesota Historical Society who over the years have been so accommodating in making archival material readily available for examination. Appreciation is due also to the University of Minnesota for providing academic leave without which this project could not have been completed, and to Emilie M. Gieske for her assistance in typing the manuscript and otherwise tolerating many inconveniences during its preparation. It is also fitting to thank several friends and colleagues, including Professor William Hathaway who insisted that the project be completed and especially Carl H. Chrislock who for many years provided personal insight into the progressive mood as it touched Minnesota parties and personalities.

Millard L. Gieske

Minneapolis, Minnesota
January 4, 1979

Contents

Left to right: Farmer-Laborites Henry G. Teigan, Magnus Johnson, and A. C. Townley, ca. 1930.

Senator Henrik Shipstead (*left*) confers with Governor Floyd B. Olson, ca. 1931. Photo: St. Paul Dispatch.

Governor Olson talks about farm relief to thousands of farmers who have gathered at the state capitol, March 1933. Photo: George Luxton.

All photos courtesy Minnesota Historical Society.

Governor Elmer Benson and his wife, Frances, March 1937. Photo: St. Paul Dispatch.

Henry G. Teigan (*left*) campaigns for Congress in the third district, ca. 1937.

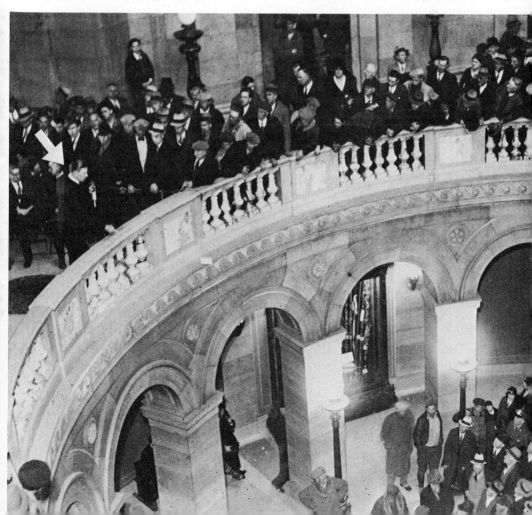

Above: Recruiting for the Farmer-Labor party, ca. 1930. *Below*: Farmer-Laborites hold a rally in the summer of 1935 to promote their plan for cheap rural electrification through cooperative power plants.

CHAPTER 1

The Roots of Farmer-Laborism

Farmer-Laborism was a political and economic movement that firmly believed workers and farmers should unite for the mutual advancement of both. Underlying this feeling was a common assumption about the system of economic distribution and social justice: The American dream of an equitable society could be realized only by adopting a fairer method of distributing income. Consequently, Farmer-Laborism attacked concentrated wealth, monopoly, capitalism, the power of the few over the many, and the prevailing American two-party system.

As a third-party movement, Farmer-Laborism grew gradually, evolving from two rather distinct ideological traditions. One was reformist, moderate, and had as political and economic objectives the overall improvement of existing institutions. The other was more sweeping in its alternatives to capitalism, and was usually more attracted to the notion of creating a third party. To these differences has to be added the sometimes clashing interests of workers and farmers.

THE POPULIST AND PROGRESSIVE TRADITION

Farmer-Laborism's ideas extended back to the Populist movement of the 1890s and appeared a generation later in the Midwest Progressive revolt. Populism and Progressivism provided Farmer-Laborism with its general faith in institutional reform. For the Progressives and later for many Farmer-Laborites, the objective was not so much to displace institutions as it was to reform and open them to popular influence.

"Popular government" and reforms like the referendum, initiative, recall, open primary, popular election of senators, trust busting, and governmental regulation of business and the economy fell considerably short of public ownership and socialism. Capitalism was an enemy that should be regulated but not so vile an evil that it had to be completely destroyed.

By 1918-20, these moderates were fighting for the legal right of labor to organize and bargain collectively, and the right of farmers to combine into producer cooperatives as an effective check upon large corporations and the free-market system. This was essentially the traditionalist's vision of political and economic pluralism working for a better society. It expressed faith in an incremental process of change. Other reforms were added from time to time: a merit system of civil service, governmental regulation of trade practices and competition, the income tax, child labor laws, pure food and drug acts.

THE SOCIALIST ALTERNATIVE

There was, however, another side to Farmer-Laborism. It provided the movement with a much more radical alternative, caused it to be controversial, and produced internal strain which never subsided during its nearly thirty-year lifespan. Although few Farmer-Labor radicals were violent revolutionaries, they did have a considerably different attitude about established institutions in organized society. Their vision of moral man beset by immoral social institutions largely dictated their task: to root out the evil institutions in order to cultivate those which were good.

The radical program was to substitute some form of socialism for capitalism, and cooperatives were to supersede corporations as industrial democracy and national planning displaced individual consumptive choice and the free- or monopoly-market system. Although a few Farmer-Laborites, if they did not advocate severe upheaval, were prepared to excuse violent acts as a natural consequence of farmer and worker exploitation, the majority of the left faction were evolutionary social democrats content to follow the slower road of plebiscary democratic socialism. These socialists often came from agrarian backgrounds, and as a result they frequently stressed more limited public ownership programs which readily served the particular interests of farmers without otherwise collectivizing the highly individualistic agricultural sector.

Consequently, the Farmer-Labor movement, from its beginning to its dissolution, developed in both Minnesota and North Dakota along two rather mutually exclusive tracks, one socialist, the other reformist.

Both were well established before the Russian upheaval of 1917, yet buffeted by it. This ideological split likewise divided the movement's two major constituent interests, farmers and workers. Farmer-Laborism remained, as a result, a loose coalition and never a union either of factions or of economic or political ideologies. That in time the movement would wither and dissolve was not at all surprising.

THE AGRARIAN PROTEST MOVEMENT

Continuing farm discontent was most responsible for the broad appeal of Farmer-Laborism. In Minnesota and North Dakota the farm economy served as the base industry around which much early industrialization, and consequently prosperity, developed. Farmers, however, had long believed that they had become victims of exploitation by commercial and corporate enterprises.

Special targets of farmer indignation were the large milling firms and the midwestern grain-marketing system, especially the Minneapolis Chamber of Commerce (the grain exchange) and the Duluth and Chicago Boards of Trade. A common agrarian belief was that these exchanges robbed farmers of fair prices for commodity crops and therefore forced them to accept an artificially low standard of living. Farmers blamed "commissionmen," or the buyers and sellers of various grains. These "speculators" farmers saw as vicious middlemen who robbed them by skimming off huge profits.

Spokesmen for farmers believed that two major policy approaches could improve this situation. One approach was federal and state regulation of railroad rates, warehouse storage charges, grain-trading practices, dockages, weighing, and anything that left farmers at the mercy of the railroad and grain "trusts." The second approach bypassed corporate and commission middlemen in one of two ways: by socializing banks, millers, elevators, (crop) insurance companies, terminal warehouses, railroads, or by creating the farmer-owned marketing corporation, the farmers' cooperative. Whereas the Nonpartisan League (NPL) preferred the first way of avoiding the middlemen, a kind of agriculturalists' "socialism for the other fellow," the Equity Cooperative Exchange (Equity) was a prime example of the farmer-owned marketing corporation.

The Equity Cooperative Exchange

Equity was important because it served as an early prototype of the Farmers Union Grain Terminal Association (GTA) and the Central Exchange (Cenex). Although Equity, too, favored some limited public ownership — a state-owned terminal elevator in North Dakota, for example, that would serve farmers and provide a "yardstick" method of checking private elevator rates — it was primarily interested in farmer cooperative enterprise and regulatory reform, not socialism. The NPL, by contrast, attracted more socialists and initially championed socialist enterprise.[1]

The Equity name first appeared in 1902 when the American Society of Equity was established in Indianapolis. Its objective, the "ever normal granary," was to use grain holding or storage as a means for obtaining higher, more stable commodity prices. Within the American Society of Equity a Grain Growers department was created, and in May 1908 the department established the autonomous Equity Cooperative Exchange (Equity), the first cooperative exchange in the United States. Equity soon united with a few small private grain-marketing companies which had attempted in 1907 to compete against the large "grain combine." In 1911 Equity incorporated under North Dakota law, and by August 1912 the first grain shipments arrived in Minneapolis for sale through the Equity terminal.[2]

Important politically for later Farmer-Laborism was the fact that Equity emerged almost simultaneously with the 1912 Bull Moose Progressive movement. While Equity and the cooperative movement developed a following among Minnesota and Dakota farmers, the third-party Bull Moosers in 1912 carried Minnesota for Theodore Roosevelt. The result was evidence not only of Roosevelt's personal popularity but of increased public dissatisfaction with the performance of Minnesota's two major parties. Progressives generally distrusted old party labels, and their leaders combined with reformers and Democrats to pass nonpartisan election laws, first in 1912 for state and local judges and elected city officials in St. Paul, Minneapolis, and Duluth, and then in 1913 for state legislative candidates. In such fashion the nonpartisan Minnesota legislature came into being, lasting fifty years, until 1973.

Meanwhile, Equity continued to expand as a grain-selling agency for farmers. It hired employees, paid fixed salaries to its officers, and operated as an economic — and political — competitor of the "grain combine." Equity stock shares paid 8-percent interest; any "surplus" earnings above this were returned as dividends to its farmer patrons in proportion to the amount each producer (i.e., farmer) shipped and sold through the Equity exchange. High profits, which the "grain trust" was suspected of creating through market price control, would thus eventually be channeled back to the producers who marketed through Equity.[3]

It was understandably easy for farmers, who had a keen sense of the injustice of their situation, to overlook larger economic and social causes which contributed to the plight of agriculture. A farm-to-city migration already was under way. Farm production tended to outrun demand. Mechanization and other technological changes were beginning to require greater capital outlays. Those who could afford such investment usually enjoyed greater earnings, improved working conditions, and the benefits of large-scale operation. But many others could ill-afford both capital investment and increased personal consumption or home improvements.

This brought many farmers to turn against the interests that served and, to their way of thinking, exploited them. Railroads, bankers, millers, monopolists, trusts, "Big Business" were all seen as joining in unfair competition against farmers, who as an unorganized group were no match for either a price-manipulated market or even a free-market economy. Farmers attacked commission firms and large millers like Van Dusen-Harrington, Heffelfinger, Pillsbury, Crosby, Washburn, Crocker. "The sacred 550" members on the Minneapolis Chamber of Commerce dominated the grain exchange market through their seventy-five firms which in turn, Equity claimed, were dominated by the large elevators and millers.[4] Indeed, malpractices that injured farmers could be documented: overcharges for impurity dockages, improper weighing, grain loss through vacuum clearing, sometimes high speculative profits for grain never even leaving an elevator, false supply reports to manipulate prices, high-interest loans, excessive storage fees.[5] Equity calculated farmers' economic losses in the millions.

It was inevitable that Equity and the Chamber of Commerce would be not only economic competitors but also bitter political adversaries. Attracted to the cooperative were the smaller commission independents, small millers, and reformers associated first with the Populists and then with the Progressives. Among the reformers were political mavericks like St. Paul lawyer James Manahan, the Equity legal counsel, a 1908 Minnesota Bryan Democrat who was elected as a Progressive congressman in 1912. From the Minnesota Progressive Republican League came Magnus Johnson, the future Farmer-Labor senator, and George Loftus, Equity's director-sales manager who with Manahan had challenged the Great Northern and James J. Hill interests in cases brought before the Interstate Commerce Commission involving Pullman rates, hay-moving rates, and express charges.[6] Loftus and Manahan had cooperated to help push a rate reform bill through the 1907 Minnesota legislature.[7]

When Loftus assumed direction of Equity in August 1912 he launched an aggressive campaign against the Minneapolis chamber and brought serious allegations of wrongdoing before the 1913 legislature. Both houses carried on committee investigations. The most spectacular was in the House where Manahan, just elected congressman-at-large, served as special committee counsel; the hearings were spiced with frequent clashes between Manahan and the chamber's executive secretary. As Manahan and Loftus levied charges against the chamber, accusing it of abusing farmers and small grain-marketing companies, the embattled interest attempted to discredit Equity and destroy its independent ability to market grain outside the regular buying and selling channels.[8]

The chamber's incorrigibility intensified farmers' distrust. This situation was politically and demographically important because agrarian grievances came at a time when the farm population in Minnesota was about to reach its highest level ever. Equity, however, gained little immediate advantage from the hearings, though continuing bad feelings invited exploitation by a more politically-oriented movement — like the soon-to-be-launched Nonpartisan League in North Dakota. Equity did retain, as Loftus hoped it would, the "economic freedom for the grain grower" to market his product through the cooperative system.[9] And in special congressional hearings Manahan attempted (unsuccessfully) to build farm bloc support for marketing legislation.[10]

Equity's impact in North Dakota did help prepare the way for later Nonpartisan League success. In 1912 and 1914 Equity led a constitutional referendum campaign establishing the right of the state to erect terminal warehouses for grain storage. With three of four North Dakota voters coming from rural areas, the proposal received 75-percent approval in the two elections. By February 1915 Equity joined with the otherwise independent North Dakota Society of Equity in convening the annual Equity state convention at Bismarck. St. Paul economic and commercial spokesmen delivered welcome news by pledging to help the cooperative arrange financial backing for the building of terminal storage facilities in St. Paul to compete with those in Minneapolis. However, Loftus failed to gain majority support in the North Dakota legislature, which refused to appropriate funds for the now constitutionally authorized elevators.[11]

Support for farmer protest came from several sources. The 1912 Progressive candidate for Minnesota governor, as publisher of *The Northwest Agriculturalist*, repeatedly flailed the grain monopoly and praised cooperative ventures like Equity.[12] Small grain processors like Lindeke Roller Mills used Equity's buying facilities. In August 1914 Equity was assured by St. Paul banks of financial backing to construct a large Mississippi River terminal for grain storage and shipping. And the November 1914 elections appeared to extend support for moderate protest when Democratic congressman Winfield S. Hammond was elected governor, the last Democratic gubernatorial candidate to win in the next forty years.

Equity and the farmers' political revolt were making steady if not spectacular progress. At Equity's November 1914 convention special trains carried hundreds of delegates to St. Paul, where advance circulars promised "the Dark Chamber methods of the [grain] combine will be exposed!" The mayor, outgoing Republican governor Adolph Eberhart, Senator Moses E. Clapp, and even the head of the St. Paul Association of Commerce addressed supporters of the new cooperative exchange.[13]

Equity's economic and political headway was more than just worrisome to the Minneapolis chamber, which in one instance resorted to coercive retaliation against a Minneapolis accounting firm for agreeing to audit Equity's books. When the young accountant, M. W. Thatcher, learned why his firm had dropped the unfinished account, he resigned in protest and continued to work for Equity,[14] beginning his long career in the farm cooperative movement which lasted until the 1960s; Thatcher eventually became an adviser to presidents and the best-known cooperative leader in the nation.

Whether out of growing sympathy for depressed conditions or increased recognition of developing farmer political sentiment, economic and policy leaders drew closer to this new farm movement. The 1915 Equity convention attracted the sympathy and attention of Wisconsin senator Robert La Follette and Minnesota congressman Charles Lindbergh. To the usual litany of Chamber of Commerce abuses Equity convention resolutions added criticism of the Railroad and Warehouse Commission for not seeking expanded regulatory powers, and Equity now showed an isolationist concern about foreign policy, attacking "preparedness" mentality which, it claimed, aided "the big business enterprises, and the jingoes who advocate enormous expenditures of the people's" taxes.[15]

Although the outbreak of European war did contribute to Equity's problems, it was not the basic source of Equity's financial instability. Nor was the cooperative's weakness the outgrowth of the obvious hostility of the grain combine and the Minneapolis Chamber of Commerce. Equity, in fact, had expanded quickly but not in a sound businesslike way. Thatcher, in a 1917 audit of the exchange, issued a

stern warning to its directors after discovering it had a working deficit of $125,000. He criticized employee working conditions, improp-
er accounting methods, low capitalization, overdrawn banking ac-
counts, poor internal communication, low morale, and generally un-
satisfactory management practices.[16] Popular with farmers, Equity
by July 1922 owned 80 elevators (including 52 in North Dakota and
26 in Minnesota), and managed 12 locally owned farmer elevators;[17]
nevertheless it was forced the same year into receivership.

More important than its demise was that Equity pioneered one significant path in the emerging Farmer-Labor trail. As an economic alternative, it served as forerunner of the GTA and the Central Exchange (Cenex). Pluralist in its approach, it gained support for the
cooperative movement among influential rural newspaper editors and
publishers, including men like future Republican governor (1925-30)
Theodore Christianson,[18] who found its more moderate program
sensible and appealing; and it helped make Farmer-Laborism appear
to be a legitimate form of reasonable protest. It was this Farmer-
Labor wing which not only moderated the originally more radical
NPL program but broadened its base of appeal during the 1920s and
later.

The Nonpartisan League

Where Equity relied upon primarily an economic weapon — the
farmer cooperative — and traditional regulatory control, the Nonpartisan League began as a political organization (but not a party) committed to significantly greater reliance upon programs of government action, especially public ownership. There was an unmistakable
difference in strategy and style between Equity and the NPL. Equity
men were petty bourgeois, rather at ease among progressive Republicans. By contrast, the men who started the NPL came directly from
the North Dakota Socialist party and retained enough of their socialist principles that they seemed radical in comparison with Republicans or Democrats. Yet this radicalism was more apparent than real.
The NPL appealed to farmers who prided themselves on their independence, their right to own property, and their small businesses.
And league leadership was demonstrably flexible and willing to
compromise socialist ideology since its immediate objective was to
gain and retain political power, which could not be done by too rigid
an application of socialist principle.

Although the extent of the NPL's socialism was unsettled, one
thing appears very certain. The success of the movement during its
first five years was due to the organizing ability of one man, Arthur

C. (A. C.) Townley, a political genius who through charismatic and demagogic appeal was most responsible for developing the NPL and then launching Farmer-Laborism in the late teens. Townley was a legendary folk hero to farmers and, ironically, may never have been a socialist at all in spite of what he said and did. A native of west central Minnesota and a graduate of Alexandria High School, he briefly taught school before moving in 1904 to Beach, North Dakota, where he farmed the western prairie with a brother. Townley was a natural organizer. He convinced local residents to form a syndicate to purchase seed and equipment at a discount. Then he traveled to Colorado where he unsuccessfully tried his hand at bonanza, or large-scale, wheat farming.

In 1907 Townley returned to North Dakota and again became his brother's partner, this time in massive flax farming. Soon the two operated one of the state's largest flax-growing enterprises. A man never content with moderate success, Townley as "flax king" put 8,000 acres under cultivation in 1912, expecting to earn $100,000 with a market price of $3.00 a bushel. This dream ended in disaster when drought, early frost, and a price drop to $1.00 a bushel put him $50,000 in debt and forced him into bankruptcy.[19]

Disillusioned, Townley turned to the Socialist party, where he met a small cadre of exceedingly capable men who, for unknown reasons, had been drawn to this rural-agricultural-nonsocialist state. At Minot the party published a paper, *The Iconclast,* and in a special appeal to the state's politically dominant farmers it began proposing by 1908 a system of state-owned elevators and flour mills, state hail insurance, and state credit banks. What the Dakota Socialists lacked in numbers they made up for in talent. One party member, Minot attorney Arthur LeSueur, ran as the Socialist candidate for Congress in 1912 and once had served as vice-president of the protest-populist People's College in Fort Scott, Kansas. In a few years LeSueur moved to Minneapolis where he and his family later became active Farmer-Laborites. Another tactician was Henry Teigan, a Socialist candidate for superintendent of schools who likewise moved to Minnesota and then served as a state legislator and one-term (1937-38) third-district congressman.

Because they made so little political headway, Socialists looked for ways of introducing the party to skeptical, Republican-voting farmers. Someone came up with a unique idea: permit non-Socialists to participate as "nonpartisans," literally nonparty members of the party! Just as he had taken to bonanza farming, so Townley quickly took advantage of the opportunity to serve as nonpartisan organizer of the farmers. Soon he had the party's "organization department" humming. Indeed, his success so outstripped expectations that orthodox Socialists became uneasy as the number of dues-paying nonpartisans, who contributed dues of one dollar per month, quickly equaled that of regular party members. Fearful that farmers under Townley's leadership might take control—not an unlikely outcome with Townley in command—the regulars voted at the next party convention to discontinue their nonpartisan program.

Townley, predictably enough, would not allow this new opportunity to slip away. First, he convinced another Socialist, A. E. Bowen, to join him in his organizational drive and — a short time after the February 1915 Equity rally at Bismarck had ended — the two launched the Nonpartisan League. LeSueur, Teigan, and a dozen or so expatriates from the Socialist party became members shortly thereafter. Organizers now crisscrossed the state in new Model T Ford cars, a practice that not only gave rapid transportation from farm to farm but was visually impressive to farmers. Annual dues started at $2.50 but soon were increased to $9.00, or $16.00 for two years, and each farmer-subscriber received the league's newspaper, the *Nonpartisan Leader,* and the New York socialist publication *Pearson's Magazine.*

Although organizers did not entirely discard their old Socialist habits — "Dear Comrade" and "Red" remained affectionate greetings — the league was otherwise pragmatic throughout its existence. Its immediate objective was singular: political power. And its means to power was, for former Socialists, unorthodox: through the Republican party! Simply put, the NPL planned to take organizationa command of the Republican party and modestly socialize some of the Grand Old Party's program. Using two issues which Equity had developed so well during the past five years, the grain exchange controversy and public-operated elevators, Townley and the NPL focused their attention on the 1916 North Dakota Republican primary election.

Once more, Townley left little to chance. There was to be no tripping over ideological obstacles. Candidates were carefully selected. The NPL even endorsed veteran United States senator Porter J. McCumber for reelection. Farmers, not socialists, ran for the legislature. The results were amazing. Nearly every NPL candidate was nominated, from Lynn Frazier for governor and William Langer for attorney general to scores of legislative and other candidates. In the lower house 81 league endorsees won, but only 32 regular Republicans. In the senate, half of which was up for election, league candidates won 18 of 24 contests.[20]

The campaign ended as a NPL landslide, and the league claimed an 80-percent mandate. Governor Frazier followed up the victory by proposing a comprehensive social program to the 1917 legislature. He asked for better schools, improved roads, civil service reform, minimum wages, nonpartisan ballots, lowered interest rates, and the league program of state-owned flour mills, cement plants, a state-owned bank, hail insurance, and state-owned utilities. First, however, the constitution had to be amended by referendum so that the state could legally operate each of these commercial enterprises.

League proposals were carefully drawn up for the farmer-legislators by lawyers like future congressman William Lemke, LeSueur, Teigan, and Vince Day, who in the 1930s served as personal adviser to Minnesota Farmer-Labor governor Floyd Olson. To introduce the inexperienced farmers to rudimentary parliamentary procedure, the league leased a Bismarck hotel where training sessions were held and where the new legislators later met in secret caucus to learn daily league strategy. Despite these preparations, most league bills were deadlocked by Republican regulars in the state senate.[21] Not until the league gained its second election victory in 1918 was it possible to get the bills through the senate, which in 1919 approved many of the utilities and public service bills. In time, North Dakota was introduced to this experiment in midwestern socialism when a state flour mill (Dakota Maid Flour) and the Bank of North Dakota were established.

Townley, meanwhile, immediately began to look beyond North Dakota. No sooner had the 1917 North Dakota legislature convened than Townley announced the shifting of national NPL headquarters to St. Paul. This was to be a national, or at least a regional, movement. Teigan already was publicizing "The Revolution in North Dakota" in obscure socialist journals like *The Western Comrade*.[22] Immediate plans were to organize farmers in Minnesota, South Dakota, Montana, Idaho, Colorado, Nebraska, and Texas. Even before its 1916 primary victory the league in July had dispatched organizers into Minnesota, South Dakota, and Montana. By fall, Townley had deployed to Minnesota between eighty and ninety organizers — Teigan called them "trained agitators" — each with his own Model T, in preparation for the 1918 election.[23]

By March 1917 the league claimed 12,000 Minnesota enrollees; 50,000 had joined by mid-1918. Minnesota, however, was not North Dakota. Old-line Socialists were deeply troubled by the unabashed pragmatism of their renegade comrades who jumped party and made a mockery of sacred ideological principle. This, the Socialist regulars contended, was crass opportunism which undermined solidarity and threatened the Socialist party's chances for success.[24]

These were but the first rumblings of internal division in the emerging Farmer-Labor movement. Drawing together in the name of protest and reform were four groups of somewhat incompatible backgrounds. One was Socialist and willing to adopt the Farmer-Labor name but not otherwise abandon socialist goals. The second included former Socialists who in their willingness to compete in plebiscary democratic fashion were prepared to drop unpopular socialist proposals (which as socialists they preferred) whenever the public seemed certain to reject them. The third group would shortly come from organized labor, sometimes as socialists and sometimes as Gomperite conservatives. And the last would come directly from the ranks of Progressivism, the Bull Moose movement, and the Equity Cooperative Exchange, would be Farmer-Laborism's moderates, and would provide most of its candidates for public office.

CHAPTER 2

The Emerging Coalition

In mid-1916 when the Nonpartisan League launched an intensive drive to organize Minnesota farmers, the immediate political objective was not to create a third-party movement. Two years later when the Farmer-Labor party was conceived, it was not by choice. Because the league preferred to work with the two major parties, it employed a pragmatic and opportunistic strategy, patterned after what A. C. Townley called the tactics of "balance of power."

Townley reasoned that neither Republicans nor Democrats could gain victory if a large, well-organized interest withheld support. He believed a disciplined, cohesive group with mass membership could take command of a party and then win the subsequent election. Which of the two parties should such a group work in? To Townley and the league it mattered very little; they held no ideological predisposition toward either Democrats or Republicans. The choice should be determined by opportunity for success. In Republican states it was the Grand Old Party since it was dominant. That was the case in North Dakota; it would be the same in Minnesota. By capturing party nominations through the direct primary, the group would control the party, its platform, the campaign, and ultimately the legislative agenda.

There was both risk and error in the assumptions and in the strategy. Although such logic worked well in North Dakota in 1916, it failed to consider the reaction of regular party leaders and voters whenever infiltration contaminated a major party. One effect of such a change might be a "united front" campaign by, say, Democratic leaders and voters who temporarily switched support to the more dominant Republicans in order to save that party and the state from radical infidels. This, indeed, would occur in 1918 in Minnesota. Another erroneous assumption was that, once recruited candidates were in office, they would behave largely as the socialist creators of the Nonpartisan League and later the Farmer-Labor party wanted them to. This did not usually happen, and in later years socialists were constantly bewildered and dismayed as control over the movement slipped out of their hands.

MINNESOTA POSES OBSTACLES FOR THE LEAGUE

The ease with which the NPL took command in North Dakota would be difficult to replicate in Minnesota. North Dakota had a one-industry economy, agriculture. Minnesota, too, had a strong farm sector, but it was far more diversified. In addition to having North Dakota's wheat, flax, and small grain, Minnesota was a dairy, corn, and cattle-producing state. Its geographic divisions were much sharper than North Dakota's and included a rich southern corn-cattle belt, a western/northwestern prairie-farming region, a northern timber production belt, a northeastern mining industry, and the large metropolitan Twin Cities with its light industry, manufacturing, banking, distribution, and marketing. Owing to the existence of Minnesota's Twin Cities, there was also a more severe urban/rural split in politics than existed in North Dakota.

Even if each region and each sector contained significant potential for the development of political protest, organizing and integrating it on a statewide basis presented sizable logistical problems for any movement, since each region and sector had a different need and some were not harmonious with others. Protest in North Dakota could focus exclusively on "the farm problem"; in Minnesota such an emphasis would quickly bog down without the active sympathy and support of the movement to organize urban labor unions. In addition, opposition to the NPL was much better organized in Minnesota.

Two other unanticipated problems compounded the league's efforts to organize Minnesota. It had absolutely no control over the course international events would take. No sooner had the league drive picked up momentum than the war in Europe took an ugly turn, which led to American intervention. Almost at the same time two revolutions took place in Russia, the first by the parliamentary-like (Kerensky) social democrats, the disquieting second by the revolutionary (Lenin) Bolsheviks. The league had not counted on these political issues and would have preferred that they had not occurred since they diverted public thinking away from local and regional economic reform.

Fundamentally, league priorities began and ended with domestic reform. Its organizing socialists tended privately to be highly skeptical about a "war to save democracy" and equally suspected British, German, and American capitalists of being economically motivated in whatever position they took on national foreign policy. Because the league's organizing effort continued to make progress, its leaders pressed on despite the war. As a result, the league gained new and sometimes unexpected sympathizers, but the price it paid was intensified opposition and increasing distrust by those who perceived Minnesota politics as turning radically leftward.

THE EROSION OF PARTY IDENTIFICATION

Nonpartisanism and then Farmer-Laborism marked an important transitional period in Minnesota political evolution. For fifty years, from the Civil War to World War I, the Republican party dominated state politics. The first challenge to its hegemony came with the Populist upheaval in the early 1890s. As Republican majorities declined, Democrats began to campaign more effectively for office. Although this realignment had little impact yet on the legislature and most state offices, Democrats occasionally won a congressional election and were highly successful in campaigns for governor; between 1898 and 1914 Democrats won five of nine gubernatorial contests. St. Paul had been bossed by a Democratic city machine since the turn of the century, and in the midteens a Socialist, as a city reform candidate, was elected mayor of Minneapolis. And in 1916 Woodrow Wilson ("He Kept Us Out of War") came within 392 votes of being the first Democratic presidential candidate to carry Minnesota.

These were the changing general conditions when first Nonpartisanism and then Farmer-Laborism moved to and expanded in Minnesota. Party ties had been further undercut by events leading up to and then following the 1912 election. The Bull Moose Progressives were saying, in effect, that regular party labels sometimes should be abandoned. This irregularity worked against both major parties. For example, Equity counsel James Manahan, a Bryan Democrat, switched to Robert La Follette and the Republican Progressives in 1912 and the same year ran for at-large congressman; four years later he supported Republican Charles Evans Hughes for president, in part because as a Progressive Manahan protested southern Democratic influence.[1] In 1912 Theodore Roosevelt, the Bull Moose candidate for president, carried Minnesota, whereas incumbent Republican president William Howard Taft unimpressively gained but about one vote for every five cast (19 percent). In the 1912 campaign for governor of Minnesota Republican candidate Adolph Eberhart won election. However, the combined protest vote (Public Ownership, Progressive, and Prohibition) was 28.5 percent, nearly equal to the 31.5 percent cast for the Democratic candidate. Two years later, however, a Democrat was elected governor!

These politically unstable times caused voters to shift from party to party under the influence of major national and economic events. The possibility of Minnesota's becoming a competitively balanced two-party state seemed real. Nevertheless, several factors worked against this. One was just plain bad Democratic luck. Three-time governor John Johnson, on the threshold of national recognition, unexpectedly died in office; his successor was a Republican lieutenant governor.[2] The same thing happened to Democratic congressman Winfield Scott Hammond, an unexpected gubernatorial winner in 1914 who died the following year; he, too, was succeeded by a Republican.

In 1916 a bitter midyear iron miners' strike, from June to September, caused further political unrest; during the same year Republicans regained votes and Democrats could not keep pace, Wilson being the major exception. Because St. Paul Irish Catholics suspected John Lind of being antipapist, they vetoed any attempt by him to run for the U.S. Senate even though he had served as Wilson's envoy to Mexico and was well known. Constituency differences in religious affiliation now contributed to the increasing degeneration of the Democratic organization.[3] Generally unprepared to take advantage of protest politics, whether by farmers, city workers, or miners, Democrats did not expand their appeal and became increasingly conservative and cautious. Soon they would be bypassed as the new Farmer-Labor movement displaced them.

REPUBLICAN RESURGENCE

In 1916, the year the Nonpartisan League moved its major organizational effort into Minnesota, the state Republican party gained one of its major triumphs, arresting what seemed to be the steady erosion of its popular support. The league had endorsed Hughes for president, which may have been just enough to give him a razor-thin state victory over Wilson. Newcomers to protest politics were often still voting Republican in 1916; for example, future Farmer-Labor congressman (1923-27) Knud Wefald supported Hughes.

Minnesota Republicans, however, were far from united. They had badly squabbled over presidential candidates, dividing themselves between Taft, Roosevelt, Elihu Root, Albert S. Cummings, and even two University of Minnesota presidents.[4] The most serious rift occurred in the 1916 contest for United States senator. The November outcome, though a solid Republican victory, would contribute to Farmer-Laborism's first significant breakthrough.

Republican senator (1901-17) Moses E. Clapp, the incumbent, usually enjoyed substantial support from his party's Progressive wing. Facing his first popular election, Clapp was poorly organized, ineffective, and entered the primary contest much too late. The other candidates, Progressive Republican congressman Charles Lindbergh, who had long antagonized party regulars, and former governor Adolph Eberhart, did little better. The primary nomination victory went to St. Paul lawyer Frank Kellogg, who had quietly directed a very small group of men in a carefully orchestrated "draft" Kellogg movement.[5] Kellogg actually could lay some claim to a progressive past. He had served as special counsel to the U. S. Department of Justice while it successfully brought to trial important antitrust cases against the paper industry, Standard Oil, and the Union and Southern Pacific railways when they sought to merge.

Kellogg, however, was also a charter member of a prestigious St. Paul law firm whose clients included the United States Steel Corporation, which in Minnesota then and for years to come would be referred to by labor and the protest movement as "the steel trust." Kellogg was an urbane and polished lawyer, one reason why he was selected American secretary of state in the mid-1920s, and this served him well in 1916, though it proved much less of an asset in the 1922 election. Because Kellogg had long-established contacts in Washington, he warned Democrats there, including Senator William Borah and Wilson's secretary of the interior, to stay out of Minnesota since he confidently believed it was futile to oppose his election.[6]

Kellogg and the entire Republican slate won an easy victory. Whatever influence the Progressives were having in 1916 was in the Republican, not the Democratic, party.

URBAN SOCIALISTS AND ORGANIZED LABOR

The 1916 election results proved to be a poor general indicator of the strength of Minnesota's protest forces even though they reflected overall public support and confidence in the Minnesota Republican party. There were still concentrated pockets of dissatisfaction. One was in Minneapolis, where a Socialist mayor, three aldermen, and a school board member were elected.

Organized labor increasingly was separated by factionalism and ideological differences as old-line craft unions remained politically and economically cautious and carefully avoided partisan entanglements. Strict followers of Samuel Gompers's American Federation of Labor, these traditional unionists dominated the Minnesota State Federation of Labor, largely ignoring both the new industrial union movement and the bitter iron miners' strike in 1916. Gompers's men stayed a safe, respectful distance away from the newer unions which they feared were too often contaminated by urban socialists and a labor-party mentality. This was one reason why the political left so frequently took command of industrial unionism while preaching the benefits of public ownership. Many urban socialists enthusiastically joined hands with industrial unionists to organize a single business, shop, or industry. The same socialists-industrial unionists were pleasantly surprised to discover an ideological affinity with the socialist organizers in the Nonpartisan League, an attraction that helped draw them together in 1918 Farmer-Laborism.

While socialists, industrial unionists, agrarian protestors, timber workers, and iron miners all shared general grievances against powerful economic interests, these grievances by themselves were insufficient to bring about political union. Instead, the catalyst that first propelled protest into third-party union was American intervention in the European war. Those opposed to Americans' fighting in Europe to help the British and French against the Germans did not adhere to any single economic or political ideology, but the interventionists treated them roughly, as though they all were radical misfits, and in the process of wartime condemnation helped establish what was essentially a domestic protest movement. Shunned as disloyal, unpatriotic, and un-American in 1917-18, emergent Farmer-Laborism thus turned out to be a polyglot of political protest which included conservatives, moderates, reformers, agrarians, unionists, socialists, and northern and east European ethnics.

THE NEW COALITION

As Nonpartisan organizers moved into Minnesota, they hoped to gain the support of the state's progressives. Already the NPL relied upon former congressman James Manahan who had served as special counsel to the Equity Cooperative Exchange and who in January 1917 began acting as league counsel, helping plan the move of its headquarters to St. Paul.

At the 1917 Minnesota legislative session the league was understandably attracted to earthy advocates of Equity like Magnus Johnson ("Yonson," as he pronounced his name), a Swedish immigrant dairy farmer from Kimball, who led insurgent legislators pushing hard for the Equity program to tax grain-futures trading, regulate the Minneapolis Chamber of Commerce through supervision of grain exchanges, and increase regulatory powers of the Railroad and Warehouse Commission.[7] Hearings before the house Grain Inquiry Committee produced a new flare-up when M. W. Thatcher repeatedly clashed with the committee chairman after refusing to violate what Thatcher described as a confidential relationship with Equity, thereby not fully disclosing the cooperative's weakened condition and financial instability. Manahan was even more agitated and once threateningly shouted at the chairman, "Did you ever hear [what happened to] the Czar of Russia. . .?"[8]

No longer new issues, these reoccurring disputes nevertheless reinforced in the minds of dissatisfied farmers the belief that the "forces of privilege" could be toppled from power only by improved methods of political organization. There was also an unmistakable feeling that Democracy was on the march; shortly its presence was felt in a catchy national slogan, "A War to make the world safe for Democracy." When the Kerensky government came to power during the first phase of the Russian Revolution, the legislature in late March adopted a resolution of support and the normally conservative *Minneapolis Tribune* described it as a "revolution [of a] kind that American citizenship can endorse with whole heart."[9]

Before Congress declared war in early April, economic and political conservatives fretted over the Nonpartisan League's advances, but the generally expressed attitude toward it was cautious respect even though most Minnesota political leaders were skeptical about its program, particularly those features calling for public ownership. When reactionaries and militant opponents of the league, bankrolled apparently by league-threatened industries, incorporated a bogus but well-financed rival called the "Minnesota Non-Partisan League" on March 21, many Republican leaders including state auditor J. A. O. Preus rallied to the genuine league's defense and condemned the impostor.[10] Most regular Republicans, business and industry, and the leaders of the older, more secure craft unions were well aware that many of the original founders of the league had come to it from the Socialist party. Before war began, however, Nonpartisanism remained primarily a farmer's protest movement, separated from the new, more militant union organizers in the Twin Cities and especially the urban radicals and socialists who were increasingly active.

This condition was altered considerably as the country moved closer to war. Not only did German-American farmers fail to identify with the English and French, even in agriculturally prosperous southern Minnesota, but they strongly objected to English and American anti-German propaganda and the constant drumming against Deutsch Kultur. Rarely were these first- and second-generation immigrants supportive of the German government; nevertheless, they had an understandable reluctance to spill their own blood or that of friends and relatives in the "old country," and they were strongly attracted to a national policy of "strict neutrality." These German-Americans, some conservative, others moderate or progressive, were usually not comfortable allies with city socialists and urban radicals. The war, however, transformed the entire protest movement as it attracted, willy-nilly, workers, farmers, socialists, and antiwar ethnics, binding them for better or worse into a loose coalition. For a time it mattered less that some resisted the war as a mere imperialist struggle for markets of exploitation while others resented being forced to fight against their homeland. Advocates of patriotism and loyalty considered them one and the same. Nonpartisanism and its offshoot Farmer-Laborism remained skeptical about the touted high purpose of the war.

In fact, German- and Scandinavian-American isolationists were rather clearly to be distinguished from the militant Socialist antiwar resistance. In February, almost two months before war was declared, Minneapolis's Socialist mayor Thomas Van Lear bitterly denounced growing "war hysteria" and demanded that no American soldiers be sent to fight overseas.[11] A state Socialist party letter to the *Minneapolis Tribune* blamed the war on capitalistic profit mongering in food and munitions exports. The Socialists condemned the Wilson foreign policy, demanded a munitions and foodstuffs embargo, and, in the event of an American declaration of war, urged "the workers of the United States to refuse to fight."[12] To rouse popular support, Van Lear called a mass rally at the Minneapolis auditorium, where an estimated 10,000 to 13,000 overflow crowd listened to impassioned denunciations of the "kept press" and corporations by prominent local and national Socialists.

Wide ideological differences continued to separate the groups which for one reason or another opposed American intervention.

The Nonpartisan League was no exception as it carefully sought to avoid close association with men like Van Lear out of a fear that it would be politically damaging to the movement. Southern Minnesota German-Americans were even more cautious. Nevertheless, the war was slowly drawing these groups closer to coalition.

THE POLITICAL IMPACT OF THE LOYALTY ISSUE

Within two days of the Socialist antiwar rally a Loyalty League was formed, headed by aged Cyrus Northrop, president emeritus of the University of Minnesota. At the loyalty rally speeches by faculty, university president George E. Vincent, fabled rhetoric professor emeritus Maria Sanford, and Catholic archbishop John Ireland preached duty and service to country. Thirty thousand people signed loyalty petitions, which Senator Knute Nelson forwarded to President Wilson.[13]

Recognizing the risk in advocating reform during a national crisis, the NPL attempted to steer a pragmatic course away from the danger. In countless speeches the league and Townley claimed to be loyal, avoided insofar as possible the appearance of resisting war preparation or the draft; slogans were adjusted accordingly: "Conscript wealth," tax excess corporate profits, loyalty plus reform. But Townley and the league were fashioning their own propaganda as an economic protest, and on countless occasions he bluntly told farmers that it was a "rich man's war." That could mean many things.

To outsiders, however, this seemed a political masquerade. It was relatively easy, even natural, to associate the league with socialism and disloyalty, particularly so for large corporations, utilities, and the grain trade, all of whom would likely be heavy losers if the league succeeded in achieving its goals. To these interests the evidence was disquieting. When in late March a prominent rural Republican editor and a league organizer debated before several hundred farmers, the editor charged the league with being a "hidden brand of Socialism which will destroy every farmer's cooperative"; the organizer admitted "I am a Socialist," as were many other league leaders. The *Minneapolis Tribune* made it front-page news.[14]

The admission was relatively mild compared with the league's embarrassment over the actions of some urban radicals. Before some 1,500 Minneapolis courthouse demonstrators a militant Socialist complained about a conspiratorial juggernaut dragging the nation toward war, led by the Army and Navy, capitalists, the churches of Jesus Christ, and the major metropolitan newspapers. "Refuse to fight," he told his sympathizers, because even German invaders would find a peaceful population unwilling to make war. Those were not league words, but the league's enemies judged it guilty by associating it with the same thoughts. Said a *Minneapolis Journal* headline: "Socialist Would Give Country To Enemy If Invaded."[15]

The congressional war declaration of April 2 did not by itself bring on political realignment, but it did blur the antiwar groups' ideological differences while separating sides into two distinct political camps, one prowar, the other antiwar. The Socialists' strident militancy in opposing the war unwittingly created suspicion, anxiety, and distrust. When the First Minnesota Regiment of the National Guard was federalized, its first deployment was to protect railway bridges and the milling industry from possible sabotage![16] Minnesota entered the war in apparent division over the wisdom of American intervention. For example, the House congressional war vote, 373 to 50, included four Minnesota nay votes: Ernest Lundeen (R-Minneapolis), Harold Knutson (R-St. Cloud), Carl C. Van Dyke (D-St. Paul), and Chester R. Davis (R-St. Peter); none of these men were socialist or radical but all came from heavy German-American constituencies.

Skilled observers recognized that the war had added significantly to the resources which the league could use to expand in Minnesota. No one knew this better than conservative senator Knute Nelson, an astute political veteran with fifty years of public experience. Nelson was a staunch exponent of intervention and supported censorship powers under the Espionage Bill. But he also partly agreed with the league and Equity in that he defended farmers against the charge they were unduly benefiting from the inflated commodity market and were responsible for rising consumer food prices. Publicly and privately he blamed price inflation on the grain trade, millers, processors, and commissionmen, and he sponsored federal legislation to restrict futures trading, thereby drawing strong protest from the giant millers who otherwise considered him a safe and sound friend.[17]

Wartime Repression of Protest

Intense as the hostility was between the Nonpartisan League and its antagonists, this tension was not yet sufficient to boost substantially league prospects for political victory or to force it into adopting a third-party strategy. However, in the passion of wartime league opponents resorted to a severe policy of political repression. Not only was this constitutionally reckless, but it also turned out to be politically shortsighted. Repression gained temporary advantage for Republicans, inflexible conservatives, and those corporate interests which believed, incorrectly, that league collectivism could be successfully resisted only by resorting to heavy-handed law enforcement where the objective was to muzzle proponents of reform by denying them First Amendment freedoms.

Well intended or not, the vehicle for this assault was the war-spawned Minnesota Commission of Public Safety (MCPS), proposed two days before war was declared. The legislature funded it generously and gave it powers to register and intern aliens, recommend removal of officials from office by the governor, and conduct broad investigations designed to ferret out and silence "treasonous speakers" who denounced government, advocated revolution, or spoke against military enlistments. During the war it was responsible for the removal of several officers, and its agents kept close watch on Townley, league counsel A. C. Gilbert, and a few radical socialists who were jailed, tried, and eventually forced to serve short prison terms for seditious speech. Its chairman, Minneapolis judge John F. McGee (who as a postwar federal judge committed suicide) likened its powers to enforcement "teeth eighteen inches long."

The five-member, governor-appointed commission was bipartisan and included former Democratic governor John Lind, a conservative Republican who was president of West Publishing Company, and the conservative Democratic publisher of the *Duluth Herald*.[18] Those who opposed the war, either militantly or mildly, including progressives, league leaders and rank-and-file members, industrial unionists, German- and Scandinavian-Americans, and socialists, began to sense that Republicans and Democrats had united in opposition to them.

Most commission activities dealt with war mobilization; food, fuel, and clothing conservation; and war propaganda. It was, however, the investigations and harassment of various protest groups that earned the commission its reputation. For decades aliens had been solicited and welcomed as immigrants; now they were singled out for suspicion and required to register with the commission. There were a quarter million aliens in the state, and Germans were the largest single national group. Opponents of the Nonpartisan League quickly discovered the commission was an invaluable tool to discredit, harass, and even bring to trial those who made bold and politically inflammatory assaults upon capitalism and orthodoxy.

Armed with a "secret service" and a cadre of special agents directed by an ex-Pinkerton detective, the commission conducted a dragnet of investigations. Civil liberties were withdrawn for the war's duration and "Patriotism Plus" was expected. All forms of social criticism became suspect. An investigation was made of the Industrial Workers of the World (IWW) headquarters. Foreign-language newspapers drew special attention, including the conservative St. Paul Catholic paper *Der Wanderer.* The editor of the St. Paul German newspaper *Volkszeitung* was arrested August 9 for allegedly belittling the war; by mid-September he was carted off to a military prison at McPherson, Georgia. Progressive newspapers friendly to the Nonpartisan League, like the *Faribault Referendum* and the (Alexandria) *Park Region Echo,* were subjected to investigation and their editors intimidated, jailed, and fined. University regent Fred B. Snyder, on a complaint from the commission, led a move before the Board of Regents to fire political scientist William A. Schaper, a faculty member since 1901. With just two hours' notice, Schaper was terminated for what the commission called "rabid pro-German" conduct which rendered him unfit for university service.[19] After a July investigation of the People's Council of America, a national Socialist group which included Eugene V. Debs, Morris Hillquit, and Max Eastman as members, the commission recommended that it should not be allowed to hold a convention in Minnesota. Governor J. A. A. Burnquist banned it in August. By summer 1917 every meeting other than patriotic rallies was viewed by the jaded commission with grave misgivings. These excesses and the wholesale setting aside of constitutional rights were bound to encourage a broad political reaction, open or submerged.

Nothing better illustrated the terrifying extremes of the commission's behavior than its handling of a July 25 rally at New Ulm in Brown County. Among the most concentrated areas of German settlement in Minnesota, Brown County was prosperous, conservative, and largely Republican, with its Democrat voters mainly in New Ulm. Some 10,000 spectators came to the New Ulm gathering to hear speeches that opposed sending American troops to Europe. None of the rally organizers attempted to mask the general unpopularity of the draft or of the sending of draftees overseas. But the peaceful rally was otherwise a model of German restraint and self-discipline.

No oratorical firebrands were present at the rally, and speaker after speaker followed the same general reasoning. All expressed loyalty and pledged to defend the nation from aggression or invasion. No attacks were made on the economic system. The New Ulm mayor, Dr. L. A. Fritsche, warned against draft resistance and counseled the audience to obey the draft law and only use peaceful legal means to seek its reform. City attorney Albert Pfaender delivered a thoughtful constitutional résumé of the national war power, noting that there could be no appeal once Congress issued a declaration of war. To Pfaender the only unsettled constitutional question was whether the state militia (National Guard) could be ordered overseas. A few speakers condemned press censorship. The strongest criticism came from a theologian and president of Martin Luther College, who warned against foreign involvement, interference in German internal affairs, and waging war for either Wall Street or "John Bull" (Great Britain), and who declared it more important for the United States to first extend full civil rights to American Negroes.

To agents of the Public Safety Commission, these speeches seemed to be a form of seditious heresy. On August 1 rally participants were called before the commission for questioning, and it quickly recommended to Burnquist that Fritsche, Pfaender, and county auditor Louis Vogel be suspended and after a hearing removed from office for misfeasance. The governor complied, though Vogel was later reinstated owing to insufficient evidence. The removals were justified on the grounds that the officials had been disloyal, un-American, and had encouraged antidraft sentiment. To ensure compliance elsewhere, the governor and the commission encouraged local communities to form monitoring councils — actually community vigilantism — to ban future rallies like the one in New Ulm, and on August 18 Burnquist issued an executive order closing the state to antidraft meetings.[20]

The Nonpartisan League and the War Issue

Well aware of the increasingly hostile environment within which it had to work, the NPL nevertheless continued its effort to build a strong base of support in Minnesota. This meant attracting rural antiwar sentiment even though NPL programs continued to focus squarely upon economic discontent, not war opposition.

Enemies of the league saw the issues it raised much differently. Certain the league was guilty of fomenting revolutionary schemes, they easily could believe it a hotbed of disloyalty which it kept hidden from public view. NPL leaders recognized this suspicion and carefully avoided open or public association with groups that opposed the war, and professed loyalty even as they demanded "conscription of profits" to finance the war. Such sloganeering had two advantages. It allowed the league to adapt a catchy wartime phrase to political advantage, since according to a popular aphorism war should not be profitable for any interest — other than farmers. A second advantage was the attention it drew to the conscription issue among those opposing the draft. Because profits and wealth in fact were not being conscripted, farmers opposing the war might well ask, then, was it proper to conscript men? Neither the league nor Townley answered that question directly, but Townley repeatedly said it was a rich man's war. League membership increased accordingly.

Futively speculating about the league's impact in 1918, conservatives grew increasingly apprehensive. Attitudes polarized as both left and right thought in terms of the other's conspiratorial intentions. Vexed by the seeming ability of the league to avoid entrapment on the war issue, MCPS chairman John F. McGee predicted privately that riots were possible throughout the Northwest if the league succeeded in gaining political power.[21] Sensing its improved opportunity, the league made use of wartime issues and sponsored a three-day Producers and Consumers Conference on the High Cost of Living. Townley carefully planned its agenda. War protest groups were scrupulously weeded out as participants; the league went so far as to keep the People's Council out of North Dakota lest it bring embarrassment. Speakers who might unwisely bring up the war protest issue were warned not to do so. When delegates assembled in St. Paul on September 18 they included a cross section of organized labor, farmers, and socialists.

Conferees wrapped themselves in patriotic bunting. Some speakers asked for increased governmental regulation of industry and for selected programs of government ownership, but these usually were advocated in close association with "winning the war" and taking the profits out of war. Resolutions were offered for:

1. Taxation of idle land and income taxes on earnings over $2,000.
2. An absolute limit on annual income, with a ceiling of $100,000.
3. Government ownership of public utilities and state ownership of Montana copper mines.
4. Government policy encouraging producer and consumer cooperatives.
5. Possible commandeering of key industries, including milling, terminal elevators, mines, packinghouses, rail and communication, and steel *if* price controls and conscription-of-wealth taxation failed to pay for the war.
6. Cognizance of labor unionization as a principle, but government operation of any industry that failed to settle a strike quickly.
7. Stricter immigration laws.
8. Just price fixing, and wheat price reductions passed back to consumers.
9. Low-interest farm loans.
10. Regulation of grain exchanges.

11. Praise for participatory democracy, including the initiative, referendum, and recall.[22]

These proposals were moderate, at least by radical standards. To Nonpartisans, they seemed nothing more than a legitimate attempt to unite, into a political coalition, the interests of farmers, workers, and moderate socialists. To conservatives and many orthodox minds, the proposals had the ring of revolution and confiscation. Republican and Democratic party regulars were less than charitable in their assessment of them.

Nearly all the conference's speakers lent a degree of legitimacy to the league's goal of simultaneously dedicating itself to winning the war while pursuing domestic social reconstruction. Those who addressed the delegates were a past commander of the Grand Army of the Republic, a representative of the new Federal Trade Commisssion, spokesmen for industrial unionism, North Dakota attorney general William Langer who would become a Senate maverick. U.S. Senator A. J. Gronna (R-North Dakota) complained about uneven wartime sacrifices and big business profiteering. "If this organization must disrupt parties to accomplish its purpose," Gronna concluded, "then let parties be disrupted."[23] Rather methodically the league went about its business as delegates listened, often listlessly, to congressional veterans like U.S. Congressman George M. Young (R-North Dakota) and Senator William Borah praise loyalty while complaining about corporate influence in government-administered war programs. Five hours before adjournment a resolution easily carried pledging members' lives, fortunes, and honor to the flag and "OUR war." The *Minneapolis Tribune* found little to fault in the league's call for patriotism.[24]

For the good of the league the conference should have ended then. But Wisconsin's Progressive senator Robert M. La Follette was yet scheduled to speak. He had faithfully promised Townley not to discuss the intervention controversy. However, after speaking for a time he departed from his prepared text, the reason never being clear; possibly it was the result of some intemperate heckling. Suddenly he launched into the forbidden subject. Yes, he admitted, the United States had legitimate grievances against German interference on the open seas, but these were insufficient causes for going to war, especially since right of passage was being defended in the name of carrying munitions to England.

That was all the delegates needed to hear. As a body they catapulted to their feet, thundering their approval. The damage had been done. Worse, La Follette was followed by none other than Mayor

Thomas Van Lear, who compounded the unplanned blunder by declaring that

> when it comes to conscripting the wealth of the nation, the profiteers rushed to Congress and cried "save our wealth." No one dared say "save our boys." But they dared say "save our wealth." And their voices were heard.[25]

The two speeches provided the vital opportunity which the league's enemies had been awaiting. Newspapers quickly seized it. "Extreme pacifism" and "radical socialism" were declared to be in command of the league after all. On September 21 the *Tribune* carried the headline "Blaze of Disloyalty Ends Conference of the Nonpartisan League." This issue would now be exploited and the league forced into a defensive position, often outlawed in local communities by patriotic city fathers.

Two-Party Counterattack

Governor Burnquist immediately ordered the Public Safety Commission to investigate the "seditious" outbursts, and on September 25 it called on the United States Senate to expel La Follette.[26] Three days later Theodore Roosevelt, popular in Minnesota, delivered speeches in St. Paul and Minneapolis to rally the forces of patriotism and loyalty. Roosevelt ridiculed pacifists, "neo-copperheads," and "microbes and lesser microbes."[27]

A giant Loyalty Day Rally was planned for November 16 to help recover patriotic ground lost to league subversion. Planning was entrusted to the university president, the leadership of the Minnesota State Federation of Labor (AFL), mayors, educators, businessmen, bankers, industrialists, lawyers and publishers. The *Duluth News Tribune* called the November rally the "opening of a campaign to combat the traitorous and seditious influences . . . which have centered very largely in the Nonpartisan League."[28] League abuses were chronicled: disloyalty, economic and social disruption, discouraging subscriptions to the Second Liberty Loan (war savings bonds), intimidating small-town businessmen, threatening the mining industry, stirring up sedition, even terrorizing loyal citizens in predominantly German-settled areas. Sometimes simple remedies were offered by the more vigilant critics, who declared that foreign-language newspapers should be banned, insurgent leaders locked up, and "such men as La Follette and Townley" shot!

Loyalty Day drew thousands to hear Knute Nelson, Frank Kellogg, J. A. A. Burnquist, the Iowa governor, and the assistant secretary of agriculture.[29] Other international events would further harden resistance to the league. The November Bolshevik Revolution added to the uncertainty conservatives and moderates felt about the league's intentions. A common fear was that radicalism was taking hold everywhere like a political Hydra's head.

It mattered little that the Nonpartisan League was anatomically separated from the revolutionary serpent. During the war and the immediate postwar period conservatives thought the league was the ally and not the antagonist of revolution. In Minnesota the state Democratic party seemed prepared to sacrifice itself in a united two-party front against the league threat. Both sides now drew exaggerated pictures of the other, and though the NPL still did not consider itself a third-party movement, the farmer, labor, and ethnic interests to which it appealed were being isolated outside the two major parties. Impatient and disillusioned, many of these varied forces of political reform and victims of wartime persecution came slowly to the conclusion that relief could be obtained only in a Farmer-Labor third party.

CHAPTER 3

From Primary Campaigns to Early Confederation

Neither Nonpartisanism nor Farmer-Laborism was content to play the role, so common to third parties, of social critics without power. The movement's first priority was to win elections, and to achieve this objective its leaders were prepared to compromise on policies, parties, and candidates. That electoral success counted most in the minds of Nonpartisans was obvious from the way its leaders and candidates approached the elections of 1918 and 1920. In both years the NPL first attempted to capture the Republican party nominations by offering popular progressives as alternatives to "regular" Republicans. Only when this strategy failed twice—the NPL barely lost the primaries—did the league reluctantly agree to create a third party, the Farmer-Labor party.

Farmer-Laborism thus was part accident, part design, and the Nonpartisan League and its labor union affiliate acted much of the time as a highly organized special-interest coalition comprising two major interests, farmers and organized workers. During the first years Farmer-Labor campaigns were largely separate and often unequal attempts by these two to form a partnership while carrying on independently within a single new party. Such an approach lacked discipline and was particularly appalling to former Socialists, yet throughout Farmer-Labor history the movement's majority stressed pragmatism over ideology because it preferred successful compromise to noble electoral defeat.

FACTORS CONTRIBUTING TO THE APPEAL OF THE NPL

Political insurgency in 1918 was not the exclusive property of Non-partisanism but had been developing independently in four or five different movements. Early in the decade the *Socialist party* enjoyed modest expansion, and in 1914 when the European war broke out American Socialists often bitterly denounced both Allies and the Central Powers, charging that the holocaust was a fatal extension of capitalistic lust for more wealth. Although separated from the Socialists, the *Prohibitionist movement* (known in 1918 as the National party) also preached reform and shared some of Socialism's attitudes about the need for public ownership in selected industries. Many politically active Minnesota Prohibitionists fought for social justice while they battled the threat of demon rum. Both Socialists and Prohibitionists contributed protest votes to fledgling Farmer-Laborites in 1918, and some of them became dedicated Farmer-Labor leaders in 1920.

The *war issue,* however, galvanized much of 1918 NPL appeal. Opposition to American intervention cut across party lines, drawing together antiwar Republicans, Democrats, Socialists, Prohibitionists, and a politically significant mixture of Minnesota ethnic groups: Germans, Scandinavians, and more recent arrivals from Eastern Europe. In depth and breadth, 1917-18 antiwar sentiment anticipated much of the postwar isolationist appeal in Minnesota, both in Farmer-Laborism and within the dominant Republican party.

A fourth general source of insurgency was *economic discontent,* which found expression not only in Equity and the NPL but also in increased *labor strife.* During the midyears of the decade workers, striving for corporate acceptance of labor's right to organize, came to the realization that in Minnesota unions had to unite politically with the more numerous farmers in order to match the organizational and structural might of Big Business. Those who doubted this need for alliance were convinced by the unsuccessful industry-wide strike in 1916 of iron miners in the northeastern part of the state and by the equally bitter 1917-18 street railway strike in the Twin Cities. Labor leaders and rank and file alike saw St. Paul and especially Minneapolis as "open shop" cities "run" by business and commercial interests to the exclusion of trade and industrial union influence. Militant labor socialists were prepared to go a step further; they believed it was time for a more aggressive form of class struggle to take hold.

Last, although the Democratic party provided the insurgent realighnment neither leadership nor a sizable bloc of votes, it did leave an opposition-party vacuum. Perhaps in a nonwar period the social and economic dislocations of 1916-18 would have strengthened the

Minnesota Democratic party and even introduced balanced two-party competition then rather than thirty years later. When the Democratic party's opposition evaporated, the Nonpartisans moved in.

The Street Railway Strike

Political insurgency received a solid boost from a volatile 1917-18 street railway strike in the middle of which were caught the Republican state administration and particularly Governor Burnquist. After the bitter dispute had run its course a large part of urban organized labor drew politically closer to the Nonpartisan League.

The strike began in October 1917 when the Amalgamated Association of Street and Electric Car Employees sought to organize workers and replace the management-favored company union, the Co-operative and Protective Association. Soon the dispute expanded from a single attempt at organizing and bargaining collectively to a general local conflict over open versus closed shops as Minneapolis business, commercial, and industrial leaders urged the company to hold firm and break the strike lest it undermine Minneapolis's antiunion shop tradition. Accordingly, the company discharged fifty-seven union men, justifying its action by claiming that employees were already content with their working conditions.

Before long, the strike was a major public controversy affecting thousands of workers for whom streetcars were the sole means of transportation. A union appeal to the state Public Service Commission resulted in an order to the company to reinstate the discharged unionists. This turned the struggle into a "button war"—union button versus "company union" button—causing hard feelings and a daily exchange of curses between employees of the two factions. When the continuing dispute led to a second hearing, the commission did an about-face and issued a declaration favorable to management, stating that nonunion employees preferred "to work under the open shop."[1] However, not wishing to add organized labor to his already substantial political opposition, Burnquist removed Charles W. Ames from the commission, claiming Ames was "obnoxious to Union labor."[2] In Washington, both Senators Knute Nelson and Frank Kellogg urged the secretary of war to invoke federal emergency powers to force a settlement.

By early December enflamed strike sentiment had fanned into political controversy. The union had openly split with the commission while union critics charged it with exploiting wartime conditions to force unionization upon company and workers. A national union vice-president came to Minnesota to lend assistance, and NPL leaders gave the union moral encouragement; but the real climax came De-

cember 2 at a downtown St. Paul rally when Equity-NPL legal adviser James A. Manahan delivered a speech in which he strongly supported the union, backed higher wages, declared watered-stock burdened the company, and accused the Public Safety Commission of
attempting to strike a death blow at union labor. Afterward, a "small
riot" broke out; downtown streetcars were stoned, and 1,500 police
and home guardsmen were called in to patrol the area.

With the St. Paul Trades and Labor Assembly behind the streetcar union, a December 5 rally drew between 10,000 and 15,000 sympathizing workers and brought them a feeling of working-class solidarity remarkably akin to what farmer-NPL delegates had experienced
at the Producers and Consumers Conference three months before.
But among conservatives rumor overtook reason: the *Minneapolis
Tribune* speculated that federal agents were combing the area looking
for IWWs and "terrorists from the Iron Range." The Ramsey County
attorney and a Ramsey County grand jury moved quickly against
Manahan, St. Paul public works commissioner Oscar Keller, and state
representative Thomas J. McGrath, indicting them for speeches they
delivered at the December 2 rally.

Although a presidential commission investigating the strike tamed
the worst tempers and received a signed pledge from the union to call
off a general strike, President Wilson privately admitted to Knute
Nelson that few situations "puzzled me more.[3] When the commission returned to Minnesota in March, it reinforced the impression
among many workers that very little had been uncovered that was
critical of either the union's behavior or its cause.[4] Organized labor
had been drawn together in a classic dispute against owners and management, and many members were moved by the strike to seek closer
fellowship with agrarian protest, the NPL, and even the Socialists.
When neither Republican nor Democratic regulars appeared interested
in lending assistance to labor, the unions began to look for a new political alliance and possibly even a new third party to help them.

Republican and Democratic leaders saw the same set of events in a
much different light. This was wartime and therefore an improper
time to exploit economic and social grievances. Many conservatives
in both major parties believed that only revolutionaries and the irre-
sponsible would resort to work stoppages, and they blamed Iron
Range radicals, discontented aliens, union agitators in cities, militant Socialists, IWWs, Communists, and "Bolsheviki" for assaulting
both capitalism and "Americanism." Thus threatened, the conservative forces in Minnesota prepared to unite into an impregnable defense against impending political and social attack.

A Weakened Democratic Party in 1918

The steady coalescing of protest — antiwar, agrarian, urban — offered the Minnesota Democratic party opportunity and challenge. Unfortunately, this came at a time when much of the party was bewildered about what its response should be. Indecision would cost the party dearly in the future, because failure to respond left a political vacuum into which stepped nonpartisans and then Farmer-Laborites.

The Democratic tragedy was deepened because it occurred after a steady, if not spectacular, twenty-year revitalization of the party. In 1916, for example, Minnesota seemed on the verge of accepting two-party presidential politics, just as it already had accepted Democratic governors. Two months before the war, publishers Anton C. Weiss (Duluth) and Fred Schilplin (St. Cloud), Fred B. Wheaton, and a few other outstate Democrats formed the Minnesota Democratic Association to help recruit able party candidates for 1918.

Suddenly, the war made state Democrats cautious, and the party began a steady withdrawal and with that a long decline. Important as the war issue was in undermining Democratic partisanship, reasons for the party retreat went beyond debate over foreign policy. For one thing, a distinct incompatibility existed between urban socialists, or militant unionists, and the more traditional Democratic leadership. There was also an erosion of liberal influence within the party, or the liberal wing simply failed to grow and keep pace with changing socioeconomic conditions. Another weakness was a split between Catholic and Protestant Democrats. And many Democrats believed 1918 an improper time to exploit discontent. Combined, these factors provided insurgents an unchallenged opportunity to take the lead of those forces demanding change, reform, and a redistribution of both power and wealth.

The Prohibitionist Support of the NPL Movement

In contrast to Democratic party indecision, the Prohibitionist party was not the least bit hesitant to use the war issue for rallying support against commercial sales of alcoholic beverages. Unlike Democrats, most of whom were considered "wet" on the liquor issue, Prohibitionists espoused a "dry" America as one necessary way of improving the quality of life, preserving the family, and protecting women, children, and the home from abuse. These goals were reformist but conservative. However, the Prohibitionist name was often unrepresentative of the ideological range of interests which some fervent Prohibitionists believed in, and between 1918 and 1920 many of their active leaders would be absorbed into Farmer-Laborism.

While crusading against the liquor industry as an exploiter of human misery for capitalistic profits, many Prohibitionists as devoted social reformers were content to cement political alliances outside their own movement. For example, when a faction of Socialists bolted a St. Louis convention and reassembled in Chicago as the National party, an even larger group of chanting Prohibitionists asked to be admitted into the new convention. Thus fused, the Nationists adopted a platform urging wartime prohibition and other planks which easily merged with Minnesota Nonpartisanism: female suffrage, government ownership of railroads, packing plants, and other fundamental yet unspecified parts of the economy. Veteran Minnesota Prohibitionists E. E. Lobeck and Willis G. Calderwood returned from the National convention and became candidates for Congress and the Senate.[5] In the general election, as the sole opponent of Senator Knute Nelson, Calderwood won one vote in every three cast, his major support coming from Nonpartisans.

THE 1918 CAMPAIGN AND ELECTION

Nonpartisanism entered the initial phase of the 1918 election with many advantages. It gained much of its new strength when the Democratic party suddenly stopped providing political opposition to Minnesota Republicanism. All state officers, ten congressmen, the entire legislature, and seventy-six-year-old Senator Knute Nelson faced election. Since this was a nonpresidential year, the Nonpartisan League was better equipped to focus its campaign on state issues and personalities and not become burdened with national parties and presidential choices.

Election Strategy

The most vulnerable of the Republican incumbents was the 1917-18 governor, Jacob A. A. Burnquist, who had become controversial and unpopular among those reluctant to go to war. Burnquist pressed forcefully for strict loyalty, enthusiastically carried out the recommendations of the Public Safety Commission, and was seen as the symbolic head of a state government bent not only on suppressing antiwar discussion but on cutting off any rallies and demonstrations that questioned the correctness of intervention and conscription. Consequently, Burnquist was especially unpopular with German-Americans and antiwar Norwegians and Swedes. The NPL quickly recognized the governor's vulnerability and concluded it would be easier to defeat him than any other Republican incumbent.

Acting both cautiously and pragmatically, the Nonpartisan League decided to concentrate on defeating weak Republican incumbents and not oppose Nelson, who after fifty years of public life seemed near retirement. Before war came, Nelson seriously considered stepping down, and no less than six congressmen, university regent Fred B. Snyder, and antiwar critic James A. Peterson (who had run against Nelson as the 1912 Progressive candidate) wanted to succeed him.

Born in Norway, Nelson was one of Minnesota's acutely astute politicians. He had never been defeated for public office, and as the first Scandinavian candidate for governor he was responsible in 1892 for stopping the Populist challenge in Minnesota. Although a Nonpartisan opponent and a staunch supporter of the war, he remained characteristically silent about the league and therefore the NPL found him difficult to attack. Prudent Republicans and Democrats began urging him not to retire but to stand for reelection one more time, to help stop the league momentum, and publishers of the *Minneapolis Journal* and the *Duluth News Tribune* privately begged him to run.[6]

Social ferment now began to alter substantially the overall Minnesota political environment. Neither outstate Democrats nor the Lawler-O'Connor Democratic machine in St. Paul displayed any enthusiasm for supporting the increasingly militant Twin Cities labor movement. As war widened this gap, the state Democratic party was further undermined by the president's apparent preference to see Nelson run again.[7] By March 1918 many active Minnesota Democrats had decided, in the interest of wartime unity, not to challenge Republican incumbents. Furthermore, Democrats offered little or no assistance to the striking streetcar union even though Wilson's presidential commission encouraged mediation by the Council of National Defense. Both the company and the Public Safety Commission opposed mediation or rehiring discharged unionists, and business interests, especially a group called the Minneapolis Citizens Alliance, fought the union, knowing as they did that the Public Safety Commission, Burnquist, and the Republicans would defend the business point of view.[8]

In the name of wartime patriotism Democrats waved aside opportunity, turned their back on labor and two-party responsibility, and prepared to help Republicans conquer insurgency and protest. Politically neutralized or worse, Democrats agreed to the reelection of Knute Nelson, J. A. A. Burnquist, and most Republican incumbents. In Minneapolis a joint committee was formed by Democrats, Republicans, and conservative labor leaders to ensure defeat of Socialist mayor Thomas Van Lear.[9] When state Democratic chairman Fred B. Wheaton issued a call for a March 27 convention, the party was nearly moribund. Only the actions of John Lind prevented an open party endorsement of Nelson, but most Catholic Democrats and the top party names — Wheaton, Schilplin, Weiss, and Lawler — gave Nelson a personal endorsement anyway.

To see the party name survive for future elections, Wheaton formally ran for governor. But the party was becoming a hollow shell, and an entire generation would pass before the strength of the state Democratic organization was reestablished and the party reaccepted the role of vigorous opponent to Republicans.

The Nonpartisan League Convention

The NPL willingly stepped into the vacuum left by state Democrats and quickly assumed major responsibility for opposing Minnesota Republicans in 1918. Several hundred farmer delegates gathered in mid-March for the NPL state convention, and organized labor was invited to send special representatives. To guard against the charge of disloyalty, convention organizers carefully screened speakers and topics, and the same caution was exercised in choosing candidates, who were handpicked in a secret caucus by some forty league leaders.

Making every effort to overcome an image of disloyalty and war opposition, the league invited the White House to participate in its convention. Messages to the delegates came from Carl Vrooman of the Department of Agriculture and George Creel of Wilson's Committee on Public Information, and Federal Tariff Commissioner William Kent attended. The last was a former California congressman who spoke personally for Wilson and claimed the president was not fearful of radical measures when they were needed to correct economic abuses.[10] To erase the stigma of La Follette's and Van Lear's speeches delivered the previous September, the league pledged full assistance to the nation in "this supreme hour of trial," endorsed the president's war aims, and supported the goal of worldwide democracy. "Let our victory over the forces of disloyalty and reaction at home be as great as [the] victory over the forces of autocracy abroad," the league said in answer to the unconstitutional assaults which were then being inflicted upon it.[11]

However, incredulous conservatives, whether Republican or Democratic, disbelieved league assertions of loyalty. Instead, these critics looked at and even beyond what the league proposed as public policy. The 1918 league platform, though not radical, was nevertheless sufficiently collectivized to send a sharp chill up the spine of a sizable sector of private industry. It included a call for:

1. Lowered farm taxes, exemption of farm improvements from increased tax assessment.
2. State-owned packing plants, cold-storage plants, elevator terminals, warehouses.
3. State-owned pulp and paper mills, newsprint sold at cost.
4. State hail insurance.
5. Reform of grain inspection and grading practices.
6. An eight-hour workday, except for agricultural labor.
7. A state system of life, accident, and old-age insurance.
8. Progressive income taxes, taxes on excess profits.
9. Government-owned munitions plants.
10. Government control when labor and private management fail to negotiate differences.
11. Increased ore taxes through a tonnage tax on iron ore.[12]

The conservatives asked themselves, If this is the beginning, what is likely to follow? After all, in Russia Kerensky came first but now the Bolsheviks were taking firm command.

To conserve strength, the league largely avoided seeking congressional seats and concentrated upon state offices. It endorsed only two congressional candidates and worked hardest for Glenwood dentist Dr. Henrik Shipstead, and it followed Townley's recommendation not to endorse any opponent of Knute Nelson. Its major goals were to deny renomination to Governor Burnquist and to recruit qualified candidates for the state legislature. League candidates were carefully selected from the dominant ethnic groups as German, Scandinavian, and Irish surnamed individuals like Mueller, Malmberg, Tjosvold, and Sullivan were chosen to widen its overall appeal.

In choosing a gubernatorial candidate the league gambled with maverick progressive Charles A. Lindbergh, who had served ten years in Congress (1907-17). Lindbergh spoke, voted, and wrote as a longtime adversary of business. His *Banking and Currency and the Money Trust* (1913) had established him as a bitter enemy of the banking system, as early as 1915 he had contributed articles to the Nonpartisan *Leader,* and his *Why Is Your Country at War, and What Happens to You after the War, and Related Subjects* (1917), though hastily and poorly written, had summarized his antiintervention attitudes. The league needed a sufficiently well-known candidate to oppose Burnquist, and Lindbergh seemed well fitted; unfortunately, his candidacy made the league more vulnerable on the war loyalty issue because his endorsement seemed sharply in contradiction with league professions of standing solidly behind Wilson's war policy. The *Minneapolis Journal*[13] and other newspapers drew immediate headline attention to the inconsistency, and regular Republicans made it the centerpiece of their primary campaign.

Political Harassment during the Primary Campaign

The 1918 Minnesota primary campaign was important because it combined bitter political conflict with ideological confrontation. Only two other primaries in the state (1920 and 1938) were as bitter as this one, and no primary since has come close to matching the level of harassment inflicted upon the losers.

Lindbergh courageously traveled the state as hundreds of farmers turned out to hear him almost everywhere he spoke. He bravely endured threats, tomatoes, stones, and on one occasion a shot. From late winter right through the primary election there was an unmistakable increase in prosecutions against league officials under state and federal emergency statutes. League secretary Joseph Gilbert stood trial five times in five months. Townley was arrested several times, and both he and Gilbert were convicted in Jackson County for allegedly inciting draft resistance, though appeals delayed their sentences until 1921. Nineteen counties literally closed off all league meetings and rallies.[14]

Perhaps the worst fate befell Minneapolis lawyer James A. Peterson, running against Nelson. The Democratic U. S. Attorney hauled him before federal judge Page Morris for indictment the first week of April on a charge of printing a seditious article that obstructed the draft. Nine days later, after the judge ruled against a defense claim of freedom of the press ("I have no doubt as to the constitutionality of the law in war and not much in time of peace"), Peterson was convicted and sentenced to Leavenworth, Kansas.[15] Then in late April the Democratic state central committee formally voted Nelson's endorsement, which John Lind had blocked at the Democratic convention.

Methodically, a triumvirate of church, press, and orthodoxy went solemnly forward in holy mission, united against a dangerous heresy. The Catholic bishop of St. Cloud, in a heavily-settled German region, spoke against the league and literally prayed for a regular Republican victory. The principal daily newspapers, led by the *Tribune, Journal, Pioneer Press,* and *Dispatch,* and the *Duluth Herald,* consistently reported the campaign in biased, unfair, and often dishonest ways.

Proleague papers like the (Alexandria) *Park Region Echo* were intimidated, their editors threatened or fined. Under the guidance of Charles J. Moos, a future St. Paul postmaster who had worked for Kellogg's election in 1916, the German-language press cooperated with the Republicans, faithfully rallying to "loyal" candidates. Republican regulars were, as they told the party's national chairman, waging war "against socialism and allied radical elements."[16] Almost overnight expensive campaign magazines appeared to expose the league.

Few could confidently predict the primary result. The league was well organized, but it also faced a united front opposition. And, since it was a new, largely unknown political pressure group, there was widespread uneasiness about the league: Was it radical, disloyal, disruptive, or secretly associating with foreign revolutionaries? Was it guilty of creating disturbances and unnecessary dissatisfaction when the nation was at war? Such questions were not always asked in order to gain partisan advantage but were genuine concerns since league candidates sounded sensible and moderate; but what about its platform? Many people found the league a puzzle, a political departure yet too new and too unknown to be fully accepted or trusted.

Harassment both hindered and helped the NPL. Looking more martyred with each passing day, the league quickly expanded its membership as over 1,000 farmers joined each week during the spring, with 7,000 new members enrolling in May.[17] In outstate areas where the league was strong, Republican activity fell off sharply. A veteran Republican campaign organizer, finding he could learn little about what was happening because local Republicans were fearfully silent, complained "We have no organization. It is simply chaos...."[18]

And league advantages were substantial. Besides the war issue, it had gifted leaders, superior, disciplined organization, and a crusading zeal. In 1918 it easily rallied Minnesota's protest forces after they had been all but abandoned by Republicans and Democrats. It also had a popular theme, "conscript wealth," and a now vulnerable opponent, Burnquist. The governor had been invited to speak to the league convention, but he treated the invitation with contempt and his reply abused the movement. He charged that it was being led not by "real farmers" and "real workers" but by pro-Germans, IWWs, "Red Socialists," and "self-seeking demagogues" who, like wolves, paraded "in sheep's clothing."[19]

Republicans tried their best to save him. A contrived letter, written to Knute Nelson by Republicans but actually signed by eighty-three-year-old Cyrus Northrop, sounded like a legitimate inquiry about Burnquist and the election. Nelson's reply, not surprisingly, endorsed Burnquist and described the governor as a clean, honest, hardworking, fearlessly loyal public servant who was entitled to renomination. The two letters were "boiler plated" and sent to 36 daily newspapers and some 544 country weeklies for publication in early June. Coming at a time before the appearance of radio and television, this kind of endorsement from Nelson — always a cautious politician — was important.

As the primary ended, the Twin Cities papers acted almost as an adjunct to the Republican state central committee. On pages one and four the *Minneapolis Tribune* printed a headline-type message to the electorate: "Vote in Minnesota the Way the Boys Shoot in France." Needless to say, the tide turned sharply against the Nonpartisans.

Primary Results

No primary and few if any general elections have been taken as seriously by Minnesota voters as that of June 17, 1918. It was the last primary before the woman's suffrage amendment took effect. An estimated 94 percent of eligible enrolled male voters cast ballots, 369,000 as Republicans, 33,000 as Democrats (there were no Democratic congressional contests and only two gubernatorial candidates). The primary vote exceeded the 1916 presidential vote and was only 21,000 votes below the November 1918 turnout.

Republican regulars were victorious. Knute Nelson, without leaving Washington or making a speech, received almost two votes for every three cast and led all nominees. Burnquist, once considered a likely loser, won 54 percent and a 50,000 margin of victory. The only regular who lost was Supreme Court Clerk I. A. Caswell, a victim more of long-simmering factional dispute with Minneapolis Republicans; Caswell was defeated by a conservative German-American Catholic from Stearns County who, though he had supported McKinley in 1896, had won league endorsement. And antiwar district congressman Ernest Lundeen was defeated for renomination.

Nevertheless, the NPL threat to the Republicans could not be taken lightly. League candidates for lieutenant governor and attorney general polled only 6,500 and 11,000 fewer votes than the regulars, and in the seventh district Shipstead with 46 percent came close to winning; a switch of just 1,500 votes from nationally prominent congressman A. J. Volstead to Shipstead would have changed the outcome. League candidates did better in contests for the nonpartisan-designated legislature. In active league-organized districts it claimed nomination for three-quarters of its endorsees and expected to have a visible minority in the 1919 session.[20] For eight state offices, the range of league votes was from 118,000 to 151,000, its percentage between 28 and 41; this compared well with the regulars' 116,000 to 205,000 votes, or 31 to 55 percentage. The NPL showing was an impressive start, since every regular was an incumbent. Still, the league had failed to win in Minnesota, and it fell considerably short of equaling the victory it had gained in 1916 and repeated in 1918 in North Dakota. Impatient leaguers were forced to consider a change in strategy.

Labor Insurgency and the Third Party

Few years match the political destabilization of 1918. Republicans, though much less disorganized than Democrats, nevertheless were disspirited over Burnquist's political performance and continued to worry that some kind of unholy alliance might yet take place between Democrats and Nonpartisans, unlikely as this seemed.

After the primary the major catalyst for disestablishing the prevailing Minnesota party system was the Minnesota State Federation of Labor. When the MFL met in annual state convention at Hibbing on July 17, the normal expectation would have been for it to follow cautiously the Samuel Gompers tradition of avoiding partisanship, rewarding political friends and supporters, and opposing third and particularly labor third parties. The two leading MFL state officers proposed to do this very thing.

Insurgents challenged it. More militant than Secretary George Lawson and President H. G. Hall, younger labor socialists active in and sympathetic to the industrial union movement equally distrusted the two parties and the large corporations. Organizational setbacks on the Iron Range and in the street railway controversy suggested to socialist and rank and file alike that labor was vulnerable and badly in need of political friends. Business had been protected by Burnquist, the MCPS, and local trade associations like the Chamber of Commerce, the Association of Commerce, and the Citizens Alliance. But who was willing to defend labor?

Labor insurgents thought they knew the answer. Led by three socialists — Juls Anderson, John Emme, and William Mahoney — they secured an invitation for Nonpartisan League counsel Arthur LeSueur to sit in the MFL convention as an NPL delegate. LeSueur, a socialist himself, delivered a fervent plea for a third party. At a crucial moment of debate on this issue, Mahoney took the floor and in an emotional, eloquent address urged organized labor, socialists, and Nonpartisans to unite and oppose Burnquist's reelection. To the surprise of federation conservatives, Mahoney and his supporters gained an affirmative vote for the third-party proposal, and a reluctant George Lawson agreed to call a joint Federation-NPL conference in August to negotiate an agreement.[21]

After a fashion, this turned out to be August lovemaking between farmers and workers, but not the birth of a party. On August 20 a committee began negotiations over possible candidates. On August 24 what some claimed to be a convention convened — in disagreement. Militants and socialists argued that its purpose was the formal creation of a third party. Federation president H. G. Hall denied this and declared it was only to select a slate of legislative candidates endorsed jointly by workers and farmers, a position which the (NPL) *Minnesota Leader* rejected.[22] Whatever its purpose, this rapidly changing series of events upset regular Democrats who realized, too late, the threat to their future. State Democratic leaders Fred Lynch and Fred Wheaton made a hurried trip to the White House to confer with presidential secretary Joseph Tumulty in the hope of securing administrative help for Wheaton's gubernatorial candidacy. None was forthcoming and the panicky Democrats understood at last that protest, which could have been channeled to their party, was now weakening their coalition and being drained into Farmer-Laborism.

The final agreement on August 25 was much less than the third party advocates had hoped for. Within the MFL Hall and Lawson continued to resist fusion and third-partyism. When farmer delegates mixed in joint convention with some ninety union local representatives in St. Paul's Trade Union Hall, there was no agreement to sire a third party, nor were precautions taken to prevent its conception. Rather, two committees met, one from the unions and the other from the NPL, and they negotiated a settlement on candidates. By and large, farmers fared the best, which would be the pattern of the future. Endorsed for governor was Tracy implement dealer David J. Evans, an unknown political novice, with a lawyer from Marshall, Thomas Davis, for attorney general. The agreement gave the impression that in the new movement farmers were first among equals, and candidates, at least those for major office, were petty bourgeois and not socialists.

This was but a beginning, a mere loose federation into which only part of the protest movement had been funneled. The hyphenated "Farmer-Labor" symbolized the separateness rather than the unity of its two branches. Only three Farmer-Labor candidates were offered for statewide office, including primary-winner Herman Mueller for supreme court clerk, a league-endorsed Republican. Part in the movement and part outside it was William L. Carss, a Proctor locomotive engineer running for eighth-district congressman as a Union Labor candidate. The National party had seven candidates, several of whom competed against Farmer-Laborites.

The Working People's Political League

What had been created in August 1918 was a name rather than a party, which in turn was organizationally overshadowed by two distinctly separate leagues, a farmers' Nonpartisan League and now a Working People's Nonpartisan League (WPPL). The newer WPPL had a state committee, an executive committee, and district committees which were completely independent of the NPL. Each league ran its own campaign for Farmer-Labor candidates; liaison was rare to nonexistent. The WPPL manifesto asked "the working people of Minnesota and their sympathizers to unite in a political movement that will protect and promote the welfare of those who toil." Remembering labor's organizational defeats, the WPPL blamed them on Burnquist and the Public Safety Commission, and it promised to fight against postwar control of working people by a "class of discredited and incompetent plutocrats."

For labor socialists the WPPL manifesto was a moderate beginning, cautious, pluralistic, and a significant compromise between ideal principles and political reality. In this respect Mahoney and the men responsible for it were following the practice of the Socialists who had abandoned their North Dakota party and developed the NPL. But the labor manifesto contained seeds of future discord:

> We maintain that the prime duty and highest function of government is to provide ample opportunity for all to earn an honest living. When the government assumes industrial functions, labor as the most vital factor in the production of wealth, should become the dominating element in government so that the interest of the producing class may receive proper consideration, and the non-producing rich may not be in a position to exploit and oppress the masses of mankind.[23]

If labor was to dominate, what would be the rank of independent farmers in this hierarchy?

That already there were differences could be seen in the given name, Farmer-Labor. Some preferred to use the better known name, Progressive, for the new "party." A joint committee thrashed out this problem. Mahoney insisted that "Labor" be included, and William Lemke of the NPL held out for "Farmer." Eventually the two men, with James Manahan, Fred Pike, and Thomas Fraser, reached the inevitable hyphenated compromise.[24]

The Four-Party Fall Campaign

To generalize about the 1918 election is difficult. Four parties competed — Republican, Farmer-Labor, Democratic, and National — and a referendum on the Prohibition amendment was held. The only certain things, aside from the names of candidates and parties, were that voters cast 380,604 ballots and that four candidates received higher "approval" votes than the 189,614 in favor of Prohibition.

The Democrats were neither politically alive nor dead but badly injured by fratricide and the new Farmer-Labor movement. First John Lind and his followers sought to petition a competitor to Wheaton onto the ballot, but the Republican secretary of state rejected it. Then the Democrats petitioned seven more candidates onto the ballot but left Knute Nelson unopposed. A frustrated John Lind and Democratic St. Paul mayor Lawrence C. (Larry Ho) Hodgson followed by publicly endorsing Nelson's Prohibitionist opponent, Willis G. Calderwood. The national Democrats added to the confusion when in late October they launched a drive to elect Democrats, although the national committee had already endorsed Calderwood. Under these unstable and confused conditions it was little wonder why only the Republicans were in a position to benefit.

Election Results

For the last all-male general election in Minnesota, 89.5 percent of enrolled voters turned out, and a clear majority gave the Republican party a vote of confidence. Republicans won all nine state offices, eight of ten congressional seats, solid control over the nonparty-designated legislature, and Knute Nelson carried seventy-seven (of eighty-seven) counties and 54 percent of the vote. Burnquist, however, did poorly; his 44-percent vote was enough to win, but it fell considerably below the 50-percent combined vote of his Democratic and Farmer-Labor opponents. The only major loss came with the defeat of eighth-district congressman Clarence B. Miller.

For Democrats the result was an ominous forewarning. With its organization in disarray and its leaders split along religious lines, the party was unprepared to cope with economic protest and political opportunity. Yet pockets of Democratic strength remained. One was the fourth district (St. Paul) where congressman Carl C. Van Dyke was overwhelmingly reelected (62 percent). The party could also claim partial credit for the eighth-district congressional victory of William L. Carss, a brotherhood of railway trainmen engineer who was helped by Lind Democrats and who received limited financial contributions from the national Democratic congressional campaign committee. Two years later he was reelected as a Democrat. Overall, the Democratic vote for state offices averaged only 23 percent, and it would soon plummet lower.

Political protest had made inroads in Minnesota. Each of the three Farmer-Labor candidates for state offices outpolled his Democratic counterpart, averaging together 28 percent of the vote. In Minneapolis socialist mayor Thomas Van Lear barely was defeated (28,955 to 27,650) by a two-party coalition. And the NPL claimed legislative victory for 11 of its 37 endorsed senate candidates (out of 67 seats), 22 of its 49 house nominees (out of 131 seats).[25] In wartime or any other this would be called a moral victory. Unfortunately, Farmer-Laborism was seeking much more. Its goal was political power, not just social criticism, economic protest, or the honor of displacing the Democrats as the Republican party's opposition. Three of every four Farmer-Labor votes came outside Hennepin, Ramsey, and St. Louis counties, leaving largely unsettled the greater issue of effective long-range strategy and the kind of candidate appeal necessary to gain major victory.

PREPARING FOR 1920

Although pleased with their 1918 victory, Minnesota Republicans neither overestimated the extent of their appeal nor underestimated the postwar threat of Nonpartisanism. Nor did Republicans or insurgents understand current public feeling about the policy disputes over which they jousted. Both stumbled about looking for a balance of issues and tactics that would bring future success.

Republican-Sponsored Reform

Victory gave Republicans the time to assess critically the impact of recent protest. Nevertheless, they were deeply divided by party factionalism as well as by two major economic interests, each of which fought against becoming the political sacrifice of the other. Such an economic split was nothing new. For example: Duluth millionaire Chester A. Congdon (he died in 1916) had vast holdings in iron mining property and securities; he and his followers were sometimes known as the "steel Republicans." Senator Frank Kellogg had once served as counsel for the United States Steel Corporation. Aligned against them in the party were powerful lumber and milling interests concentrated in Minneapolis.

Progressives and Republican pragmatists believed some kind of accommodation had to be made in order to offset the protest movement's complaints against the established system in Minnesota. The question was: Who or what interest might be sacrificed for the good of the party? Milling and grain interests? Mining interests? Or both? Neither sector was about to volunteer. Equity and the NPL focused first upon the grain trade. After the miners' strike the league broadened its program to include protections for workers and miners, and there was talk of a "just" or higher tax — an iron ore tonnage tax — on the mining industry and of financing internal improvements (like schools) in the northeast by the industry and not by individual homestead property taxpayers.

To retain power, Republican officeholders would soon take up the cause of cooperatives, tax relief, especially for farmers, and higher mining taxes. As political strategy, it became the stitch in time that would help save nine Republicans for every one that would lose to the new protest movement. In the process of accommodation Republicans demonstrated greater flexibility than Democrats, who were now so debilitated by the insurgent movement that they were becoming a third-rate party about to be displaced by Farmer-Laborism for the next quarter century.

To the credit of the Minnesota Republican party, it recognized the political need for going beyond a campaign of congressional or legislative investigation of alleged subversion by radical revolutionaries, though the party by no means gave up this approach as a way of discrediting 1919-20 protest. The wiser course, however, and the one that better served the party, was the decision to offer some policy reforms in partial answer to agrarian demands for economic justice. This response was essential, though not easy, since it required usually conservative party professionals to resist the pressure being exerted by agribusiness and the mining industry not to give in.

One of the wiser hands dispensing political wisdom was none other than Knute Nelson, who, after all, had successfully lived through and compromised with the Granger, Alliance, and Populist movements in the nineteenth century and the Progressive in the twentieth. Nelson never directly attacked the league, and when the vote came to expel Robert La Follette from the Senate for his speech before the Producers and Consumers Conference in 1917, which the Public Safety Commission had recommended, Nelson and Frank Kellogg voted against the resolution. Nelson well understood the need for a positive

Republican program. Privately, he chastised grain millers and emerging conglomerates like the Washburn-Crosby Company (the forerunner of General Mills and the initials of which were later used by radio station WCCO), for profit mania. In spite of bitter Washburn-Crosby opposition, Nelson sponsored a bill backed by the Minnesota Railroad and Warehouse Commission for U.S. government-owned grain warehouses in New York, and he bluntly told the grain industry they should not "take such a narrow view of the question." When the Supreme Court threw out congressional power to tax stock dividends, Nelson sponsored a constitutional amendment to restore the power.[26]

In Minnesota the 1919 legislature more than sensed the Nonpartisan presence and began what for many conservatives was a painful adjustment. Despite Burnquist's wish to have legislative party labels restored after a 1913 reform removed them, the legislature rejected the move even though NPL legislators were but a small minority. Progressives, moderates, or sometimes just ordinarily astute Republicans in the legislature recognized the political wisdom in increasing taxes on the mining industry. Tax reform through the imposition of an iron ore tonnage tax, something the Nonpartisans had been demanding for several years, became the session's most controversial issue, created sharp divisions in the majority caucus, and ended in a stalemate at the regular session as supporters of the steel industry blocked it, only to have it pass in the special session that followed. Nelson advised his conservative protégé, State Auditor J. A. O. Preus, to support the tax. But the foolish Burnquist, already a political liability, vetoed the bill as the steel forces wanted him to do, bringing Nelson to lament that the governor's action had put the Republicans "in a very sad condition."[27] Wiser heads could see Burnquist's stigma infecting the entire party, and to offset it the 1920 Republican platform included a tonnage tax plank.

NPL Disadvantages in the Postwar Period

Attacks upon Nonpartisanism diminished little if at all when peace came abruptly in November 1918. They left its leadership in doubt about what was appropriate strategy to follow in the postwar period, since victory at the election polls remained the first objective. NPL leaders sometimes were embarrassed by radicals, communists, and overzealous socialists who were certain that class warfare had begun in earnest, yet the league needed both assistance and dedicated organizers, and the Farmer-Labor coalition was still in the process of being formed.

Because the league needed broad popular support to win in 1920, it could ill afford to appear radical rather than moderate. Unfortunately, world political conditions were rapidly changing, and as Lenin communists — "Bolsheviki" — came to power in Russia, the tremors were felt in the United States. Neither left nor right knew what to expect next. Some feared that capitalism and representative democracy were about to be besieged by violent revolutionaries; a few looked forward to a coming new order. In the Senate a powerful Judiciary subcommittee simultaneously launched investigations of wartime German propaganda, communist subversion, and the Nonpartisan League. Examples of subversion, occasionally real but usually imaginary, were exposed in the subcommittee hearings held between September 1918 and March 1919, and fearful conservatives were eager to cite its reports both to educate the public and to gain political advantage. The *Red Scare* was on. Knute Nelson reasoned that the investigations were a legitimate attempt to "smoke out the disloyal elements and the Bolsheviki," and in a matter of time government agents were paraded before the committee, vividly describing Midwest Nonpartisan League activities in ludicrously threatening and misrepresentive detail. League patriotism was questioned, its reputation slandered, and its leaders were judged guilty by association with socialists and communists. Who could tell the difference? In a Senate speech of February 8, 1919, Nelson claimed anarchists and Bolshevists were beyond First Amendment protection and subject to prior censorship and repression under a doctrine of inherent governmental right to self-preservation.[28] Yet in spite of conservatives' hallucinations about radicalism, local evidence usually did not sustain the reality of a revolutionary threat even though *Minneapolis Journal* editor H. V. Jones claimed radicals had taken command of both the NPL and local labor unions.[29]

Despite these attacks, the Nonpartisan League continued to grow, but its period of rapid expansion was nearing an end. Old and new problems plagued it. The sedition trials of Townley and Gilbert resulted in July 1919 convictions. Campaigns were slowly being undertaken to narrow its influence. Knute Nelson had a Norwegian-American publicist placed in the Chicago publicity office of the Republican national committee to work with the three largest Norwegian language papers against the league. More important was the appearance of sharp disagreement with the NPL apparatus itself. In North Dakota William Langer attacked Townley's leadership and an Independent Voters Association (IVA) was formed to offset NPL election influence; in Minnesota socialist Arthur LeSueur resigned from the league and commenced a long and bitter denunciation of Townley, his "schemes," and his strategy of nonalignment.[30]

Political insurgency was still far from becoming muted, but as a movement it was increasingly uncertain about which party it would work within to secure its objectives. Nonpartisans largely ignored the now weak Democratic party. In a special 1919 election held in the Fourth Congressional District to replace the deceased Democrat Carl C. Van Dyke, the winning candidate, to the dismay of business interests, turned out to be St. Paul public works commissioner Oscar Keller, a Republican who had spoken out in support of striking streetcar unionists in 1917. Keller was no radical or even a Farmer-Laborite, but labor had not forgotten his courage, and in returning the favor labor caused orthodox Republicans to speculate about an unholy alliance between Keller and the NPL in the 1920 gubernatorial campaign.

The Working People's Nonpartisan Political League

Uncertain whether to follow a third-party strategy in 1920 and recognizing that the NPL generated three times as many votes as labor did in 1918, MFL insurgents chose to imitate farmers by formally establishing a workers' league in 1919. At the thirty-seventh State Federation of Labor convention, held at New Ulm in Brown County where the German vote had gone strongly against the state Republicans, William Mahoney and Thomas Van Lear worked through an adjunct Labor Political Conference which created an NPL counterpart for labor named the Working People's Nonpartisan Political League (WPNPL).

Dominated by labor socialists and beyond the control of the regulars in the state federation, the WPNPL borrowed heavily from the NPL platform by combining progressive reforms with moderate socialism. Condemning "monstrous schemes" led by military-industrial political imperialists, the WPNPL defended First Amendment freedoms as the best defense against tyranny, revolution, and reaction, stressed complete equality of women with men, sought a guarantee for workers to organize and bargain with employers, called for an eight-hour workday and a forty-four hour workweek, the elimination of unemployment, and government work programs during depressions. Middlemen in production and distribution were to be eliminated, cooperatives encouraged, and income and inheritance tax laws reformed. To displace "autocratic selfish private interests" in control of the economy, the WPNPL called for nationalization of transportation, communication, packing plants, grain elevators and terminals, public utilities, and natural resources. In this revised economic system the workers league foresaw a withering of control by selfish interests and its replacement by those "who work by hand and brain."[31]

The program blended progressive and utopian principles, but was it a strategy which, at last, would bring the downfall of orthodox interests and Minnesota Republicanism? The Old Party pros thought not. "I sometimes get discouraged," a veteran party organizer and former U. S. marshal confessed, "but usually wind up believing that our [Minnesota voting] people will level up and that it will come out all right in the end." His 1920 campaign strategy was simple:

> In this state it seems to me that instead of letting the league and labor make the issue—we should make socialism and radicalism the issue and show that Townley and radical labor stand for these ruinous things.[32]

THE 1920 CAMPAIGN AND ELECTION

Foreign Policy Issues

Armistice Day November 11, 1918, quickly ushered in a return to domestic politics and a postwar controversy over peace, the Versailles Treaty, and American affiliation with the League of Nations. State debate over the loyalty issue did not just abruptly end, but it now was displaced by other matters and effectively neutralized by careful selection of candidates. Any difference between Republican and Nonpartisan foreign policy was relative, not absolute, the Republicans being more internationalist, the Farmer-Laborites more isolationist. Both Knute Nelson and Frank Kellogg supported the peace treaty and the League of Nations, whereas the isolationists, initially, remained skeptical and continued to question the wisdom of intervention in international affairs. Displacing the war issue in 1920 was an intense economic argument: the ideological clash over the nature of the economy and the intrusion of socialist alternatives to private enterprise.

Competing for the Vote of a Vastly Expanded Electorate

Republican ability to remobilize popular support was about to be severely tested, and Farmer-Laborites now had before them a grand opportunity to expand as the Nineteenth Amendment went into effect. For the first time, large numbers of Minnesota women would vote for state and national offices. With returning Doughboys added, the size of the electorate more than doubled, an increase of 420,000 voters since 1918, or a growth of 110 percent! For whom would the new voters cast their ballots? What most appealed to their values and interests? Insurgency, equal rights, socialism, a social democratic ideology? Or the more "traditional" platform: private ownership, an appeal to sacred family relationships, limited change through modest reform? Whatever it was, the Minnesota NPL was better prepared than it had been two years before; its membership increased in early 1920 to 50,000,[33] about 6 percent of the total vote, and potentially double that number if farmers' wives voted the way their league husbands did. If WPNPL and labor votes were added, and if all workers behaved in disciplined response to the command of insurgent leaders — an unlikely expectation — the insurgent voting bloc would be sizable.

Republican Factionalism

These changes should have been a great help to any broad new political coalition, and they coincided with growing differences among Republican factions: city versus countryside, lumbering and milling versus mining, old guard against Progressives, the "interests" competing with the professionals seeking election. Factional discord was sufficiently worrisome to bring in national Republican chairman Will Hays to mediate differences, and it spilled onto the four major competitors seeking the gubernatorial nomination: Secretary of State Julius Schmahl, Lieutenant Governor Thomas Frankson, Congressman Franklin Ellsworth, and State Auditor J. A. O. Preus. Broadest support was going to Preus, and an official of the *Duluth News Tribune* made it no secret that Republicans in northeastern Minnesota were "necessarily forced to look" for an aspirant who was not antisteel.[34] Schmahl, Frankson, and Ellsworth had irritated steel spokesmen by supporting the tonnage tax proposal, whereas the steel industry liked the fact that Preus had kept his tax thoughts to himself as long as he could. The auditor was helped still more by his popularity with influential Minneapolis Republicans.

The Nonpartisan Slate of Candidates

The general challenge facing Nonpartisans was the need to popularize their cause with the electorate. Each league issued a call for a separate but simultaneous convention on March 24-25, and between them communication was carried on through a joint conference committee. Leaders from both negotiated a slate of candidates to be entered in the Republican primary, with emphasis on the governorship where six candidates — Lindbergh, Manahan, Shipstead, Van Lear, Hibbing mayor Victor Power, and former University of Minnesota professor Willis M. West — were considered by the joint screening and conference committee before its recommendation was passed on to the two conventions. The endorsed slate led by Shipstead once more clearly showed greater deference to farmers' preferences, and it hinted strongly that the agrarians would be the most influential in determining the direction Minnesota insurgency would take.

Two possible, and contradictory, impressions were being formed about 1920 Farmer-Laborism. Many of its legislative and policy objectives appeared to be steered along a social democratic byway which over time seemed capable of widening into a road leading to public ownership. But, in contrast, its populist candidates seemed to be progressive political moderates, generally more content with economic and regulatory reform than with limited socialism.

Henrik Shipstead well illustrated this dualism. After graduation from Northwestern University he set up a dental practice at Glenwood in central Minnesota, served three routine years as village mayor, ran successfully for the legislature in 1916 before the Nonpartisans had taken hold, and nearly upset veteran seventh-district congressman A. J. Volstead in the 1918 primary. Shipstead was a worthy challenger: he projected a handsome, impressive, almost patrician image, he spoke moderately and intelligently, and his cautious, vague reformism sounded anything but radical.

The candidate for lieutenant governor, George H. Mallon, a former captain and winner of the congressional Medal of Honor, was the obvious league answer to the loyalty issue. The candidate for attorney general again was NPL legal counsel Thomas V. Sullivan, who had run strongly (42 percent) in 1918. Seeking the position of secretary of state was Thomas V. Vollom, a farmer and cooperative manager. Another farmer, Paul Ostby, won endorsement for the regulatory Railroad and Warehouse Commission. At later district conventions endorsements were added for fourth-district congressman Oscar Keller, William L. Carss who sought congressional reelection as a Democrat, and Lutheran minister O. J. Kvale in the seventh.[35]

The Republican "Eliminating Convention"

The existence of a league candidate slate made organizational discipline imperative for Republican regulars. It was imposed by resorting to an endorsing convention, which Iron Range Republicans first proposed in July 1919 and old Knute Nelson recommended in the fall.[36] Republicans normally allowed factional disputes to be settled for better or worse in the primary, but because the NPL was more disciplined and had a moderate slate of candidates the regulars could not afford this luxury. Facing potential defeat, Republicans made a call for a May 7 "eliminating convention."

The gathering was anything but harmonious. When Secretary of State Julius Schmahl angrily withdrew, he condemned "certain interests" for dictating the nomination of Preus. Ellsworth and Frankson were more defiant; both refused to drop out, ran in the primary, and paid the price of having their political careers cut short. Endorsed with Preus were two incumbents and Mike Holm for secretary of state (1921-52) as a replacement for Frankson.[37]

Steel Republicans were highly pleased by Preus's endorsement but dismayed by convention approval of the ore tonnage tax. To counteract it the industry helped create a Fair Tax Association, a move which upset the shrewder party professionals. "It looks as though the Steel Trust [U.S. Steel Corporation] were trying to sandbag our State Convention," Knute Nelson complained to his protégé Preus, "and the movement [by steel] can only aggravate and tend to unite the farmers on the other side." Steel, however, was not quite that suicidal and one of its sympathizers told Nelson, "We will do our best to help save the State from Socialism in spite of the tonnage tax plank."[38]

The Primary Campaign against Socialism

The short intensive 1920 primary campaign was not what Nonpartisanism wanted, nor was the movement able to control the issues under debate to its best advantage. In a general way the regular Republicans said: If Nonpartisanism represents an economic and political break with past practices, if its end is to be a special midwestern blend of socialism and public ownership, then let that fact be debated openly and let it not be distorted by disguising the outcome with a blend of moderate-appearing candidates and misunderstood reforms.

Nonpartisans wanted to continue the strategy that had carried them to near victory before. They carefully built upon familiar abuses which agrarians had campaigned against for a decade, stressing the old Equity-type programs of replacing outdated institutions, eliminating questionable and disputed trade practices, and in other ways reforming, regulating, or displacing the old socioeconomic power elite. The two leagues had now added unfair labor practices to the complaints of farmers, and they hoped to escape what to them was the misrepresentation of being identified with radicalism and alien revolutionary movements.

Both Nonpartisans and Republicans believed Minnesota was at a turning point. Republican elderstatesman Knute Nelson recommended an "education campaign" much like the crusade against silver inflation in 1896; he counted heavily upon newspaper editors and speakers to arouse farmers against the league "menace"; and he asked Republicans "to put a new and more conservative spirit in the hearts of our [Minnesota] people."[39] Larger, wiser, and better financed than before, Nonpartisans sought to convert old weaknesses into new strengths. As an answer to the daily metropolitan "Republican press," a group of Nonpartisans incorporated the *Minnesota Daily Star* in February 1919 and printed its first edition in August. *Star* presses printed the *Nonpartisan Leader* and the *Minnesota Leader;* in March the corporation signed a contract with the *Minneapolis Labor Review;* and the *Star* building also served as headquarters for the NPL, the WPNPL, and a Women's Nonpartisan Club.[40]

With these tools of communication and a central command, Nonpartisans enthusiastically launched their 1920 primary campaign. Beginning well ahead of the faction-torn regulars, the still dynamic Townley and Shipstead were stumping the state a full two weeks before the "eliminating convention" had finished its business. Recognizing the curious interest of farmers and rural people in newfangled "flying machines," which was made even stronger by popular wartime stories of heroic aerial combat, Townley rented a small plane to fly Shipstead to the farthest reaches of the state. Shipstead campaigned hard and well, and Nonpartisans were partly helped by new Republican disagreement over presidential candidates. The Minnesota Republican convention delegation split three or four ways over presidential candidates, and Frank Kellogg insisted upon "favorite son" candidacy, hoping for a convention deadlock.[41] Finally, Nonpartisans correctly understood Preus's major political vulnerability to be his acceptability to the steel, lumber, and milling interests, an affection they exploited as best they could.

The major burden for stopping insurgency therefore rested with Preus. Despite all his weaknesses he was a tough, durable attacker who appeared to his audiences as strong, confident, and, like Shipstead, publicly handsome. A religious man who came from an already well-known immigrant family with deep ties in the Norwegian Lutheran Church, its schools, and in orthodoxy, both religious and political, Preus was well suited to the type of campaign being waged against Nonpartisan collectivism. He had once clerked for Knute Nelson in Washington, and now he jumped into an aggressive crusade "to save the state from the menace of socialism."

Much to the dismay of the two leagues, Preus and other enemies of insurgency were able to steal the initiative and take wrathful offensive against what they said was the institutional infidelity of the leaders associated with leagueism. Preus began late, starting with a slashing May 3 kickoff speech at Mankato, and he proceeded to paint a stark picture of Minnesota being under siege by teachers of false doctrine. The major issue was said to be a "fight of the honest God-fearing electorate of Minnesota to prevent the government and resources of this state from being exploited by professional Socialist agitators." Sacred traditions and institutions — like private property, religious freedom, the sanctity of the home — were allegedly under attack by impractical socialist visionaries pledged to destroy the good things in American life. The scourge had to be stopped.

> Let us not despoil ourselves of our heritage; let us cherish the institutions of our fathers; let us preserve the Republican form of government instituted by our forebears and perfected by ourselves. Let us still believe in our American institutions, our familes, and our homes.[42]

Not only did Preus speak fire and brimstone, but he believed his words as fervently as the socialists and agrarians who found so compelling a need to alter and replace the prevailing financial, industrial, and commodity systems. Decades later the most cherished memory Preus retained about his Minnesota political career was his 1920 contribution in saving, as he said, the state from socialism.

Ideologues of the left and right found little ground between them upon which to compromise. Preus and the Republican campaign around him wisely chose to make no direct attacks upon Shipstead, but he, Republican orators, and editorial writers in the dailies carefully separated Shipstead, league moderates, and farmers from the conspiracy of "Socialist schemers and agitators" who were said to be in actual command of the league. A vote for Preus was made into a rejection referendum against radical league socialists rather than a call for Minnesotans to defeat Shipstead. The strategy worked well in 1920, but it also had the unintended effect of purging Shipstead of any personal connection with radicalism and, unknown at the time, made him an even more appealing Farmer-Labor political commodity in 1922.

In a simplified way the primary ended as a series of dichotomies: socialism versus capitalism, unions versus corporations, farmer cooperatives opposing grain exchanges, the people versus the interests, Republicans against radicals, reform versus reaction, Preus versus Shipstead, family versus free love, God versus atheism. With both sides prophesizing dire consequences, the outcome remained in doubt to the very end.

The Nonpartisans' Primary Defeat

The Nonpartisan movement was every bit as strong as Republicans feared, was greater than it had been in 1918, but still it could not dislodge Republican regulars. With over 92 percent of the total votes cast in Republican contests—a good indication of the now lagging interest in the Democratic party—Republican regulars won all six party nominations for state office and the Nonpartisans were left with near- and moral victories

Preus's 8,000 plurality barely defeated Shipstead; the percentages were 41.7 and 39.2 respectively. Even closer to victory was Thomas V. Sullivan who was only 1,133 votes from defeating the incumbent attorney general. The two leagues found some consolation in Oscar Keller's fourth-district renomination, Carss's successful switch to the eighth-district Democratic nomination, and the seventh-district victory of O. J. Kvale over prohibition congressman A. J. Volstead (17,369 to 15,059). The latter outcome was clouded by a state supreme court decision declaring that the Lutheran minister engaged in an unfair campaign practice when he accused Volstead of being an atheist.[43] Among the disappointed Democrats was twenty-eight-year-old Minneapolis lawyer Floyd B. Olson, who lost his party's fifth-district nomination for Congress and with it interest in his party.

The second Nonpartisan defeat forced the movement to take stock of its strategy and determine exactly what kind of a role it would play in the November election; meanwhile, Republican confidence grew and many regulars believed the tide had turned against the Nonpartisan movement.[44] Not only had workers and farmers failed to unite, but defeat brought out internal differences even more. The more socialist-leaning left wing of the movement preferred to change the insurgent organizational structure into an outright third-party system. The right wing and the moderate NPLers resisted this maneuver out of a general suspicion of third-partyism and a fear that it was designed to literally strip away the league organization and supersede it with a new party organization over which they would have much less influence. Shortly after the primary these differences came to light when a fight broke out within the Cooperative Wholesale Society of America, ostensibly over internal staffing; a sharp clash ensued between lawyers James Manahan, who said the society was unalterably opposed to state-ownership policy, and Arthur LeSueur, who represented three socialists whom the society had sought to dismiss.[45]

RESULTS OF THE 1920 MINNESOTA REPUBLICAN PRIMARY
(Candidate, No. of Votes, and Percentage of Total Vote)

OFFICE	"REGULAR"	NONPARTISAN LEAGUE	OTHER			
Governor	J. A. O. Preus 133,832 (41.7%)	Henrik Shipstead 125,861 (39.2%)	Thomas Frankson 27,421 (8.5%)	Franklin Ellsworth 7,754 (2.4%)	Sam G. Iverson 7,383 (2.3%)	Thomas Keefe 5,060 (1.6%)
Lieutenant governor	Louis Collins 155,432 (48.4%)	George H. Mallon 138,707 (43.2%)				
Attorney general	Clifford Hilton 118,932 (37.0%)	Thomas V. Sullivan 117,799 (36.7%)	John C. Larson 29,434 (9.2%)	Stelle Smith 17,298 (5.4%)	Elmer C. Patterson 12,560 (3.9%)	
Secretary of state	Mike Holm 134,689 (41.9%)	Thomas Vollom 112,210 (34.9%)	A. M. Opsahl 40,479 (12.6%)			
Treasurer	Henry Rines 153,260 (47.7%)	Charles A. Lund 136,975 (42.6%)				
Railroad and warehouse commissioner	O. P. B. Jacobson 166,767 (51.9%)	Paul T. D. Ostby 120,537 (37.5%)				

Note: The total percentage for each office is less than 100 because some voters cast blank ballots and some ballots were spoiled.

Minnesota Farmer-Laborism, by Millard L. Gieske, © 1979 by the University of Minnesota.

Independent Candidates and a Farmer-Labor Party

Nonpartisans agreed that they should continue to pursue political power. But how? In early July 1920, they decided to launch a fall campaign much like their 1918 campaign. Technically, the name Farmer-Labor was still available to them since they had run a single candidate in the June primary with the understanding that he would withdraw to let Shipstead run in November either as a Farmer-Laborite or as an Independent.[46]

At an informal July 7 NPL convention in Minneapolis Townley announced the plan to some 700 delegates and exhorted farmers to raise a million-dollar campaign fund. Twelve days later in Rochester William Mahoney assembled his WPNPL at the annual convention of the State Federation of Labor, expecting to endorse the same candidate slate as NPL farmers.[47] Unfortunately for Farmer-Laborism, activities between its two main interests became even more poorly coordinated, and national political developments suddenly forced the two even farther apart.

One reason for the widening split was the creation in an August convention at Chicago of the national Farmer-Labor party, which nominated a little-known progressive, Parley Parker Christiansen, to run for the presidency. The convention was a motley assemblage which included the Committee of 48 (a group of intellectuals and socialists who preferred political effectiveness to doctrinal rigidity), the Labor party, the Chicago Federation of Labor, and various dissident insurgencies. Minnesota delegates had little or no desire to enter presidential politics since they preferred to concentrate on state politics and feared a further deterioration of relations with the NPL (Townley refused to have anything to do with national Farmer-Laborites).[48] Even the presence of Minnesota delegates in Chicago irritated Townley; three weeks after apparent agreement had been reached in Rochester, Townley bluntly rejected the idea of a Minnesota Farmer-Labor party and announced instead that Shipstead would run as an Independent. Distrustful of socialists and of what he thought they were doing to the NPL, Townley now was dissatisfied with the third-party alternative, and in national Farmer-Laborism he thought he detected the guiding hand of radicals and IWWs; if this was true, he said, any state movement or party affiliated with it would be discredited.

Minnesota insurgency thus split during the fall into two divided camps, the pro-NPL Independents and the more labor-oriented Farmer-Labor party candidates. Each sponsored three candidates. Townley and the Nonpartisan League ran Shipstead, Mallon, and Sullivan as Independent candidates for governor, lieutenant governor, and attorney general,[49] and the laborites supported three new candidates, Lily J. Anderson, John P. Wagner, and Emil C. MacKenzie, and ran them as Farmer-Labor candidates for secretary of state, treasurer, and railroad and warehouse commissioner. Through the NPL's *Minnesota Leader* Townley and the league repeatedly asserted independence from Republicans and Democrats.

In the last weeks before the election Republican campaign managers were satisfied they had properly anticipated the public mood and with the help of the Twin City newspapers, the outstate dailies, and the country weekly papers the crusade against radicalism which had begun in May was continued into November. A. J. Volstead was petitioned back onto the ballot—as an Independent—and Knute Nelson went to his aid. As the campaign reached the final stretch direct Republican attacks upon the NPL were abandoned but hundreds of billboards throughout the state carried a single blunt message: "Stop Socialism." On September 7 the state party even lured presidential candidate Warren G. Harding off his Marion Ohio front porch and to the Minnesota state fairgrounds, where he was more warmly greeted than the Democratic nominee, Governor James M. Cox, had been the previous day. By mid-October Nelson and Kellogg were predicting a major Republican victory, and Nelson sensed that many NPL farmers would vote for Harding, who had received only one unenthusiastic Minnesota vote on the tenth and final convention ballot.[50] Preus and the regulars ended the campaign with slashing attacks upon Townleyism, socialism, and radicalism.

The Republican Landslide

Two general conclusions can be reached about the 1920 Minnesota election. First, the outcome was a Republican landslide. Harding tallied over 65 percent of the presidential vote, Cox only 18 percent; every state office and the legislature was in Republican hands; and all ten congressional seats, including the seventh-district seat for which Volstead campaigned as an Independent, went to Republicans. Second, the election had an impact on the relative roles of the opposition parties: through a minor-party realignment NPL "independents" and Farmer-Laborites displaced Democrats as Republicanism's major opposition. Shipstead led all the insurgents with 281,000 votes (35 percent), and O. J. Kvale came within 1,500 votes of unseating Volstead. Statewide and in most congressional races Democrats captured about 10 percent of the vote. Cox did only slightly better, the fourth-district Democratic congressional candidate (with 34 percent) was another exception, and Carss in the eighth district barely lost reelection by 1,000 votes. The

RESULTS OF THE 1920 MINNESOTA GENERAL ELECTION

OFFICE	REPUBLICAN	DEMOCRATIC	NONPARTISAN LEAGUE	FARMER-LABOR	SOCIALIST	NATIONAL	OTHER
President	65.1%	17.9%			7.0%		2.2%
Governor	52.1	10.2	33.3%		.6	.8%	
Lieutenant governor	54.2	10.0	28.1		1.3	.8	
Attorney general	56.0	6.7	31.5				
Secretary of state	54.4	10.0		24.3	2.4	1.0	
Treasurer	56.2	8.6		24.0	2.8		
Railroad and warehouse commissioner	55.8	9.1		22.2	3.0		

Note: Results are expressed as a percentage of the total vote cast in the election. The total percentage for each office is less than 100 because some voters cast blank ballots and some ballots were spoiled.

Minnesota Farmer-Laborism, by Millard L. Gieske, © 1979 by the University of Minnesota.

state Democratic party had entered a near catatonic stupor which would last almost a quarter century.

The election left insurgency facing the critical question whether it was possible to challenge successfully Minnesota's dominant economic interests within the framework of the Republican party. Or had the time come to abandon Townley's "balance of power" tactic and start operations within a new permanent Farmer-Labor party? The socialists preferred the latter. But it also was true that Independent, NPL-backed candidates led by Shipstead outpolled Farmer-Labor candidates, on the average, by 9 percent, or 65,000 votes.

The dilemma was further complicated by the observable fact that insurgency and protest had the greatest appeal in the western and northwestern agricultural sectors, and in the northeast where the moderate Carss narrowly lost reelection. The urban labor, socialist, and radical protests seemed to have added little to Farmer-Labor appeal, indeed they may have hurt it, and the presence of the labor left wing posed a serious question about who would and who should control the movement as it entered the 1920s.

CHAPTER 4

Third-Party Breakthrough and Retreat

After two unsuccessful attempts by the Nonpartisan movement to gain political control by working through the Republican primary, a growing number of Nonpartisans and their sympathizers began to question the wisdom of continuing this strategy which had worked in North Dakota but which could not be duplicated in Minnesota. Because in 1918 and again in 1920 the movement had been forced belatedly to fall back upon a third-party campaign, many, though not all, insurgents concluded that the next campaign should begin with the third party rather than just end with it. This feeling was by no means unanimous, and its greatest support initially came from socialists and the more militant members of the labor movement.

THE GROWING STRENGTH OF FARMER-LABORISM

For the third-party strategy of the Farmer-Labor movement to succeed, it needed wide appeal, the cooperation of the farm protest movement, and new converts from splinter groups and even from the Democratic party. Fortunately for Farmer-Laborism, postwar economic dysfunction in the agricultural sector, the erosion of two major issues—patriotism and radicalism—upon which Republicans had hitherto been most able to rely, renewed factional discord among Republicans, and loss of popularity of the NPL all combined in 1922 to give Farmer-Laborism its best opportunity yet to displace the majority party. Spurred by sharply declining agricultural commodity prices and boasting attractive moderate candidates, a strengthened Farmer-Labor movement won a major senatorial election in 1922, repeated this success in 1923, and just as suddenly allowed these gains to slip away in 1924 when it foolishly ignored the formula for victory and permitted the Republican charge of radicalism to return in all its fury.

Converts to Farmer-Laborism

Several groups were attracted to this revised Farmer-Labor strategy. Best known of those who came from the small National party of splinter socialists and Prohibitionists was pacifist-socialist Susie W. Stageberg of Red Wing, a pious, evangelical Lutheran crusader who was attracted to Farmer-Laborism's high purpose and moral activism. Once committed and converted, she discovered in the movement the "fit and worthy torchbearers of the principles of truth and justice to all men. . . . Oh, may we measure up."[1] Over the years she was the very personification of the religious disciple in politics.

Another group attracted to the postwar Farmer-Labor movement was the small Minnesota branch of the Committee of 48. The committee's national headquarters were in New York, and its national secretary, J. A. A. Hopkins, had dipped into the North Dakota Nonpartisan League to recruit Walter Liggett as its director of publicity.[2] Although the committee was sympathetic to a variety of protests which included the Nonpartisan League, many of its members, including University of Minnesota intellectuals, mostly wanted a new third party that would retain some socialist principles but not the burdensome socialist name.[3] They would soon find the Farmer-Labor party attractive.

Members of the state Socialist party, particularly those active in the organized labor movement, were already in or close to Farmer-Laborism. They included William Mahoney, Arthur and Marian Le-Sueur, S. A. Stockwell, John F. Emme, Roy C. Smelker, and Benjamin Drake. Other proponents of Farmer-Laborism, like Henry Teigan, had started in the Nonpartisan league but had come to question Townley's capacity to lead the movement; or, like James Manahan, they had moved to the league from the Progressive movement and were now ready to support a third party. Howard Y. Williams, a Congregational minister from St. Paul, had been drawn as a student toward the Social Gospel by the theologians at Union Theological Seminary and stood ready to join the new party. A few political nomads — Gustavus Loevenger, Roger Rutchick, Max Conrad — wandered into the party, some to stay, others to drift away.

Both the Socialists and the Committee of 48ers sought peaceful alternatives to radical politics and revolutionary schemes. The Minnesota committee did "not wish to go with the extreme radicals," demanded strict adherence to constitutional process, and change "by the ballot and not the bullet."[4] As such goals were blended they came to mean some public ownership, reform, and a new third party both in the state and nationally. Following Shipstead's loss in the 1920 primary, these groups believed the time had come for the NPL to drop its Republican strategy and accept the third-party alternative.[5]

New Attacks upon the Nonpartisan League

The Nonpartisan League had withstood rather well the Republican attacks of the past three years.[6] But by late 1920 some NPL expatriates began to denounce it for reasons somewhat different from those which motivated Republicans. In late 1920 Arthur LeSueur, who had helped draw up much of the league's proposed legislation but had broken with it in April 1919, began a string of assaults upon the league. These he published in the *Socialist Review*[7] and in an extensive antileague pamphlet which was distributed throughout North Dakota and sent to every member of the North Dakota legislature. LeSueur charged the league with political mismanagement, especially within the agency responsible for managing the state public enterprises, the North Dakota Industrial Commission, and he asked for an end to political influence in public administration. Naturally enough, these broadsides drew front page coverage in the Twin Cities and in North Dakota.[8] LeSueur's purpose, he admitted, was to destroy the league while preserving the public ownership programs it had fostered.

Another person turning against the league was William L. Langer, who now began calling Townley and the league a radical threat to North Dakota.[9] LeSueur renewed his antileague drive in the fall of 1921. This time he charged Townley and William Lemke with illegally squandering several hundred thousand dollars and with virtually controlling thirty-eight league corporations, including the Consumers United Stores Company which they had allegedly mismanaged and brought to near ruin.[10]

The cumulative impact of these attacks, from left and right, Socialist and Republican, was to weaken league popularity and to increasingly channel protest away from it and toward a third party.

Postwar Economic Adjustment and Republican Dissension

While Nonpartisanism was buffeted by its postwar adjustment, the Minnesota legislature and the new Preus administration started to put their own modest reform program into operation. The 1921 legislature accomplished this by approving a 1922 constitutional referendum permitting an iron ore tonnage tax and by passing the controversial Brooks-Coleman Act granting the Railroad and Warehouse Commission the authority to regulate street railway fares. The latter had the appearance of regulatory reform, but Farmer-Laborites long criticized it as a disguise designed to thwart local home rule and municipal ownership of the street railway system.

As governor, Preus talked enthusiastically about the agricultural benefits of farmer cooperatives, but for Republicans in general this poorly offset the effect of a growing postwar "farm problem," which was then just beginning and still had not been totally contained a half century later. To understand the source of farmers' bitterness, one needed to look no farther than at the price of wheat. After reaching a high of $3 per bushel in May 1917, the price fell steeply in the postwar period when European production rose to prewar levels; it would take fifty-six years for the price to climb to $3 again. Already dissatisfied in 1915-17, farmers in 1922 were again in a mood for political revolt.

These changes in the economy were difficult for any party to manage, and they caused divisiveness within the Republican party. Some business interests already believed the party had made too many concessions to farmers, at the expense of business. Further injuring the party was the continued conflict between Minneapolis and St. Paul Republicans, and the tension between steel industry Republicans and the interests of the Minneapolis trade groups. The individual most vulnerable to intraparty bickering was Senator Frank Kellogg, who unexpectedly encountered a set of opponents eager to challenge him for the party endorsement. His competitors were state supreme court justice Oscar Hallam, who was widely supported in Kellogg's own Ramsey County, and Minneapolis mayor George Leach who was about to begin a twenty-year quest for higher state office.[11]

Because Kellogg himself had successfully unseated an incumbent in 1916, many party regulars were not worried about Kellogg's fate. Nevertheless, he survived these challenges and won an April Fool's Day endorsement on the first convention ballot after rural Republican delegates came to his aid.[12] Preus, by contrast, had a much easier time and looked forward to reelection and then, in 1924, to entering the Senate as Knute Nelson's successor.

THE 1922 CAMPAIGN AND ELECTION

The Farmer-Labor Ticket and Platform

Political insurgency entered 1922 more advantaged than ever before. Yet, despite the successful skirmishing by those who would defrock Townley from the movement and the increased willingness of many to start with a third-party campaign, farmers and workers were not drawn firmly together into one organization. Divisions were both organizational and ideological, and it would prove difficult to negotiate a mutually acceptable Farmer-Labor ticket. As had happened before, farmers met in an NPL convention at the *Star* building, labor gathered at Richmond Hall in Minneapolis, and not far away at the West Hotel the Democratic party met in the hope of reaching a March agreement with the farmers.

At the NPL convention Townley, a growing liability, vehemently opposed sacrificing the "balance of power" strategy and warned farmers against allowing a party to absorb the NPL. But he had already been rebuffed by the North Dakota NPL convention, had been seriously undermined by the Langer and LeSueur attacks, and was losing interest in the cause. As a result, he resigned as league president.[13]

Townley's resignation would have played directly into the hands of the WPNPL, Mahoney, the socialists, and those most active in pushing the idea of a Farmer-Labor party had it not been for Democratic interference. The labor-leftist forces were suddenly thrown into a panic when Democrats, led by John Lind, came to the Nonpartisan League convention with a five-member conference committee which proposed to farmers that Democrats and the NPL negotiate a common ticket to oppose the Republicans. To the utter disgust of the left wing, an NPL conference committee voted to accept the proposal. The Democrats then offered their party Senate endorsement to Henrik Shipstead in return for the withdrawal of the NPL gubernatorial candidate, Magnus Johnson, and his replacement by Edward Indrehus. To farmers this seemed a very tempting offer, but Mahoney had the labor convention send a strongly worded ultimatum to the farmers, accusing them of being "trimmers" and demanding that there be no fusion with Democrats, who were described as a dead party. Rather reluctantly the farmers terminated negotiations and the disappointed Democrats returned empty-handed. Having been forced to withdraw their support of Shipstead for the Senate, Democrats then made history by endorsing Mrs. Anna Dickie Olesen, the first Minnesota woman to seek the office.

Nevertheless, the Democratic scare had a major impact upon the emerging party and the 1922 ticket. It forced the third party along a much more moderate pathway, and it strengthened the negotiating hand of farmers. Labor now had to accept farmers' choices for the two major public offices — Shipstead for senator and Johnson for governor.[14]

The near fusion into a single NPL-Democratic ticket left a lasting impression on labor and gave farmers and moderates a kind of veto power. For the next two decades Farmer-Laborism would continually debate its mission in politics. Was it a reform movement patterned after the Progressive tradition, an early version of the coming Democratic New Deal, or a genuine American version of socialism and public ownership?

The 1922 Farmer-Labor ticket evolved over a period of weeks. The feminist 1920 Farmer-Labor candidate for secretary of state was passed over, and endorsement was given to Susie W. Stageberg, a recent convert from the Prohibition movement. The uncertain selection of other candidates resembled a comic opera. For example, Benjamin Drake declined to run for attorney general; he was replaced by a former St. Paul legislator who surprised the ticket makers by withdrawing his name so that he could run as a Democrat; a third choice accepted the candidacy. The candidate for lieutenant governor (who became lieutenant governor fourteen years later) also withdrew and again the ticket settled on a third choice. The Farmer-Labor negotiators were further rebuffed when they proposed to endorse a Democratic judge from Mankato for the nonpartisan-designated state supreme court. Negotiations between representatives of the two leagues did not end until April 29, well over a month after they had begun.[15]

The 1922 NPL platform, however, went far enough to satisfy the laborites. It criticized the return of railroads from wartime government control to peacetime private management, asked that natural resources be developed under "government control," and advocated abolition of the use of the labor injunction and militia during strikes, public service jobs for the unemployed, a state-owned cement plant and flour mill, a 10 percent iron ore tonnage tax, and — somewhat illogically — tax economy (i.e., reduction) and elimination of governmental inefficiency!

Although Farmer-Labor candidates and the 1922 Farmer-Labor state campaign reflected a certain point of view, there still remained serious differences separating the ideological extremes of the new coalition. When the state labor convention was about to assemble,

Minneapolis labor assembly radicals were strongly criticized for their willingness to associate with IWWs, Communists, and Leninists. In return, left wing Minneapolis alderman Irving G. Scott sponsored an assembly resolution that denounced the AFL, called for labor participation with Communists in a May Day parade, and invited American Communist William Z. Foster to address the assembly.[16] These were associations which Farmer-Labor moderates and men like Shipstead and Johnson would refuse under any circumstances.

Republican Strategy

Republicans had good reason to be apprehensive in 1922. For cumbersome though the Farmer-Labor mechanism had been in selecting candidates, when the negotiations finished the fledgling party appeared self-disciplined and harmonious despite its divisions and wide ideological diversity. Farmer-Labor endorsements for state offices went unchallenged, and the only primary contest occurred in the Ninth Congressional District where former Republican Knud Wefald won a close race for the nomination.

Republicans went into the June 12 primary unsure whether Farmer-Labor voters would cause trouble by voting against incumbents and party endorsees. Although 85 percent of the nearly half million primary ballots were cast for Republicans, it did not seem to have changed the nomination pattern. Kellogg defeated former congressman Ernest Lundeen (52 percent to 30 percent), and Preus once again withstood the challenge of just retired second-district congressman Franklin F. Ellsworth (58 percent to 33 percent). All regulars won nomination.

Few were deceived into believing that the 1922 general election would be like those of 1918 and 1920 and that Republicans would finish as they had before. The issue of radicalism and revolution, which the party had used in the two previous elections, had grown increasingly thin and did not seem to apply to Shipstead and Johnson. Neither Kellogg nor Preus was able to make it an effective issue, and they had no good substitute. Worse, they now had to work for reelection amid a growing agricultural depression and falling farm prices, a condition that played directly into Farmer-Labor hands.

Preus had opened his primary campaign by renewing the charge that once more the Republican mission was to stop socialism's offensive against capitalism and private property.[17] Both he and Kellogg made an issue of a strike by John L. Lewis's coal miners, who, some worried, might deny winter coal to Minnesota. Kellogg promised coal by harvest time, and the antisocialist Preus called a governors' conference to ask for federal seizure of the mines!

Kellogg faced by far the most difficult reelection campaign. He was an advocate for the Great Lakes-St. Lawrence Seaway project, which was popular in northeast Minnesota and with farmers looking for a better way of marketing their growing surplus. At Walnut Grove in mid-August he told the farm community that agriculture was the key to prosperity. Kellogg's speech sounded reformist. He supported an emergency tariff preventing the dumping or undercutting of American products, greater federal control over meat packing, putting a farmer on the Federal Reserve Board, lower (i.e., subsidized) loan rates to farmers, reduced rail rates, and cooperative marketing.[18] There was nothing unusual about what he was saying, nor was it even a departure from progressive Republican policies of the past; yet, for years, these issues were included among the demands made by Equity, the NPL, and other reformers. When the amendments on state rural credits and the tonnage production tax were endorsed in speeches like Kellogg's, it appeared that Republicans and Farmer-Laborites were seeking common objectives, which hardly was a way of distinguishing sane policy makers from those whose policies had been and would be described as radical departures from the American tradition.

Even when a radical issue appeared, Republicans found it difficult to exploit. Late in August Michigan police and federal agents arrested seventeen alleged Communists, including William Dunne and William Z. Foster. Dunne, who for many years to come would be a leading American Communist party member, came from Minnesota. Urged by Irving G. Scott and Robley D. (Red) Cramer to help Dunne, the Minneapolis Trades and Labor Assembly voted to raise $1,000 in bail.[19] But other issues had attracted public attention, helping to obscure and otherwise neutralize the Red Scare.

Republican concern escalated as summer waned. Farmers followed with interest a Minneapolis hearing of the Interstate Commerce Commission on whether the Chamber of Commerce had been guilty of illegal restraint of trade against the farmers' Equity Cooperative Exchange.[20] Republicans sensed further trouble after Robert M. La Follette won an impressive primary victory in Wisconsin; they drew little comfort from the traditional Republican September victory in Maine despite a meaningless *Minneapolis Tribune* headline[21] —seven columns wide!— that attempted to bolster sagging party morale. As Maine went, so went Vermont but not Minnesota.

Shipstead's "New Deal" Campaign

To a large degree, the fate of Farmer-Laborism rested on the politically impressive shoulders of Henrik Shipstead, the Glenwood dentist. Almost the exact opposite of his running mate, farmer Magnus Johnson, Shipstead proved to be the most difficult political target the Republicans had yet encountered. The politically experienced Shipstead was no radical and in two previous elections had campaigned as a moderate and a reform progressive. Now that Townley was out of the league, Shipstead appeared an even more valuable political commodity who maintained a frustratingly safe distance (in the eyes of both Republicans and Farmer-Laborites) from the socialists and the militants within his own party.

Shipstead insisted upon running his campaign in a highly independent fashion, with only loose attachment to the Farmer-Labor party; he studiously avoided as much as possible any association with the advocates of public ownership. When he opened his fall campaign at Detroit Lakes in the northwest section of the state, he pledged to work for what he called a "New Deal" for agriculture. Farmers and laborers had the same right to a just livelihood as owners of mines, railroads, and munitions factories. He pledged to work with the "farm bloc, the labor bloc, the small businessmen's bloc, the soldier's bloc," and for good measure he added, "the mother's bloc." He explained that this meant working with the Senate's Republican and Democrat progressives — Borah, La Follette, Norris, Frazier, Brookhart — and against the politicians who served Standard Oil, Wall Street, the railroads, and the mine owners. Shipstead praised Norris's agricultural bill, favored a soldier's bonus, condemned high tariffs for the injury they caused the poor through higher prices, and charged Kellogg with doing nothing to help farmers and with working against a widened Senate investigation of the Newberry election controversy,[22] where the issue was excessive campaign spending for a Michigan seat in the U.S. Senate.

Shipstead, in short, was a nonradical candidate who carefully avoided talk about a coming new social order or public ownership, and his 1922 candidacy represented the most serious challenge to the Republican party in the first quater of the twentieth century.

A Shortened Republican Campaign

Shipstead's moderation, party independence, and political attractiveness were not underestimated by Republicans, and both Farmer-Laborites and Democrats concentrated their oratorical fire upon Kellogg. Worried and unsure about what next could go wrong for them, Republicans decided their best chance was to gamble with a short campaign and rely upon Republican newspapers to present the senator and Preus as dedicated public servants too busy with official responsibilities to campaign actively.

The Republican "campaign," therefore, was cut short. The state committee scheduled Kellogg's keynote address for St. Cloud on October 4, and Preus had his delayed until October 10 at Montevideo near the western border. Before 2,500 faithful, Kellogg introduced the ticket and talked about peace, the need for disarmament and lower tariffs, Minnesota's winter coal requirements, and Republican gains and accomplishments. He issued a solemn warning that "quacks and demagogues and state Socialists and Bolsheviks . . . will tell you that if they were in Congress they would immediately legislate prosperity to the farmers."[23] But who were these phantom socialists and Bolsheviks?

A week later, in introducing Preus at Montevideo, Kellogg bleakly referred to "these days of depression when our producers are receiving such low prices for their commodities" while costs were higher than in what he called "normal times." Neither he nor the governor had a solution; nor could they promise much relief. Preus was a conservative, more so than Kellogg, though he had sought to adjust to the changed economic and political conditions. He too supported the veterans' bonus. But his most natural tendency was to stress efficiency and economy in government and a reduction in taxes which, he said, had reached the breaking point until his first administration had forced them lower. Preus pledged to eliminate more waste, cut school expenditures while attracting and retaining competent teachers; "frills and fads" would no longer be tolerated.[24]

To Republicans outside Minnesota, this political situation appeared to be reaching the critical point and the state seemed in danger of slipping away from Republican control. Aged Knute Nelson, eighty years old and with only six months yet to live, was called upon to help offset this trend, and he was joined by Wisconsin senator Irvine L. Lenroot for speeches at Alexandria and Minneapolis.[25] Their appeal to resave Minnesota was quickly counterbalanced by the Democrats, who brought in William Jennings Bryan and William G. McAdoo to speak for Mrs. Olesen and thus lend their voices to the growing attack upon Kellogg.[26]

Shipstead grew stronger as the campaign progressed. The only setback came when unpredictable Ernest Lundeen reversed himself and refused to endorse and appear at a Shipstead rally.[27] Continuing as he had begun, Shipstead stressed a New Deal and Progressive reforms.

His campaign reached a climax when Robert La Follette, bent upon settling some old political scores, traveled first to North Dakota to help Lynn Frazier and then into Minnesota, where he spoke for Shipstead. With the postwar spread of isolation, La Follette once again belittled the war and charged Wall Street with pushing the United States into intervention.

At Mankato La Follette told a large crowd that Kellogg did not represent the people. By the time he reached the Twin Cities it was as though he had launched a new national campaign. In front of 20,000 enthusiastic listeners gathered in and around the Kenwood armory, he blistered big business and charged Kellogg with serving corporate interests. At the St. Paul Auditorium over 16,000 turned out to hear him deliver an emotional explosion in which he called Kellogg a creature of monopolies whom the state should replace with Shipstead.[28] As the campaign closed Shipstead seemed to have engineered a skillful rise to power, La Follette had enjoyed his revenge, and Farmer-Laborism was about to secure its first major breakthrough.

Election Results

The election of 1922 firmly established a three-party state system in Minnesota, one which survived for two decades. This election tended to stabilize party realignment, a process which had undermined Minnesota's evolution to a competitive two-party system and which had begun with the 1912 Progressive Bull Moose revolt, the decline of the state Democrats between 1916 and 1918, and the appearance of the Nonpartisans and Farmer-Laborites in 1917-18.

Farmer-Laborites could celebrate three major victories, led by Shipstead's 84,000 (45 percent) plurality over Kellogg (34 percent), and the elections of O. J. Kvale in the seventh district and Knud Wefald in the ninth. Coming near to victory was former congressman William L. Carss (47 percent) who had switched to the Farmer-Labor label and lost by just under 4,000 votes to incumbent Oscar J. Larson. The strength of Shipstead's appeal was seen in his total vote; only the Republican candidates for treasurer and secretary of state outpolled him. Liberals also claimed 29 of 67 state senate seats, and with tripartisan support voters approved constitutional amendments for the iron ore tonnage tax (66 percent) and rural credits (75 percent).

Republican popularity had suffered, but the party had not lost its dominance. It still controlled the legislature and its eight candidates for state office were all elected, though Preus (43 percent) narrowly defeated Johnson (41 percent) by only 14,000 votes. Democrats, however, were now playing the role of a third party whose vote averaged

RESULTS OF THE 1922 MINNESOTA GENERAL ELECTION
(Candidate, No. of Votes, and Percentage of Total Vote)

OFFICE	REPUBLICAN	DEMOCRATIC	FARMER-LABOR
Senator	Frank B. Kellogg 241,833 (33.8%)	Anna D. Olesen 123,624 (17.3%)	Henrik Shipstead 325,372 (45.5%)
Governor	J. A. O. Preus 309,756 (43.3%)	Edward Indrehus 79,904 (11.2%)	Magnus Johnson 295,479 (41.4%)
Lieutenant governor	Louis Collins 322,700 (45.2%)	Silus M. Bryan 88,441 (9.6%)	Art A. Siegler 269,417 (37.7%)
Attorney general	Clifford Hilton 319,529 (44.7%)	James E. Doran 72,157 (10.1%)	Roy Smelker 254,715 (35.6%)
Secretary of state	Mike Holm 348,559 (47.8%)	Claude Swanson 66,613 (9.3%)	Susie Stageberg 247,757 (34.7%)
Treasurer	Henry Rines 339,832 (47.6%)		Frank H. Keyes 214,131 (30.0%)
Auditor	Ray P. Chase 315,089 (44.9%)	James Doran 72,157 (11.2%)	Elizabeth E. Deming 253,913 (35.5%)
Railroad and warehouse commissioner	Ivan Bowen 290,084 (40.6%)	Wm. J. North 75,027 (10.5%)	W. W. Royster 270,752 (37.9%)
Clerk of the Supreme Court	Grace Kaercher 293,173 (41.0%)	Frank Kelb 74,285 (10.4%)	Harold T. Van Lear 273,542 (38.3%)

Note: The total percentage for each office is less than 100 because some voters cast blank ballots and some ballots were spoiled.

Minnesota Farmer-Laborism, by Millard L. Gieske, © 1979 by the University of Minnesota.

about 10 percent; just as important, they had begun to cooperate with Farmer-Laborites whenever the new party united to run moderate candidates in districts where they had a strong chance of winning. Major benefactors had been Kvale, Wefald, and Carss.

The competitive performance of four women candidates—a Democrat, a Republican, and two Farmer-Laborites—likewise implied another important change in state politics was under way. Only Republican Grace Kaercher (Davis) of Ortonville won election and though she did not do as well as other Republicans she began an elective career as clerk of the supreme court which lasted, with one interruption, through 1954. With some national Democratic party assistance, Anna Dickie

Olesen (17 percent) ran slightly but not impressively ahead of males in her party. In general, the women fared about as their parties did, but, ironically, over fifty years would pass before there again would be as many women candidates for state office as there were in 1922.

FARMER-LABOR PROGRESSIVES IN 1923

The 1922 election reaffirmed the thinking in the rural-dominated 1923 Minnesota legislature that some additional relief was due farmers and that there was a proper place, whether expedient or otherwise, for reasonable reform. The session devoted a considerable amount of time to taxation matters. After voters had given wide approval to the iron ore tonnage tax and the rural credits amendments, majority conservatives found it much easier to follow the electorate's wishes.

Conservative (usually Republican) legislators really had not turned very far to the left, since the legislature as a body had traditionally been sympathetic to farmers, although much less so to workers. Indeed, the political wisdom of listening to farmer complaints already had reached Washington, D.C. It was no accident that, in 1922, Congressman Andrew J. Volstead (who was defeated in November) had coauthored the far-reaching Capper-Volstead Act which exempted farmer cooperatives (which are corporations organized in a special way) from the national antitrust laws. This Republican law was probably the most important legislation ever enacted to favor cooperatives. The 1923 Minnesota legislature was just keeping pace with these changing times.

When the legislature ended its session, 1924 voters were asked to approve or reject five constitutional amendments, including one which created a special dedicated fund from gasoline excises to build a network of state highways, and "Amendment 3" which proposed construction of a state-owned terminal elevator to be financed through the sale of public bonds. Politically, these referendums offered some advantage to the Republicans. First, they lessened interest group tension within the Republican party because the decisions were rooted in *vox populi* guidance. Second, they transferred some burden for approval to Farmer-Laborites since "letting the people decide" controversial issues could hardly be taken as an example of Republican resistance to protest and the popular will.

The Special Senate Election

Nevertheless, Farmer-Laborism was still in an upward cycle when it was presented yet another opportunity to advance. In late April 1923, octogenarian Knute Nelson quietly died on a train near Baltimore after bidding a final, lonely farewell to Washington only a few hours before returning home for a summer on his Alexandria farm. He had but nine months remaining in his Senate term (1895-1923), and his logical successor, probably his choice, was Governor J. A. O. Preus.

A nominating primary was scheduled for June 18 and filing for the office were, besides Preus, eight Republicans, including four congressmen (Sydney Anderson, Thomas D. Schall, just-defeated Halvor Steenerson, and ex-congressman Ernest Lundeen), ex-governor J. A. A. Burnquist, and supreme court justice Oscar Hallam. Farmer-Laborites were more fortunate because only three candidates, L. A. Fritsche of New Ulm, Charles A. Lindbergh, and Magnus Johnson, filed in the primary. And during the primary Farmer-Laborites helped their own cause by an unusual display of tolerance and personal courtesy toward one another when they campaigned in joint appearances and forums. In the six-week campaign Preus finished first with 33.6 percent of the Republican vote (60,000 of 172,000), about 27,000 ballots ahead of Hallam, his closest challenger. Although fewer votes (118,000) were cast for Farmer-Laborites, at 49 percent Magnus Johnson seemed a clearer party favorite since he also received the general endorsement of his competitors following the primary.

The special election procedure was used only this one time, since shortly thereafter the legislature changed the law to gubernatorial appointment; this was not modified until 1978 when the special election requirement was reestablished following the unpopular "self-appointment" of Governor Wendell A. Anderson in 1977. The July 16, 1923, special election rematched the moderate agrarian Johnson against the conservative Preus in a three-way contest which included Democratic state senator James A. Carley of Plainview (in the state house 1909, in the senate 1915-29, 1935-51). Johnson deliberately patterned his campaign strategy after Shipstead's and avoided any association with radicals and those exponents of public ownership who might embarrass him and unnecessarily cost the movement its chance for victory. At the very moment when the campaign was in full swing, the national Farmer-Labor party met in convention under the shadow of a take-over by William Z. Foster and the Communist party. Minnesota sent no delegation, though its state party chairman used the convention as a forum to declare the Minnesota organization an independent, nonaffiliated, nonclass party which appealed to farmers, laborers, professionals, teachers, and editors[29] — in short, a progressive protest movement in the populist tradition.

This message registered with Minnesota voters. Magnus Johnson, the Swedish-immigrant dirt farmer who as a champion of Equity had served in the state house (1915-17) and senate (1919-21), won a near landslide victory over the Republican governor. Preus carried only eleven counties, his political career was aborted, and Farmer-Laborism now had two of its members, both of whom were from the moderate wing of the party, representing Minnesota in Washington. The impressive victory made the Farmer-Labor future appear bright.

RESULTS OF SPECIAL MINNESOTA SENATE ELECTION, JULY 16, 1923

PARTY	NUMBER OF VOTES	PERCENTAGE OF TOTAL VOTES
Farmer-Labor	290,165	57.4%
Republican	195,139	38.3
Democratic	19,311	3.8

Note: The total percentage for each office is less than 100 because some voters cast blank ballots and some ballots were spoiled.

Minnesota Farmer-Laborism, by Millard L. Gieske, © 1979 by the University of Minnesota.

The Right Wing's Political and Economic Goals

These good times presented no particular problem to the progressive right wing of the state Farmer-Labor movement, since its reform goals were largely conventional, incremental, pluralist, and sought assistance for workers and farmers from a government that better represented their interests and organizational needs and that promised a "square deal," "new deal," the right to bargain, cooperate, and compete equally against "big interests" regulated in the public interest. If the right wing advocated public ownership, the objective was largely peripheral rather than central to economic organization, a yardstick to measure corporate performance for fairness, or it was a last resort when other measures fell short of preserving the public interest.

Labor conservatives too remained adamant in their opposition to post-1917 radicalism. Nothing better illustrated this position than the 1923 outcome of the American Federation of Labor's national convention at Portland, Oregon, when Samuel Gompers, John L. Lewis, and William Green led the speechmakers in heated denunciation of "reds," labor radicals, communists, and any others who rejected traditional labor cautiousness and substituted for it third-partyism and revolution. Although critical of the Ku Klux Klan and the rise of Italian Fascism, Green personally offered the resolution that led to the expulsion of Communist William F. Dunne who had moved from Minneapolis to Butte, Montana, where he now represented the Silver Bow Labor Council. Upon his expulsion, which the Minneapolis Trades and Labor Assembly opposed, Dunne shouted, "I will meet you at the barricades."[30]

Newly elected Magnus Johnson reinforced the progressive image when he went on display in Washington as a unique Midwest political phenomenon. Although Wasington was curious about Johnson, it soon perceived him to be no more radical than Shipstead, less abrasive than LaFollette, and less polished but more entertaining than either of them. Johnson introduced himself to newspaper reporters by telling stories: one, that the Department of Agriculture had developed a new flat-sided pea to help him eat the vegetable off a knife; another, that he had been honored by a new dance, the Johnson three-step, which he illustrated as a scraping motion to remove mud and manure from his boots.

Johnson's speeches quickly dispelled the radicalism myth of Farmer-Laborism and made it and him appear as current populist substitutes for traditional Democratic and Republican progressivism. He delivered his first eastern speech in Carnegie Hall, where he attacked the Federal Reserve Board for helping kill farm credit expansion and spoke as an isolationist. "I do not think it our business to engage in crusades to make the world safe for democracy," he said, nor for the United States to determine for any nation its kind of government. Newspapers like the *New York World* and the *New York Post* soon found in him a nonradical, midwestern agrarian who reflected a protest tradition which extended back to the Granger era.[31]

BUILDING A NEW FARMER-LABOR ORGANIZATION

Success in 1922 and 1923, rather than unifying the Farmer-Labor wings, pulled them farther apart. Not only was there no agreement upon what conditions and strategies had given the movement its victories, but there was growing dispute about what direction Farmer-Laborism should take, how it should organize, who should be in command, and what ideology and principles should prevail. The net result of these basic differences created internal upheaval and, within a year, brought political disaster.

The Minnesota Farmer-Labor left wing took a much less contented view of the world of protest. Johnson's victory caused socialists and militant labor leaders to veer toward a much more active radicalism in an effort to turn the movement in the direction of collectivism, bureaucratic self-discipline, and democratic centralism. For whatever reasons, perhaps a misinterpretation of the causes which led to Shipstead's and Johnson's victories, or possibly a fear the left was losing its grip and with this the ability to control the movement, the left wing began in the fall of 1923 a systematic attempt to recapture power and remodel Farmer-Laborism on its own purposes and dimensions.

The Mahoney Plan

Through 1922 Farmer-Laborites operated in a very loose confederal way through their farmer and labor leagues, an extremely weak party apparatus, and with highly independent candidates like Shipstead. Labor socialists and some NPL members were never comfortable with this arrangement and were acutely distressed by poor control, irregular organization, and lack of disciplined coordination. To change this, in early 1923 some members created a political corporation, called the Farmer-Labor Educational Association, which held publishing rights to the *Farmer-Labor Advocate* and otherwise served as a propaganda vehicle and the prototype for the soon-to-be-formed Farmer-Labor Federation.

At conception, the Education Association was cautious, and in February 1923, speaking through the *Advocate,* it continued to discredit Townley's "balance of power" tactic, attacked Farmer-Labor fusion with "other parties," and called for political realignment through the medium of a Farmer-Labor party.[32] These were the judgments of people like William Mahoney, Henry Teigan, Susie Stageberg, Charles Lindbergh, Farmer-Labor party chairman Fred A. Pike, and others who followed them. Until spring, when the group made a critical assessment of state Republican performance, it blamed the incumbent administration for shortcomings which the left otherwise would consider largely superficial issues: excessive governmental spending, an increasing state debt, tax favoritism, and reputed insolvency in state government.[33]

Mahoney was determined to bring disciplined order to the Farmer-Labor movement and to align it with the national Left. The reorganization plan taking shape was largely his political brainchild. Behind his thinking lay two general goals: first, to revitalize a national Farmer-Labor party and make the Minnesota party a critical element in this development; second, to create a "super league" that combined the farmers NPL and the laborers WPNPL into a single body called the Farmer-Labor Federation. This federation was to be a highly self-disciplined party-within-a-party with controlled membership, and its function would be domination of the Farmer-Labor party, including its policies and nominations. But the Mahoney plan was not accepted at first. When the two leagues met, separately, in September 1923, the farmers, led by NPL chairman A. C. Welch of Glencoe and A. C. Townley, stoutly resisted it. So, too, did state Farmer-Labor party chairman Fred A. Pike and the party executive committee, which recommended a strengthened party, not one dominated by some outside federation or association.

Mahoney and the militant socialists worked the proposal before the Working People's Nonpartisan League, where it was introduced by communist Clarence Hathaway of St. Paul.[34] Resistance quickly developed, and the Mahoney plan was debated within the movement for the remainder of the year. The *Leader* accused Mahoney of seeking to create a "super political machine" which by design would place farmers in a subservient position within the Farmer-Labor party.[35] Undaunted, Mahoney and his allies refused to drop the proposal.

Temporarily, however, Mahoney postponed further effort on the local federation plan and turned his attention to the national movement. He and Robley D. Cramer were key participants in the national Farmer-Labor negotiations, which Mahoney brought to St. Paul on November 15 by inviting some 350 national representatives for preliminary discussions about the 1924 election. With Minnesota Farmer-Labor success as the example of what could be accomplished, plans were made to hold a national Farmer-Labor convention in St. Paul on May 30. A polyglot of left protest showed up for the quiet fall sessions, including eighteen from the Communist party,[36] plus Norman Thomas-Morris Hillquit Socialists, the National Farmer-Labor party (as distinct from the communist-infiltrated Federated Farmer-Labor party), John A. H. Hopkins's largely defunct Committee of 48, and various splinters and pieces from the left.

The invitation to the communists proved an unnecessary gamble and eventually Mahoney bitterly regretted it. At the time, however, Henry Teigan assured Hillquit the Minnesotans expected to be able to contain the communists, saying "it is quite probable that we can defeat their plans and altogether eliminate them from the National Convention next May. . . ."[37]

Political Reaction to the Mahoney Plan

Strong currents of resistance to Mahoney's ambitious efforts to reorganize the state movement and expand national Farmer-Laborism continued throughout the winter and into spring. Opponents were not necessarily weaker nor a minority within Farmer-Laborism, but they suffered several reverses at a crucial time. Although the NPL had not collapsed, it was in decline, and one avenue of NPL-Farmer-Labor communication was about to collapse: the *Minnesota Star,* after four years of publication, teetered on the brink of economic ruin. When the paper reemerged, it was beyond the Farmer-Labor pale and had been reorganized into the *Minneapolis Star.*

Within the formal Farmer-Labor party strong criticism was expressed against the Mahoney plan. In announcing the call for the 1924 state convention, party chairman Fred Pike denounced it, called the leagues' merger into a Farmer-Labor Federation a scheme to "sovietize" the movement, and was as blunt in opposing Mahoney's May 30 national convention. To socialists like Mahoney and Teigan, such a reaction was expected; Teigan rather lightly dismissed the accusations because he found that Pike was "just out of the Democratic party and still [carried] with him many of the inclinations and practices of the Democrats."[38]

By contrast, the response from the far left was much more positive. Working with Mahoney and Teigan was Joseph Manley, then the secretary of the communist-controlled Federated Farmer-Labor party. Manley's objective was to help create, at the national convention, a class-conscious party free of more well-to-do property-owning farmers and petty-bourgeois businessmen. To Manley, progressives like Shipstead, Johnson, La Follette, Frazier, and Smith Brookhart were unnecessary and unwelcome. Knowing Manley's radical attitudes, Mahoney foolishly continued associating with the far left, even though he had received a timely warning from the Chicago Federation of Labor advising him of the peril of continued involvement with leaders of the Federated Farmer-Labor party and with representatives of the Workers (i.e., Communist) party.[39]

At a two-day March planning conference, representatives from seven states and the District of Columbia made final arrangements for the convention, now rescheduled for June 17. Mahoney was elected permanent chairman, communist Clarence Hathaway secretary, and Minnesota's Farmer-Labor party was directed to issue the formal call for national delegates.[40] Right until the convention began, the single issue most dividing the planners was communist participation, but a majority voted to let them attend. Red Cramer best summarized left-wing Farmer-Laborites' attitude on communists when he argued, inaccurately to say the least, that Minnesota's success was due to its "open" policy on communists. "They are not very numerous, they are good workers, and a splendid dynamic force. . . . They can help a great deal if they are with you, and they can make a lot of trouble if you keep them out."[41] Although many disagreed with Cramer's reasoning, it came to be a standard judgment shared by many Farmer-Labor leftists over the next twenty years.

A Merged Farmer-Labor Federation

Ever since he had introduced it in September, Mahoney had worked quietly yet tirelessly to gain support for his federation merger plan, and once the national convention issue appeared to be settled he returned full of confidence to the local issue. Already he had renamed his WPNPL the Farmer-Labor Federation, which gave him and his allies a psychological edge over those Nonpartisans and Farmer-Laborites who questioned it. At the Farmer-Labor Federation convention in mid-March Mahoney easily commanded a sufficient number of votes to approve formal merger with the existing NPL. Of the 300 delegates and observers, however, only 30 came from outside the Twin Cities. Spokesmen from rural areas, especially the strongly NPL region of the northwest, charged Mahoney with overrepresenting labor and underrepresenting farmers, and he had to agree to compromise on the apportionment issue.

Strategic considerations lay at the root of Mahoney's enthusiasm for the federation. In addition to merging Farmer-Labor forces into one unit, Mahoney was determined to create a *unique political organization* designed to dominate the legal Farmer-Labor party. In that sense it was a variation of the old Nonpartisan League principle. The *apparatus for control was narrow* rather than general, and the public was excluded from effective influence over the organization, since it was not a party and therefore public law affecting parties did not apply to the federation. For the general public the only avenue of influence was by voting in primary and general elections, and organizational participation was limited to those who were qualified for and accepted into federation membership. In practice, membership came only through affiliation with a labor union, a farmer organization (e.g., a cooperative), or a veterans organization or club acceptable to the federation. Its unifying *ideological principle* was expected to be Farmer-Labor socialism, collectivism, or cooperative marketing, and its span of control a disciplined democratic centralism.

Mahoney, in short, had chosen to attack the existing Farmer-Labor party, the followers of Fred A. Pike, and political moderation, and he described the existing party as a "miserable shell and a delusion."[42] Rather strangely, this implied a rejection of those who had been successful in gaining public office, but it remained rhetorical so long as the NPL existed as a separately functioning body. It was one thing for Mahoney to gain approval from his own organization, but the real test would come at the NPL convention. He sent a special committee, headed by James A. Manahan, to plead with the farmers for merger acceptance. A tense four-hour debate erupted. Farmer-Labor party chairman Fred Pike opposed the merger, some veteran leaguers from as far back as 1915-16 spoke against it, and in letters Senators Magnus Johnson and (North Dakota's) Lynn Frazier denounced it, sarcastically pointing to the coming June 17 national Farmer-Labor convention which they predicted would be "dominated by Communists." By a narrow 84 to 78 margin the merger was approved. Losers wept, and in a funeral oration chairman A. C. Welch admitted he regretted seeing the NPL's demise.[43]

When delegates of workers and farmers met in their first joint session as the Farmer-Labor Federation, the amalgamation nearly ended before it started. Mahoney had hoped to steamroller a quick approval of endorsed candidates. An acrimonious three-hour debate ensued, and, with labor supporters still overrepresented, an endorsement motion actually carried (166 to 151). Sensing disaster and dissolution if this vote should stand, Mahoney again capitulated by issuing an extraordinary parliamentary ruling that declared the motion defeated because farmers had in fact exercised a veto by virtue of their underrepresentation. Mahoney's fusion had not produced unity.

The federation had to surmount one more hurdle, at the Farmer-Labor state party convention in St. Cloud. The party had the option of continuing as it had before and otherwise ignoring the federation. Mahoney and the left therefore tried to gain influence and a following among the delegates. Pike continued to attack Mahoney's "soviet" plan, but with lessened impact following Mahoney's retreats of the past ten days. Farmer delegates, however, still outnumbered labor delegates, and 1918 gubernatorial candidate David Evans of Tracy was selected temporary convention chairman over labor-backed Irving G. Scott. Pike urged caution while Mahoney soothed moderates with assurances that the sole purpose of the June 17 national convention was to endorse Robert La Follette as a Farmer-Labor candidate for president. The party and the federation platforms included nearly identical public ownership planks.[44]

A significant evolution in Farmer-Labor organizational form was now taking place, but this had not necessarily altered the ideological impasse. Yet to be settled was the wisdom, electoral effectiveness, and composition of the Farmer-Labor coalition, the communist question, and whether the new federation would be able to discipline Farmer-Labor candidates and officeholders. The left wing's cherished desire to speak the last word on the meaning and scope of the Farmer-Labor mission was far from being a reality.

The Attack on the Radicals

Mahoney's and the socialist's design to move Farmer-Laborism farther from progressivism and closer to collectivism soon met with rebuke. Old Samuel Gompers denounced the scheduled June 17 convention. On May 1 Magnus Johnson leaked word that he had serious reservations about it, and when pressured to recant, the most favorable thing he would say about it privately was that he was "neutral."[45] Shipstead was less kind and announced his flat opposition to what he called "the launching of a new third party with communist cooperation," a position from which he refused to budge despite pleas from the convention arrangements committee.[46]

Minnesota AFL unions drew ever farther away from the new variant of Farmer-Laborism. By contrast, the Minneapolis Trades and Labor Assembly planned a May Day parade, inviting Workers (Communist) party leaders Earl Browder of Chicago and Alexander Bittleman of New York[47] as speakers. Serious damage to the Farmer-Labor movement spread as newspaper after newspaper picked up the theme of an apparent radical drift in the federation and the party. Throughout May and June stories appeared about the alleged linkup of Mahoney, Farmer-Laborites, communists, and agitators from the new Soviet Union.[48] The final blow came on May 28 when La Follette himself denounced the June 17 convention and announced he would refuse to attend it.[49]

Worse for Minnesota Farmer-Laborism, efforts by Shipstead and Johnson and successful candidates to alter its image, shift the movement away from radicalism, and convince the voting public that the party could be entrusted with public responsibility, and would govern in accordance with traditional norms of progressive change, were now being questioned. Suddenly the wild 1918-20 claims of Republicans and Farmer-Labor enemies that the movement had become radical gained new credence and appeared to justify the previous campaigns to save the state from socialism and radicalism. One important difference was increasingly apparent. Now Red-baiting came from within Farmer-Laborism itself. Old-time NPLers charged Mahoney with using communists to destroy the farmers' movement. Left-wing Farmer-Laborites either ignored or denied it and blundered on. "There is," Teigan confidently predicted, "no danger in my opinion of the communist element, so-called, exercising any control over the [June 17] convention."[50] Nothing he said could have been farther from the truth.

THE 1924 CAMPAIGN AND ELECTION

The June 17 Convention

The national Farmer-Labor convention began and ended just as badly as the skeptics had predicted. The disaster was a near-repeat of the 1923 national Farmer-Labor convention sponsored unwittingly by the Chicago Federation of Labor. In 1924 529 delegates came from 29 states to St. Paul, and the communists clearly had a majority for they literally pulled into the station by a trainload. Legitimate Farmer-Laborites favoring La Follette's nomination were inundated, and communists nominated Illinois mining leader Dwight MacDonald for president and editor William Bouck of the *Western Progressive Farmer* for vice-president.[51] Three weeks later they dropped these candidates and replaced them with Workers party candidates William Z. Foster and Benjamin Gitlow.

Mahoney was left only with a platform, similar to the federation's and state party's, that called for nationalization of monopoly industry, banks, mines, public power, transportation, communication — and immediate American recognition of the government of the Soviet Union.[52] He had learned the bitterest and most lasting political lesson of his life. But Minnesota Farmer-Laborism was dealt a crippling blow for the remainder of the 1924 campaign. Tardily, the Farmer-Labor Federation denounced the communists, and the *Farmer-Labor Advocate* reprinted a Bouck article denouncing the communist duplicity at the convention.[53] It came too late.

The State Primary

The convention disaster was not the only sign of deterioration in the Farmer-Labor party. It started well before the June 16 primary election, for, unlike the situation in 1922, Farmer-Laborites were now in a combative mood as three dozen candidates fought for but seven statewide nominations; three filed for the Senate, eight for governor, and not less than four for every other state office. The Republicans had only about half as many in the primary, but even this was too many.

Magnus Johnson, with 85 percent of the vote, easily gained nomination for the Senate, but consensus on the governorship was nonexistent. Four major candidates fought for the nomination. Charles

Lindbergh campaigned until a terminal brain tumor forced his withdrawal; Tom Davis, a one-term legislator (1917) and now a Minneapolis attorney, had previously campaigned statewide as a Farmer-Laborite and had a strong following among NPLers; Dr. Albert Fritsche was popular among antiwar Germans and isolationists in southern Minnesota; and Hennepin County Attorney Floyd B. Olson, a former Democrat, had the support of the left-wing Hennepin County Farmer-Labor Federation, leaders like Mahoney, Robley Cramer, and Irving G. Scott, and was the favored candidate of labor.

The primary election drew 238,000 Republican and 205,000 Farmer-Labor voters. Had Mahoney not been forced to back down on endorsements, Olson's nomination would have been more secure. Nevertheless, Olson won nomination (27.3 percent) with a 293-vote victory over Davis (27.1 percent), an outcome which may have been decided when Lindbergh withdrew and his campaign leaders endorsed Olson. His Republican opponent, Theodore Christianson, won party nomination with only 22.6 percent! In a total of eleven contests, only one Republican and two Farmer-Labor candidates won nomination with over 50 percent; the rest gained victory by a plurality vote that ranged between 20 and 34 percent, an outcome which was repeated in most congressional contests.[54]

The Left Wing in Retreat

With the disastrous convention coming on the heels of the indecisive primary, Minnesota Farmer-Laborism was in a summer shambles as moderates and old-line progressives vented their wrath on Mahoney and the left for the predicament they had brought the state movement and the La Follette presidential campaign. At Cleveland on July 4, when La Follette was nominated at the Progressive party convention, Mahoney was attacked by delegates who wanted to ostracize him from any connection with Progressive protest. At first Mahoney and the *Farmer-Labor Advocate* made a halfhearted attempt at defending the June convention, but within a fortnight he and noncommunist labor socialists realized how untenable such a position was. Consequently, the executive committee of the Farmer-Labor Federation met July 8, reversed itself, urged support for La Follette, and repudiated the June 17 convention and any connection of the federation with it.[55]

Mahoney and the Farmer-Labor left quickly learned that extricating themselves from their radical contacts was no easy task. Moderate and right-wing Farmer-Laborites had no intention of letting them off so easily. Those who had opposed his federation plan still suspected it was a factional coup led by city labor leaders and radicals to seize control of the movement, and they now were eager to use Mahoney's blunder as a means to recapture command of the party and movement. The counterattack against the left came July 10 when A. C. Gilbert wrote a letter to Farmer-Labor candidates demanding immediate expulsion of communists from the party central committee. Claiming the moderate faction represented the Farmer-Labor majority and the time had come to end "pussy-footing on the issue," Gilbert charged that Mahoney's ill-conceived federation plan and the St. Paul convention now made drastic action imperative to rebuild the party. After he made a point of Mahoney's expulsion at Cleveland, Gilbert expressed what came to be the general Farmer-Labor right-wing position on affiliation with communists during the next twenty years:

> The League farmers do not subscribe to communist doctrines and their organization has received the foulest attacks in its history from this source. Their interest in the state ticket cannot be strong enough to force them to sacrifice their principles and their organization for political folly.
>
> With communists on the committee our hands would be tied in answering the campaign arguments which our opponents could make. Thousands of unattached voters would be driven away and few added by playing with extremists.
>
> Every move made by the candidates should suggest worthiness and ability on a high plane as has the British Labor party. The British Labor party excludes communists.[56]

The Fall Campaign

These factional skirmishes snarled the organizational makeup of the 1924 campaign. Progressives quickly set up an entirely separate campaign for La Follette and ran him as an Independent in spite of Mahoney's complaint that this discredited the federation and undermined Farmer-Labor unity.[57]

Republicans' sudden advantages did not make them immediately confident of victory, and Farmer-Laborites, left and right, continued to believe that Magnus Johnson and Floyd Olson could bring another pair of victories to the movement. Olson was an extraordinarily skilled campaigner, Johnson a recognized populist, and neither had been severely tainted by Mahoney's and the left's radical flirtation. Both campaigned in the moderate style of Shipstead in 1922 and Johnson in 1923. Olson abandoned almost entirely the public ownership planks of the federation platform.[58] The two Farmer-Laborites probably still could have won had they not lost some votes to the marginal Democratic candidates, Carlos Avery for governor and John J. Farrell for senator.

Johnson faced intemperate Thomas D. Schall, the blind tenth-district Republican congressman who made slashing personal attacks against him, aided by a vicious, widely distributed campaign newspaper called the *Minnesota Harpoon.* This scurrilous sheet was edited for Schall by Arthur Jacobs, who oddly enough ultimately joined Farmer-Labor ranks in the 1930s. Among other things Johnson was accused of having a drinking habit, stealing, and taking bribes.

Theodore Christianson opened his fall gubernatorial campaign at Madison in mid-September.[59] His message was largely a repetition of Preus's campaign literature from 1920 and 1922: the need for tax reduction, efficiency and economy in government, and another call to stop the march of Farmer-Labor socialism. Olson avoided a discussion of public ownership, sidestepped the federation and Farmer-Labor party platform, and found himself repeatedly accused by Christianson of avoiding these key issues.

During the final week of the campaign, Republicans made an all-out assault upon alleged Farmer-Labor radicalism. It was a chronicle of conspiracy, Mahoney's federation plan and its sponsorship by communist C. A. Hathaway, the March merger, the ill-fated movement for a June 17 convention, communist domination of Farmer-Laborism, the pushing aside of moderates like Gilbert and Pike, and radical lust for power.[60] The climax came at a mass rally in the St. Paul auditorium, where 10,000 listeners heard a parade of speakers charge Farmer-Laborism with becoming a tool of communist infiltration and the featured speaker, American secretary of state Charles Evans Hughes, appealed to Minnesota voters to avoid becoming prey for dangerous third-party quacks.[61]

Every major metropolitan newspaper became a political sounding board for these Republican charges. The political grotesqueness of the Red Smear suddenly gained renewed creditability when the Communists aggravated an already bad Farmer-Labor situation by announcing during the last week of October that the Workers party was endorsing the entire Farmer-Labor ticket! Friendly editors and publishers spread the story across front pages of the *Tribune, Journal,* and *Dispatch.*[62] It was a political embrace that could well have been designed to kill, and it came after the Communists had identified Mahoney and St. Paul labor leader Frank Starkey as political scoundrels for having endorsed Republican congressman Oscar Keller over the Communist-backed Farmer-Laborite Julius Emme.

Republican Victories

Farmer-Laborism had squandered its opportunities in 1924 and had needlessly snatched defeat from victory by a series of ill-considered attempts to move the party politically leftward. Strategic errors of judgment cost the movement the reelection of Magnus Johnson, undercut the farm protest movement, and gave Minnesota's slipping Republican party renewed vigor. Nevertheless, Farmer-Laborites had apparently displaced Democrats as the party of opposition, for the Democratic statewide vote, including that for president, fell to about 6 percent for each office. Republicans won every state office, though they did so with only a plurality of the vote; only their candidate for secretary of state, Mike Holm, won with greater than 50 percent. Coolidge's 48 percent carried the state, but this was a sharp drop from the 65 percent received by Harding four years before. And as an Independent La Follette (39 percent) ran just 80,000 votes behind Coolidge but 280,000 ahead of the pathetic John W. Davis.

The legislature remained conservative and the Minnesota mood of the twenties seemed to be a dislike for public ownership proposals. The best illustration of the latter, and the ill-timing of the socialists to move Farmer-Laborism leftward, came in the defeated constitutional amendment referendum to authorize a state-owned public grain terminal. The "no" vote was 29 percent, slightly higher than the "yes" vote; 41 percent failed to cast a ballot on the issue.

The most distressing Farmer-Labor setback was the 8,000-vote defeat of Magnus Johnson, which left a feeling that half the election had been stolen from him by the unscrupulous Schall and the other half given away by Mahoney's colossal blunder. Floyd B. Olson won the second highest number of Farmer-Labor votes (42 percent) but was 40,000 votes short of Christianson. The important long-range question to be faced by Farmer-Laborites, now that Minnesota was operating under a three-party system, was whether the remnant 50,000 Democratic vote would perpetually prevent the new party from successfully challenging the Republicans. What would have to sustain the Minnesota Farmer-Labor party in the 1920s was rural protest in the west central and northwest and among the timber and mining regions of the northeast. Indeed, seventh-district congressman O. J. Kvale and ninth-district congressman Knud Wefald won landslide reelections, and in the eighth district William L. Carss once more returned to Washington. They and Shipstead were the symbols of success around which a majority of the movement would have to rally.

RESULTS OF THE 1924 MINNESOTA GENERAL ELECTION
(Candidate, No. of Votes, and Percentage of Total Vote)

OFFICE	REPUBLICAN	DEMOCRATIC	FARMER-LABOR	SOCIALIST-INDUSTRIAL	INDEPENDENT	WORKER'S	OTHER
President	Calvin Coolidge 420,759 (48.4%)	John W. Davis 55,913 (6.4%)		Frank F. Johnson 1,855 (.2%)	Robert La Follette 339,192 (39.0%)	William Z. Foster 4,427 (.5%)	
Senator	Thomas Schall 388,594 (44.7%)	John J. Farrell 53,709 (6.2%)	Magnus Johnson 380,646 (43.8%)		Thomas Keefe 4,994 (.6%)		Merle Birmingham 8,620 (1.0%)
Governor	Theodore Christianson 406,692 (46.8%)	Carlos Avery 49,353 (5.8%)	Floyd B. Olson 366,029 (42.1%)	Oscar Anderson 3,876 (.4%)			Michael Ferch 9,032 (1.0%)
Lieutenant governor	W. I Nolan 410,433 (47.2%)	Fred Schilplin 50,330 (5.8%)	Emil Holmes 345,633 (39.8%)				
Attorney general	Cliff L. Hilton 417,376 (48.0%)	Robert C. Bell 42,913 (5.1%)	Thomas V. Sullivan 342,236 (39.4%)				
Secretary of state	Mike Holm 473,577 (54.5%)	Ole C. Halvorson 45,622 (5.3%)	Susie Stageberg 288,946 (33.2%)				
Treasurer	Henry Rines 422,389 (48.6%)	Henry H. Reindl 48,302 (5.6%)	Carl Berg 322,585 (37.1%)				
Railroad and warehouse commissioner	Frank W. Matson 403,332 (46.4%)	J. J. Lanin 46,031 (5.3%)	A. E. Smith 334,174 (38.4%)				

Note: The total percentage for each office is less than 100 because some voters cast blank ballots and some ballots were spoiled.

Minnesota Farmer-Laborism, by Millard L. Gieske, © 1979 by the University of Minnesota.

The Legacy of 1924

A few Farmer-Laborites still clung to the fantasy that victory was possible through a socialist platform, and some still were not ready to give up all ties with radical protest. There was no end to the excuses and reasons given for defeat. Mahoney blamed the communists and would for the rest of his life. The Farmer-Labor candidate for lieutenant governor privately charged Olson with being "not very much of a Farmer-Laborite," possibly even working against Magnus Johnson.[63] But the major issues which the movement faced for the rest of the decade remained conflict over ideology, party versus federation, farmers versus workers, city versus country, socialists versus pluralists, reformers against radicals, moderate officeholders impatient with intractable ideologues.

Yet Mahoney had given the movement a major face-lift, the innovative federation plan which was modified slightly in 1925 and changed into the Farmer-Labor Association. Organizationally, it attempted to structure Farmer-Laborism around Farmer-Labor clubs, composed of dues-paying members at the ward, village, and township level. Parallel to them, and in fact more dominant in the large counties (Hennepin, Ramsey, and St. Louis) were the interest group "affiliated" clubs associated with union locals, cooperatives, veterans groups, and similar social and economic agencies. The association otherwise had a hierarchy of command much like a political party, with final authority resting in county and state conventions. Officers, committee structure, central committees, executive committees, and most of the other accouterments of parties were found in the association.

Mahoney had also succeeded in gutting the regular party apparatus, though in practice the term "Farmer-Labor party" survived in daily use. The official party met but one day every two years when nominated candidates, after the primary, caucused at the capitol and elected party officers who then ceased to carry out any political function. The idea behind this unique "federation" method of operation was unity in command, interest, ideology, and to the socialists a hoped-for change in basic public policy concerning ownership and distribution of production. In practice, such unity was seldom achieved. The alliance remained as shaky as ever. The strength of the Mahoney federation was at once its major weakness. Farmer-Labor chairman Fred Pike put his finger squarely on this Farmer-Labor problem when he originally criticized the federation units, or clubs, as "easily manipulated in the interest of special groups and interests," with the political danger being that this would create too narrow an appeal in a much larger democratic society[64] than the socialists were willing to admit existed in Minnesota.

The left's misunderstanding about the necessity of appealing to nonsocialist protest, and its inability either to recognize or to accept the fact that Minnesota voters normally were conservative to moderate, was the major Farmer-Labor failure in 1924. Such faulty judgment begged the issue of what Farmer-Laborites could or should do with Democrats. Those who survived in the larger constitutencies had usually moderated their political appeals and demands and had made peace with the Democrats, openly or sub rosa.

CHAPTER 5

The Unsuccessful Attempt to Rebuild Farmer-Laborism

Farmer-Laborites, left and right, foresaw that their 1924 election defeat would lead to the political demise of the movement unless steps were taken to rebuild it. Even while remedies were prescribed, lack of agreement on goals, policies, candidates, and organization kept the movement at odds with itself. Two major factions remained. One was more pluralist, moderate, and amenable to seeking a working relationship with Democrats. The other retained a sometimes overpowering need to push Farmer-Laborism to the left and merely had postponed its plans to displace private enterprises with collective ownership. The moderates, or right-wing, Farmer-Laborites tended to be more pragmatic than ideological about their politics, but the left too had hardly abandoned practical considerations for ideological purity during the period of postwar "normalcy." Even those who seemed least likely to dishonor collectivist ideology sometimes were guilty of doing it. No less a Farmer-Labor disciple than Henry Teigan, usually a consistent socialist, was then engaged in stock speculation in a Pacific northwest mine, anticipating that his 1,500 shares would "reap a handsome profit . . . in a short time."[1]

Factionalism during this troublesome period was symbolically and functionally tied to the "communist problem." After 1924 and for the remainder of the decade communists were made to feel unwelcome in the Farmer-Labor movement, constitutionally "outlawed" as it were. When Farmer-Laborites dealt with this issue in 1925, their solution—expulsion—was based on the supposed violent revolutionary nature of Workers party communists. The left distinguished them from radicals. The right usually did not. The reason for this difference was perpetual disagreement over whether Farmer-Laborism was pursuing progressive or socialist alternatives.

Another fundamental problem for the movement was interpreting the Minnesota popular mood in the twenties. If leaders could not accurately recognize it, neither could the rank and file, nor, for that matter, the voters. In the state very few were calling for a return to the "good old days" of the prewar period or for solutions that relied upon statism and public ownership. Plumbing the public mood for attitudes was, as it always has been, an inexact art. Like most American citizens, Minnesotans were neither *laissez faire* nor socialist but reacted to issues and problems that most affected their personal interests. One such area of concern was the continuing "farm problem," the major destabilizing agent of the decade. Besides debating where the movement was to stand on the public policy issues of the decade, Farmer-Laborites fought to keep what they had not yet lost to Republicans while working to erase an image of radicalism that had been reattached to the movement.

REBUILDING FARMER-LABORISM, 1924-25

The Protest against Schall's Election

Farmer-Labor reconstruction began when an attempt was made to overturn Thomas Schall's election and prevent his seating in the Senate. To many people, Johnson's defeat appeared to be an unjust and improper outcome of a distorted campaign, even though some of his closest supporters — Henry Teigan for one — admitted privately the populist was somewhat intellectually overmatched in the Senate. Within days of the election Teigan, the senator's personal secretary, undertook a systematic search for evidence upon which to base Johnson's appeal against Schall.

This appeal demonstrated that, on balance, moderate Farmer-Laborism was the preferred strategy to follow. Urging Johnson to contest the outcome were well-known Democrats such as John Lind and Edward Indrehus, and conservative Republicans like Elmer E. Adams of Fergus Falls (who served intermittently in the legislature from 1905 to 1941) and Rudolph Lee (publisher of the *Lone Prairie Leader*). Affidavits were collected which reputed to disclose that Schall had taken campaign contributions from "bootleggers" in return for his promises to protect them against government prosecution. One contributor sued for return of an $850 contribution. In May

Schall's campaign coordinator, Arthur Jacobs, was sentenced to sixty days in jail for criminal libel in connection with his anti-Johnson articles in two smear papers, the Minnesota *Harpoon* and *Scandal;* these stories said Johnson took bribes and had stolen farmers' money from the Equity Cooperative Exchange. After a year of investigation, however, the Senate concluded that the charges against Schall had not been proved, and in June 1926 they were dismissed.[2] Schall was by now a Republican embarrassment, and a great number of people in his party organization preferred to see him pushed from office in 1930. Although Farmer-Laborism had lost the appeal, many felt the defeat was one more illustration of how far the unscrupulous opposition would go to defeat the new party.

Moving against the Communists

Another step in Farmer-Labor rebuilding was the expulsion of known communists from the federation and the local labor movement. In St. Paul it was led by Frank Starkey and resulted in the expulsion of Clarence Hathaway from the Trades and Labor Assembly. At first Red-hunting was resented by left-wing Farmer-Laborites on the civil libertarian grounds that American radicals were to be considered innocent until proven guilty. In June 1924 a spirited debate over communist presence in the Farmer-Labor Federation broke out in the executive committee following introduction of a Starkey resolution to bar them. Susie Stageberg "reserved judgment" and preferred toleration, though she worried that communists might seek domination of the federation and frighten away more orthodox progressives. The anticommunists lost the vote seven to four[3] after Hathaway and Minneapolis communist C. R. Hedlund argued they wanted to see the Farmer-Labor party develop as a proletarian class movement.

Following the November 1924 election a sharp change in attitude toward communists set in, and on January 1 (1925) William Mahoney opened the attack by charging them in the *Minnesota Union Advocate* with undermining the Farmer-Labor Federation and sabotaging La Follette. At a meeting of the federation's central committee on January 17, a resolution carried to expel Hedlund and J. O. Johnson of Minneapolis as Robley D. (Red) Cramer, once their defender, argued against communist participation.[4]

The Farmer-Labor "Unity Conference"

Communist expulsion was preliminary to a careful effort by Mahoney and his labor supporters to reconcile Farmer-Labor ideological factions, create a more permanent and secure federation, change the movement's external image, and save the federation principle.

Socialists and labor were willing to take one step backward (toward moderation) in the hope that sometime in the future they could take two steps forward (toward the economic left). The call announcing the March 1925 convention of the state federation was deliberately made as broad as possible. Invitations were sent to old Nonpartisan League members, the NPL Women's club, "friends of the movement," feminists. To further buttress moderation and bring back farmers, state senator Richard T. Buckler (congressman, 1935-43), a Crookston farmer, was chosen temporary chairman. And the call mentioned that Workers party members were excluded from the federation. Communists made these changes appear more creditable when they denounced the convention as a betrayal of the Farmer-Labor party and the working class.[5] Popular as the communist purge appeared to be, Mahoney and federation treasurer Ralph L. Harmon continued to encounter strong opposition to Red-baiting and political moderation from the traditionally left-leaning Hennepin County Federation.

When the 250 convention delegates assembled in St. Paul, it seemed unlikely that the movement would be able to rally around a pole of unity. Several delegates were denounced as communists and, based on these accusations, Emil S. Youngdahl (state representative, 1927-33) of Minneapolis and Julius F. Emme of St. Paul were expelled. Emme, a Farmer-Labor congressional candidate in 1924, prophetically warned the convention that it could not effectively bar communists from participation.

The Formation of the Farmer-Labor Association. A more substantive issue at the conference was Mahoney's reorganization plan to strengthen the federation and rename it the Farmer-Labor Association of Minnesota. The proposal reopened the issue of workers and farmers acting in political concert through a body operating *outside* the legal Farmer-Labor party. This matter was as controversial now as it had been in September 1923, and Mahoney, most labor leaders, and the socialists worked to have the federation principle strengthened and extended. Their chief antagonist was lame-duck senator Magnus Johnson, still hostile toward labor and convinced that ideological adventurousness by the left wing had cost him reelection. Johnson proposed to revive the old two-league system of NPL and WPNPL. In blunt language he argued that federation put farmers at a disadvantage by pitting them against "silver-tongued" labor union orators who, through their organizational and negotiation experience and fast-moving union debate, would tend to dominate and control the body, to the injury of farmers.

Johnson may have half-believed his own argument, but he too was a dozen-year veteran of organization struggle, was politically shrewd, and knew that farmers produced a majority of the Farmer-Labor votes. His long speeches against federation had the result of forcing Mahoney, labor, and the left toward more moderation and even acceptance of a dominant farmer role in the new association. Mahoney compromised by offering the association presidency to Johnson, the vice-presidency to state representative Louis Enstrom (1919-29, 1939) of Roseau County, and the secretaryship to labor anticommunist Frank Starkey. To give Farmer-Laborism a fresh start and further purge its suspected communist past, the federation name was dropped, replaced with the association, and the executive committee was divided between city and country: Johnson, Mahoney, Starkey, Floyd B. Olson, and Victor Lawson of Willmar.[6]

To firmly establish this new Farmer-Labor organization as a substitute for the regular party, the *Constitution of the Farmer-Labor Association of Minnesota* was drawn up at the convention, under the direction of Floyd B. Olson. The association was a peculiar adaptation of functional representation — unions, cooperatives, clubs, groups — and, ironically, this change would come to be a plague for none other than Olson himself in the 1930s.

Olson and the other constitution framers deliberately cast the movement in moderate, progressive, but not socialist, language. In the constitution's Declaration of Principles, the Farmer-Labor goal was announced as the uniting of workers, farmers, and their friends to secure protective legislation against "special privilege," monopoly, industrial oligarchy, and control of the government by the privileged few.[7] Conspicuous by its absence was any mention of a comprehensive or long-range socialist blueprint calling for a basic reorganization of the economic and political system. Socialists and the left wing in the association had not abandoned these goals, but their words were muted now as a price of union. Socialists, however, hoped these goals could in some way be introduced and quietly advanced through a subordinate agency, the Farmer-Labor Educational Association, whose function was the dissemination of ideas and propaganda.

The framers thought they had put the communist question to final rest when article 2, section 1, was inserted to bar from membership any group or person adhering to a doctrine advocating "political or economic change by means of force or by means of revolution or advocating any other than a representative form of government. . . ."

The language was stronger than that used in a preliminary version, favored by the left wing, excluding those who advocated "violent revolution"; the earlier version had been attacked on the convention floor for being weak and unacceptable because it allowed communists in "by the back door."[8]

Reorganized and with a new name, Farmer-Laborism hoped its recent stormy past had been put to rest and the illusive goal of unity had finally been achieved. Nevertheless, despite the association's claims, it was not the sole voice speaking for the farmer. A decimated NPL still limped along; it stubbornly refused an invitation to merge its *Minnesota Leader* with the association's *Farmer-Labor Advocate;*[9] and its state chairman planned a series of summer picnics, having been assured by Shipstead that he would attend them to speak before NPL farmers.[10] Shipstead in particular and all Farmer-Labor officeholders in general remained a continuing irritation to the association bureaucracy for the independent course they often pursued. As Farmer-Labor political times worsened, their independence increased, to the distress of the left wing. Even in Minneapolis, conservatives in the labor movement — Teigan called them "labor reactionaries"[11] — were regaining strength, and the left worried it was losing control of the city labor movement.

THE 1926 CAMPAIGN AND ELECTION

The Farmer-Labor Convention and Primary

The association had a year to put its new house in order before learning, in the 1926 campaign and election, how well the changes would be received. The results proved disappointing. Although a wide-open primary was avoided, disharmony persisted through lack of real union and a dogged continuation of the communist problem even in the new association.

The association state convention met in the St. Paul Labor Temple on March 26 while, elsewhere in the same building, the crippled NPL stubbornly met in deviant independence. To avoid a costly and divisive primary, association leaders hoped to negotiate a slate of candidates acceptable to the Nonpartisans. They were successful to some extent, except where it counted most, in the selection of a gubernatorial candidate. Initially, there were six candidates, including Magnus Johnson, Tom Davis, and Victor Lawson. After the first ballot Johnson almost won majority endorsement, which he subsequently obtained. However, the Nonpartisans refused to accept him and instead endorsed Davis, forcing the deadlock to continue into the primary.[12]

Both Davis and Johnson were from the ranks of the Farmer-Labor right, and in keeping with the times the 1926 association platform was moderate: lower farm and home property taxes, rural electric cooperatives, workmen's compensation, "home rule" rather than state regulation of utilities (repeal of the then controversial Brooks-Coleman Act), a St. Lawrence deep-channel seaway to Duluth, public works jobs for the unemployed. Ironically, Johnson found new allies among the labor left and within the strong association bureaucracy which he heretofore had opposed.[13] By contrast, Davis, now a city lawyer, claimed much of his support from the old NPL.

The communist expulsions of 1925 had not ended that controversy nor quieted the right wing's suspicion of the left despite Johnson's being taken as the association's favored candidate. Just as the Nonpartisan Leaguers continued to press the charge that labor dominated the association, so they still believed there was a communist link to the Farmer-Labor movement, even if it was not visible to the naked political eye. About the latter they were correct. During the middle of the primary campaign the Communist International, or Comintern, in Moscow, in an effort to eliminate a source of dispute among American Communists, changed the international party line by permitting American communists to work through established Farmer-Labor parties.[14] In Minnesota this meant working for Magnus Johnson. Henry Teigan took advantage of it through an intermediary, Thomas Canty, by submitting to the *Daily Worker* a story eulogizing Johnson and the progressive forces behind him while claiming Davis was backed by the forces of reaction. Teigan excused this ploy, pointed to the depleted Johnson campaign treasury, and argued that the strongly organized and disciplined Communists could prove helpful to Johnson.[15]

Such lapses by the Farmer-Labor left did not mean it had completely abandoned its course of nonalignment with radicals since it otherwise remained cautious and refused to associate with national third-party movements.[16] However, these lapses were endemic to Minnesota left-wing thinking, and occasional backsliding on the communist issue occurred throughout Farmer-Labor history. This is why the Farmer-Labor right distrusted the left. O. M. Thomason, a former Nonpartisan *Leader* editor and at the time the publisher of the *Ortonville Star,* for that very reason had advised Johnson not to run for governor because — as he told none other than Teigan — schemers and "extremists" still dominated the association[17] and were merely using Johnson to cover up their activities.

The primary election outcome was a genuine cause for Farmer-Labor concern. Although Republican votes increased dramatically, up 200,000, to 420,000, the Farmer-Labor vote fell, down 50,000, to only 155,000. Johnson eked out a 12,000-vote victory (53 percent) over Davis (45 percent), and the nomination for lieutenant governor went to Emil Holmes (39 percent) in place of the association-backed candidate who finished a poor third (18 percent).

"Agreements" with Democrats

Farmer-Laborites were not the only group experiencing hard times in 1926. Minnesota Democrats were still unable to win back old supporters who had defected to Farmer-Laborism. Consequently, their common political depression brought factions within both parties to explore ways in which they might reach agreements about uniting against the dominant Republicans.

Not all Farmer-Laborites welcomed such a shift in third-party strategy. As a general rule, the left resisted it throughout Farmer-Labor history, and in 1926 believed that it already had compromised enough on candidates and platform. Nor did all Democratic factions desire a formal or informal linkup with Farmer-Laborites. Some envisioned Farmer-Laborism as a composite of left-wingers, radicals, communists, whatever, and to them it seemed only prudent to avoid associating with a source of political contamination. It was also believed that the more numerous Farmer-Laborites would dominate a common campaign, control a merged party, or monopolize the benefits and leave little or nothing for the Democrats. C. A. Quist, leader of one Democratic faction, demanded complete Democratic independence and nonalliance,[18] and the 1926 Democratic gubernatorial candidate, Duluth judge Alfred Jacques, talked ambitiously of rebuilding his party along progressive liberal lines that completely rejected new totalitarian radicalism, communist or fascist.[19]

Different from these positions were the attitudes of some of the more flexible Democratic moderates located in outstate regions or pockets where both Farmer-Laborites and Democrats pursued rather modest public policies which largely avoided the strident ideological appeal of left or right. One region where this especially held true was the St. Cloud area. In the 1924 campaign for sixth-district congressman, Democrat Edward Indrehus had withdrawn from the race in favor of Dr. S. C. Shipstead, brother of the senator. In 1926 this principle of cooperation was reversed when district judge Joseph B. Himsl, a lifelong Democrat, ran as a Farmer-Laborite and won the primary nomination. Such agreements were made under the watchful eye of Fred Schilplin and his regionally powerful *St. Cloud Times,* the leading Democratic paper in central Minnesota. And they were almost always condemned by the more dogmatic Farmer-Labor socialists who rejected the principle that being a Democrat or Farmer-Laborite could be an interchangeable act of political allegiance.

Farmer-Labor success depended upon obtaining fresh voter defections from the Republican and Democratic parties to the third party. Now, however, the major defections were not toward the new party but away from it. The Republican governor Theodore Christianson had not uncovered a popular new theme for his reelection campaign; instead, he relied upon the claim of running an efficient and business-like state administration and he promised to pass on the savings to the taxpayers.[20] Speaking for Farmer-Laborism through the *Minnesota Union Advocate* and the *Farmer-Labor Advocate,* editor William Mahoney predicted voters would reject Christianson for Johnson, but Mahoney also had to speak harshly against defectors from the NPL and Farmer-Laborism, "self-seekers" he called them, men like O. M. Thomason ("a former socialist soap box orator" and "turn-coat") who were urging farmers to defect to Republicans.[21]

The "Round Robin" Movement. Probably the most serious threat to Farmer-Laborism in the mid-twenties was the so-called round robin movement, the brainchild of Walter Quigley, a backer of Tom Davis and the "Progressive Reorganization Volunteer Committee." It asked Farmer-Laborites to abandon their party by voting Democratic in preparation for merging the two parties in 1928. Quigley argued that Farmer-Laborism had lost momentum, Democrats were near extinction, voters were defecting to the Republicans, and the chances of political reaction increased as Republican opposition dwindled and divided. The only effective way of countering these changes was through a reformed and rebuilt Democratic party into which progressive Farmer-Laborism had merged.

Quigley's merger plan was to be kept secret until October 6, 1926, but word of it came to the association, forcing publication a week earlier. Signed by twelve lesser-known Farmer-Laborites (Oscar Brekke and R. A. Trovatten were the best known among them), the letter urged defection to Democratic candidates preparatory to Farmer-Laborite participation in the 1928 Democratic caucuses in which they were to take active command. The third-party idea, Quigley and the signers concluded, was futile and therefore should be abandoned.[22] Weaknesses in the scheme were all too obvious. For one, it was cavalier in its treatment of Democratic leaders, appeared to have entirely ignored them, and undoubtedly made them suspicious. The plan also was premature, poorly developed, and involved far too narrow a segment of the movement.

The association's response to Quigley was predictable. To discredit the plan, it slandered Quigley's character, not altogether difficult: he was described as having connections with prohibition bootleggers, and pointed references were made to his disbarment by the courts.[23] Journalistically, Quigley could be a gunslinger and he countered with Red-baiting, claiming Communists like J. Louis Engdahl and William Dunne of the *Daily Worker* were behind the personal attacks against him and had come to Minnesota to give speeches in behalf of the Farmer-Labor ticket.[24] The net result was that the Farmer-Labor party continued to distrust the Democratic party and vice versa.

Farmer-Laborism's Dismal Fall Campaign

Quigley's round robin had failed badly, but it did underscore the weakness of the Farmer-Labor campaign. By the end of the campaign nothing really seemed to work well for the protest movement. Campaign funds were depleted. The Farmer-Labor nominee for lieutenant governor, Emil Holmes, bolted the party and announced his support of Democratic Alfred Jacques over Magnus Johnson; Holmes further embarrassed the party when he released a letter by Charles E. Ruthenberg, national secretary of the Workers party, announcing Communist support of the Farmer-Labor slate.[25]

Little help was forthcoming to Farmer-Laborites, although they tried hard to reverse their slide. To replenish campaign funds, the association hired fund-raising solicitors on commission, allowing them to keep as pay one-third of their gross collections. The association leadership even sought to make some use of Democratic speakers when they could; former governor John Lind delivered speeches on behalf of Himsl, Kvale, and Wefald. Henry Teigan had sought further Democratic cooperation and blamed the Democratic state chairman for resisting it.[26] Editorials about Theodore Christianson from the 1917-18 issues of the *Dawson Sentinel* were reprinted in an effort to portray the governor as anti-German and anti-Catholic. One of the more foolish efforts was to bring Chicago Republican mayor William (Big Bill) Thompson to Winona, St. Paul, and Minneapolis to address mass rallies for Johnson. Thompson promised almost magic results, but it was clear that what worked in Chicago had virtually no appeal in Minnesota; his presence drew little interest and provided almost studied silence by the press.[27] Emil Holmes's charge that Farmer-Laborism was aligning itself "with extreme Reaction or extreme Radicalism"[28] was hardly the full truth, but many of the old issues which Farmer-Laborism had successfully touched in the past now seemed to have turned to dust.

Election Results

That the Farmer-Labor condition would become still worse before it improved was no consolation in November. Statewide, Farmer-Laborites could be thankful there had not yet been widespread defection to the Democrats, who ran only four candidates in the eight races and received between 5 and 8 percent of the vote. Among the Farmer-Laborites, Magnus Johnson performed the best, but his 37-percent showing hardly was encouraging when compared with Theodore Christianson's 55-percent mandate for "businesslike administration." Somewhat puzzling was Emil Holmes's showing (33 percent),

RESULTS OF THE 1926 MINNESOTA GENERAL ELECTION
(Candidate, No. of Votes, and Percentage of Total Vote)

OFFICE	REPUBLICAN	DEMOCRATIC	FARMER-LABOR
Governor	Theodore Christianson 395,779 (54.8%)	Alfred Jaques 38,008 (5.3%)	Magnus Johnson 266,845 (36.9%)
Lieutenant governor	W. I. Nolan 373,940 (51.7%)	Charles D. Johnson 53,189 (7.4%)	Emil Holmes 236,307 (32.7%)
Attorney general	Clifford L. Hilton 384,724 (53.2%)	George Cahill 45,049 (6.2%)	Frank E. McAllister 214,781 (29.7%)
Secretary of state	Mike Holm 449,447 (62.2%)		Charles Olson 217,424 (30.1%)
Treasurer	Julius A. Schmahl 384,724 (53.2%)		Thomas J. Meighen 244,861 (33.9%)
Railroad and warehouse commissioner	Ole P. Jacobson 387,677 (53.6%)		Thomas Vollom 236,131 (32.7%)
Clerk of the supreme court	Grace F. Kaecher 341,597 (47.3%)	Winnifred McDermott 61,952 (8.6%)	Minnie Cederholm 227,520 (31.5%)

Note: The total percentage for each office is less than 100 because some voters cast blank ballots and some ballots were spoiled.

Minnesota Farmer-Laborism, by Millard L. Gieske, © 1979 by the University of Minnesota.

which matched the performance of the strongest Farmer-Laborites despite his persistent attacks upon the association.

Where protest was sustained it was primarily agrarian, not urban. O. J. Kvale won easy reelection (59 percent) in the rural seventh district and William Carss (55 percent) won in the eighth, but further decline was apparent in Knud Wefald's 972-vote loss. Republicans had reached a plateau, won eight of ten congressional seats, all state offices, and retained solid legislative control.

ISSUES AFFECTING FARMER-LABORISM, 1927

The 1926 election was a vote of confidence in Republicans, for these seemed to be Republican days of wine and roses. Reform measures fared poorly in the legislature. A bank deposit guarantee bill lost in the lower house, 66 to 55, and in the senate James Carley led an investigation of the activities of Arthur N. Jacobs. Republicans were confident. Business was expanding. A new Sears-Roebuck store was under construction on Lake Street in Minneapolis, and there was talk of new buildings like the Foshay Tower. Republicans invited President Calvin Coolidge to move the summer White House to northern Minnesota (he chose South Dakota's Black Hills).[29] Because Republicanism seemed so impregnable, Farmer-Laborites were beset by disagreement as they searched for issues to revive their lagging movement.

The Debate over Ideology

Both factions in the Farmer-Labor party recognized the need to rebuild; they differed substantially over how this should be accomplished. The progressives and those on the right continued to defend their belief that policies of modest reform, appeals to the political center, and working relationships with Democrats were the alternatives most worthy of consideration and most likely to bring future success against Republicans. The left wing had never been fully comfortable with moderate or reform politics and was suspicious of plebiscary democracy as practiced by Republicans and Democrats. Having compromised collectivism and accepted moderate candidates in the 1926 election, the left found the outcome as disappointing as it had been in 1924. So the left reopened the debate about goals and strategy.

Many left-wingers were now tempted to reassemble a left-leaning coalition and return Farmer-Laborism to collectivist principles. To Henry Teigan, it was natural enough to be asked by *Daily Worker* editor William Dunne to write unsigned articles on the Minnesota "political situation."[30] And to Susie Stageberg, who was always religiously philosophical, setback and defeat were but ways to test the depth of one's faith. "It amazes me," she confessed two weeks before Christmas, 1926, "to see how easily our flock of Faithfuls can be dispersed. It gives me an inkling of what the Master must have felt when He said 'Oh ye of little faith.'" For the elect, perseverence and hope in the future were qualities wedded to a Joblike patience. Devout social critics such as Stageberg continually gained inspiration in their fidelity to the "people's crusade" and were determined to keep it alive as a

> protest movement hanging as a club over the heads of the despoilers of the people's wealth and happiness. . . . Personally I am content to carry on tho we never elect our candidates. We compel them to adopt our issues. . . . I feel like fighting it out along this line if it takes a half century.[31]

A week after the election the *Farmer-Labor Advocate,* reflecting the left wing's point of view, abandoned some of its self-imposed caution, called for a national Farmer-Labor party, and pleaded for a program of "unqualified" governmental control over transportation, natural resources, and fiscal and monetary policy. Although it avoided the word "socialist," the clear implication was an association return to collectivism. At the same time the left attacked the centrists, and singled out Holmes, Quigley, Brekke, and the fusionists for being either unscrupulous or ignorant of what it saw as basic Farmer-Labor principles. Political merger with Democrats was a contradiction, the left claimed, because the two parties were incompatible and antagonistic. Democrats were said to be nearing extinction and were little different from the Republican or any other "plutocratic party." Farmer-Laborism had to return to basic principles, "fundamental changes" were required in American industry, and as a movement Farmer-Laborism was a vanguard obligated to oppose "private ownership of the vital necessities of the people, and monopolies of every nature."[32]

Such a call to action was too ambitious. No storming of the political barricades occurred, and in spite of rhetorical bombast the moderates apparently had not been displaced, weakened, or impressed with the most recent argument to turn the movement leftward. At the state association conference in January 1927 at the St. Paul Labor Temple, the left's proposals to 200 delegates were much toned down, though there were appeals for growth of regional Farmer-Labor parties and for a revitalized national Farmer-

Labor party, and speculation about a possible 1928 Farmer-Labor presidential ticket.

Even these modest projections were beyond the means of the association to accomplish. Teigan's financial report showed the central committee to be nearly bankrupt; it had been forced to run its 1926 campaign on a budget of $3,000, $1,000 of which was borrowed. To pay for convention expenses, the "hat was passed" and exactly $61 collected. Little wonder that the *Advocate* suspended publication the next month.

More serious was a flare-up of differences between organized labor and farmers over the program of manufacturing farm implements at Stillwater prison. Labor demanded an end to the practice because it competed with regular factory labor, but when it was vigorously defended by a Scott County delegate, state senator Henry Arens (lieutenant governor, 1931-33, congressman, 1933-35), as a way of checking the (International) Harvester trust, labor accepted a state Federation of Labor compromise offered by Frank Starkey not to expand implement production to other state institutions.

While radicals were proposing, moderates retained the power to disapprove of the collectivist alternatives, and the farmer and moderate vetoes were usually sustained. The general program endorsed by the conference was largely in keeping with the values of farmers and the more conservative state Federation of Labor: workmen's compensation, unemployment insurance, national prohibition of child labor, teacher tenure, state guarantee of bank deposits, reclassified property taxes, approval of a constitutional amendment allowing state-owned electric power, and opposition to a state police ("state constabulary") force (to be distinguished from the "highway patrol"). The majority still opposed general programs of socialism, and strong opposition was expressed when Mahoney and Teigan sought approval for public ownership of rail transportation.[33]

Foreign Policy

Although constituency interests often seemed to force workers and farmers into intraparty competition, left and right generally agreed on foreign policy and would do so for another decade. A resolution of the 1927 Farmer-Labor conference condemned American policy in Mexico and Nicaragua and demanded the impeachment of the Coolidge secretary of state, Frank B. Kellogg. The mood was isolationist and antiwar, to fight only when attacked, an attitude not exclusively Farmer-Laborite for Republicans were equally taken up with the apparent retreat from Wilson's earlier internationalism. Kellogg himself had joined the idealists of his day by helping draw up, in August 1928, the sixteen-nation Kellogg-Briand pact renouncing war as an instrument of national policy.

While the Communists watched the 1927 conference closely, someone, probably Teigan, wrote a "special to the Daily Worker" article on the convention, and the Communist general secretary praised the Farmer-Labor Association for being a bona fide workers' and farmers' movement, for rejecting fusion with Democrats, for demanding what the Communists said were socialist reforms, for opposing American imperialism, for expressing interest in a 1928 national party, and for considering a resolution to seat "former Communist" (as the Communists identified him) Emil S. Youngdahl in the Minnesota legislature (1927-33).[34]

The Farm Problem

Minnesota in the 1920s was still highly agricultural, and the major economic and political problem of the decade involved that sector. The insoluble farm problem was simple to describe: overproduction accompanied by depressed prices. Basic causes for this condition were equally simple: technological development, a changed economy especially in agriculture, rising expectations (or a continuation of wartime prosperity), and, as a result, production which exceeded demand and brought sharply falling farm commodity prices. This combination of circumstances prevented incumbent Republicans from becoming an even more entrenched political majority, and helped the last pockets of Farmer-Laborism last a little longer, possibly through the decade or until Democrats displaced them.

During the years that employment remained high, tariff protection appeared to offer workers some security against foreign goods and low wages, but even though the 1922 tariff act was designed to protect farmers as well as workers, in practice it could do little, if anything, to boost farm prices. As a result agrarian spokesmen pursued a different policy: Have the government purchase commodity "surplus" to bolster (or inflate) farm prices, and then sell (or "dump") the "surplus" on the world market. In 1924 the McNary-Haugen Bill was introduced in an attempt to make this the basic national farm policy. Although it started as primarily a midwestern wheat bill, it had to be expanded to cover the so-called basic staple commodities of wheat, corn, cotton, tobacco, and rice, which politically joined the major sectional interests of the farm bloc. When President Calvin

Coolidge twice vetoed the bill in 1927 and 1928, a contentious policy issue was born, which lasted into the 1930s and beyond.

Agricultural interests saw the vetoes as a major setback, and farm bloc attacks upon the national administration became bipartisan. In Minnesota most Republican and Democratic progressives favored the McNary-Haugen Bill — Charles McNary of Oregon became the Republican candidate for vice-president in 1940 — and the discontent that followed rejection was almost a lifeline for Farmer-Laborism. At the Northwest Farm Conference held in July 1927, a typical reaction occurred. The speakers were neither socialist nor radical, and whether Republican or Democrat (like young Kentucky Democratic senator Alban W. Barkley who became vice-president under Harry S. Truman), they poured out a message of farmers suffering under prices which kept many in near bondage. McNary-Haugen was said to be an avenue of escape. Even the tone of the usually conservative *St. Paul Pioneer Press* was somber, sympathetic to the farmer, as it communicated in headlines the "Plight of the Farmer" and dutifully reported the gloomy tales about farmers suffering from low prices and low returns.[35] An issue of major proportions was developing for 1928. The question now was whether Minnesota Farmer-Laborism remained strong enough and capable enough to use the issue to recapture the political initiative which had been slowly slipping away.

THE 1928 CAMPAIGN AND ELECTION

Despite growing uncertainty about agriculture's lag in prosperity when compared with the rest of the economy, Republicans enjoyed good times and even better intraparty relationships. Party dissension was the lowest it had been for a dozen years, perhaps as long as several decades. After their 1926 success the major challenge was to defeat Henrik Shipstead in the Senate race; Governor Theodore Christianson seriously considered becoming a senatorial candidate until January 1928 when he announced his decision to seek a third term. One reason why Republicans appeared so formidable was that their strength contrasted greatly with the weakened condition of Democrats and Farmer-Laborites.

The Uncertain Candidacy of Olson and Shipstead

The chances for reviving the Farmer-Labor party did not appear bright. Nearly broke, the association had lost its newspaper, the *Advocate,* and now relied almost exclusively upon the *Minnesota*

Union Advocate, which Mahoney and Teigan edited for the state Federation of Labor. Worse, the party and the association had apparently run out of strong candidates around which to build a campaign. Association leaders had one ace in the hole, Hennepin County Attorney, Floyd B. Olson, and they tried desperately to sell him on the need to run for governor. Olson's disinterest led some to suspect his conversion to Farmer-Laborism had not been genuine, and there was speculation he planned to turn Democrat once again.

The situation was not one bit better when the association leadership looked to the cautiously independent Shipstead. Because he largely ignored the association and had nothing in common with its socialists, the association hierarchy viewed him with distrust and anxiety. In Washington he sat on the right side of the Senate among the Republicans, and though Shipstead remained popular with the AFL leadership — president William Green had announced support for his reelection six weeks before the association convention — the Farmer-Labor left wing would have liked to remove his name from the ticket and defeat him with another candidate.[36] Politically, however, this was impossible because the association now needed Shipstead more than he needed the association. Association leaders pleaded with Shipstead publicly and privately to attend the March 27-28 state convention. He said nothing, however; no one knew what he was thinking, whether he would bolt the party, run as an independent, or turn Republican.

The Farmer-Labor Convention

Observers found it difficult, even impossible, to chart the direction in which Minnesota Farmer-Laborism was moving at the 1928 state convention. Despite the 1925 communist exclusion clause, a few current or former communists served as convention delegates: C. R. Hedlund, Vincent R. Dunne, and state representative Emil S. Youngdahl. Spokesmen from the national Farmer-Labor party urged the association to send delegates to the July 4 national convention, but a motion for this was defeated (109 to 63) after Hedlund spoke in favor of it. Labor leader Robley D. Cramer warned against affiliating with "extreme radicals."[37] And socialist Henry Teigan supported a motion to endorse George Norris, the progressive Republican senator from Nebraska, for president, and it carried (146 to 78)! Norris was an exponent of McNary-Haugenism and government development of hydroelectric power at Muscle Shoals in the Tennessee Valley, ample reason why he was popular with agrarians and reformers, but, just the same, Farmer-Laborism had endorsed a Republican for president.

The association platform was moderate, and socialist proposals were absent. It supported such programs and policies as the St. Lawrence Seaway, workmen's compensation, the McNary-Haugen plan for an ever-normal national grainery storage system so prices would stabilize and not drop during periods of overproduction, regulation of electric utility rates, government-guaranteed bank deposits, lower tariffs. In foreign policy it expressed opposition to imperialist wars of aggression. The strongest ideological statement of appeal to the left was the vague general call for cooperatives to replace monopoly capitalism, but the industries were neither named nor defined.

Farmer-Labor moderates, led by representatives of agrarian interests, were still dominant, and this condition ensured A. C. Welch's reelection as association state chairman. Nevertheless, Minnesota Farmer-Laborism was troubled and uncertain about its future and about which candidates it should put before the public. Its three endorsees for governor, senator, and president all seemed on the verge of rejecting their Farmer-Labor candidacy. Floyd Olson had long since concluded that 1928 was a very poor year in which to seek high public office. Maverick George Norris remained a critical progressive, a kind of prototype New Deal Republican. And Shipstead was such a man of political mystery that he always remained a source of agony and suspicion for the Farmer-Labor left. Although Shipstead partly relented in his self-imposed silence about the election by sending a wire of greetings to the convention, he still stayed away, saying that legislative business forced him to remain in Washington. A minority report was filed by Hedlund and backed on the floor by Workers party member Vincent R. Dunne and left-leaning Joseph A. Poirier urging Farmer-Laborites to support for the Senate the little-known William Watkins in the place of Shipstead. A few leaders and members of the state central committee continued to think well of the idea of a national Farmer-Labor ticket in 1928, but the rank-and-file members and Farmer-Labor candidates ignored it, content to try if they could to keep the party alive in Minnesota for another two years.[38]

The New Democratic Threat

Farm discontent had the potential of being an important contributor to the revival of the Minnesota Democratic party, particularly if it could heal the most serious factional disorders which plagued it. Unfortunately for the party, prospects for this were indeed poor. Two factions continued to fight one another more than they waged battle with Republicans and Farmer-Laborites. One group of insurgents (Thomas E. Cashman, J. F. D. Meighen, A. A. Van Dyke, and Edward Indrehus) favored the McNary-Haugen Bill; the "regulars" (led by Z. H. Austin, Joseph Wolf, and W. J. Quinn) did not. When party chairman C. A. Quist died, each faction claimed one of its members should be state chairman, Cashman for the insurgents, Austin for the regulars. For a time the threat was real that there would be two state Democratic conventions, though differences of that magnitude were settled practically if not amiably; by the time the national convention nominated Catholic New York governor Alfred W. Smith for the presidency, non-Catholic state Democratic leaders grudgingly accepted him.[39]

Meeting a week earlier than the Farmer-Laborites, the Democrats displayed much the same interest in issues popular within the association, like the McNary-Haugen Bill, the St. Lawrence Seaway proposal, and opposition to high Republican tariffs. They denounced the national administration for the Teapot Dome scandal, its "unauthorized" war in Nicaragua, and the Coolidge-Kellogg foreign policy of putting Americans into combat areas. As a result of the party caucuses, which were usually captured by supporters of Al Smith, party control continued to rest with the "regulars."

Yet despite the internal differences, this year Democrats made a serious effort to put together a capable slate of candidates who would attract popular support in Minnesota. The state convention delegated the endorsement process to a twenty-member committee headed by Andrew Nelson of Duluth. For the first time in over a decade the behavior of state Democrats was perceived by Farmer-Labor Association leaders as a threat to the third-party movement. This happened because the Democratic candidate search committee was instructed to make a selection that would help rebuild the party[40] and because Farmer-Laborites, especially the left wing, feared that Democrats would seek "agreements" or "campaign fusion" with willing Farmer-Labor candidates and in this way begin a process that would lead eventually to merger or absorption into the Democratic party.

That was no idle threat. In the weeks following the Democratic state convention both Olson and Shipstead displayed the type of behavior that increased association anxiety. First, neither Olson nor Shipstead indicated acceptance of their Farmer-Labor endorsements for governor and senator; thus rumors circulated about their possible plans to run as independents. Olson repeatedly asked the association for an extension of time to consider whether he would be a candidate, and he apparently was in contact with the Democratic search committee to see whether it would publicly endorse him or give private assurances not to offer opposition if he chose to run.[41] Through mid-April Olson and Shipstead refused comment about possible negotiations with the Democrats.

For their part, Democrats were unusually cautious and deliberate, and were about to begin the painfully long quest of absorbing Farmer-Laborism into their own party. But they had not forgotten the "round robin" movement two years before, particularly Quigley's plan for Farmer-Laborites to assume command of their party. Consequently, negotiations with Farmer-Laborites broke down, and in late April the Democratic ticket was announced. Nelson, the chairman of the search committee, was to run for governor and Edward Indrehus for senator — Indrehus later withdrew from the race. After these announcements, and following four weeks' haggling, Olson finally declared himself out of the 1928 campaign.[42] Shipstead belatedly followed with an announcement in late April of his intention to file as a Farmer-Labor candidate. He apparently had been more successful than Olson in dealing with Democrats, since Indrehus had long been friendly toward him and in 1924 had withdrawn as the Democrats' candidate in the Sixth Congressional District when the senator's brother, Dr. S. C. Shipstead, won the Farmer-Labor nomination.

The Primary Election Campaign

The association was in a quandary. Olson's default brought opportunistic Ernest Lundeen into the primary contest. Lundeen, who had switched to Farmer-Laborism in 1926, was equally distrusted by both the left and the right; few considered him a strong candidate; and the left refused to consider him one of their own even though he rather consistently supported collectivist policies and had announced unqualified opposition to fusion with Democrats. With no candidate for governor other than Lundeen, the association and organized labor made one more unsuccessful appeal to Olson. Again he rejected the offer, though he finally assured them that had he chosen to run it would have been as a Farmer-Laborite.[43] The association state committee refused to accept Lundeen as its candidate and instead drafted Dr. L. A. Fritsche, a party moderate from New Ulm; it asked Lundeen to withdraw, but he refused.

During the primary campaign Shipstead was denounced by William Watkins, his Communist-endorsed Farmer-Labor challenger, for being a disloyal follower of the association program.[44] Not only did the

Farmer-Labor senator ignore Watkins, but he also avoided mention of any connection to the association. When Indrehus refused the Democratic nomination and was replaced by George F. Cashman of St. Cloud,[45] it did not affect the Democratic noncampaign that would be waged against Shipstead.

The primary campaign had little or no effect on factional relationships within the three parties. Farmer-Laborites had only two contests (senator and governor), Republicans four (senator, governor, attorney general, and railroad and warehouse commissioner), Democrats none; there were but a few important races for Congress. Both Shipstead and Christianson won easy renomination, the competition between Fritsche and Lundeen was amiable, and the Republican Senate nomination went to Arthur E. Nelson over former governor J. A. A. Burnquist and state senator A. J. Rockne. The major Farmer-Labor defection came when first-district Farmer-Laborite Victor Christgau filed as a Republican, taking the nomination away from the incumbent Republican congressman.

The prosperity of 1928 had a moderating effect upon politics. Even the Farmer-Labor left sensed the mood and chastised the communists for interfering in the party. When Vincent R. Dunne in the fifth district and C. R. Hedlund in the tenth filed as Farmer-Laborite candidates for Congress, William Mahoney and the *Minnesota Union Advocate* condemned "communist meddling."[46] Mahoney also warned the state's socialists, advising them they had two choices: to join the revolutionaries in the Communist party or to support the "progressives" in the Farmer-Labor party.[47]

The early signs did not look at all promising for Farmer-Laborism. Only thirty delegates were reported to have traveled to Chicago for the so-called national Farmer-Labor convention, and Mahoney lost no time in ridiculing the folly of Ernest Lundeen, Emil S. Youngdahl, Joseph Poirier, and those Minnesotans supporting the national-party idea.[48] More disturbing were the results of the June 16 primary, not just Lundeen's 824-vote victory over Fritsche, but the sharp drop in Farmer-Labor turnout. Republicans outdrew Farmer-Laborites almost three to one (280,000 to 98,000).[49] Worse, Farmer-Laborism had a senatorial nominee who refused even to use the name Farmer-Labor in his campaign; a suspected communist, C. R. Hedlund, as a congressional candidate whom it could not support; and in the general election a communist running against incumbent W. L. Carss in the eighth district, where the loss of miners' votes could cost him reelection.

The General Election Campaign

With each passing month, Minnesota Farmer-Laborism became weaker, its strength fading as the movement approached a time of crisis. While farm discontent had stabilized, the two minority parties and especially their candidates were coming nearer each other on many public issues. Fusion grew more likely despite stubborn resistance by the Farmer-Labor prohibitionists and socialists. Democrats were in the midst of revival, at the expense of Farmer-Laborites.

Shipstead's Independence. The major irony of 1928 was that Shipstead controlled much of Farmer-Laborism's fate, a situation which Farmer-Labor partisans found unbearable and from which they would have escaped had it been possible. More than any other major candidate before or after him, Shipstead turned independence and nonpartisanism into a nearly impregnable bastion. Repeatedly he ignored his party and the association, going outside it with nonradical appeals to the dissatisfied regardless of their party affiliation. Such a strategy was made possible by the help he received from Senate Democratic and Republican progressives and by his determination not to be limited to the Farmer-Labor label even though he filed under it.

Shipstead's campaign organization completely separated itself from the Farmer-Labor apparatus. His speeches before business groups like the Minneapolis Club or a local farmers' cooperative carried the same message: party labels did not necessarily serve the best interests of the state. Understanding the reasons behind political protest, he nevertheless carefully put aside all radical appeals. In this he was aided by even the Minnesota State Federation of Labor, which at its twenty-fifth annual convention denied a seat to Shipstead's former primary opponent, William Watson, at the urging of Mahoney, Frank Starkey, and Geroge W. Lawson, because Watson was suspected of being a Communist.[50] Throughout the campaign Shipstead delivered a simple twofold message: he asked to be judged by his Senate record, not his party label; he declared farmers were needlessly suffering during a period of so-called Republican prosperity.[51]

The rudeness Shipstead inflicted upon the association hardly diminished the praise he received from its leaders and those of organized labor. Apostolic embraces came from Democrats. When Burton K. Wheeler, Montana's Democratic senator and La Follette's running mate in 1924, came to Minnesota to deliver speeches supporting Al

Smith, Wheeler made a point of praising Shipstead. The state Democratic faction headed by Thomas Cashman, after losing party control to state chairman W. J. Quinn and national committeeman Joseph Wolf, created its own independent Democratic campaign club which worked simultaneously for Smith and Shipstead.[52] Republicans brought Senator William Borah into Minnesota to rally support for Hoover, and Borah too refused to speak against Shipstead. In early October Nebraska's thoroughbred progressive, Senator George Norris, delivered several enthusiastic addresses for Shipstead in Rochester and other parts of southern Minnesota where Republican strength was traditionally greatest.

Political Independence and Democratic Comeback. In few Minnesota political campaigns were the battle lines as fluid as in 1928. By September, voters were being pushed in the direction of independence rather than drawn toward party loyalty; ticket splitting was not only necessary but made into a virtue. Voter independence was reinforced as an important cultural characteristic of Minnesota politics and would remain so for the next three decades.

Magnus Johnson was the first significant Farmer-Labor leader to call for Al Smith's election. Strangely, five days later Alfred Jacques, the Wilson administration's U.S. attorney in Minnesota and the 1926 Democratic candidate for governor, declared for Republican Herbert Hoover on the basis of Hoover's support for the St. Lawrence Seaway which Smith, as a New Yorker, opposed. Democrat John Lind, who sometimes campaigned for Farmer-Laborites, at one point announced he would not endorse a Tammany Hall Democratic candidate.

Shipstead received another tremendous Democratic boost in late September when the Democratic candidate, George Cashman, abruptly announced his withdrawal from the campaign in favor of Shipstead, who gave up nothing in return. Shipstead continued to be neutral on the presidency despite Republican efforts to draw him out in the hope of cutting away some of his tripartisan following.[53] Other Farmer-Laborites were not only willing but eager to take a presidential stand. In New Ulm Dr. L. A. Fritsche headed a Smith-Robinson club which reportedly sent out 50,000 letters on behalf of the New York governor,[54] and when Smith came to Minnesota on September 27 he was received more enthusiastically than any other Democratic candidate in the last dozen years.

The Appeal to "Save the Farmer-Labor Party." During the final campaign month Farmer-Laborism seemed on the brink of extinc-

tion. Shipstead was the one exception, but he had become almost a
three-party consensus candidate rather than a Farmer-Laborite. Fusion or Democratic absorption crept closer. In early October Henry
Arens, the Farmer-Labor congressional candidate in the third district,
came near to withdrawing but arrived just minutes too late at the
capitol to sign the necessary papers.[55] Democrats were asking and
getting Farmer-Labor assistance, though some, like Ernest Lundeen,
refused to consider withdrawal.

Farmer-Labor partisans opposed to merger with Democrats were
not alone in despairing about the trend of the campaign. Republicans
foresaw future political threat if cooperation between Democrats and
Farmer-Laborites continued, and they worried about Shipstead's
practice of nonalignment and the effect this might have in drawing
independent Republican protest votes to Smith, and about anything
which contributed to the rebuilding of the Minnesota Democratic
party. Yet Republicans were very uncertain about how to stop these
shifts, so once again the state administration of Theodore Christianson relied heavily upon the claim of Republican administrative efficiency and economy.[56]

What was a Republican concern, however, amounted to a Farmer-
Labor panic as the campaign went into the final stretch. Not only
did Farmer-Laborites worry because Shipstead refused to use the
party name, but they were upset by growing independence among
the constituent interests that supported the movement. For example,
the railroad brotherhoods endorsed only five — Arens, Carss, Kvale,
Wefald, and Howard Y. Williams — of the ten Farmer-Labor candidates for Congress.[57]

Sensing collapse, association leaders made an eleventh-hour appeal
to revive the Farmer-Labor name by convincing Floyd Olson, Thomas Sullivan, and Frank McAllister (a recent candidate for St. Paul
mayor) to tour the state delivering "save the Farmer-Labor party"
speeches. "Stick and Win" — the old Nonpartisan slogan — was revived by Olson to reestablish Farmer-Labor identity as he called
upon voters to support the entire Farmer-Labor ticket in speeches
throughout western Minnesota counties and in Duluth late in the
election drive.[58]

Republicans, taking note of these divisions, accused Shipstead
of being ashamed of the Farmer-Labor party and refusing to campaign for it. The senator responded over radio stations WCCO and
KSTP by charging Republicans with operating a huge slush fund
and falsifying his stand on the presidential election.[59] Confident of
his election, Shipstead admitted during the final week he was still

a Farmer-Laborite, his first personal reference to the party since early spring.

Olson's and Sullivan's efforts to stave off further defections by appealing for Farmer-Labor neutrality in presidential politics had little impact, nor did they appear to rally lagging support. Some old-time Nonpartisan Leaguers like Thomas Vollom and Martin Odland campaigned for Hoover. Another group released a "round robin" letter on October 21 in an open appeal to Minnesota political insurgents to vote for Alfred E. Smith. Signers included many well-known state and local Farmer-Labor leaders: Magnus Johnson, L. A. Fritsche, Tom Davis, Walter Quigley, Richard T. Buckler, Frank Day, Emil Holmes, R. A. Trovatten, Joseph B. Himsl, Steve Lush of the Brotherhood of Railway Trainmen, editor William McEwen of the *Duluth Labor World,* and Farmer-Labor members of the legislature.[60]

Election Results

Dynamic shifts in Minnesota political behavior were under way even while Republican majorities dominated every level and branch of government. For the first time over a million votes (1,070,274) were cast, an increase of almost 350,000, or 48 percent, from the 1926 election and nearly 600,000 more votes than were cast in the first Farmer-Labor election, in 1918. But new voters were not turning to Farmer-Laborism.

Office	*1928 Percentages*			*Change from 1924-26*		
	Repub.	*Dem.*	*FL*	*Repub.*	*Dem.*	*FL*
President	52%	37%		+ 4%	+32%	
Senator	32%		62%	–13%		+18%
Governor	51%	20%	21%	– 3%	+15%	–16%

Note: The total percentage for each office is less than 100 because some voters cast blank ballots and some ballots were spoiled. Changes in percentages for the offices of president and senator are calculated from 1924; for that of governor, from 1926.

In overall outcome, Republicans could claim a tremendous mandate. The party retained all state offices, kept control of the nonpartisan lower house (the senate was not up for election), and won nine of ten congressional elections. Nevertheless, there was weakness in this performance which few perceived at the time. The Republican gubernatorial vote declined 3 percent, its vote for senator was down

RESULTS OF THE 1928 MINNESOTA GENERAL ELECTION
(Candidate, No. of Votes, and Percentage of Total Vote)

OFFICE	REPUBLICAN	DEMOCRATIC	FARMER-LABOR	SOCIALIST	INDUSTRIAL	WORKER'S
President	Herbert Hoover 560,977 (52.4%)	Alfred E. Smith 396,451 (37.0%)		Norman Thomas 6,774 (.6%)	Verne L. Reynolds 1,921 (.2%)	William Z. Foster 4,853 (.5%)
Senator	Arthur E. Nelson 342,992 (32.0%)		Henrik Shipstead 665,169 (62.1%)			Vincent R. Dunne 9,380 (.9%)
Governor	Theodore Christianson 549,857 (51.4%)	Andrew Nelson 213,734 (20.0%)	Ernest Lundeen 227,193 (21.2%)		Harris A. Brandborg 3,279 (.3%)	J. O. Bentall 5,760 (.5%)
Lieutenant governor	W. I. Nolan 526,413 (49.2%)	Fred Pfaender 180,449 (16.9%)	Thomas J. Meighen 235,133 (22.0%)			
Attorney general	G. A. Youngquist 524,151 (49.0%)	George Cahill 205,861 (19.2%)	C. F. Gaarenstrom 192,472 (18.0%)			
Secretary of state	Mike Holm 625,712 (58.5%)	Ruth Haynes Carpenter 163,371 (15.3%)	Susie Stageberg 178,096 (16.6%)			
Treasurer	Julius Schmahl 541,981 (49.2%)	William A. Just 187,950 (17.6%)	Peter J. Seberger 205,228 (19.2%)			
Railroad and warehouse commissioner	C. J. Laurisch 463,791 (43.3%)	Viggo Justesen 171,954 (16.1%)	J. L. Peterson 259,823 (24.3%)			

Note: The total percentage for each office is less than 100 because some voters cast blank ballots and some ballots were spoiled.

Minnesota Farmer-Laborism, by Millard L. Gieske, © 1979 by the University of Minnesota.

13 percent (to 32 percent), and in eight statewide contests, including those for president and senator, only three Republicans (Hoover, Christianson, and Holm) in eight won with a majority.[61]

Farmer-Laborism suffered a serious decline in popular support. From the 1926 range of 225,000-250,000 votes, it fell in 1928 to 178,000-260,000. Aside from Shipstead (665,000 votes), the strongest Farmer-Labor candidate received 24 percent. The only successful congressional candidate was O. J. Kvale (67 percent), and Farmer-Labor eighth-district congressman W. L. Carss (43 percent) lost by 1,269 votes — a result which could have been reversed had he not faced either a Democratic candidate (9,800 votes) or a Communist (3,000 votes). In five districts both a Farmer-Laborite and a Democrat ran for Congress; in three the Democrat outpolled the Farmer-Laborite.

The popularity of the extraordinary Shipstead won him a 62-percent landslide, one of the greatest in any Minnesota Senate campaign. Although his election was a triumph for nonpartisan alignment, persistent rumors soon circulated about Shipstead's shifting to the Republican party.[62] Yet despite his indifference to the Farmer-Labor label, Shipstead continued to be more help to the party than either he or his critics realized because he had preserved and extended the use of the Farmer-Labor name, giving it a nonradical reputation which in two years would draw thousands of new protesters to it as the Great Depression of the 1930s began claiming new economic victims.

After a decade of stodgy quiesence, Farmer-Laborism faced a new rival, the Democrats, who, if they continued to grow at their 1928 pace, were certain to be a serious challenge to Farmer-Labor existence. Leading the Democratic comeback was presidential nominee Alfred E. Smith. Normally, a 37 percent (400,000) showing would have been anything but impressive, yet compared with John W. Davis's 6.4 percent (55,000 votes) in the 1924 election, it pointed toward a reversal of a twelve-year decline. Democratic and Farmer-Labor candidates each shared about approximately 20 percent of the total vote. If the trend to the Democrats and away from the Farmer-Laborites continued into 1930, the third-party movement was certain to collapse. Already the shifts which took place would bear importantly upon the kind of Farmer-Labor campaign Minnesota would experience in 1930.

CHAPTER 6

Economic Tragedy and Farmer-Labor Revival

The dismal political ending to the 1928 campaign undermined the faith of all but the most dedicated Farmer-Laborites. Few remained who still firmly believed it likely that collectivist programs would soon displace capitalistic concentrations of wealth or that the exploited and dispossessed would shed economic and political shackles to turn upon longtime tormentors. For most of 1929 few dared to believe Farmer-Laborism's revival could be near. The nation was prosperous and exhibited economic confidence, greeting its new president, Herbert Hoover, a man more forceful and flexible than his two immediate predecessors, with a climbing stock market and rising popular expectations of better times coming. As the economy expanded, credit was plentiful, a building boom was under way, markets were bullish, and millions of Americans and thousands of Minnesotans took up speculation in search of quick rich dividends. Employment was high, corporate profits were up, and prices remained stable. Critics pointed to an apparent weakness, that workers' wages had increased only 12 percent between 1923 and 1928,[1] and they remained convinced that distribution benefits were inadequate for both blue-collar workers and farmers.

Somehow Farmer-Laborism lasted through the Republican years. Part of the credit for sustaining it belonged to the small band of founders who carried on. More important, its name was sustained by a handful of skillful officeholders, led by Congressman O. J. Kvale and Senator Henrik Shipstead, who gave the movement a "safe" nonradical reputation even though they were cursed by the movement's ideologues. The better-known Shipstead provided Farmer-Laborism with a model for moderate independent action and a style of campaigning which most future Farmer-Labor candidates would imitate in one way or another. And fortunately for the protest movement, as the new decade approached, Republicans were becoming less united than at any time in the past ten years.

Nevertheless, for most of 1929 there was little apparent reason for the disunited Farmer-Laborites to be optimistic about their future. In Minneapolis organized labor was badly divided, and the Hennepin County Farmer-Labor Association split hopelessly into two cantankerous factions. The labor groups each backed rival mayoral candidates, neither of whom survived the city primary election, and Republicans furnished the finalists, incumbent George Leach (mayor for eight years) and his challenger. Farmer-Laborism was at political perigee. Only two labor-endorsed aldermanic candidates survived the primary. Even the normally optimistic Henry Teigan was pessimistic about the immediate future.[2]

Liberal legislative success was as rare. Governor Theodore Christianson, an honorable and honest man, made little effort to face current problems in the midst of general prosperity — he apparently believed that boom times would automatically bring benefit to all — nor did he (or could he) anticipate the future. Instead, Christianson was immersed in planning his 1930 challenge to unseat blind Republican senator Thomas Schall, building his popular case around the theme of his six-year administration, "efficiency and economy in government." The conservative-dominated 1929 legislature was noted more for what it rejected — reforestation, small loan regulation, university expansion, tax reform — than for what it approved. These modest remedial measures were not radical changes recklessly scattered about by socialist wildmen, but conservative Republicans and the interests they often represented defeated them anyway. The few new innovative programs that emerged came out of the state senate, usually to be vetoed by Christianson in order, he routinely said, to "save the taxpayers' money." Ever since 1925 Christianson had clashed with the senate leadership.

State Republicanism's "do-little" image was, in the environment of 1928-29, of little consequence, perhaps even an advantage. That Farmer-Laborites would be critical of it came to be expected. Now, however, the normally patronizing "Republican press" began to express misgivings over the course of state public policy. Both the *Minneapolis Star* and *Tribune* complained about inadequate legislative funding for schools, state institutions, and the university, and veteran *Minneapolis Journal* political reporter Charles C. Cheney's résumé of the 46th session was a flat declaration which claimed the session had left little or no record of accomplishment.[3] The major story involved an investigation of the Cochran "Gold Note" swindle in which hundreds of small investors had lost thousands of dollars, in some cases life savings, in a furtive scheme designed to refloat the floundering *Volkszeitung* (German) newspaper company.

For protest, only one event in 1929 offered much consolation. In the west central prairie region of the seventh district former clergyman O. J. Kvale had kept Farmer-Labor fortunes alive, but he died unexpectedly, forcing a call for a special congressional election. Republicans chose Morris newspaper publisher J. C. Morrison, who faced Paul Kvale, son of the congressman.[4] A not very exciting campaign followed and only 35,000 people took time to vote. The younger Kvale, however, won 73 percent of the vote and the district stayed in moderate Farmer-Labor hands.

THE CAREFUL BUILDUP OF FLOYD B. OLSON

Nevertheless, Farmer-Laborism's fate lay in the more talented hands of Floyd B. Olson, the Hennepin County Attorney. Through much of 1928 Olson kept politically silent, coming to his party's aid only late in the disastrous campaign. But in 1929 Olson began a deliberate effort to erect a positive public image, encouraged by the Shipstead campaign and style, prospects of Republican divisiveness, and the knowledge he would not face an incumbent governor. In May Olson launched a "law and order" campaign by calling into session a special Hennepin County grand jury to investigate graft and crime in Minneapolis during the period when the city was administered by Republican mayor Colonel George Leach. Although the jury's report was not directed against Leach, Olson well understood that it could be a valuable campaign tool; he profited politically from the investigation and the report when several jurors insisted upon commending him for crime detection and law enforcement in spite of the fact that other jurors resisted such a citation as unnecessary.[5]

By summer Olson was firmly committed to running in 1930, and in September he told a Farmer-Labor conference, "If the party sees fit to draft me, I will be a candidate."[6] That is how it would be. Steps were taken to eliminate any serious challenge to Olson, and few disputed that he was the best available Farmer-Labor candidate (no new talent had been uncovered in the movement during its hard times).

While Farmer-Labor ranks were closing, Republican gaps widened. Irascible Tom Schall opened another breach in December by recklessly accusing several hundred small Minnesota newspapers of selling out to eastern financial interests, a wild outburst which brought quick rebuke from the papers and the Minnesota Editorial Association.[7]

THE BIRTH OF A NATIONAL THIRD-PARTY MOVEMENT

Nationally, as in Minnesota, third-partyism staggered under 1928 Republican normalcy. Intellectual and ideological critics of two-partyism were little impressed by the Al Smith campaign and the apparent reversal of Democratic party fortunes after a decade of decline. Instead, they looked toward new political alternatives in much the same way as had the founders of Minnesota Farmer-Laborism: something that offered socialist and collectivist organization, national "planning" for production and distribution, ultimate replacement of capitalism and the profit motive, (usually) non-Marxian social criticism, and political reorganization to produce a "new majority" which was neither Republican nor Democratic.

At its conception this new national movement borrowed rather heavily from the Minnesota experiment, and it suffered on an even larger scale the same problem of putting a variety of insurgent factions into a common third party. Intellectually, the political engineers of the movement were talented and capable. Most were from one socialist strain or another, active in academic, intellectual, or social criticism, and aligned with groups like the League for Industrial Democracy. And like the Minnesotans, a majority — but not all — had reluctantly concluded that neither the Socialist party nor any other then existing radical party could sufficiently break through the grip the two major parties had upon the masses of American voters. Therefore, in late 1928 the planners made a decision to assemble economists, statisticians, and "other qualified people" to erect an American-type Fabian Society as a forerunner of a yet unnamed mass labor party. Those called to the task included members of the Socialist party and sympathetic trade unions like the International Lady Garment Workers, Greenbackers and monetary inflationists, Single Taxers, and others from the reform movement.[8]

On October 31, just days before the Hoover victory, economist Paul H. Douglas, Socialist Norman Thomas, and Sherwood Eddy signed a call for a December 15 conference in New York's International House. The delegates were expected to perfect an "American

Fabian Society, under some appropriate name" preparatory to building a new American opposition party.[9] The intellectual celebrants
answering the summons were impressive: John Dewey, Frederick V.
Field, Nathan Fine, J. B. S. Hardman, Arthur Garfield Hays, Harry
W. Laidler, Robert Morse Lovett, Kirby Page, H. S. Raushenbush,
L. H. Sage, John Nevin Sayre, Constance L. Todd, Harry F. Ward,
Colston E. Warner, and Oswald Garrison Villard. Lofty discussion led
the conference to an ominous conclusion: little hope and no relief
could be found in the liberal faith of salvation through the social
problem-solving capacity of the Democratic party because this party
could not survive, let alone win electoral victories. Consequently,
progressives were asked to leave both major parties and "help build
up another party which would become for this country what the
British Labor Party is for England." This was to accompany an ambitious social program of "rapid expansion of public ownership" in
the electric utility industry; "public ownership and democratic management of the coal industry"; "high progressive taxes" on incomes,
inheritances, and land values; health, industrial, and old-age protection; farm relief; and elimination of "the economic and political
causes of war."[10]

To help launch the movement, University of Chicago economist
Paul H. Douglas was elected provisional chairman of the executive
committee. Choosing the proper name for the movement proved
troublesome. At first the intellectuals decided to call it The Third
Party League, but wisely changed it to the more acceptable *League
for Independent Political Action* (LIPA). To carry its social message,
the league expected to work with the People's Lobby, trade and industrial unions, the Federal Council of Churches, Farmer-Labor parties, and to communicate through Kirby Page's futurist *The World
Tomorrow,* Villard's *The Nation,* and with Bruce Bliven in *The New
Republic.* Armed with good intentions, a mimeograph, and letter-
head stationery, LIPA recruited black intellectual W. E. B. Dubois,
civil libertarians Alexander Meiklejohn and Paul Blanshard, and
Minnesota Farmer-Labor unionists William Mahoney and Henry
Teigan.

LIPA reached even deeper into Minnesota in its search for a permanent director. In June 1929 it extended a call to St. Paul's Rever-
end Howard Y. Williams, the pastor of The People's Church and an
active disciple of Minnesota Farmer-Laborism.[11] A firm believer in
the social gospel, Williams was a graduate of the University of Minnesota and the Union Theological Seminary, had run for St. Paul mayor
in 1926, had finished a poor third in the fourth-district congressional

campaign in 1928, and was an accomplished speaker who during the summer of 1928 had traveled the Chautauqua circuit in Kansas.

Williams welcomed his new career as LIPA executive director, but political proselytizing proved not always easy. For LIPA to become a new majority, it had to broaden its appeal beyond the Socialist party. Opinion differed on how this could be done. John Dewey saw some virtue in the old Nonpartisan League "balance of power" strategy,[12] and Williams was able to enlist some former NPL organizers as members.[13] But there was resentment too as a skeptical Norman Thomas warned LIPA to stay away from active socialists if the objective was to undermine and displace his party with a yet unnamed new one.[14] Sometimes organized labor proved to be hostile. The president of the Chicago Federation of Labor, which had been victimized by communists during its 1923 association with the national Farmer-Labor party, firmly declined an invitation to join LIPA.[15] Harold Ickes bluntly described the third-party movement as a "hopeless venture" destined to fail.[16] Felix Frankfurter declined "any kind of political association in these fluid days," and in her polite refusal Jane Addams added insult by confessing she had voted for Hoover.[17]

Even among its early members arcane and otherwise pedestrian jealousies surfaced. Union Theological Seminary's religious philosopher H. P. Van Dusen found fault with Paul Douglas's public statement on LIPA goals, calling them "extraordinarily dull and uninspired."[18]

However, Minnesota's left-wing Farmer-Laborites generally welcomed the new national movement. Since 1920 William Mahoney had been a fervent exponent of the necessity for "our independent Farmer-Labor movement to expand into a national force before it can accomplish its fundamental aims,"[19] and Henry Teigan, though he had formally abandoned the Socialist party fifteen years before, saw renewed promise in the willingness of some national socialists "to cooperate in the building of an independent political party."[20] Not only would the LIPA movement further complicate Minnesota Farmer-Laborism, but it would serve as an additional source of internal division. Officeholding Farmer-Laborites generally preferred Shipsteadian nonalignment, disputing the collectivists' contention that attachment to a national political realignment was an appropriate base upon which to build majority support in Minnesota.

FARMER-LABORISM, 1930

The sparks that had ignited Minnesota Farmer-Laborism in the previous decade had come not just from workers' and farmers' economic discontent but from wartime protest against American intervention in Europe. Indeed, 1918 and even 1920 had been relatively good income years for Minnesota's workers and farmers. The year 1930, by contrast, signaled the beginning of real economic deprivation and growing political reaction to worsening times. For nearly ten years the movement had awaited this grand opportunity, so essential to rebuilding its cause.

At issue now was deciding which group should be entrusted with the movement. Should it be the leftists, like Mahoney and Teigan, who had formerly severed membership in the Socialist party, but who otherwise retained limited socialist goals which they espoused through Farmer-Laborism and a strong attachment to the expansion of organized labor? Or should it be those Farmer-Laborites who were party dualists, that is, who retained formal membership in the Socialist party even when they belonged to the Farmer-Labor Association? For example, Albert G. Bastis and Lynn Thompson had served as 1928 presidential electors of the Socialist party, and Farmer-Laborites Sigmond M. Slonim of Duluth and I. C. (Dutch) Strout of Brainerd were state committee members of the Socialist party.[21] Or was control best entrusted to moderates and the right-wing, to men like Shipstead for whom ideological determinism and collectivism had little and sometimes no appeal?

From a practical and purely empirical standpoint, Farmer-Labor candidates and officeholders seemed more like Shipstead in their activities; they were exponents of reform and incremental changes in politics and social policy, rather than radicals demanding fundamental reorganization in the instruments of production. Shipstead in fact had done much to set the basic tone for Farmer-Laborism's 1930 campaign. Popular and apparently aloof to the crass appeals of party, class, and special interest, Shipstead had largely made it possible for 1930 Farmer-Laborism to turn its more radical face to the wall. As a result, it was difficult for Republicans to rail against radicalism and collective ownership under the Farmer-Labor banner. Also helping the movement was the tremendous attention given Shipstead during the first six months of 1930 as he drew attention and coverage on many current public issues, not a single one of which was tied to socialist proposals. Intended or not (probably the latter), Shipstead proved to be crucially important in Farmer-Laborism's resurgence.

Further boosting Farmer-Laborism was the bitter struggle for the Republican Senate nomination being waged by Theodore Christianson and Thomas Schall. By far the favorite of organization Republicans, the three-term governor enjoyed newspaper support throughout the state. Schall, on the other hand, was never liked, let alone trusted, by active politicans but still campaigned stubbornly. The primary contest thus turned into one of the great Republican brawls. Neither candidate gained much from it, Schall because it reinforced his already poor reputation and made him appear unpopular with his party, Christianson because he seemed ambitious for attempting to dump a member of his party. When the primary campaign had ended, former Republican governor (1901-5) Samuel R. Van Sant (who had supported Christianson) summed it up by describing the donnybrook as the "worst mudslinging fight" he had witnessed in following Minnesota politics for nearly three-quarters of a century.[22]

Other good signs developed. In early January the Farmer-Labor state central committee revived its newspaper, the *Farmer-Labor Leader* (formerly the *Advocate*), which had last been published three years before. In the very first issue it called upon the state convention to draft Floyd Olson;[23] growing unemployment it did not blame on the emerging depression but on the capitalistic practice of replacing human labor with machines. At the March 28-29 convention of the Farmer-Labor Association, moderates were strongly in command, the left wing was at times self-disciplined and otherwise quiescent, and the association exhibited a becalmed air of mature responsibility with almost no hint of reckless radicalism on the loose.

The convention was well managed and Olson served as its master director. His only concern was whether to run for U.S. senator or governor. Shipstead's success and Republican mayhem tempted Olson, but finally and at the last possible moment he announced his intention to seek the governorship. The left wing and the Farmer-Labor ideologues were forced to accept Olson on his terms, not theirs. He issued a stern warning that he would run an independent campaign as he saw fit; doubtless he had Shipstead's successful strategy in mind. Welcoming the delegates, Olson also warned the association against falling prey to spoils and patronage, pledging his administration to the merit system of appointment rather than basing it upon service given to the Farmer-Labor party.

Olson, in short, intended to be a moderate candidate, not a radical, and he was not about to introduce new schemes into traditional Minnesota government. He asked for and got a "practical, sound and progressive" platform restoring "American ideals." There was to be no storming of the political barricades; his letter of greeting to delegates made this clear for it was cautious, even conservative, in tone. "As I regard the political situation in Minnesota," Olson wrote, "it is not up to the Farmer-Labor party to introduce new and unique ideas in government. In my vision of its purpose, it is up to this party to restore the fundamentals of good government and suit them to the present needs."[24]

Olson's platform sounded much like a rather mild new deal for old problems, and Democrats and Republicans were made to feel comfortable with it. Planks included support for the St. Lawrence Seaway, improved inland waterways, better state administration of rural credits, adoption of a standardized state budget, improved protection of investors by the state securities commission, support and encouragement of small businesses and small banks, endorsement of the McNary-Haugen farm program, tax reduction, pay-as-you-go tax withholding, uniform primary elections, legislative party designation, repeal of the Brooks-Coleman Act, opposition to labor injunctions, and opposition to railroad mergers.[25] There were no planks calling for public ownership or confiscation of wealth, and platform drafters claimed to have created the broadest-appealing document in association history. Confessed the *Leader,* in partial agreement: "the average voter is conservative by nature and yields only under the severest economic pressure. That pressure has now arrived."[26]

Some radicals were deeply disappointed by the turn of events, but moderates were in control and held them at bay. W. W. Royster of Glenwood was elected convention chairman over two radicals, Albert Bastis and Emil Youngdahl. A few delegates openly expressed sentiment for merger with the Democratic party, and Magnus Johnson proposed an even trade of offices with Democrats. On the floor impatient and disillusioned radicals protested the platform and the exclusion of left-wing planks; most delegates were unmoved by the charges and when Walter Frank moved for convention approval of American recognition of the Soviet government his resolution was defeated. Frank then sought to substitute a plank calling for government ownership of industry, but conservatives soon learned of it, put a motion to adjourn, and Royster gaveled the meeting to an abrupt ending, leaving radicals bitter and angry.

Association endorsees likewise were carefully drawn from among the moderates. Olson's running mate for lieutenant governor was Henry Arens, a first vice-president for Land O'Lakes Cooperative Creamery. For U.S. senator, former ninth-district congressman Knud Wefald won easy endorsement over Ernest Lundeen by a margin of four to one, though Lundeen filed in the primary. Ties with the Democratic party were renewed by the endorsement of St. Cloud

judge Joseph B. Himsl for attorney general. Farmer-Laborites continued the party tradition of endorsing a woman, this year Anna Deter-
man, for secretary of state, and Elmer G. Johnson of Hibbing was the
candidate for railroad and warehouse commissioner. The position
remaining for the left wing was state auditor; after William Mahoney
withdrew, he was replaced by Henry Teigan who, though a socialist,
exercised restraint in what he did or said in public.

Farmer-Laborism's sometime radical image of the past was gone
now. The remarkable transition drew attention and favorable mention from even its staunchest opponents, like the normally hostile
editors of the *St. Paul Pioneer Press*, who commended the ascen-
dency of the movement's moderate interests and the excision of public ownership theories from its political lexicon. Its former critics
admitted: the old Farmer-Labor reputation of radicalism was largely
"undeserved," many current Farmer-Laborites accepted Olson's goal
of merger with Democrats, and the few remaining radicals were largely harmless carry-overs from pockets of metropolitan protest. The
majority, the *Pioneer Press* concluded, were conservative farmers
and workers, a kind of modern extension of Thomas Jefferson's
nineteenth-century yeomanry who sought above all else to make
farming into a "profitable" venture.[27]

Olson and the cadre of strategists around him made no effort to
undo this favorable image of restraint, moderation, and mild reform.
Simultaneously in Washington, Henrik Shipstead's performance was
consistent with Olson's and the Farmer-Labor platform, bespeaking
not so much a new but what had come to be the dominant element
in Farmer-Laborism. Week after week, headlines about Shipstead reinforced the impression that he was a fighter for liberal reform in the
progressive tradition. Shipstead championed environmental conservation, fought against damming of the Rainy River and commerical
timber exploitation of the wilderness, pushed for a nine-foot Mississippi River channel, introduced an antilabor injunction bill, opposed
the open shop, sponsored with Congressman Melvin J. Maas a bill for
a new St. Paul post office building, spoke out against European
foreign policy entanglements and a Great Powers naval treaty. The
Farmer-Labor senator, growing in prominence, gained praise from
many different quarters, from Thomas Schall to the *Minneapolis
Labor Review.*[28]

These changing political fortunes significantly boosted Farmer-
Labor chances for success, and with the burgeoning of the Great Depression the party suddenly was catapulted into being a near-equal

competitor with the Republicans — provided it could hold off the Democrats. Those farmers for whom Farmer-Laborism had spoken in the 1920s were joined now by many others suddenly injured by the rapidly falling farm commodity prices and rising capital costs associated with modern farm mechanization. The ranks of workers espousing Farmer-Laborism swelled as those made unemployable by the depression joined the movement.

In 1930 the full force of the economic turndown was not yet deeply felt, but speculators, both plutocratic and common, were severely injured whether they had gambled with stocks, bonds, land, fur farms, or industrial real estate. The 1929 stock market had begun to decline October 21, plummeting on the 29th. The trading value of stocks fell 40 percent in a month; in several months the *New York Times* stock index dropped from 452 to 224. National unemployment was 3 million in 1930, escalating to between 12 and 15 million by 1933. Factory payrolls, $55 billion in 1929, fell in 1931 to $33 billion.[29]

At first few people recognized the seriousness of what was happening or anticipated how bad things would get. But by spring 1930 the Farmer-Labor campaign began to adjust to conditions, and Olson picked up the depression issue soon after the association convention. At a well-attended rally in the Minneapolis auditorium in late April, the always politically fluent Olson started making capital by sounding ominous: the unemployment picture had to be improved and the productive gains of monopoly and industry had to be more broadly shared, or, he warned, the government would be forced to take drastic measures.[30] Olson wisely avoided saying what these would be; he offered no radical solutions though he made vague reference to possible restrictions on large individual property holdings. Above all else he was a skillful campaigner who had few peers in speaking before groups large and small, rich and poor.

Politically more important, however, was the psychological advantage that he and other Farmer-Laborites had gained and would maintain provided they stayed clear of radical rhetoric and the nostrums of socialism. Republicans had come to symbolize an attitude of keeping government out of the economy and allowing business a free hand to capitalize prosperity. Once Minnesota Farmer-Laborism had discarded its most offensive socialist slogans, it symbolized the need for increased governmental intervention and regulation. And the pendulum was rapidly swinging toward the side of the interventionists.

THE DEMOCRATS, 1930

One possible major challenge to Farmer-Labor realignment had to be met. Minnesota Democrats were also potential benefactors of an economy gone sour. Already in 1928 the party had begun its long upward climb, and at Farmer-Labor expense. This posed a dilemma for both groups. A significant portion of the Democratic leadership recognized Farmer-Laborites as political competitors and sometimes campaign allies. Nearly every Democrat accepted the long-term solution: merger or fusion, that is, joining Farmer-Laborites or absorbing them outright. The question left open was not whether but when. Those in both parties who most resisted it were found at the ideological extremes. In between stood the accommodationists who for years had engineered campaign agreements, withdrawals, and occasional joint candidacies in partial fulfillment of future amalgamation. At the state Democratic convention in late April the accommodationists had a slight upper hand even though there was much talk about a coming Democratic renaissance. One fact stood out: just as Democrats could not yet win unless they gained a significant measure of Farmer-Labor voter and organizational support, so Farmer-Laborites needed Democratic assistance to gain state victory. Divided, both would surely fall.

Democratic optimism unfurled where Farmer-Labor strength and Republican weakness were at their greatest. This happened to be in the race for U.S. senator, where the hopeful Democratic candidate was Einar Hoidale of Minneapolis. Once Floyd Olson—who in 1920 had been a Minneapolis Democratic candidate for Congress—had decided upon the governorship, the way was cleared for, if not secret agreements, then common understandings and expectations between Olson (as distinct from the Farmer-Labor Association) and the Democrats. It was no accident that the Democrats chose Edward Indrehus of Foley as their candidate for governor. Indrehus had a rather weak political history: he had withdrawn in 1922 as a congressional candidate in the sixth district when Shipstead's brother ran as a Farmer-Laborite, and he had refused to run against the senator in 1928. This year Indrehus played the role of filling a ballot slot but otherwise not campaigning in a serious or vigorous manner. Olson helped manage this situation to near perfection and now was able to concentrate upon the Republicans.

Democrats, at least those in control, believed the pattern was being established for eventual fusion. This idea now received strong support from the Democratic national committee and at the annual Jefferson day dinner preceding the state convention the acting national chairman expressed interest in some sort of fusion.[31] The strategic question left unanswered was whether state Democrats had timidly underplayed their hand, failing to recognize the scope of state and national Democratic revival.

THE 1930 CAMPAIGN AND ELECTION

The Primary Campaign

This year the Farmer-Labor primary campaign, and for that matter the Democratic, differed significantly from the Republican. The only statewide Farmer-Labor contests were for governor and senator. Olson faced and ignored token opposition from Carl E. Taylor, whom Olson supporters derisively dismissed as a communist outsider.[32] The more interesting contest involved Ernest Lundeen's challenge to the endorsed Knud Wefald for the senate seat. Lundeen won by 12,000 votes (53 percent to 37 percent) but only 75,000 votes were cast. This contrasted with the nearly half million (477,816) Republican primary vote, which suggested that a strong popular shift away from Republicans and toward Democrats and Farmer-Laborites had not yet been completed.

Distressing as Wefald's defeat was to some in the association, Lundeen's victory may have presented Olson a new opportunity and advantage. Neither left- nor right-wing Farmer-Laborites trusted Lundeen, though on issues he appeared to have moved closer to the collectivists. In the fall, the left suspected Olson of doing nothing for Lundeen and of tacitly aiding Einar Hoidale in whatever way he could, short of disavowing Lundeen's nomination.

For Republicans, however, the primary sometimes turned brutal. Of the seven candidates who filed for governor, state auditor Ray P. Chase won the race (42 percent), followed by wartime governor J. A. A. Burnquist (24 percent). Seven candidates sought the lieutenant governorship, which was won with just 17 percent of the total vote. The primary also introduced Stafford King, who was to become a near forty-year incumbent as state auditor.

The main Republican event, however, featured Schall and Christianson, with the latter attempting to move from Minnesota governor to senator, always a difficult transition. The last to succeed had been Knute Nelson in 1895, long before the days of popular election; it was not repeated again until 1946 (though it likely would have succeeded in 1936), and several governors had been frustrated in attaining the goal, including Eberhart (1916), Lind (1916), Preus (1923), and Burnquist (1924, 1928).

Schall, a tough man of few principles and fewer scruples, treated Christianson not only rudely but as though he should be counted among the bitterest betrayers of the Republican party. By early April the blind junior senator was drawing blood freely from Christianson by charging the governor with responsibility for the Cochran Gold and and Ten Thousand Fur Farm scandals, and for failing to protect small investors from fraudulent loss of some $2 million. Christianson never escaped the trap. Two weeks before the primary vote Schall predicted federal indictments would soon implicate state administration leaders, and he blithely charged the Christianson administration with responsibility for the "biggest stench in the state's history."[33] A week later eighteen individuals were indicted, among them two relatively minor former state officials.

Such timing well suited Schall's campaign, which coincided in a general way with Floyd Olson's law-and-order drive early in the year; Olson had pursued, unsuccessfully, the same fur farm case in Hennepin County district court.[34] Schall may have gained a victory over Christianson in the primary, but the lingering effect was to help Olson and the Farmer-Laborites "restore the principles of good government" in the autumn.

Farmer-Labor Crossover. A more mysterious element in the Schall campaign was the participation of Farmer-Laborites and former Nonpartisans in its planning and execution. Never proved, it still raised suspicions that Floyd Olson was secretly involved in order to disrupt the state Republican organization. Schall in fact had support from a rather broad scattering of individuals and interests, including Harold Knutson, Senator William Borah, AFL president William Green, and the Brotherhood of Railway Trainmen.

However, Schall's primary campaign was largely planned by Walter Quigley, the originator of the 1926 round robin (merger) scheme, and Tom Davis of Minneapolis, who several times had sought office as a Farmer-Laborite—in 1924 he had lost the gubernatorial nomination to Olson. Davis and Olson were friendly acquaintances, and Schall appointed Davis campaign manager. The astute Davis made a strong appeal for a Farmer-Labor crossover in the primary, and to reinforce it German-American voters saw reprints of 1918 Christianson editorials from the *Dawson Sentinel*, which seemed anti-German and even anti-Norwegian.[35] A mass-circulation letter signed by Davis and other one-time NPL leaders and fusion advocates was distributed to former NPL members urging a crossover to Schall.[36]

The appeal worked to near perfection. Nearly a half million votes were cast in the Republican primary, which was 100,000 more votes than those received by the leading Republican in the fall. Schall himself came within 23,000 votes of his Novermber vote! An angered Christianson planned to file suit in an effort to block Schall's nomination, and he backed down only at the last minute following an appeal to him by Ray P. Chase, who argued that the suit would bring him sure defeat against Olson because of its shattering impact upon Republican organization.[37] To the delight of Democrats and Farmer-Laborites, however, the damage had already been done. Only three Republican-aligned papers had endorsed Schall, the Republican party remained badly split, and Olson, Hoidale, and other Farmer-Laborites and Democrats welcomed their best opportunity in a decade.

The Olson Campaign

Minnesota Republicanism of 1930 had not yet been eclipsed, nor would it be, but rapidly changing economic conditions had taken away its initiative and given it to the Olson campaign, around which Farmer-Labor effort primarily revolved.

A product of the north Minneapolis melting pot and possessing the innate ability to make an audience feel its cause was his, Olson spoke with forceful political fluency, interspersing his speeches with a storehouse of dialect jokes that poked fun but never seemed to be ethnically offensive, then making listeners laugh with others and at themselves. Olson witnessed, first hand, neighborhood poverty, and he grew up identifying with political, economic, and social underdogs. He stressed the common good; his image of Republicanism, which the growing depression reinforced, was of a party too often subservient to well-to-do special corporate interests. Although a law graduate and unlike the protest radicals, he had no well-developed and organized economic ideology or systematic public philosophy. Rather, he sensed economic injustice, deplored poverty and suffering, and pledged to act against it if elected.

The strength of his 1930 appeal, which was the greatest of his public career, was built solidly around a nonraidcal image, a skillful working arrangement with cooperating Democrats (which he never again was able to repeat so successfully), and his own adaptation of the Shipstead strategy of political independence. His appeal was never to a parochial Farmer-Laborism but was tripartisan, and the mechanism through which he campaigned was the "Olson All-Party Volunteer Committee." This ad hoc organization functioned independently of the Farmer-Labor Association, and the all-party theme caused the left-wing third-partyists to be distrustful of it because it undermined the basic third-party spirit of political and ideological realignment. Leftists and radicals were further dismayed by Olson's choice for chairperson of the All-Party Volunteers, Mrs. Jean (Frederick) Wittich, a woman of moderate political attitudes who had been a Republican and who had served as state vice-president of the League of Women Voters.

Farmer-Labor chances continued to improve each month as the depression deepened and grain prices slipped ever lower. The *Farmer-Labor Leader* depicted in stories and cartoons the agricultural disaster that seventy-five-cent wheat and seventy-cent corn were bringing to Minnesota's hard-pressed farmers. The war issue was once more dragged out of political archives not so much to help Olson, who was an isolationist, but to aid Lundeen. The *Leader* accused Schall of supporting the military draft and of having "voted with the war crowd" in 1917, and it bluntly denounced 1917 American intervention. "There never was a shadow of justification for America's declaration of war on either Germany or Austria. Our troops had no more business in the affair than a burglar has in another man's house," *Leader* editors declared without qualification.[38]

From outside Minnesota the League of Independent Political Action tried to help Minnesota Farmer-Laborism by backing its entire slate, but it ultimately rode Olson's coattails; elsewhere, as in New York and Milwaukee though with less success, LIPA endorsed socialist candidates like Norman Thomas running for Congress. Olson did ask for a personal endorsement from John Dewey,[39] probably more because of Dewey's academic as opposed to his political reputation and Olson's unfamiliarity with the disarming name "League of Independent Political Action" rather than out of an understanding of LIPA's third-party goal and ideology. Both Henrik Shipstead and Paul Kvale were more cautious and rejected an invitation to serve on the LIPA national committee,[40] and a leading member of the Minnesota cooperative movement, George W. Jacobson, criticized the league for being top-heavy with intellectuals and incapable of understanding the problems of farmers.[41]

Coming to Minnesota from New York was LIPA executive director Howard Y. Williams, who spent two weeks in October speaking, distributing posters, and sending out 100,000 LIPA leaflets in support of Olson. Such assistance came late and well after the pattern of the election had been set, yet it served to inflate Williams's and LIPA's own impression of their contribution to the Minnesota Farmer-Labor campaign.

As the campaign drew to a close, Olson felt confident about the outcome. Former Democratic governor John Lind had joined the Olson All-Party Volunteer Committee but died before he was able to deliver speeches.[42] Shipstead long remained noncommittal,[43] breaking his silence only after Olson's victory seemed reasonably certain. Shipstead's tardy endorsement of Olson was nevertheless promptly used by the All-Party committee in late campaign flyers.

Republicans found Olson a difficult target upon which to inflict serious injury. In late October Ray Chase resorted to "law and order," charging that Olson had failed to push vigorous criminal investgations and had allowed law breakers to escape prosecution.[44] For Republicans such an issue now carried limited appeal, probably contrasted unfavorably with Olson's own early attempts to publicize law enforcement, and was hardly a suitable replacement for the issue of the depression which so heavily weighed down Republicanism as it entered a new unsettled decade.

Sharing Victory with Republicans and Democrats

Farmer-Laborism's confidence in Floyd Olson as the candidate who would rescue the movement by bringing about its first gubernatorial victory in twelve years was well placed. Olson won 57 percent of the vote (473,000 votes), second only to Republican secretary of state Mike Holm (59 percent, or 488,000 votes). Olson's popularity appeared to help Henry Arens, Farmer-Labor candidate for lieutenant governor, whose 43 percent resulted in a narrow 16,667-vote (2-percent) victory. Aside from Paul J. Kvale's massive 81-percent landslide in the seventh district, the rest of the major offices remained Republican.

Republicans had not yet fallen victim to a sweeping Farmer-Labor realignment, the governorship being more a personal Olson victory than an unqualified Farmer-Labor triumph. Seven of nine state offices, nine of ten congressional seats, and a solid nonpartisan legislative majority remained in Republican hands. The voting public was keeping a cautious eye on what Olson would do in office, and Einar Hoidale (with 34 percent of the vote) kept the Democratic renaissance alive. Hoidale came within 11,000 votes of defeating Schall, ran over 100,000 votes ahead of Lundeen, and outpaced nearly every Farmer-Labor candidate other than Olson and Arens. There was no Democratic candidate running for clerk of supreme court, and the Farmer-Labor candidate for railroad and warehouse commissioner outpolled Hoidale by over 6,000 votes.

In the election of 1930 there was increased voter instability and the process of partisan realignment continued. Two Republicans, Schall (35 percent) and railroad and warehouse commissioner Frank

W. Mattson (39 percent), won reelection with less than 40 percent
of the vote, and no Republican besides Mike Holm won statewide
with as much as 47 percent. Farmer-Laborism had gained a limited
victory with a campaign, molded along lines set so successfully by
Henrik Shipstead, that deemphasized partisanship and collectivist
ideology. When voters faced a choice between a moderate Democrat
like Hoidale and the more left-leaning Lundeen, over 100,000 more
chose the Democrat.

To Olson the outcome suggested the necessity of programmatic caution, moderate policy, a better deal for workers and farmers, and less
empathy for business than was the case under Republican administration. However, to Farmer-Labor left-wingers and intellectuals, Olson's
victory signaled the beginning of far-reaching change.[45] For them the
third party's time was at hand. "I have been a socialist for more than
20 years," Henry Teigan confessed privately, and "I expect to continue to be that till I pass in my checks as it were."[46]

Most left-wingers agreed that Democrats were a major threat to
the exponents of the third-party American alternative. To Howard Y.
Williams, Democrats were nothing less than the "false face of Republicanism," and he admonished Minnesota LIPA members for
tolerating Farmer-Labor support, in whatever form, of the Hoidale
campaign. Schall was a demagogue, Williams admitted with Machia-
vellian charity, but he still was preferred over Hoidale. "A victory
for Hoidale," Williams told Olson's All-Party campaign manager
Jean Wittich, "would have meant the building up of the Democratic
party in Minnesota, and no permanent good would come of the result."[47] For the left wing and the socialists, "increased social planning and social control" (by which they often referred to public
ownership and redistribution of wealth) were not to be realized
under either Republican or Democratic administration. LIPA's "Four
Year Presidential Plan," the goal of which was the creation of a new
third-party presidential ticket in 1936 and even as early as 1932, was
threatened by Democratic victories and buildup.[48] Williams ignored
or failed to realize the reasons for Olson's victory and its heavy reliance upon Democratic assistance, goodwill, and "agreements" between the Farmer-Labor candidate for governor and the Democratic
candidate for United States senator.

THE SHIPSTEAD BRAND OF FARMER-LABORISM

Farmer-Laborism now could be judged at two levels: Shipstead (and
Kvale) were in Congress, and there was a newly evolving state admin-

RESULTS OF THE 1930 MINNESOTA GENERAL ELECTION
(Candidate, No. of Votes, and Percentage of Total Vote)

OFFICE	REPUBLICAN	DEMOCRATIC	FARMER-LABOR	INDEPENDENT	COMMUNIST
Senator	Thomas Schall 293,626 (35.4%)	Einar Hoidale 282,108 (34.0%)	Ernest Lundeen 178,671 (21.6%)	Charles Lund 20,669 (2.5%)	Rudolph Harju 5,645 (.7%)
Governor	Ray P. Chase 289,528 (35.0%)	Edward Indrehus 29,109 (3.5%)	Floyd B. Olson 473,154 (57.1%)		Karl Reeve 5,594 (.7%)
Lieutenant governor	John Hougen 341,718 (41.3%)	Andrew Roine 14,719 (1.8%)	Henry Arens 358,385 (43.3%)		
Attorney general	Henry N. Benson 358,995 (43.3%)	Walter F. Dacey 86,037 (10.4%)	Joseph B. Himsl 256,581 (31.0%)		
Secretary of state	Mike Holm 487,695 (58.9%)	Mary C. MacGregor 56,535 (6.8%)	Anna Olson Determan 209,596 (25.3%)		Henry Bartlett 12,326 (1.5%)
Treasurer	Julius Schmahl 375,946 (45.5%)	J. Pierce Wolfe 77,894 (9.4%)	Fred Miller 271,286 (32.7%)		
Auditor	Stafford King 385,406 (46.5%)	Benjamin Loeffler 78,183 (9.4%)	Henry Teigan 260,272 (31.4%)		
Railroad and warehouse commissioner	Frank W. Mattson 323,217 (39.0%)	August Bloomquist 84,593 (10.2%)	Elmer G. Johnson 288,553 (34.8%)		Nich Maki 8,753 (1.1%)
Clerk of the supreme court	Grace K. Davis 338,154 (40.8%)		Roy C. Smelker 337,157 (40.7%)		

Note: The total percentage for each office is less than 100 because some voters cast blank ballots and some ballots were spoiled.

Minnesota Farmer-Laborism, by Millard L. Gieske, © 1979 by the University of Minnesota.

istration. In addition, during 1931 between 65 to 70 Farmer-Labor legislators (roughly one-third) were in the 198-member state legislature. What path would they follow, collectivism or incremental progressive reforms?

The Senate was evenly divided, and, ironically, Shipstead represented the swing vote when party lines held (which they rarely did). Kvale held almost the identical position in the 435-member House. Speculation centered on the intentions of these two Farmer-Laborites, particularly Shipstead, who sat on the Republican side and who it had been rumored for years was likely to formally switch parties. This was less likely now. He told the *New York Times* the 1930 election was a rebuke to Republicans.[49]

Whatever Shipstead did or thought to the contrary, he still was formally listed as a Farmer-Laborite and many thought of him as the model of Farmer-Laborism in office. Since few others were prominent enough to compare with Shipstead, the yardstick he created was of personal independence, nonalignment, nonpartisan behavior, reform, foreign policy isolationism, and criticism of monopoly power. A few people even saw him as a potential 1932 presidential candidate. As always, he remained anathema to the Farmer-Labor left.

Barely a week after the 1930 elections, on November 16, Shipstead delivered over CBS radio a comprehensive nationwide address outlining a seven-point program to combat the deepening economic depression. His proposals updated progressive reforms and anticipated much in the coming "New Deal." (He had first used this expression in 1922.) Shipstead urged passage of the Robert F. Wagner Bill for unemployment relief, public works projects, conservation projects and controlled development of national resources, restriction against use of the labor injunction, inflation controls but lowered credit rates, credit reform, improved distribution of national income, and public works programs in navigation and communication to help relieve unemployment. He blamed depression not on overproduction but on underconsumption.

Shipstead's moderate reforms fell light-years short of the basic economic overhaul demanded by Farmer-Labor collectivists. Nonetheless, they drew wide coverage in the *Washington Star* and the *New York Times* as well as front page coverage and high praise from Minnesota's large daily papers.[50] At year's end the *Minneapolis Tribune* applauded them, describing the senator as the very embodiment of true Farmer-Laborism. *Tribune* editors assured readers that Shipstead was neither revolutionist nor radical but "conservative at heart, an old-fashioned constitutionist." Wisconsin senator Robert La Follette obliged him further by inserting the praise into the *Congressional Record*. And in mid-January Shipstead reviewed for the *Washington Herald* the soon-to-be-classic *A Treatise on Money*, by John Maynard Keynes, claiming it must reading for every American voter![51]

THE OLSON ALL-PARTY ADMINISTRATION

Shipstead's mild variant of Farmer-Laborism served as suitable introduction to Olson's first Farmer-Labor administration. For a dozen years Republicans and conservative interests had predicted dire consequences if the Farmer-Labor party gained power and control over the reins of government, warning about fretful assaults upon private property, the home, the family, womanhood, and traditional American morality. Now Minnesota was about to judge the real consequences of the Olson victory.

Patronage and the Farmer-Labor Association

Independently, the new governor began to select his administration, and soon it became evident a serious rift existed between him and the Farmer-Labor Association. Merit-based state civil service was still eight years and two administrations away. Theoretically, thousands of rank-and-file state employees faced dismissal and replacement by Farmer-Laborites.

Olson had anticipated patronage pressure and in March 1930, before accepting Farmer-Labor endorsement, he had extracted the promise of a free hand in civil service matters; in return, he had pledged nonpartisan appointment by merit. Once he was governor, however, association jobseekers beseiged him with demands for dismissals and replacements by certified Farmer-Laborites. As the depression grew more intense, so too did the pressure on Olson to hire association members exclusively. The association hierarchy turned into a screening committee which catalogued everything from the lowest and poorest jobs to the very top positions and had a candidate — often a needy one — for each.

Job placement soon became a major headache for Olson as he resisted the pressure, sought to avoid a too narrow-appearing administration, and attempted to build his administration with representation from all three parties and sometimes outside all of them. The Farmer-Labor left wing in particular wanted nothing to do with such a policy. Claims were advanced that only bona fide association members would remain loyal to the administration, and Olson was flooded with hundreds of appeals from throughout the state to place needy, Farmer-Labor club-endorsed candidates who, it was said, had rendered him crucial assistance in the campaign. The situation never improved, in fact it worsened, developing into an albatross for both Olson and the Farmer-Labor movement.

Olson did put together a coalition administration, and, ideologically speaking, it sustained beliefs which stretched from moderate right to socialist left. By and large, however, the men at the top were not political or economic ideologists, nor had most been long prominent in the Farmer-Labor Association, but they were indeed considerably different from those in previous Republican administrations.

Olson's key personal adviser ("personal secretary" in the lexicon of the day) was his longtime friend Vince Day, a Minneapolis lawyer who had hitherto led nearly a celibate political life away from active Farmer-Laborism. What service he had rendered was largely professional, but he was rational, liberal, and otherwise accepting of some forms of government ownership if emergency conditions required it. Day was a University of Nebraska law graduate, had first settled in Spokane and later in Bismarck, North Dakota, where he gave legal advice to the Nonpartisan League, drawing up legislation the most important of which he considered to be workingmen's compensation. In 1919 he moved to Minnesota where he continued to advise the league, and in 1922 he became a law partner of Benjamin Drake, the two serving as legal counsel to the ailing Equity Cooperative Exchange which was being phased out of existence as the Farmers Union movement evolved as a replacement.

Staffing the Key Administrative Agencies. During the 1930s the vital organs of state administration were the "Big Three" commissions: Administration and Finance; Budget; and Purchases. Control over state government — and beyond — largely rested with these three units and a handful of specialized function agencies like conservation, highways, and welfare. Whoever controlled them controlled government, patronage, and greatly influenced politics.

Olson took care to place in command of these agencies individuals who he was reasonably certain were administratively competent, loyal to him rather than the association, and not likely to recklessly abandon orthodoxy for radical change. For comptroller, the chief state budget and planning officer in the Commission of Administration, Olson chose Edward J. Pearlove, a nonpartisan, nonpolitically active lawyer who for over ten years prior to his appointment had served in the Federal Bureau of Internal Revenue, spending some time as a revenue agent. The post of commission secretary went to former one-term congressman Knud Wefald, who years before had switched from progressive Republican to Farmer-Laborite.

In October Olson appointed Carl R. Erickson commissioner of purchases. A Swedish emigrant who in his late teens had joined the Social Democrats in Canada, Erickson had served as an organizer for the Scandinavian Socialist Federation until he came to Minnesota where he first joined the Socialist party and then the Farmer-Labor party.[52] Still later, Olson appointed as budget commissioner Jean W. Wittich, a Phi Beta Kappa, ex-Republican, and former League of Women Voters officer who had headed his All-Party volunteers.

To the increasingly sensitive position of banking commissioner — a critical one as it turned out owing to the depression-spawned "run on banks" — Olson appointed John N. Peyton, a conservative small banker from Duluth who carried the endorsement of the (small) Independent Bankers Association and the Minnesota Bankers Association.

Olson's insistence that he select agency heads independent of the association brought him into sharp disagreement with its patronage exponents, especially when he designated W. D. Stewart director of the Department of Game and Fish. The governor refused to back down, though local Farmer-Labor clubs sought to impose a strict patronage system upon the department, which under previous Republican administrations sometimes had succumbed to political favoritism in the appointment of game wardens.

The wholesale housecleaning of incumbents from state positions demanded by the Farmer-Labor Association built up tensions. Stewart's heading of the Department of Game and Fish was especially galling to Farmer-Labor spoilsmen, who worked strenuously for the candidacy of Joseph Poirier, a staunch supporter of both Farmer-Labor third-partyism and collectivism. Soon Olson had an association revolt on his hands, led by Brainerd railway telegrapher I. C. Strout, who was not only a leader in the demand for more patronage but also a committed socialist who resented Olson's nonpartisan and tripartisan appointments in administration. Strout did not talk idly; in private he began to advocate "tough methods" to force the issue and change the practice. In due course Strout would succeed, winning a patronage appointment as state hotel inspector, a position from which he slowly began to force open the door to widespread Farmer-Labor patronage.

During Olson's first administration he held firm in other appointments. For example, R. A. Trovatten, the new commissioner of agriculture, had been a one-term legislator (1923-24), a former member of the NPL, a signer of the 1926 "round robin" letter, a sometime advocate of fusion, and was generally a conservative Farmer-Labor voice. His appointment was further evidence that Olson's first administration was cautious, liberal but not radical, and patterned to be rather remote from the ideological expectations of the left, though it made a conscientious effort to include representation from every ideological corner of the movement.

Olson's 1931 Legislative Program

Olson's pragmatic liberalism was fueled by an emotional commitment growing out of injustices and sharpened by the depression catastrophy. He had no well-formed public philosophy. The policies he advocated and the programs he advanced tended to be reactions to circumstances, often dismal ones, confronting government and his administration. Upon taking office, he did not attempt to introduce the state to an American variant of socialism.

The political realities Olson faced in January vis-à-vis the nonpartisan legislature were not encouraging. The majority membership was conservative, Republican, and unaccustomed to bargaining with either a liberal or a non-Republican governor. Olson set limited objectives. He wanted a series of reform measures passed but none of them were in any sense radical, and he initially sought to be reasonably cooperative with the leadership. The legislature rather quickly dismissed even these meager accommodations. Almost 40 percent of the state senators were liberals (Democrats, Farmer-Laborites), and for forty years the lieutenant governor, as presiding officer, had appointed the standing committees. But such a custom was guarded only by a senate rule and not law, and the lieutenant governor heretofore had always been a Republican and one of the majority. Henry Arens now was a Farmer-Labor lieutenant governor but he also was a ten-year legislative veteran (1919-30). Olson and Arens attempted to negotiate an agreement but an impasse was reached over composition of the Senate Rules Committee. Whether this doomed the effort or merely provided an excuse, senate Republican leaders decided to strip Arens of this power, and the rule change carried with a vote of 38 to 29.

Olson anticipated the outcome. Nevertheless, the tone of his inaugural message was moderate, he avoided impossible and implausible policy objectives, and there was no careless or futile bravado about future socialist remedies under the banner of Farmer-Laborism. By most standards, certainly by Farmer-Laborism's, Olson's program was modest; indeed, Farmer-Labor critics of Olson declined even to give it high marks as reform. Specifically, he asked for a reorganized conservation program, reform and reclassification of real estate property evaluations, better law enforcement, improved securities regulations to protect investors, prohibition of labor injunctions, minimum wage floors and improved working conditions on state projects, aid to small business, a state old-age pension system, and a state building program to help provide relief for growing unemployment.[53]

Compared with Preus and Christianson, Olson had mounted a liberal program, but it hardly could be said to have raised the hackles of the Red-baiters. It was in step with Shipstead's proposals of 1931, and its severest critics were those members of the ideological left who believed growing economic emergency a sufficient reason or excuse to resurrect more politically risky proposals for some forms of public ownership.

The Legislative Liberals

Olson was not alone in thinking that Farmer-Laborism should move cautiously, even in opposition to the movement's militants. The left had a tendency to overestimate Farmer-Labor strength. Henry Teigan, editor of the association's *Farmer-Labor Leader,* calculated it as 28 (of 67) senators and 41 (of 131) representatives,[54] an overall average of 35 percent. This was accurate only if it included fusionists and Democrats like Mankato's conservative John E. Regan and St. Paul moderate liberal John J. McDonough. These men and the moderate Farmer-Laborites had much less in common with passionate third-party partisans like Teigan, Howard Y. Williams, and the collectivists than they would have with the coming New Deal and even conservative Democrats. If a generalization had to be made, it was safer to classify the majority of the Farmer-Labor legislators with Shipstead than to place them with the socialists.

Few legislative proposals could test this hypothesis. One that did in part was the call to return party labels to the legislature. Third-party disciples had long included it in the association platforms. When a midsession vote to reintroduce party designation was held, it failed 46 to 82 against, gaining support of only 11 Farmer-Labor representatives while 29 others in the liberal (Democratic, Farmer-Labor) coalition rejected it.[55] Republicans actually gave the measure greater support than Farmer-Laborites. Willmar liberal senator Victor Lawson even proposed removing all party labels from the Minnesota ballot, a move which drew Shipstead's approval and a coinciding attack upon the convention system of *de facto* nomination.[56] Labor socialists were aghast at the callous rejection of party labels; William Mahoney (in the *Minnesota Union Advocate*) immediately denounced Lawson and Shipstead for being "Out of Step with the Farmer-Labor party."[57]

Olson's Accomplishments in 1931

Olson inherited a series of problems from previous administrations. One of them was rural credits. In 1923 the (Republican) legislature had created the Rural Credits Bureau, a quasi-government corporation which extended credit to farmers. It was, ironically, a conservative, Republican experiment that put state government into the ("socialist") business of financing farmers when credit was otherwise unavailable to them from private commercial sources or when private bank loan rates were (in farmers' eyes) too high or risky. The political reasoning behind it was obvious: those Republicans sympathetic to or weary of farmer reaction considered it a way of undercutting early Farmer-Laborism.

In a qualified sense rural credits were a success — or failure, depending upon one's bias. The bureau proved highly popular owing to its low rates, a mortgage policy of securing loans on poor or low production land, and because farmers could obtain loans otherwise rejected by banking and commercial sources. During years of declining farm income and falling land prices, especially in the agriculturally marginal areas of the northern and northwestern counties, the bureau experienced hard times. By 1930 farmers had defaulted on hundreds of these loans, the bureau was insolvent and floundering, capital available for loans was exhausted, the "efficiency and economy" attitude of Republican administrations precluded pouring still more funds into the agency, and the state had become the unwilling owner of thousands of acres of low production farmland.

Olson was caught in a dilemma. The Rural Credits Bureau languished with an indebtedness of $58 million and interest-earning loans of only $43 million. To continue its operations Olson could have permitted the bureau to issue bonds (for needed capital), but the existence of loan defaults meant that state taxpayers would have been required to subsidize bond interest because the financially unsound bureau was certain to continue losing money. This would have necessitated a tax increase, hardly popular during a depression when state revenue was already declining. State land could have been sold, but only at a fraction of its previous value, and there was little demand for it. Consequently, Olson hesitated, hoping the economy would improve. The problem continued and there was some political relief in 1931 when a legislative investigation uncovered previous Republican malfeasance, but this in no way dealt constructively with the basic problem.

Olson's successes were limited, yet he steadily built the impression of a hardworking governor attempting to struggle with depression-related public issues. During the legislative session he pushed a public works program to give work to some of the unemployed, he worked hard to reorganize and centralize the Department of Conservation, and to guard against investment frauds he sought stronger "blue sky" legislation.[58] A $15 million bonding authorization for highway construction was a central focus of public debate, and Olson added to the controversy on February 26 when by executive order he required contractors on state projects to pay a minimum hourly wage of forty-five cents for up to forty-eight hours weekly, with overtime pay beyond these hours. Farmer legislators viewed such a scale with suspicion — even if they were Farmer-Laborites — since they feared farmers would be forced to pay "hired help" more and they questioned the propriety of such a "short" summer workweek. Some accused Olson of being "prolabor" but not profarmer. Nevertheless, he succeeded in helping pass the highway construction bill and signed it into law April 1.

Olson brought some excitement to the end of the session by vetoing three relatively important bills. Minnesota governors normally do not veto substantial legislation, and Olson did not violate this tradition; but he vetoed a metropolitan sewage bill which passed a large part of the sewage cost not to South St. Paul meatpackers but to the general public; a Republican-gerrymandered congressional reapportionment bill designed to help Republicans and disadvantage Farmer-Laborites and Democrats; and a truck regulation bill which the railroad lobby had worked hard to pass.[59]

Olson and Farmer-Laborism had not been injured politically in their clash with Republicans, and the governor had significantly increased his stature as a man working to meet a rising tide of serious public issues. Even the normally staunchly Republican *Minneapolis Journal* sided with Olson and condemned obstructive tactics of the Republican legislative leadership.

Attacks upon the Governor

But cross-pressures upon Olson and the state administration grew with each passing month. Any step Olson took proved costly in one way or another, either economically, as a tax burden, or politically. Depression in fact did not automatically unite workers and farmers; sometimes it drew them farther apart. Olson's forty-five-cent wage code for highway laborers was one example of this, since it appeared to some farmers the governor had actually increased wages while farm income continued to fall drastically, and it brought Republicans and rural editors to accuse him of being antifarmer.

Solutions to general economic problems would have to be largely national, yet Olson, like Democratic and Republican governors everywhere, was held accountable for help and leadership during the economic emergency. Organized labor demanded a special legislative session for an unemployed workers relief bill. Farm groups called for fixed commodity price floors, tax reform (actually, a transfer of tax burden away from farmers), and credit and mortgage relief. Yet, if Olson were to satisfy both these groups, it meant higher state taxes, a much larger state budget, deficit spending, and a state debt (which the Minnesota Constitution forebade).

Criticism mounted. A. C. Townley traveled the state advocating a five-year moratorium on mortgage interest payments and accusing Olson of doing little to help farmers. Olson's chronic stomach disorder made him feel even more miserable. Nevertheless, the governor was a premier politican and not one to be blamed for problems and conditions which he had not created and for which he had only limited resources to solve or control.

His first effort, therefore, was to shift the political burden while building support for national action, rallying popular sentiment behind his state program, and strengthening the leadership case for his reelection. In October 1931 Olson called a farm conference at which he proposed to farm representatives a broad program, including basic commodity price floors, passage of the McNary-Haugen Bill, a refinanced Rural Credits Bureau and subsidized 2-percent farm loans, and reduced assessed values for farms and homes with the tax burden apparently to be transferred to business and industry.

Unfortunately, it was much more difficult and costly to provide state assistance to unemployed workers. Farmers who retained land (even by a moratorium) could feed themselves, but unemployed workers frequently faced starvation. Given the state tax structure at the time — neither a sales tax nor an individual income tax existed — there literally was no way for the state to finance unemployment relief and emergency benefits, unless new taxes were passed, which Republicans and the legislature were sure to reject and make into a damaging political issue. For an accused "labor" governor, Olson faltered badly, though it must be said he did no worse than Republican and Democratic governors everywhere.

As a result, Olson was extremely cautious in 1931 when he discussed unemployment relief. An advocate of increased governmental intervention, he proposed a private system of voluntary relief contributions! It revealed how inadequately Olson had thought through his liberalism and public policy. Politically, however, it bought him time even though it increased left-wing dissatisfaction with his administration. More important, initiative had been returned to Olson and the state Farmer-Labor administration.[60]

Such an economic environment forced Olson to analyze his own liberalism and to act cautiously. He was determined to govern compassionately, to help the victims of economic collapse, to maintain public order and manage conflict — and to be reelected. He had no wish to become an economic and political prophet who could claim to have once held high public office briefly.

As economic stability disintegrated, new converts joined Farmer-Laborism and old prodigals returned. One of the returnees was A. C. Townley who in the early months of 1931 once again traveled the NPL speaking circuit. Townley was critical of the unwillingness of Farmer-Labor legislators to lead a fight for more fundamental changes in public economic policy. Left-wing Farmer-Laborites echoed this sentiment and grew increasingly restive.

Left-wingers continued to believe, or at least hope, that Olson would eventually support the basic issue of the day — socialism — and lead a political campaign for expanded programs of public ownership. These collectivists manifested a missionary and crusading spirit, almost a feeling of revealed predestination and of being among the chosen elect. "We, the real Farmer-Laborites," Henry Teigan was now chanting, "are going to put over a program next year that will be truly progressive and fundamental in the best sense of the word."[61] Visions like these and dismal times made it increasingly difficult for the left to compromise its basic values much longer.

WHICH DIRECTION FOR FARMER-LABORISM?

The turbulence wrought by the depression and the responsibility of managing state government buffeted Minnesota Farmer-Laborism after the 1931 legislative session and throughout 1932. At issue within the movement were how it wished to present itself to voters, how to define its prevailing ideology, and what relationship (if any) it should have with other state third parties and the national movement to include a third party in presidential elections. The issues went far beyond the symbolism of a "common people's" party whose goal was the creation of a "people's government," which symbolically at least was equally claimed by the two major parties. Farmer-Laborism was now being pulled in two directions. Moderates regarded it as a unique, independent alternative to the two parties, but one which did not reject cooperating with progressive Republicans and Democrats, and they shied away from the left wing, socialism, and the national third-party movement. By contrast, the left wing rejected liberal Democratic and Republican policies, incremental changes and "superficial" reforms, and insisted instead upon aligning Minnesota with the national third-party movement and an ideology stressing evolutionary public ownership policies as a replacement for capitalism.

By 1932 one person in five was without work, a condition which brought insecurity even to those who still held jobs. Catastrophic as this was, another political reality for those who rejected revolutionary seizures of power was that at least three-quarters of the public were still gainfully employed as before, and many farmers, probably a majority and especially those in the richer agricultural portions of southern Minnesota, were solvent even though they faced reduced incomes. Minnesota voters were not likely to vote a socialist movement into power.

An adjunct to the regrowth of Minnesota Farmer-Laborism, and shortly to be a substantial contributor to both its cause and controversy, was the unmistakable revival of the left wing in Minneapolis and Hennepin counties. In 1931 Republican Minneapolis mayor George Leach was challenged by William A. Anderson, a moderate socialist with a rather mild disposition. To say a socialist was elected mayor requires qualification. The Anderson campaign largely played down his socialist background, and his supporters politely declined assistance from the League of Independent Political Action, fearing it would make him more vulnerable and add very little support.[62] In St. Paul William Mahoney was somewhat more generous, for he invited Howard Y. Williams to return home and become a candidate for mayor (or congresman),[63] though Mahoney himself eventually became the candidate.

GOALS OF THE NATIONAL THIRD-PARTY MOVEMENT

Complicating matters for Farmer-Laborism were national events, presidential politics, and the fledgling League for Independent Political Action. Some LIPA spokesmen even thought it possible to run a 1932 ticket though their real plan aimed at the 1936 election. Somewhat mistakenly, LIPA looked upon Olson as a model individual for third-partyism. However, when the governor was invited to address a 1931 LIPA convention, he politely refused on the grounds of pressing state business,[64] though the reasons were probably much more practical.

Division over LIPA objectives already undermined its potential for success. A. J. Muste, a militant socialist and pacifist, resigned with a sarcastic denunciation of John Dewey's attempt to induce George Norris, the progressive Nebraska senator, to be a third-party presidential candidate in 1932, and charging LIPA with failing to become a genuine socialist working-class party. Shortly after, Norman Thomas resigned from the LIPA executive committee because he believed the Socialist party was the proper existing vehicle through which to channel growing protest.[65]

In spite of these splits, Howard Y. Williams assured 500 delegates to the 1931 LIPA convention that the third-party idea was becoming popular. Traveling extensively and addressing university, YMCA, LWV, and liberal groups, Williams attempted to set up small organizations in every state he visited. His speeches and LIPA pamphlets carried these messages: "Does the United States Need a New Political Party?" "Capitalism, Communism, and American Politics." "Can Capitalism Survive?" "A National Plan for America." The best written was Professor Paul Douglas's "Why a New Political Alignment."[66]

Much of this appeal was visionary rather than politically realistic. The LIPA Four-Year Plan depended upon an untested hypothesis and, as it turned out, faulty logic. The simple dialectic found voters abandoning Hoover and the discredited Republican party. First, they would turn to the Democrats, who (LIPA assumed) would nominate a conservative 1932 presidential candidate. Then, as a result (because no "fundamental changes" would take place), the Democrats would drive away literally millions of voters still in search of a responsive political alternative. By skillful political engineering, LIPA would realign these millions into a new political party, launch a coordinated 1936 congressional and presidential campaign, and as a triumphant new majority win the presidency in 1940.

Williams sensed but one major problem in the strategy. Al Smith and New York governor Franklin D. Roosevelt (to Williams a "great straddler") were threats. "Neither of these men," Williams observed, "are real progressives" yet he feared liberal political forces might rally behind them.[67] If this happened, it would undermine the entire third-party realignment. Moreover, in Minnesota Olson and the moderates were not worried by such a circumstance and when their own reelection seemed to hinge on making an accommodation with the Democrats, Olson for one joined in endorsing Roosevelt.

THE FARMER-LABOR PRAXIS, 1931-32

For all their brilliance, no matter how systematic their logic and philosophy, and in spite of (or because of) their academic and often scholarly attainment, the socialists and the intellectuals did not shape the future course of Farmer-Laborism. The political pragmatists did. Immediately and in the long run the pragmatists had an impact upon and took a toll of the third-party movement whether in Minnesota or outside it. Floyd Olson was a practitioner, not a philosopher. He would compromise whenever and wherever it seemed necessary, and to Hell with the socialists and the left wing.

Of course, brilliant men like Norman Thomas were correct. Thomas suspected "muddle-headed" liberals would follow the Franklin Roosevelt Democratic bandwagon, and he classified the New York governor a subservient creature of Tammany Hall whose reasoning was conspicuously devoid of "any thought out policy on any of the larger issues."[68] Thomas's alternative was a "small size mass movement" into the Socialist party. Philosopher John Dewey, considered one of the pragmatic progressives in the intellectual arena, saw the future in a national Farmer-Labor party. And Howard Williams hoped to see an American counterpart to the British Labor party emerge.[69]

These were astigmatic images of the early thirties. Although many people were being called to the intellectual's third-party realignment, few were gathering. Williams asked some thirty Minnesota Farmer-Labor leaders to help LIPA build a national third-party realignment; the request was viewed with cold skepticism. The national Socialist party likewise rejected the LIPA invitation.[70]

For politicians like Floyd Olson and before him Henrik Shipstead, something, perhaps a practitioner's instinct, warned them not to stray too far from the two major parties. This was the way it would be in 1932 and beyond.

CHAPTER 7

The Temptation to Socialize Farmer-Laborism

The first Olson Farmer-Labor administration improved popular impressions of this Minnesota third party. Both Farmer-Labor factions — as well as some Democratic and (usually former) progressive Republican members — were represented in the Olson administration. The general expectation was that this style of administration, with its tone of moderation, would continue if Olson was joined by other elected Farmer-Laborites in 1932. Yet both Olson and the state of the economy contributed to Farmer-Labor (and Democratic) troubles, and Olson himself had to question increasingly whether he should continue to follow the same cautious approach to problems.

Olson was a crafty political stylist whom contemporaries and history have found difficult to judge accurately. He could be lion or fox, radical or reformer, and he unquestionably expressed a deeply felt humane desire to protect those who suffered in the depression. The bad times made his public life difficult. Farm and home foreclosures, 25-percent unemployment, starving individuals without income, and too often an opposition's rigidly conservative values conflicted with his need and wish to take prompt remedial action. But the Farmer-Labor Association also added to his increasing turmoil as its left-wing members began to pressure him and Farmer-Laborism into becoming militant social advocates of public ownership as a replacement for capitalism.

How far Olson was prepared to move in changing public economic policy remains unsettled, largely because Olson was deliberately ambiguous out of sheer political necessity. And during the economy's darkest hours he, like many others, came to question some old values and assumptions about ownership of wealth and distribution of income. Franklin Roosevelt did not wish to destroy but rather preserve capitalism, yet he too used colorful political language when he ridiculed "robber barons" and "malefactors of great wealth," terms not really original with the Democratic New Deal. Politically and personally, Olson admired Roosevelt.

Republicans were now at an even greater political disadvantage than before. Temporarily at least, they found it difficult to charge Farmer-Laborites with being rampaging radicals. Democrats were divided into two camps: those who wished to continue cooperating with Olson and Farmer-Labor moderates and those who opposed such agreements because they were too one-sided and tended to delay rather than speed up the resurgence of Minnesota's state Democratic party. In general, the liberal, or Roosevelt, Democrats opposed them. And Farmer-Laborites were divided between moderates who argued for all-partyism and reform, and the ideological left which believed the time long overdue to march toward public ownership and "fundamental change." Economic suffering brought on by the depression caused a left-winger like Henry Teigan to once again denounce the private system of corporate enterprise and reassume the role of a critical socialist. "Stalin and his crowd in Soviet Russia are after all the only real patriots worth while," Teigan charged in one of his more bitter moments. "They are administering government in behalf of workers, farmers and the useful members of society and not in behalf of a pack of plunderers as is being done in the United States and other capitalist countries."[1]

DISSENSION IN THREE PARTIES

Minnesota's three parties each faced a different set of organizational disorders and none entered the formative stages of the historic 1932 campaign united by a single purpose. Economic miseries tremendously handicapped Republicans everywhere, providing a grand opportunity and handsome political advantage for both Democrats and Farmer-Laborites.

The Farmer-Labor Dilemma

Both wings of the Farmer-Labor movement were prepared to exploit the economic issue, but they disagreed over the kind of ideological appeal that should be directed toward Minnesota voters. The left wanted a bold, unique, partisan Farmer-Labor drive which set its name off sharply from both Republicans and Democrats. This year congressional candidates were running at-large rather than from districts, and socialists were prepared to tie them and all Farmer-Laborites to public ownership proposals. This contrasted sharply with the position of Olson and the moderates who preferred the all-party, nonpartisan, nonradical approach which had brought them earlier and recent victories.

The left wing grumbled on in dissatisfaction. Oscar Behrens, secretary to Minneapolis mayor William A. Anderson, typified its frustration and criticized (not necessarily accurately) the quality of Farmer-Labor leadership outside the association. Henry Teigan "lacked good judgment," William Mahoney "went off half-cocked," Anderson "lacked initiative," and Olson was "not committed to the Third Party idea."[2] This attitude would improve only rarely over the next few years, and worse, as far as the left was concerned, its suspicions about 1932 election strategy were about to be confirmed.

Financing the movement, despite the recent growth in association membership, proved increasingly a challenge, and the association treasury had literally run out of funds. Circulation of the *Farmer-Labor Leader* had leaped by an astounding 5,000 percent, yet the paper carried a $500 operating deficit and was on the verge of suspension.[3] To help relieve its creditors, the association resorted to a capitalistic selling practice by hiring newspaper salesmen who received 50-percent commissions on each dollar subscription sold. And in April 1932 the executive committee hired George Creel as its $75-per-week editor, gaining an experienced professional who had served in 1917-19 as the Wilson administration's chief war information officer.[4]

The Democratic Split

Bleak unemployment figures also raised Democratic expectations; in February the job market had deteriorated so badly that the Minneapolis American Legion and the Chamber of Commerce began a door-to-door canvass to locate "off-job" work for the unemployed.[5] Democrats anticipated their potential gains by recalling how close Hoidale had come to being the first elected Democratic senator. Taking all these things together, the party should have been united by opportunity, but instead it was split along liberal and conservative lines and by debate over relations with Farmer-Laborites.

Such a breakdown was exacerbated by religion, ethnicity, and especially presidential politics. The Minnesota Democratic party was unpleasantly divided into those supporting Roosevelt and those following Alfred E. Smith, the first Roman Catholic to gain a presidential nomination. Smith Democrats tended to be Catholic, causing German and Scandinavian Protestant Democrats to complain privately about Irish dominating (and politically injuring) the Minnesota party. A second factor in the division was the tendency of Roosevelt backers to be party liberals and Smith backers party conservatives. Finally, Democratic liberals usually were fusionists who looked toward continuing "agreements" with Farmer-Laborites, whereas conservatives were determined to end one-sided agreements with Olson and instead immediately began rebuilding the Democratic party at every level rather than waiting for the unknown future. A good case could be made for either position. Conservatives were essentially correct in contending that Democratic strength occurred at more than just the presidential level (and was greater there than both factions realized), but conservatives erred in failing to recognize which Democratic candidates had done well historically in Minnesota: John Lind, John Johnson, and Winfield S. Hammond, i.e., Scandinavians and non-Irish Anglo-Saxons.

Conservatives resolved to block liberal "agreements" with Olson and to otherwise nullify secret negotiations between the governor and compromising Democrats willing to trade silent assistance to Olson for help and/or endorsement for Roosevelt. The Roosevelt group, led by Hoidale, national committeeman Joseph Wolf, St. Paul financier Adolph Bremer, state chairman J. J. Farrell, and Z. H. Austin, continued efforts to reach an understanding with Farmer-Laborites. Such persistence was ominous, for not only did it help bring on a Democratic schism which lasted ten years, but it provided substantial proof that Democrats were in a position to critically limit the Farmer-Labor realignment.

The first evidence of the intensity of animosity toward fusion came in Hennepin County when Neil Cronin succeeded in pushing an antifusion resolution through the state Democratic convention of March 9. However, Roosevelt-backers, directed by Wolf, were in solid command, and Hoidale defeated Cronin for temporary chairman by more than four to one (542 to 115). The conservative reprisal was swift. Led by Ruth Haynes Carpenter, Smith delegates angrily bolted, set up a rump convention, drew to their side a sizable bloc of individuals who (besides Carpenter and Cronin) would long remain influential in state Democratic politics, some for twenty years: Ray Moonan, John E. Regan, A. J. McGuire, Jerry Harri, Pierce Butler, Jr., and Margaret Drips.

The regulars, however, retained organizational command and their members, too, often came to be well known: John J. McDonough, Anna D. Oleson, John F. D. Meighen, and Robert Butler. The regular party platform was very much like moderate Farmer-Labor resolutions and supported tariff reform, a veterans' bonus, a referendum on prohibition, the St. Lawrence Seaway, the McNary-Haugen Bill, and an income tax-based old age pension.[6]

The Republican Search for Candidates

Minnesota's traditional majority party was not sanguine about its prospects. Demoralized when it met in convention the third week of March, the party had to start almost from the beginning after the three leading gubernatorial contenders—John Hougen (whom Olson had defeated in 1930), state auditor Stafford King, and highway patrol chief Earle Brown—all withdrew. The Hennepin County Republicans, normally very influential, were sharply divided, and there was little enthusiasm for Hoover.[7]

At a closed door meeting Brown was asked to reconsider and come to the aid of his foundering party, which was nearly bankrupt of issues upon which to campaign. He agreed to enter the gubernatorial race, and Brown County Attorney T. O. Streisguth ran for lieutenant governor, appealing more or less for strict enforcement of "law and order." Republicans pledged to cut $5 million from the state budget, condemned the Olson administration for excessive spending, called for a return to efficiency and economy in government, and ignored references to the depression. Additional pledges were made for an income tax to replace "other" (usually property) taxes, continuation of prohibition, and lower agricultural taxes, and charges of political meddling were levied against the embattled Rural Credits Bureau.

Symbolically, however, nothing better expressed the Republican fall from grace than its selection for convention keynote speaker, eighty-eighty-year-old former governor (1901-4) Samuel R. Van Sant, who doted upon his seventy-two years of political experience.[8] Nostalgia proved a poor prescription for 1932. Such a prologue hardly was a fit remedy to cure a depression or save an old party from its dying ways.

A CONVENTION VICTORY FOR FARMER-LABOR MODERATES

Floyd Olson was determined not to sacrifice an early Farmer-Labor advantage over faction-torn Democrats and demoralized Republicans. Such a wish was more easily expressed than realized. Working skillfully to retain party command, Olson was careful to avoid indiscriminate use of sheer political muscle as he labored to prevent the left from either wrecking his party's chances for victory or angrily denouncing Farmer-Labor candidates and the state administration for ideological malfeasance and in the process bringing on an irreconcilable schism. This required a thespian performance by the governor before the Farmer-Labor Association state convention in late March, a challenging role for him because the depression had generated rising left-wing agitation for sweeping economic changes and the demand that the Farmer-Labor movement adopt a socialist program of economic relief.

Never was the left more convinced that it was time to seize the political initiative. Right before the association convention began, the state Socialist party met in annual session, the call being made by Albert G. Bastis, who also served as Farmer-Labor vice-chairman. He, with Lynn Thompson and state senator (1919-25, 1931-39) Andrew O. Devold, convinced the Socialists to drop plans to run state candidates, and the meeting ended with an endorsement, sight unseen, of the yet-to-be-named state Farmer-Labor ticket. Socialists had but one condition: there was to be no fusion with Democrats, no secret agreements to support Roosevelt, and they expected a more forward-looking Farmer-Labor platform.

The same general attitude extended to the Hennepin County Farmer-Labor Association, which in resolutions and platform gave a ringing endorsement to public ownership, demanding state ownership of banks, railroads, utilities; a six-hour workday; and creation of a state department of public works. To ensure that Hennepin delegates carried this message to the state convention, a delegate-screening committee was appointed under Bastis.[9]

Developments like these brought the left into near direct confrontation with Olson and conflicted with his preconvention maneuvering to retain the moderate Farmer-Labor program and not allow it to be transformed into a socialist bulwark. The governor was determined to restrain Farmer-Labor platform writers. And although he could hardly handpick delegates from left-wing strongholds like Hennepin and St. Louis counties, there was little doubt that his followers were in control and that his personality would dominate issues, candidates, the platform, the convention, and ultimately the campaign.

In spite of Olson's insistence upon shaping the Farmer-Labor image to his specifications, he did need left-wing support. He deployed masterful elocution to obtain it. His keynote address, a dynamic contrast to Van Sant's funeral oration, firmly put Olson's stamp upon the convention. As a forceful public speaker Olson had few peers and no masters, and he put these consummate skills to work. The plan was for him to take and keep the Farmer-Labor campaign initiative, and the 1932 election would thus result in his greatest political triumph. Olson assailed Hoover, but he disappointed Socialists and the Farmer-Labor left by an implied willingness to commit his party to supporting Roosevelt if he won the Democratic nomination. He sketched out a Farmer-Labor political program, which with few additions and to no one's surprise ultimately became the association platform. It included a state income tax, a graduated tax on chain stores (like Penney's, Sears, Ward's, Woolworth's) to save small business, a tax on wild animal pelts, low-interest farm loans, a veterans bonus, compulsory unemployment insurance, and national minimum farm support prices.

Surely this represented a restrained Farmer-Laborism, not unlike the New Deal Democratic appeal and even some Republican proposals. It was designed with the electoral center in mind and was to attract moderates and liberals, and even some conservatives who feared the economic consequences of depression and monopoly. The 1932 Farmer-Labor ticket complemented it. Henry Arens was redrafted for lieutenant governor, and when he later decided to be one of the at-large congressional candidates his replacement was K. (Konrad) K. Solberg of Clarkfield, a state senator (1923-29) from the southwest corner. Other endorsees, each from a distinct geographic region, were political moderates: John T. Lyons (secretary of state), A. H. Kleffman (treasurer), Harry H. Peterson (attorney general), and former congressman Knud Wefald (railroad and warehouse commissioner). The platform was patterned after Olson's speech and added only planks for a state-owned printing plant and a public water power generating system.

The major controversy at the convention revolved around an issue which had severely fractured Democrats: "fusion" of the two parties. Whereas Democratic conservatives rejected agreements with Farmer-Laborites (in part out of fear of "radicalism"), Farmer-Labor socialists seethed when they thought of compromising with capitalist-defending Democrats. Taking their case to the convention floor, bitterly frustrated left-wingers denounced the ever-present rumors about pending arrangements which were beyond the association's official ability to influence or veto. Olson was not involved in this debate and wisely maintained his silence, yet all knew he would be the architect of any agreement with Democrats. Duluth attorney Sigmund Slonin, a socialist, lectured the convention on its failure to pursue what the left saw as Farmer-Laborism's principles. Unlike the moderates, the left believed it could win or at least risk a campaign waged on the merits of public ownership rather than partly rely on tainted Democratic assistance.

However, the left itself was divided and too weak to bend the convention will toward collectivist policies. It suffered a defeat when a compromise proposal for a Farmer-Labor slate of presidential electors pledged to Roosevelt was rejected after encountering opposition from moderates and empassioned socialists who were fighting Roosevelt and campaigning for a national Socialist ticket.[10] In this tumultuous context Olson's 1932 performance represents the work of a political virtuoso.

OLSON, ROOSEVELT, AND THE FUSION ISSUE

Fusion debate tempered Olson's freedom of action, since he did not wish to jeopardize the tense lines of support he kept with the left. Near and far, Socialists denounced him. Clarence Senior, national executive secretary of the Socialist party, in a warning to Howard Y. Williams claimed that last-minute opposition from militant Socialists had prevented the "Olson machine" from winning convention endorsement for Roosevelt. "The only thing which will save the breakup of the Farmer-Labor party is the defeat of Roosevelt at the Democratic convention," Senior prophesized gloomily (and correctly), and he warned that the Socialist party would withdraw its members from the Minnesota Farmer-Labor party if Olson rallied it "behind a capitalist politician."[11]

Like Olson, Joseph Wolf and other regular Democrats were outwardly cautious about "fusion" since they wished to avoid an irreconcilable split with Smith conservatives. When Governor Roosevelt's April Minnesota visit was announced, antifusionist Farmer-Laborites and Democrats worried about the meaning of an Olson-Roosevelt conference.[12] Yet neither Olson nor Wolf was free to reach binding agreements (outright merger, though rumored, was unthinkable), because neither could be sole spokesman or agent for his party. In some ways Democrats were the most severely restricted; for example, there were three claimants to the post of Hennepin County chairman! And Democrats in general remained ambivalent toward Olson. Why, they wondered, was Olson's old acquaintance Tom Davis filing in the Republican primary? As evidence mounted of an emerging political realignment in Minnesota, liberal Democrats also began to worry that advantages were too one-sided. Remembering Hoidale's impressive showing in 1930, they and the conservatives questioned whether Democratic political benefits were proportional to the size of the

Democratic contribution. What they found was that Olson had appointed his noncampaigning Democratic opponent Edward Indrehus to an administrative position in the Rural Credits Bureau,[13] hardly an even trade.

Roosevelt's Minnesota April visit went well. When Roosevelt and Olson met it seemed obvious that the two governors were continuing to enjoy the good personal and political rapport which had begun the year previous at the annual governors' conference. Olson attended the Roosevelt dinner but delivered no speech; to leftists, however, his mere presence was a bad omen. Roosevelt, too, avoided in his speech any mention of Democratic-Farmer-Labor cooperation, and in his inimitable style he talked about an economic crisis more grave than war, called for lower tariffs and national regulation of electric utilities, and (rare for a New Yorker) praised the St. Lawrence Seaway proposal — themes which Olson himself frequently exploited. However, in the auditorium corridors the major topic was fusion,[14] and Henry Teigan's Farmer-Labor News Service sent newspaper releases highly favorable to the Roosevelt speech.

Why was Olson so solicitous of the Democrats? In part the answer was found in the activities of the Al Smith Democrats. At the time of Roosevelt's visit, these Democratic conservatives were assembling a slate of candidates to run against the Wolf regulars; heading the slate were Mankato's John E. Regan for governor, Ruth Haynes Carpenter for lieutenant governor, and Waseca's Ray Moonan for attorney general. If the conservatives succeeded in winning in the primary, and even if there was a national Democratic trend under Roosevelt, it held unknown consequences for Olson and Farmer-Laborism.

Another piece in the emerging 1932 campaign mosaic fell into place on May 11 when the United States Supreme Court upheld (in *W. Yale Smiley v. Holm*)[15] Olson's veto of the badly gerrymandered congressional redistricting act, which had compressed ten districts into nine and now forced candidates to run at-large. After Olson refused to call a special session, eighty-seven candidates filed in the primary: twenty Democrats, thirty-two Republicans, and thirty-five Farmer-Laborites. At-large election seemed a benefit to and a good test of comparative Democratic and Farmer-Labor strength in Minnesota.

THE PRIMARY ELECTION

Although not recognized as one of the critical primaries (like those of 1918, 1920, and 1938), this election was significant for Democrats and Farmer-Laborites alike. Republican strength had not yet withered, indeed, the 530,000 primary votes were split evenly between Republicans (50 percent) and their two-party opposition (30 percent for Farmer-Laborites, 20 percent for Democrats). Few opponents challenged the Republican state ticket, and it survived easily, as was the case with the Farmer-Labor ticket.

Democrats, however, engaged in a full-scale organizational struggle which had far-ranging consequences after 1932. Three days after the Supreme Court decision the Regan-Carpenter-Moonan rumpers called 300 delegates to a Minneapolis conference where they adopted a separate platform calling for reduced governmental spending, lower tariffs, an income tax, repeal of liquor prohibition, Philippine independence, the St. Lawrence Seaway, and federal and state regulation of water power utilities.[16] It differed from the regulars' platform in its strict opposition to D-F-L "fusion" and its almost complete rejection of the endorsed regular slate of candidates. The primary victors were the Democratic conservatives: Regan, Carpenter, Moonan, Jerry A. Harri (secretary of state), and Tim Doyle (treasurer). The liberals were left only in command of their presidential delegates and in time the politically important fruits of presidential patronage.

Another casualty of the primary was Olson's hope for reaching a more advantageous agreement with Democrats, since the governor now could rely merely on receiving subrosa liberal assistance. The Democratic split delayed that party's Minnesota rebuilding effort because it institutionalized factional disagreement; an equally important outcome was that it limited considerably the size of the political territory into which Minnesota Farmer-Laborism could expand. When Democrats vigorously contested the third party rather than aided it, Farmer-Labor risk increased substantially.

POLITICAL REALIGNMENT AND THE NEW NATIONAL PARTY MOVEMENT

Disagreement over the scope and direction of political realignment plagued the national League for Independent Political Action. Some, like Howard Y. Williams and John Dewey, sought to rally major party progressives such as George W. Norris to the movement, but more vocal socialists like Norman Thomas and A. J. Muste would resign rather than dilute the ideology in the hope of gaining new converts.[17]

More important than these setbacks was the fact that LIPA was not making popular headway where it counted. Williams appealed to the New Workers School for creation of a bona fide labor party in the United States, but his calls went largely unheeded. They did attract the interest of Benjamin Gitlow and the (Stalinist) Communist Party of the United States (CPUSA). Gitlow saw "political crystalization" on the march, argued class lines were sharpening, and claimed the time opportune for the American left to radically liberate labor from the two major parties.[18]

This was not the kind of coalition that more moderate LIPA exponents foresaw as they attempted to build a strong movement which they believed would hold a "balance of power" between the two major parties before it could win the 1940 presidential election. Most of these adherents were overburdened by intellectual brilliance and shortchanged when it came to political insight and campaign common sense. Nonetheless, Howard Williams and LIPA relied upon them for guidance in a league-sponsored conference of "experts" in social planning under the chairmanship of the distinguished John Dewey. This group drew up a seven-point "Four Year Presidential Plan" which served as the movement's cornerstone.

As a source of proposed political action the plan was a distillation of current discussion among academics and the intellectual community. Dewey wrote a section on unemployment, advocated a six-hour workday, federal relief programs, and expanded public work projects. Encyclopedist Alvin Johnson of the New School of Social Research (editor of the *Encyclopaedia of the Social Sciences*), writing on money and banking, called for an end to holding companies and chain banks, prohibition of banks from investing in stocks, and asked that banks be limited strictly to "consumer services." Tax policy was formulated by Clair Wilcox and stressed progressive income taxes, elimination of tax loopholes, and encouragement of world trade through low tariff taxes. Country Life Association president Benson Y. Landis wrote the section on agriculture which included farm tax relief, low-interest loans, cheap (i.e., subsidized) rural electricity, marketing cooperatives, federal school aid, and an end to reclamation projects. Professor Paul Brissenden put together LIPA's civil rights program (free speech, ethnic equality, economic emancipation, the right to strike) and asked for abolition of the electoral college. A foreign policy statement, written by *The Nation's* associate editor, Devere Allen, endorsed a 50-percent reduction in military and "preparedness" spending, popular referendums before declaring war, recognition of the Soviet Union, and abandonment of the Monroe Doctrine, military intervention, and conscription. A final article dealt with public ownership and, as a socialist program, was generally mild: endorsement of a federal government-owned electric utility at Muscle Shoals in the Tennessee Valley, public ownership of utilities, and eventual federal ownership of coal, oil, and rail industries.[19]

Some of these proposals were to be a part of the New Deal, but hardly because LIPA had advocated them. Williams found it difficult even to give them widely recognized publicity, though Professor Paul H. Douglas included them as he put the final touches on a McGraw-Hill manuscript, *The Coming of a New Party*, pledging 40 percent of his royalties to LIPA.[20]

Dewey, Douglas, and Williams had faith in this grand design. Held before them was the vision of a discredited and fallen Hoover, faction-torn Democrats (Roosevelt versus Smith) destroying themselves, and the new third party moving into the political vacuum.[21] What LIPA moderates had failed to anticipate was disorder in their own movement and their ability to direct it. Douglas thought of LIPA as professional, white collar, and middle class; hence a moderate policy and lack of militant socialist "class consciousness."[22] But in July when the national LIPA convention assembled in Cleveland, moderation received rather rude treatment as endorsement was given to Norman Thomas and James H. Maurer, the Socialist party presidential ticket! Not only did this undercut Williams, but back in Minnesota it reinforced in the minds of Floyd Olson and his advisers a lingering suspicion toward any national third-party movement since the state administration was determined to extend the benefits it received by working with the state's Roosevelt Democrats this year.

A Disabled National Third-Party Movement

Not only was presidential politics responsible for rearranging political priorities in Minnesota Farmer-Laborism, but it soon undermined nearly three years' recruiting and planning by Howard Y. Williams and the League for Independent Political Action. LIPA leaders, aside from those representing the Socialist party, had suffered a serious rebuff on July 9 at the national LIPA convention (which had endorsed Thomas and Maurer). More critical, however, both immediately and in the long run was the Roosevelt candidacy.

LIPA had never escaped bickering over organization and ideology. Whenever its relatively moderate leaders succumbed to reality they were charged with cheating on higher, more noble principles. Williams, Paul H. Douglas, and their allies wanted to transform LIPA into or assist it in creating a British-type labor party, and Williams believed the American Socialist party was moribund and popularly discredited for the expedient reasons that Catholics and agricultural interests rejected it outright.

Difficulties went deeper. Although Congressman Fiorello H. La Guardia of New York gave lipservice to the third-party idea, he was unwilling to go beyond predicting that 1932 "might" be the last presidential election dominated by the two major parties.[23] Defections from LIPA were occurring at a faster rate than conversions. Republican senator George Norris, whom LIPA moderates like Williams and John Dewey saw as presidential timber, endorsed Roosevelt, whom LIPA had come to fear most. And some of LIPA's early partisans such as John A. Lapp and encyclopedist Alvin Johnson had joined the Roosevelt movement.

LIPA likewise had counted on Minnesota to serve as a third-party model, but the actions of its third-party officeholders and candidates hardly proved exemplary. A few exceptions, like Ernest Lundeen, faulted Roosevelt and called him another Hoover. But some of Minnesota's most trusted and successful Farmer-Laborites had become political turncoats in the eyes of LIPA and the leftists. William Mahoney, one of the original Farmer-Labor architects and heretofore a staunch third-party advocate, had recently been elected St. Paul mayor, and either political success or a change of heart caused him to rethink party alignments and preferences. Mahoney's St. Paul victory was a product of coalition, specifically cooperation between the St. Paul Trades and Labor Assembly, Democrats, and Farmer-Laborites who jointly functioned under the name Progressive-Labor coalition; this body transcended the regular Farmer-Labor organization and was an early prototype of "fusion." As a result, Mahoney in good conscience predicted a Roosevelt victory nationally *and* in Minnesota, seemed not the least displeased by this, and told one LIPA pioneer that it was politically better to defeat Hoover than to pursue any other goal.[24]

Thwarted at the national level and defeated in the Minnesota congressional primary, Howard Williams then sought temporary refuge in Farmer-Laborism, only to suffer rebuff again. He strived to be named state Farmer-Labor campaign chairman and appealed to and received support from the association executive committee, but his past and present plagued him. Williams's major problems were his reputation of being anti-Democrat, antifusion, anti-Roosevelt, and the distrust he displayed toward those who leaned "to the Democratic crowd," like Lieutenant Governor Henry Arens (now running as a Farmer-Labor congressional nominee). Floyd Olson was not about to turn away from the Roosevelt Democrats, and, not surprisingly, he quickly vetoed the Williams appointment.[25]

THE 1932 GENERAL ELECTION CAMPAIGN

Depression economics continued to inflate Farmer-Labor and Democratic advantages, and Olson's incumbent state administration and Farmer-Labor candidates still symbolized reform and change while blaming Hoover and Republicans for current economic dislocation. Strategically, the major challenges for Farmer-Laborites were to keep popular protest peaceful and institutional rather than disorderly and violent—lest they be blamed for encouraging and fomenting lawlessness—and if possible to prevent Democrats from siphoning off any sizable part of the voter shift away from Republicans. On both scores the movement was only partly successful.

The Farm Holiday Movement and the Campaign

In general, Farmer-Laborism's state reputation continued to be patterned after Olson, Shipstead, the Kvales, Arens, and mostly moderates running for congressional, state, and local offices. But some unwelcome agitation began to appear in May 1932, beginning first in Iowa and spreading into Minnesota, when the Farm Holiday Association (FHA) was formed as an independent adjunct to the National Farmers Union movement. Farm Holiday managers condemned the "free market" pricing system for farm commodities which was based upon supply and demand, preached that farmers themselves should help set commodity prices, and called for "farmer strikes" to keep commodities from being marketed in order to dramatize their economic plight, force prices higher, and push the federal government into adopting corrective legislation to increase commodity prices.

Olson and Farmer-Labor campaign advisers quickly recognized the political danger in sympathizing with FHA. An Iowa strike in late August triggered violence and led to sixty-five arrests. Olson's closest personal adviser, Vince Day, solemnly warned him to oppose and otherwise head off publicly, privately and in every possible way all use of violence to resolve political and economic misfortunes generated by the continuing depression.[26]

Farm strikes were costly in other ways. They were opposed by conservative farm groups like the Farm Bureau, were financially damaging to liberal cooperatives which were forcibly restrained from marketing perishable foodstuffs, and they tended to hurt Farmer-Laborism's moderate appeal. In Minnesota brothers John and Richard Bosch planned an FHA strike, and Olson worked to prevent it. First, he was instrumental in calling a midwestern governors' conference in Sioux City for September 9, hoping to set in motion throughout the farm belt a political drive for new national legislation which would result in higher prices without recourse to violence-prone strikes. Then he appealed to the Bosch brothers to be restrained in what they urged upon protesting farmers. Nevertheless, when the Minnesota farmer's strike began in late September and early October, roads to market were shut down, disturbances became unruly and nasty, and local sheriffs and the state highway patrol had to disperse farmers in order to reopen highways. Fortunately, injuries were few and the disorders quickly disappeared, allowing Farmer-Laborites to escape the consequences of any major upheaval, including that of pitting farmers against blue-collar truckers.

Olson soon returned to his reelection campaign, traveling widely in the state, projecting confidence, and seeming to be a skillful master in comparison with either Earle Brown or John Regan.

The Republican and Democratic Campaigns

Republican Earle Brown was no consummate politician. He avoided debates and face-to-face confrontations, and Farmer-Labor propaganda pictured him as a wealthy landholder and "gentleman farmer" of plutocratic tastes and loyalties. (Such propaganda could have been written about Franklin Roosevelt, too, but he was a Democrat.) Furthermore, as the former head of the state highway patrol, Brown was in a very poor position to lay much emphasis on his government service since the patrol had been used to break the farmers' strke and this issue thus was neutralized.

Democrat John Regan's campaign contrasted with those of the more cautious Olson and Brown, though his lack of sound political judgment undermined the effort. A difficult man to restrain, Regan attacked both his opponents and sometimes the people in his own party. In a strictly formal sense he could claim support of Roosevelt liberals like Joseph Wolf and John F. D. Meighen, but this was given grudgingly, and in private they continued to support Olson. The last week of the 1932 campaign Olson was given endorsement by the veterans division of the Roosevelt-Garner clubs, a final blow to Regan delivered by the Wolf-Meighen faction.[27] Regan seldom concealed his contempt for the Roosevelt nomination, a fact which further weakened Democratic organizational unity and limited the number of Republican votes he was able to draw and keep from going to Olson. Nevertheless, Regan's aggressiveness, Roosevelt's rising popularity, and the example of his determination not to stand mute as a Democrat reinforced the feelings of Democratic candidates to no longer take defeat for granted.

On balance, votes for Regan did decrease the margin of Olson's victory. Had Regan been more astute politically and had he used Roosevelt's coattails to full advantage, he could have altered considerably the margins of victory and the shape of Minnesota's political realignment, though he could not have taken victory from Olson.

Farmer-Laborism and Olson were about to reach a high-water mark which would be exceeded only once (in 1936) and then largely as a result of a colossal Democratic blunder. In his march to victory the governor weathered some personal attacks. Republican state auditor Stafford King, a war veteran, charged Olson with being a draft dodger; actually a hernia (as was the case with Hubert Humphrey in 1943-45) kept him out of the service. Then others whispered about his fondness for good bourbon and extramarital female companions. The most prominent story, accepted by many knowledgeable Farmer-Laborites, linked Olson romantically with Annette (Mrs. Billy) Fawcett, wife of a prominent publisher and sport enthusiast who during the campaign was involved in a sensational divorce action.[28] Such was the price of public life, and Olson displayed neither irritation nor concern over campaign gossip, his best defense resting upon his personal popularity which was almost as great as Roosevelt's popularity in Minnesota.

Political Realignment in Minnesota

Voter shift toward Farmer-Labor candidates, which Olson first triggered or enjoyed in 1930, was extended in 1932 to two additional state offices—attorney general (Harry Peterson) and railroad and warehouse commissioner (Knud Wefald)—and four more congressional seats (for Magnus Johnson, Henry Arens, Ernest Lundeen, and Francis H. Shoemaker who joined with John Paul Kvale to give Farmer-Laborites a majority among the nine-member Minnesota delegation). Farmer-Labor influence in the state legislature was extended, and in the lower house it represented the largest single bloc of votes, yet it was not a majority; the nonpartisan liberal caucus in fact had to be fashioned as a coalition which included Democrats and a handful of progressive Republicans with whom Olson negotiated in order to enlist their cooperation. In the at-large congressional run-off where victory went to the nine candidates receiving the highest vote—an idiosyncratic type of proportional representation rarely seen in American elective politics—the four highest vote-getters were Farmer-Laborites: Johnson, Kvale, Arens, and Lundeen in order of popularity.

For a third party Farmer-Laborism had good reason to feel elated. Still, realists were justified in not exaggerating the degree of voter shift to the movement. In times past Farmer-Laborites had been elected in

three congressional districts and Shipstead twice had won impressive
Senate victories; though this comparison is somewhat unfair, the senator in 1928 *had* outpolled the governor in 1932 by approximately
143,000 votes. Republicans retained three at-large congressional seats
(won by Theodore Christianson, Ray P. Chase, and Harold Knutson),
the two state offices of secretary of state (Mike Holm) and treasurer
(Julius Schmahl), and held a statewide voting percentage which ranged
between 30 and 43 percent. By comparison, Olson led all state Farmer-
Laborites and congressional candidates, but his percentage was 49.6,
or a 188,000 plurality over Brown (31.7 percent).

The voter shift toward Farmer-Laborism had to be balanced with a
more significant occurrence, the sharp increase in the size of the state
Democratic vote, evidence that voters had not shifted exclusively toward the third party. In presidential politics Minnesota was now about
to become a Democratic state, not only for the first time, but for five
uninterrupted presidential elections through 1948. In addition to shattering a Republican presidential tradition, Roosevelt led all candidates:
he amassed 600,000 votes, or 57 percent, ran 78,000 votes ahead of Olson, and was the sole candidate to gain a majority from the 1,054,203
ballots cast. And for the first time since 1916, an organization Democrat (Einar Hoidale) was elected to Congress. Democrats statewide
were taking 16 to 21 percent, or between 170,000 and 225,000 votes,
and in the case of Hoidale, 322,000. An ominous sign (because the
Farmer-Labor party had been the major opposition party since 1918),
this performance suggested that Farmer-Laborites could not gain victory without some agreement, collusion, or fusion with Democrats, and
it seriously undermined the left-wing Farmer-Laborites who wished
to pursue public ownership policies and who resisted any agreements
with a "capitalist" political party. Although 225,000 more total votes
had been cast in 1932 than in 1930, Olson had gained only 48,000 of
these and his overall percentage had dropped seven points. The agres-
sive though inept Regan had won 140,000 more votes than Indrehus
had gathered in 1930, a rise of 16 percent, yet Regan was the weakest
of all state Democratic candidates.

Had Democrats been more unified and organizationally integrated,
their growth would have been greater. As it was, the largest gross shift
was not toward Farmer-Laborites but toward Democrats. With presidential patronage as a lure, only political ineptitude seemed to stand
in the way of state Democratic expansion. Fortunately for the Farmer-
Labor party, Democrats were not yet prepared to exploit this opportunity, seemed unwilling to settle internal differences, lacked statewide
leadership and imagination, misunderstood the depth of Roosevelt's

RESULTS OF THE 1932 MINNESOTA GENERAL ELECTION
(Candidate, No. of Votes, and Percentage of Total Vote)

OFFICE	REPUBLICAN	DEMOCRATIC	FARMER-LABOR	SOCIALIST	INDUSTRIAL	COMMUNIST
President	Herbert Hoover 363,959 (34.5%)	Franklin Roosevelt 600,806 (57.0%)	Jacob Coxey 5,731 (.5%)	Norman Thomas 25,476 (2.4%)	Verne L. Reynolds 770 (.1%)	William Z. Foster 6,101 (.6%)
Governor	Earle Brown 334,081 (31.7%)	John Regan 169,859 (16.1%)	Floyd B. Olson 522,438 (49.6%)		John P. Johnson 1,824 (.2%)	William Schneiderman 4,807 (.5%)
Lieutenant governor	T. O. Streissguth 314,669 (29.8%)	Ruth Carpenter 193,671 (18.4%)	K. K. Solberg 429,759 (40.8%)			John Lindman 10,159 (1.0%)
Attorney general	Henry Benson 345,486 (32.8%)	Ray Moonan 218,076 (20.7%)	Harry Peterson 379,418 (36.0%)			Tom Foley 8,585 (.8%)
Secretary of state	Mike Holm 451,611 (42.8%)	Jerry Harri 182,065 (17.3%)	John Lyons 342,496 (32.5%)			Robert Turner 8,180 (.8%)
Treasurer	Julius Schmahl 371,574 (35.2%)	Timothy Doyle 223,651 (21.2%)	A. H. Kleffman 360,498 (34.2%)			
Railroad and warehouse commissioner	Oscar Swenson 345,659 (32.6%)	Mathen Kraus 215,980 (20.5%)	Knud Wefald 372,105 (35.3%)			Emil Hygard 9,458 (.9%)

Note: The total percentage for each office is less than 100 because some voters cast blank ballots and some ballots were spoiled.

Minnesota Farmer-Laborism, by Millard L. Gieske, © 1979 by the University of Minnesota.

appeal in the state, proved ineffective in negotiating with Olson and Farmer-Laborites, and could not be aroused from their lethargy for another decade.

CHALLENGES FACING THE SECOND OLSON ADMINISTRATION

Some element in Minnesota's political culture helps produce able leadership. It was at work long before and survives well after the Farmer-Labor movement, and credit for its persistence must be shared. First, with the general population which expects, demands, and regularly selects leaders capable of managing conflict and effectively seeking solutions to problems. Second, with the leadership elites which encourage able, talented individuals toward community service and into public life. Leaders generally have not abused power, interests (private, public, and personal) tend to be well balanced, and major scandal is the exception. As a result, the Minnesota political system has been internally respected, maintained, and renewed, with each generation receiving and then passing on a flexible, responsible governmental process.

In responding to the times, Minnesota was fortunate in having a Floyd Olson in command, for the Farmer-Labor administration had serious blemishes and faced mounting challenges. The movement's major cultural contribution was not its third-partyism, nor its sometimes uniquely different economic theories, but rather the fact that during the turbulent mid-1930s, a crucial period of time, it preserved and carried forward the tradition of effective leadership.

Organizing for the Depression

Olson's ambition and the people's choice had kept him where he wanted to be, in charge. Yet he probably underestimated how agonizing it would be for a governor in 1933-34. Under Olson Farmer-Laborism was entrusted with emergency management of state resources. Like Roosevelt in Washington, Olson in Minnesota had to contend with panic, runs on banks, mortgage foreclosures, sheriffs' sales of farms, mass unemployment, closed factories, foodless families, and violent confrontations. But unlike Roosevelt, Olson had no compliant legislative majority; his financial and political resources were much less than a president's; and he was forced to "muddle through" the two most difficult gubernatorial years in the twentieth century. Contending with the consequences of prodigious economic dislocations and facing militant farmer and labor union movements which were in aggressive pursuit of not only their self-interest but sometimes their survival, Olson had to call upon every political skill at his command. He galvanized action, resorted to extraordinary maneuvers, and occasionally made political use of public turmoil to break a legislative stalemate. Probably no other time and no other governor would have been permitted such discretion.

Neither Olson nor Farmer-Laborism could have been effective without assistance from Democrats and even a few Republicans. Olson succeeded in fashioning a coalition with which to work while fighting off the left wing in his own party as it became increasingly defiant in demanding a state program of public ownership and more state jobs for its association members. Because of extensive turnover, sixty new state legislators had been elected. When the conservative caucus assembled November 18, fifty-five supporters attended. On November 25 Olson personally greeted the house liberals—the group had sixty-five members and could count on four likely proxy votes—but this was an engineered coalition. The house speakership had been offered to Charles Munn, a Republican progressive from Osseo who had attended the March 1932 state Republican convention but who later supported and campaigned for Olson. Other choice committee chairmanships went to liberals like St. Paul's Democratic representative (1925-33) John J. McDonough. In such fashion the liberal coalition of Farmer-Laborites, Democrats, and a few Republicans was able to organize the house by a margin of 74 to 56.[29]

Olson's 1933 Budget and Legislative Program

Although Olson's biographer claims it pointed to "the emergence of a radical,"[30] Olson's aggressive leadership early in 1933 was radical only in comparison with his immediate predecessors and with what might be called the normal pattern of executive direction in dealing with the legislature. In most respects Olson's grandest hours and greatest achievements occurred in 1933 when he skillfully mixed demands for quick action, pressure upon the legislature, emergency declarations, and direct appeals to the public for support in order to extract emergency, remedial, and reform social legislation. No Minnesota governor before or since could expect to match these bold direct confrontations or to be as successful as Olson, since the circumstances of 1933 were highly unusual and, institutionally speaking, were at variance with traditional legislative independence and the rather strict separation of powers which are the hallmarks of Minnesota's and most states' political systems. In the context of the evolution of the New Deal and the launching of the American version of the welfare state, Olson's actions and programs were not radical; this becomes clear when a comparison is made with Roosevelt's first "hundred days" and when it is understood that Olson was attempting to manage intense conflict under extreme circumstances.

The context in which Olson labored to maintain social order was charged with bitterness and anxiety. In locales where the Farmers Union and Farm Holiday Association movements were strong, some farmers were taking "direct action," that is, interfering with the legal activities of county officials and sheriffs, sometimes by openly displaying guns so as to intimidate and discourage both buyers and public officials from foreclosing against farmsteads. A logical chain of events led to the failure of local commercial banks: As land values fell, commercial "paper" (mortgages, notes) on which farm loans were secured became meaningless; then, as prices dropped, farmers could no longer meet their bank payments. Depositors feared for their savings, panicked, and withdrew them, banks became the owners of land they neither wanted nor could sell to recoup their losses, and they were forced to close. A large percentage of the population had not lost their farms, homes, or employment but still suffered a decline in income and worried over the erosion of "law-and-order" and the threat of violence. As governor, Olson found himself caught squarely in the middle. Although he identified strongly with the poor, the weak, the suffering, and with those being dispossessed of their farms and homes, he in fact was an opponent of violent confrontation and a strong proponent of policy change through regular process of negotiation and compromise in the established institutions of government.

Olson had to deal with a state senate controlled (38 to 29) by conservatives. Budget cutting was endemic. For example, the senate cut its own budget, reduced its staff from 120 to 30, and dropped salaries by 10 percent. Olson directed his commissioner of the budget, former Republican Jean Wittich, to reduce the proposed state budget to the level which had existed in 1923. Eventually the legislature reduced the budget of state administrative departments by 20 percent, cut the university budget by 16 percent, put salary reduction on a sliding scale, ordered vacations without pay (which Olson opposed) for those earning over $1,200 per year, and made other reductions (some of which Olson resisted).

Olson set the tone of his administration in his biennial address, the most comprehensive to date. Warning that "lawlessness and possible revolution" in state and nation could be avoided only be remedial social legislation, he then offered a program that staggered old-guard conservatives. He asked for partial cancellation of mortgage debts, a two-year deferment period on mortgage foreclosures, a noneviction law for delinquent mortgagors who continued to live on their homesteads and paid reasonable and fair rent, and increased state funding for the Rural Credits department. School aid was frozen at 1931 levels. His tax program requested increases in the utilities' gross earnings tax, a graduated chain store tax, and although voters had rejected a proposal for a constitutional amendment authorizing an income tax, Olson asked the legislature to enact a state statutory income tax. To help counteract unemployment, Olson called for reduced working hours and compulsory unemployment insurance (patterning it after a plan developed by economics professor Alvin W. Hanson), though he unwisely sought to fund it entirely by a 4-percent tax on employers which led to its rejection by the legislature. To this Olson added a statewide retirement, or old-age pension. And he asked that emergency powers for the state executive council (which was empowered to assist flood, fire, and drought victims) be extended to include giving aid to persons "suffering from economic causes."

These programs were basic social welfare reforms almost entirely devoid of propositions for public ownership. The one exception was a proposed amendment authorizing state government to enter the electric generating business and a suggested statutory authorization for municipalities to sell city-owned electric power to nearby farms (90 percent of Minnesota farms still were without electric power in 1933). These propositions were hardly radical and were parallel to Roosevelt's advocacy of the Tennessee Valley Authority and the Rural Electrification Administration. Olson also advocated allowing cities to maintain municipally-owned buses and street railways.[31]

The senate's response to Olson's sweeping call for economic remedy was to dig in its heels and resist these "radical" changes. But times and suffering were extraordinary, and Olson had no intention of playing a passive role. He made use of nearly every opportunity to goad, plead with, even intimidate and frighten, the conservatives. Sometimes he resorted to discussing the possibility of declaring martial law to feed the needy, and he talked about an extraconstitutional suspension of the mortgage foreclosure law. Occasionally he appeared in person before legislative committees where he verbally clashed with conservatives and suffered some defeats, the most bitter of which was the loss of his unemployment compensation bill; but overall he remained in political command.

1933 Legislative Victories and Defeats

As Olson jousted in mid-February with legislative conservatives, he and his confidant Vince Day were made deeply anxious by A. C. Townley's activities among the farmers in the western prairie counties.

Townley roused farmers with political fire-and-brimstone speeches, telling them that 100,000 farmers should besiege the capitol and (as Day put it) "if the Conservative Senators refused to vote for [moratorium] legislation, . . . the farmers [should] take the seats in the Senate and pass the legislation themselves." Day believed that such agrarian recklessness was political suicide, that it would tip the balance away from reform, and he met with Farm Holiday leaders to warn them against using revolutionary threats or making radical demands for full repudiation of debts.[32]

Actually, since Townley's threats did not materialize, they may have assisted Olson, who by a series of extraordinary maneuvers forced the conservatives and their senate leader A. J. Rockne of Zumbrota to capitulate. On February 23, when rural disorder was at its height, Olson summarily proclaimed an immediate cessation of all mortgage foreclosures sales until May 1, justifying his proclamation on the questionable constitutional ground of "higher law." He cited extreme conditions and a breakdown of law enforcement. (Most sheriffs probably welcomed the cooling-off period since they felt personally threatened and outnumbered.) Olson's *coup* literally forced senate conservatives to pass the famous Minnesota Mortgage Moratorium Bill, which became law on March 2 and gave a landholder whose mortgage was past due up to two years—until May 1, 1935—to meet his or her obligation.[33] Conservatives had acted in part because Olson had astutely put the political burden of additional relief on their shoulders and because some were not certain exactly how they would be held accountable either in an election—or on the streets of their own communities. The law eventually was sustained by the U. S. Supreme Court in the landmark decision *Blaisdell v. Home Building and Loan Association.*

This year, as a substantial portion of his program became law, Olson trounced his conservative political antagonists. Victories outnumbered defeats. Pleased with the result, Vince Day tallied up the administration's successes: congressional reapportionment (a compromise rather than a Republican-dictated measure), the morgage moratorium act, homestead tax reform (lowered taxes), passage of the state income tax, a progressive tax on chain stores (the "most drastic of any state"), a bank reorganization law, land "retirement" to take it out of production, thirteen new state forests, liquor dispensory reform authorizing municipally owned retail stores, increased securities protection for investors (especially against fraud), ratification of the national child labor amendment, settlement of a bitter and sometimes violent strike by Austin packers, and creation of the state Planning Commission.[34] Significant reforms in labor relations included limiting the number of hours worked by women (to fifty-four hours per week), outlawing yellow-dog contracts, and providing state old-age pensions. In addition, a metropolitan sewage system was created, and legislation was passed to conserve the wilderness in the state's boundary waters area.

Olson suffered some setbacks, as expected, losing fights for unemployment compensation and for state-owned hydroelectric plants; he also could not prevent a reduction in the salaries of state employees. On balance, however, the record put Olson and Farmer-Laborism in a good position for the 1934 election. Throughout the legislative session Olson had kept the Farmer-Labor appeal moderate, though he occasionally thundered warnings about how modern capitalism (in a depression) adversely affected too many people.

Nevertheless, after two and one-half years in command Olson was about to lose some of his political savvy and power. This resulted partly from sheer physical incapacity. Already in mid-1931 an ulcer attack had forced him into seclusion and rest at his summer home on Gull Lake. In February 1933 he was staggered by appendicitis and chronic ulcers, which sapped him of vital energy even while he fought with the legislature. In May he had an appendectomy. For the next two and one-half years Olson mended but never healed, and by December 1935 a sharp rapid decline in his health set in.

Another change was an increase in left-wing opposition to the governor. While Townley stirred up agrarians, Farmer-Labor socialists demanded policy redirection far more comprehensive than that offered by Olson in early 1933. Olson, too, was becoming more critical of industry and the system of income distribution, and the left succeeded in moving him farther from the political center.

His major setback occurred in the crustier realm of politics, in patronage. The association clammered for jobs, had done so incessantly since 1931, and Olson was no longer capable of holding back the job mongers.

The Patronage Deluge

For over two years Olson warred with party job seekers. During the banking crisis in February he steadfastly defended conservative John Peyton, the state banking commissioner, who had effectively sought and won legislative banking reform requiring stringent reserves for state banks; when a bank closed Peyton insisted upon full solvency before allowing it to reopen. In effect, this impounded depositors' funds, made Peyton unpopular in some rural areas, and rather than capitulate to unsound practice Peyton resigned. Olson replaced Peyton with Elmer A. Benson, an Appleton bank cashier relatively new to state government.

The appointment received little attention at the time, even though Benson and Peyton differed in their ideologies and temperaments, but more importantly in their basic political allegiances; Peyton and others like him were in Farmer-Labor eyes "outsiders" whereas Benson was well received by the Farmer-Labor Association. The change was personally important for it marked the beginning of Benson's rise to prominence; it also was symbolic of an important administrative shift in policy. The barriers were about to be lowered for the association, patronage was soon to inundate the state administration, and Farmer-Labor opponents were given a new weapon which they would use handily over the next five years.

In May and June, while Olson endured severe physical complications, his relations with the association nearly ruptured. Veteran Farmer-Laborite A. C. Welch, no longer able to contain the opposition (he was a moderate), called the association's executive committee into emergency session. A demand was made for a plenary state conference to "discuss the political unrest of the Farmer-Labor party." Welch retreated, apolgetically warning Vince Day that "nothing will satisfy the Farmer-Laborites all over Minnesota, but a general housecleaning in all departments."[35] Olson simply collapsed under the pressure.

Two political appointments set a course which opened the patronage floodgates, created a "machine" image, and ultimately combined with ideological assault and turmoil to undermine the Farmer-Labor base. The first, that of Joseph A. Poirier as personnel director of the Highway Department, came as winter ended; the second occurred in May when Brainerd railway telegrapher I. C. (Dutch) Strout, a member of both the Farmer-Labor and Socialist parties, was appointed Commissioner of Budget and Personnel (a unit in the "Big Three" departments of the Finance Commission).[36] Olson had let a Trojan horse into his administration.

DIVISION IN THE NATIONAL THIRD-PARTY MOVEMENT

Schism was not confined to Minnesota. Liberals and socialists everywhere in the third-party movement were confused by and divided over the 1932 election, and Roosevelt's victory bewildered the League for Independent Political Action. LIPA had backed Farmer-Labor candidates in Chicago and Minnesota, Socialists in California, Massachusetts, New York, Pennsylvania and Wisconsin, and Norman Thomas for president. Collectively, its leaders talked with many voices. John Dewey still espoused socialist policies but insisted they not be associated with that party's name. Liberal editor Oswald Garrison Villard of *The Nation* believed that LIPA was instrumental in the Minnesota Farmer-Labor victory, and he just as incorrectly claimed that Roosevelt's election "means not a rebirth of the Democratic party, but a desperate attempt to secure an immediate New Deal by any means."[37] And Howard Y. Williams called on Floyd Olson to order a patronage housecleaning, assuring the governor that Farmer-Laborism was now in so commanding a position it no longer was necessary for it to compromise as it had done in the past.[38]

In practice, however, Williams and his LIPA allies followed a policy of accommodation by seeking to align with U. S. Senate progressives, both Republican and Democratic, in the mistaken belief some ten senators would join the movement.[39] Williams also fought a bitter war of words in *The Nation* with Norman Thomas, arguing over the impact of the 1932 LIPA contribution (which the Socialists denied), while Thomas continued to be irritated by the rejection of the Socialist party label as a rallying point for change.

LIPA was severely handicapped by the November results, though its founders still cherished its original goals. Philosopher John Dewey denied that the 1933 choice was between Rooseveltian progressivism and old-guard conservatism; "it is between far reaching socialization and liberal capitalism." In pursuing that long-term socialist objective Dewey assigned an important though transitional role to the Minnesota Farmer-Labor party, which he and many other LIPA members including the Socialists found not all it should be. Dewey believed Farmer-Laborism was improving, "gradually moving more to the left and . . . our function is to bore from within and help make it more what it ought to be."[40] This was precisely the view of the left in Minnesota and within the Farmer-Labor Association—and in a few years it would also be espoused by Stalinists and Trotskyites.

The Farmer-Labor Political Federation

LIPA was living on borrowed time and limited funds. It was hampered by a split between those loyal to the Socialist party and a nonaligned group. Essentially intellectuals, the former included Emil Rieve of the hosiery workers, Julius Hochman of the International Lady Garment Workers' union, Devere Allen of the *Jewish Daily Forward*, theologian Reinhold Niebuhr, Jesse H. Holmes, and B. Charney Vladeck. The larger nonaligned "regular" group included Dewey, Williams, and Paul H. Douglas. In an effort to revitalize national third-partyism, the regulars along with Thomas R. Amlie, Fiorello La Guardia, Ernest Lundeen, and William Mahoney called a September 2-3 meeting in Chicago (the "United Conference for Progressive Political Action"). The conference soon was under attack, from the progressive right and men like Philip La Follette of Wisconsin and William Lemke of North Dakota, to the socialist left. Protesting still another attempt to market public ownership policies under a new label, LIPA Socialists, led by Niebuhr, Allen, and Hochman, publicly resigned from LIPA.[41]

Conference delegates represented protest organizations and a few labor unions: the Farmers Union, the United Farmers of America, the Farm Holiday Association, some AFL and railroad brotherhoods, the Farmer-Labor Association, the Wisconsin Progressive party, Technocracy (a utopian group with faith in an engineered society), and the Communist party. As the depression reached its nadir and the New Deal was about to launch its first programs, the conference tried to shore up third-partyism by creating another organization around which to rally its forces, the Farmer-Labor Political Federation (FLPF). Dispute quickly erupted over who was eligible to join. Fearing an internal monster, economist Paul Douglas of the University of Chicago moved to bar Communists from membership, and his resolution carried despite sharp denunciation by Benjamin Gitlow, a Communist who later broke with the party.

The FLPF platform was a mixture of noncommunist dialectic, utopian hope, and economic denunciation. "The old system is crumbling. We need courage and intelligence to build a new order," its preamble stated in judgment of an era which was coming to an end.[42] Claiming the "two old parties which govern us are paid and bossed by the same Wall Street bankers," it declared they had to be displaced with a new party if the United States's destiny and the dream of an annual $5,000 family income were to be realized.

Nevertheless, cosmetic alterations were not to revitalize the movement. Where LIPA had a "Socialist" party problem, the FLPF was about to assume a Communist one. Intellectual suspicion divided people of letters. Paul Douglas distrusted J. B. S. Hardman because he seemed too friendly with and acceptable to the Communist *Daily Worker*, and Douglas distrusted the radical pacifist A. J. Muste for either cooperating with or being used by the Communists. Worried about Communist infiltration, Douglas at one point suggested FLPF headquarters be moved to Minnesota for better security.[43]

By late 1933 LIPA had nearly expired, and Williams' $5,200 annual salary had become uncollectable because the treasury was empty. LIPA's replacement, the FLPF, was a political curiosity with John Dewey as honorary chairman, Alfred M. Bingham executive secretary, and Williams national organizer. On its executive board sat a group which was ideologically diverse and probably incompatible: Douglas,

Gitlow, Hardman, John Bosch, J. Huntley Dupre (later a member of the faculty at Macalaster College), Ernest Lundeen, and Franklin P. Wood.

In charge of operations, Williams had the task of concentrating 1934 third-party development in the Midwest, especially in Wisconsin, Iowa, and South Dakota where third-partyism was to be made as strong as Minnesota Farmer-Laborism. He confidently predicted that third-partyism "would spread like a prairie fire,"[44] and he was prepared to gamble. The time had come to reject Roosevelt, the New Deal, halfway compromises of Democrats, and in Minnesota the contemptibly heretical idea of fusion. "Those of us who have no illusion about the Minnesota Farmer-Labor party have got to get together before the March convention and organize a campaign of strategy," he told the editor of the *Minnesota Union Advocate*. "I regard the situation as very critical."[45] This was an understatement, and Williams's recklessness would come near to demolishing the Farmer-Labor ediface and with it a careless Floyd B. Olson.

1934: A SHIFT IN OLSON'S IDEOLOGY AND FARMER-LABOR GOOD FORTUNE

Although Floyd Olson and Farmer-Laborism became more belligerent in 1933, many liberal Democrats (and some conservatives) continued to be generally satisfied with his leadership. For Olson, Democrats were always a constraint, sometimes a barrier, and ever necessary in pursuing objectives, whether personal or programmatic. After Olson had attacked the evils of chain banking in a speech before the Independent Bankers Association, Democratic St. Paul industrialist Robert Butler offered praise as well as temptation by noting regret "that you announced that you are going to run for Governor again instead of Senator."[46] Olson rarely neglected his Democratic contacts.

Day's Plan for Olson's Reelection

Neither Olson nor Vince Day considered it possible to turn away from Democrats and still survive politically. In private Day admitted that some form of socialism would emerge in the United States (unemployment was now near 25 percent); though he did not define this, it appeared to include the welfare state. Day's view of the ideal world was not unlike that of Howard Y. Williams, but (unlike Williams) Day remained highly skeptical about joining Minnesota to any national third-party movement.

To steer Olson away from political dangers, Day reminded the governor of the reasons for 1932 Farmer-Labor success. He gave partial credit to the Democratic party split, a fight for control over national patronage in Minnesota, and the secret understandings between Democrats and Farmer-Laborites. "What made the Farmer-Labor party successful has been fusion with the State Democratic Party," Day conceded. "This destroyed the Democratic Party of Minnesota," Day continued, warning that to be avoided at all costs was any action which encouraged or allowed Democrats to reunite, for once they did so Farmer-Laborism would be undermined to the point of either giving victory to the Republicans or having the realigned Democrats displace Farmer-Laborites as the party of majority protest.

Day guided Olson away from rather than toward national third-partyism and a broad autonomous Farmer-Labor realignment independent of the Democratic New Deal, and he urged continued political restraint:

> We are now confronted with another form of slavery, that of the capitalistic system. The cause for the organization of a new party is present, but the time is inopportune. . . . If there isn't one state in this union that is willing to create a co-operative commonwealth; there is a slight chance of doing it through a national organization.[47]

The Patronage Upheaval

Ideology aside, Olson bore another growing burden which partially stripped Farmer-Laborism of its humanitarian image. Opening state government to Farmer-Labor spoilsmen rescued Olson from few of his critics and added more than it removed. By mid-1933 wholesale firing of incumbents was being justified on the grounds that Republicans and Democrats had done it previously. An old vice was suddenly transformed into a new virtue. At nearly every level of job classification the Farmer-Labor spoils machine went to work. Some employees with several decades' experience were fired, and technically the discharges were within the law; not until 1939 would civil service laws be reformed to protect state employees.

The systematically cold-blooded operation was efficiently expedited by Joseph Poirier and I. C. Strout. Strout, state hotel inspector until May 1933 when he took over as state budget commissioner and personnel director, came to the job prepared; he used a recently completed 1932 file classification system and a statewide list of all Farmer-Labor clubs to weed out the holdovers. In June 1933 he put into operation a weekly orgy of firings, his only restraint being prior clearance of the firings by the governor's office. To gain, or retain, state employment, each employee had to have a Farmer-Labor sponsor—normally this meant the endorsement of the local Farmer-Labor club in the district in which the employee resided—and an otherwise spotless political record. The local clubs enthusiastically joined in the talent search by examining local job lists within their geographic jurisdiction. Understandably enough, membership in local Farmer-Labor clubs increased accordingly!

Strout's files contained page upon page of personnel records whose notations carried gratuitous evaluations like "not a good Farmer-Laborite," "opposed to F-L Movement," "adverse to F-L Movement," "Good Republican"; rare to nonexistent were references to quality of work and competence. No one was exempt; covered were clerks, stenographers, janitors to section and department heads. Official objects of scorn were not just Republicans, Democrats (though some care had to be used since they had patronage leverage of their own), independents, but even those accused of not voting! Incumbents were guilty until proven innocent. So efficient had Strout become that he hired undercover agents who conducted background investigations to verify party regularity. "Our undercover investigator reports positive information that this whole family supported Republican candidate for governor," Strout once informed party veteran George H. Griffith, making a mockery of the secret ballot principle. Another investigator reported that a state employee could not possibly be a Farmer-Laborite because her parents were known Republicans who, in addition, collected rent money from a house they owned! Ideological heresy and guilt by association were now accepted grounds for dismissal, and relief was attainable for a variety of injustices. For example, the wife of St. Paul Farmer-Labor leader S. S. Tingle, suspecting her husband of an extramarital liaison with a new young state employee, pressed her case against the conjugal interloper by charging her before the local club of being a Farmer-Labor "pretender" which compromised her fitness as a club member. Reluctant to testify and not sure how to defend herself, the woman was forced to resign from the club and she soon lost her state position.[48] Farmer-Labor morality had triumphed!

Replacements and holdovers joined clubs in record numbers, few turned down an invitation to subscribe to the *Farmer-Labor Leader*, and the party paper was at last operating on a sound financial base. To critics, Strout offered a simple answer: "Employees must be in sympathy with the state Administration in order to serve most efficiently."[49] But those benefits came at high cost and were beginning to give the new administration its first public black eye.

Olson Moves Left

Another change occurring in late summer was the mounting criticism that Olson levied against depression-accelerated deficiencies in the American economic system. The psychological burden he bore as a governor who witnessed human suffering and disorder, and who too often was powerless to overcome its basic causes, not only proved to be wearing but also unquestionably contributed to Olson's drift toward the political left. In addition, Olson faced growing left-wing criticism, and his more acerbic attacks upon capitalism seemed in part an attempt to regain the support of Farmer-Labor collectivists who were apparently becoming more influential in the association under the spoils system.

The militant farm movement likewise presented him with a serious dilemma.[50] Farm Holiday Association (FHA) leaders looked to Olson and a handful of midwestern governors for political help in enacting the FHA national program of "cost of production plus profit," moratoriums on farm foreclosures, and the Frazier mortgage refinancing bill. FHA was split between militants like Minnesota's John Bosch and its more restrained national president, Milo Reno. Only at the last moment were Olson and Reno able to head off a May 1933 national farmers' strike, but the farm radicals were little satisfied with Roosevelt's new Agricultural Adjustment Act; Bosch demanded that Roosevelt adopt the FHA program, and when this did not occur an October 21 farmers' strike was voted.

Once again Olson was caught in the middle. In 1932 the Holiday movement had been one of his important campaign allies, and he needed its help again. Olson and four other midwestern governors met on October 29 in Des Moines, from where they moved to Washington to confront the president. Olson accepted most of the Holiday program; nevertheless, he remained adamantly opposed to the boycotts (because they often led to violence) and always worked behind-the-scenes to stop them (though when violence threatened or occurred he refused to direct the state highway police to intercede against the boycott). This policy lost him support among Minnesota's conservative southern farmers who were more economically secure and less injured by the depression and who wanted farm-to-market roads kept open.[51] The Minnesota south remained a weak Farmer-Labor area.

While contending with farm militants, Olson in his economic speeches also increasingly expressed apparent growing sympathy for the general principle of public ownership. He argued that substantial changes were imperative if economic security was to be achieved, and before an Eagles convention in August he expressed doubt whether collective economic well-being was possible until key industries were nationalized. Addressing the Junior Association of Commerce on January 22, he described the capitalistic system as vicious, based on individualism, the profit motive, and concentrated rather than broadly distributed wealth.[52] However, with Olson almost always there was a qualification which left in doubt just what he personally advocated or would do as a government official. Accordingly, he warmly embraced the new Roosevelt federal programs, the implication being that the imbalance of interests was being reversed, not by socialism but the New Deal. Citing the almost revolutionary pace of change in the past two years, more rapid than ever before with more to come, he declared

> Today we are endeavoring to save the system we call Capitalism, by attempting to curb selfish individualism, and the avaricious profit motive. . . . That there will be anything left of the so-called Capitalistic system, when the ultimate changes take place, is very doubtful, that there will be great change is certain.[53]

What did Olson mean? Businessmen might complain about growing bureaucratic regulations, high taxes, and a costly welfare state, but Roosevelt and presumably Olson were letting capitalism mend and find its own way into the future. On the other hand, radicals saw Olson's new speeches as evidence he had finally joined with them, was advocating the cooperative commonwealth and socialism, and was preparing to fight not just Republicans but capitalists and Democrats as well. Confident that it could control the gubernatorial nomination, the left even began to urge Olson to seek the Senate seat held by Shipstead, whose basic ideological imperfections and reticence to speak the left's political language caused it to number him among their targeted enemies.[54]

The Disastrous Farmer-Labor Convention

Although militants were planning to press the convention into radicalizing the party platform, apparently no one anticipated the political disaster which the March 1934 convention of the Farmer-Labor Association would bring, not even Republicans and the normally critical press. Conventional wisdom then was that Farmer-Laborism had been strengthened and would emerge more powerful after the election. After all, its advantages were greater than in 1930-32, there was a "Republican depression" worse than ever before imagined, tremendously high unemployment existed, a 1933 reform program was just now getting under way, and a dynamic, popular governor belonged to the movement.

Farmer-Laborism faced a choice. It could continue to espouse moderate reform and avoid radical change, or it could void the 1930-32 approaches and embark upon a campaign for public ownership. Previously, Olson had imposed restraint upon the left, thereby controlling it by setting a moderate tone for the movement. But with deep depression and patronage as a new rudder, the left had grown stronger and Farmer-Labor socialists were determined to break out of the past pattern. Olson, for a variety of reasons, would fail to contain them, perhaps out of indifference, carelessness, miscalculation, and because he was increasingly physically disabled and weary, worn down by ulcers (precancerous) and declining strength.

This year the left was resolved not to be pushed aside. For three years it had chaffed under restraint, cursed Olson's abominable all-party campaigns, fought appointment and retention of non-Farmer-Laborites in state government, and condemned his resistance to joining Minnesota to the national third-party realignment. In early March, reflecting this intransigence, the twelfth Minneapolis ward Farmer-Labor club distributed a denunciatory resolution charging the all-party tactic with being "the major threat to the Third Party Movement in Minnesota" and demanded an end to any Farmer-Labor policies designed "to salvage the existing capitalistic system."[55] Depression had changed attitudes and altered rhetoric accordingly; it brought University of Minnesota student Lee Loevinger, for example, to describe armament firms as being like society's gangsters.[56]

Olson was mindful of these changes and feared they could damage the party unless checked. He worked against efforts of radicals to dump Shipstead. Always very strong in Hennepin County, the left had not allowed the senator's endorsement even to be considered in the county convention, though (mysteriously) this action was reversed a week later. But the Hennepin Farmer-Laborites, determined to end agreements and trades with Democrats, asked that all candidates be divorced from "old party affiliation" (Socialists and the left were not included!) unless exception was granted by the executive committee, and to ensure ideological purity, no endorsement was to be given any candidate who had been an association member for less than six months. The Hennepin association platform was explicitly public ownership: it called for a state-owned central bank, government ownership of all utilities and natural resources, and government-developed hydroelectric power.[57]

Although the bipartisan statutory income tax law had recently been constitutionally upheld by the state supreme court, Farmer-Laborites were becoming boldly partisan. The left wanted Farmer-Laborism to cut its centrist ties and become independent. When St. Paul Democrat John J. McDonough decided to be a congressional candidate, Farmer-Laborites overlooked his record of supporting liberal state legislation, and speaking through the *St. Paul Union Advocate* the left cautioned Farmer-Laborites against supporting McDonough because he had been little else than a personal legislative spokesman for the governor.[58]

Thus the Farmer-Labor Association's mood in convention was testy, even surly.

Olson's Historic Convention Address. Olson appeared determined to capture the passion and emotion of the moment, but the motivations behind his hour-long convention address are largely obscure rather than logically clear. Had he finally joined with the radicals? Was he attempting to thwart the left by temporarily acting as one with it in rhetorical outburst? Had he really changed his economic and political thinking? And was his speech meant primarily for the 700 delegates but not the popular masses? Postconvention behavior further obfuscated the meaning and purpose of this speech, which, deservedly or not, became the classic Olson address, remembered and often quoted.

Olson spoke in general terms, as a prophet, about some future ideal republic, yet even so at times he lapsed into political carelessness and tempted the catastrophic fates of 1934. He projected a vision of a more perfect union, not to incite or enflame Farmer-Labor radical passions but to direct them toward more immediate causes and a tolerance for outside liberals. The "ultimate Cooperative Commonwealth" would eventually succeed capitalism, war was a curse of capitalism, and, he declared, "certainly no one in the light of what has happened in the last few years can defend the so-called capitalistic system."[59] At one point he sounded unequivocal; capitalism was said to be unreformable and would ultimately have to be replaced with the Cooperative Commonwealth, a term which in 1934 had important if fuzzy ideological meaning to some Farmer-Laborites. Olson, however, admitted difficulty in defining such a political state of existence except to say that it would comprise a system of cooperative enterprises, public ownership, and direct governmental control. He predicted eventual government ownership in communication (telephones, telegraphs, radios) and transportation, but food and product distribution would likely be handled through consumer cooperatives.

Beyond such idealism Olson counseled restraint and evolutionary incremental changes only through lawful governmental acts based not on narrow Farmer-Labor agitation but on broad political support beyond the party. He offered no timetable, avoided mention of immediate legislative proposals, speculated that the Roosevelt Democratic New Deal might begin taxing corporations to set up cooperative factories for basic commodity production, and appealed to Farmer-Laborites to work with liberals and moderates: "by no action of ours shall we rebuff anyone who wishes to assist us."[60] Although he admitted that Farmer-Laborites should willingly run for office under their own label (an obvious reference to Shipstead) and allow the association to exercise control over a candidate by directing his or her campaign through an association committee (something which Olson never permitted in his campaigns, and would not in 1934), no one should be expelled from the party. Farmer-Laborism needed the help of "fine liberal folks." And it should not fall prey to narrow partisan patronage.

Despite spreading ideological conflict between Communism and Fascism, Olson believed that neither movement put Americans in imminent danger because "tory conservatism" was the real enemy. Mindful of how earlier Red-scare campaigns had injured Farmer-Laborism, he seemingly dismissed the threat now: "when the final clash comes between Americanism and fascism, we will find a so-called red as the defender of democracy and the super patriot and captain of industry on the side of mass slavery."

Whatever Olson's intention, his words did not counsel political moderation in 1934; nor were they a comfort to party centrists in the movement, nor to Democrats and nonsocialists beyond it. It was not when he urged bipartisan and broad nonpartisan toleration that delegates roared approval but when he articulated collectivist dogmas and principles:

> Now, I am frank to say that I am not a liberal. I enjoy working on a common basis with liberals for their platforms, etc., but I am not a liberal. I am what I want to be — I am a radical. I am a radical in the sense that I want a definite change in the system. I am not satisfied with tinkering. I am not satisfied with patching. I am not satisfied with hanging a laurel wreath upon burglars and thieves and pirates and calling them code authorities or something else. I am not satisfied with that.
>
> I want, however, an orderly, a sane and a constructive change. I don't want any more visionary things any more than the hardest tory conservative wants it, but I know the transition can take place and that of course it must be gradual.[61]

These were the words which rang in the rafters and stayed in the minds of delegates, newspapers, the public, and his opposition. This is why they were so puzzled. Nearly always Olson was quick to include a qualification. What did he mean, what were people to believe, what would be of immediate public impact? Olson had asked that there be no sudden shifts in public policy, even cautioned against it. Change, he said, should be evolutionary, not by "jerks and spurts." Yet he had carelessly treaded an impossible political course, and he soon would pay a heavy price.

Why had Olson spoken as he had? Then, as now, those who wanted to perceive Olson as "radicalized" could easily make their case. Nevertheless, Olson had to be judged as much by his actions as by his words. After his speech he left the convention, seemingly indifferent to it, and went off to Washington to lobby for a park along the Minnesota River and to express support for the farm recovery program of Land O'Lakes president John Brandt. Worse, he left no one to expertly guide the convention, something he had not done in 1930 or 1932.

A Radical Platform Embarrasses Farmer-Labor Candidates. Although Olson and Vince Day should have known better, both apparently assumed either the left or the convention would exercise self-restraint and not carelessly press for programmatic radicalism in public policy. But there was less reason in 1934 to expect moderation, especially in the absence of Olson's direct intervention. Vince Day had argued with Olson that farmers often were more radical than Farm Holiday leaders, a point made the previous October by John Bosch, and Day speculated that Roosevelt was losing some farm support. Day had familiarized Olson with the Alberta Cooperative Commonwealth Federation ideas, and Olson's convention speech reflected this briefing. Furthermore, Olson knew that Farmer-Labor socialists, led by George Griffith, I. C. Strout, Irene Welby and Carl Erickson, were determined to expel and defeat Shipstead. Not only did Day and Olson consider such a move politically suicidal for all Farmer-Laborism, but Olson sternly warned Shipstead's critics to be diplomatic with the senator and to keep the movement broad rather than narrow. Olson, both during and after his historic convention address, sought to mediate between the antagonistic sides, which may be the reason for his rhetorical journey into the future. Day was convinced the left had to be restrained. "This group," he noted, is "determining the policy of the Party on the basis of personal grudges, and unless checked will not only drive Shipstead out of the Party, but all his friends."[62]

This feeling was conveyed to convention strategists friendly to Olson. He and Day wanted another moderate Farmer-Labor ticket which would include Shipstead, and their wish was honored. Shipstead's only announced opponent was Congressman Francis Shoemaker, who had brought an element of notoriety to himself and the movement when, after only a few months in Washington, he had been arrested for intoxication, brawling, and assaulting a taxi driver. And as was usually the case, the left had few if any popular and able candidates. At a 2 A.M. showdown on March 29, after *Minneapolis Labor Review* editor Robley D. (Red) Cramer delivered a strong defense of Shipstead, the senator received a narrow endorsement. Since Olson was believed to be running for his last term as governor, lieutenant governor K. K. Solberg was eased out and moved into the secretary of state slot; state representative Hjalmer Petersen (editor/publisher of the *Askov American*), the house sponsor and floor leader for the income tax bill, was chosen to run with Olson. John T. Lyons became the Farmer-Labor candidate for auditor, and state senator Laura Naplin of Thief River Falls was selected to run for clerk of the supreme court. In sum, as Olson and Day wanted, the ticket was moderate, not radical, in keeping with previous Farmer-Labor campaigns.

One matter remained to be settled. The platform. Unfortunately for Olson and the moderates, the platform committee was filled with advocates of public ownership and chaired by none other than recently returned Howard Y. Williams. Working closely with him were Duluth attorney Sigmond Slonin, a socialist, and state representative Emil Youngdahl, a Minneapolis left-winger. The three were determined to make the current Farmer-Labor party stand, not as planner of some futuristic Cooperative Commonwealth, but as a flesh-and-blood advocate of socialism and a true alternative to the New Deal.

Where Olson's address had been deliberately vague, general, and had espoused gradual incremental change, Williams's words called for immediate transition to public ownership. In committee and on the floor only St. Paul labor leader Frank Starkey and state senator Emil Regnier of Marshall (Lyon County) fought this radical departure. The preamble mandated swift far-reaching change:

> We, therefore declare that capitalism has failed and *immediate steps must be taken* by the people to abolish capitalism in a peaceful and lawful manner and that a new sane and just society be established.[63] [Italics added.]

Williams stirred the delegates in a manner reminiscent of his clerical days and early trips on the Chautauqua circuit. The state of Minnesota was to become owner and operator of mines, hydroelectric power plants, transportation, communications, packinghouses, public utilities, insurance, and all factories except those cooperatively owned and operated. Until all banks were nationalized a state-owned bank system would replace private state-chartered banks. School texts were to be published by the state. At the top of this list was a demand for the "commandeering [of] sufficient idle industrial plants" to provide employment for the jobless. Williams's speech in the early morning hours exhorted Farmer-Laborism to break with incrementalism and to move forward boldly with courage and dispatch. Weary delegates shouted hurrahs for public ownership and the left at last felt triumph in its grasp. However, Olson and Day would blame Williams and the collectivists for bringing on campaign chaos and disaster.

Undoing the Damage Caused by a Radical Platform

The public ownership platform immediately forced Farmer-Labor candidates and Olson into political retreat, though Olson, still in Washington, initially gave it his personal endorsement. But Vince Day minced no words. He told Olson the platform was a "major political blunder" which was certain to alienate small merchants, bankers, insurance agents, and factory owners, and to cost Farmer-Laborism thousands of supporters, maybe the election.

As Olson's key adviser on tactics and programs, Day offers the best clues about Olson's thinking on politics and political economy. Day argued that the state ownership plank had snatched away almost certain victory, shaken public confidence, encouraged the opposition, and ensured "an active and aggressive campaign over the issue of radicalism and captialism."[64] Although Day himself continued to believe that capitalism because of its seeming inability (or unwillingness) to distribute production to workers and consumers, was slowing dying and needed to be replaced by a "new political economy" or a "new political science," he saw Olson's immediate role and that of the Farmer-Labor party more as a tactical manager of social change rather than as a catalyst for rapid alteration of basic economic relationships. Peaceful social upheavals of the kind advocated by socialists and collectivists were dangerous, Day contended, because they heightened class conflict, under extreme conditions threatened physical mayhem, and might be self-defeating since they could return political power to Republicans and to those least sympathetic to economic redress and long-term programmatic reform.

Specifically, Day described Williams and the platform writers as a politically ignorant minority faction, and he warned Olson that an association brain trust composed of Carl Erickson, Strout, Griffith, and

A. R. Rathert was following a strategy of rule or ruin, was eliminating from the movement those who held different ideological views, was "intoxicated with power" and indifferent to political advice which conflicted with its socialized programmatic objectives.

> The Farmer-Labor Association is run by a group [of] jealous, ambitious, [men] and [is] greedy for power. They organize locals and then deny membership to some of the best friends of the movement. I found this to be the situation in Detroit Lakes. Men that I have known for years who have been affiliated with the movement are not permitted to join by a small group who control the Ass[ociation] for the purpose of dispensing patronage.

Finally, Day contended that the politically suicidal platform immediately obscured campaign issues and confused the overwhelming majority of campaign workers because they "do not understand it, cannot defend it, nor can they explain it."[65]

On the defensive and faced with an unwanted political crisis, Olson now was fast retreating and in less than a fortnight he delivered over WCCO radio a statewide address which sought to explain the Farmer-Labor platform. Olson denied public ownership was a Farmer-Labor goal; rather, it was said to be a Cooperative Commonwealth. Wealth was too concentrated (he claimed that 1 percent controlled 59 percent of national wealth), and he quoted Presbyterian Church Assembly resolutions and Pope Pius XI to demonstrate their concern (like Farmer-Laborism's) for modern man's economic plight. And Olson, in an obvious warning to third-party radicals, once more embraced Franklin Roosevelt and said that Farmer-Laborism stood "four-square with the churches."[66]

From editor George Creel of the *Farmer-Labor Leader* came a more curious explanation. His page-one editorial reaffirmed belief in peaceful, lawful change, and, in an elementary way, Creel explained how the system of checks and balances worked. Creel implied that although a party might propose programs, two legislative houses might change the proposals, these in turn could be overruled by courts, and it was very politically American to get less than what one wanted![67]

The first tests of the platform's impact were not long in coming. The *Minneapolis Tribune* saw a clear choice facing Minnesota voters, and other metropolitan papers suddenly turned increasingly critical of Olson and correctly identified the platform as a rather natural extension of his convention address.[68] A few defended the platform, including *Askov American* editor Hjalmer Petersen[69] (who quickly changed his mind and in 1938 undertook a massive campaign against Farmer-Labor radicals) and of course Howard Y. Williams, who saw it as suitable ignition for the 1934 midwestern campaign of the Farmer-Labor Political Federation.[70] In six weeks, however, Williams personally complained to Olson[71] and charged Farmer-Labor officeholders with backsliding and "pussyfooting" on what he said had been such a simple direct expression of Farmer-Labor principles.

The most serious test of the platform's impact came during the April 24 St. Paul city election. Mayor William Mahoney's opponent was Republican Mark Gehen, who six weeks earlier had been discounted as even a serious challenger. Then, with the platform as evidence of Farmer-Labor intent, Gehen loosened a drive to save the city from the clutches of socialism and communism, and forced Mahoney into headlong retreat by a daily barrage of antisocialist assaults.[72] After 94,000 votes were counted it seemed that the left had managed to turn certain victory into defeat, and Gehen was the unexpected victor, winning by a margin of 500 votes.

Olson needed no further warning; survival necessitated a change of direction. On May 1 Day met for five hours with Starkey, Hjalmer Petersen, and Harry Boyle to hammer out a long series of platform "explanations." Day rewrote these into a final version which was published in the May 15 *Farmer-Labor Leader.*[73] Such lengthy "interpretations" were treated as the official platform, the convention version was ignored, and previous copies of it were destroyed!

The disastrous convention platform engineered by Williams also helped undermine the LIPA/FLPF midwestern campaign for thirdpartyism. In April and May Alfred Bingham traveled to California, Washington, Montana, North Dakota, and Minnesota speaking for the cause, but he and Williams suffered new rebuffs. When Williams pleaded with Wisconsin's Philip La Follette and Olson to sponsor a midsummer FLPF conference, Olson refused to help, Minnesota criticism of Williams grew, Farmer-Labor candidates shied from him, Wisconsin's Progressive party resisted the FLPF, and North Dakota's William Lemke suggested that Progressives return to the Republican party to control it. Sales of Paul Douglas's book on the need for a new third party fell sharply.[74] Factional disorder erupted in Minnesota's small Socialist party (SP) where a majority of its members also belonged to the Farmer-Labor Association. In 1934 militant Socialists, led by W. W. Norris, seized control of the SP, sought to expel Thomasites and "moderates" who also participated in Farmer-Laborism, and demanded strict loyalty to their party.[75]

The 1934 Primary

By the June 18 primary the destabilizing effect of the platform had been arrested but not reversed, and Farmer-Laborism seemed to be losing some support to Democrats. Moderates were all nominated, Olson easily, Shipstead by a three to one margin over Shoemaker, Charles Munn for the Railroad and Warehouse Commission, Richard T. Buckler in the Ninth Congressional District (defeating A. C. Townley). The only major endorsee to lose was Laura Naplin for supreme court clerk.

Republicans, too, avoided bitter contests as Tom Davis (a maverick Farmer-Laborite) failed to upset N. J. Holmberg's Senate nomination and Austin lawyer Martin A. Nelson (a state supreme court justice in 1953-72) won nomination for governor. Democratic congressman Einar Hoidale once more was running for the Senate, and (against seven competitors) John Regan had won his second gubernatorial nomination. What had to be of most concern to Farmer-Laborites was the steady rise in Democratic votes:

Party	No. of Votes	Percentage of Total Vote
Farmer-Labor	280,152	39.3%
Democratic	267,248	37.4%
Republican	166,252	23.3%

Republican defection was not to Farmer-Laborites but to Democrats, whose primary vote had been only 15,000 in 1930, 106,000 (20 percent) in 1932, and now had more than doubled to 267,000 (27 percent), nearly equal to the Farmer-Labor showing.

Looking at the returns, Vince Day found Farmer-Labor appeal weakest in German Catholic regions, and to strengthen it he recommended that Olson appoint a representative from these localities, either Herman Aufderheide of New Ulm or John T. Lyons, as party chairman or campaign manager.

Coping with Labor Disputes

The fourth year of Olson's Farmer-Labor administration was marked by a series of severe labor organizational disputes which further tarnished though did not destroy the moderate image that Olson and other Farmer-Labor candidates sought to project from summer to autumn. As strikes turned into bloody confrontations they complicated 1934 election strategy, and they renewed concern about radicalism and leadership in the industrial union movement. Olson, the 1934 platform, the later "interpretations," and Farmer-Laborism in general had always gone out of its way to stress peacful, orderly, lawful change. Presumedly, or by implication, such a pledge extended to industrial relations since the movement claimed steadfastly that unions and their members had a special place in the Farmer-Labor firmament. Farmer-

Laborism (and city Democrats) by name and nature was very attractive to organized labor, to those who wanted and were yet to be organized, and to sympathizers with the union movement. Politically, however, the support labor gave Farmer-Laborism carried a considerable price and occasionally was in danger of becoming a net liability. Farm strikes might injure blue-collar truckers (unionized or not), and teamster and general drivers strikes closed off city markets to farmers and farm commodities. When strikes became violent and union organizational leadership was in the hands of socialists, communists, or Trotskyites, this appeared to dispute moderate Farmer-Labor claims about its intent and process.

Opening an Antiunion Metropolis. Minneapolis industry had long neutralized organized labor by working through a loose but effective local trade organization called the Citizens Alliance, giving the city a deserved reputation for being open to business but closed to unions. Union influence after 1918 was largely limited to the traditional AFL craft unions, especially in the building trades, and even those found their economic and political outreach constrained. But the New Deal, particulary Roosevelt's National Industrial Recovery Act and its section 7a, would steadily reverse labor's impotence by guaranteeing it the right to organize and bargain collectively.

The depression sharpened the union's determination to break the open shop pattern, encouraged bold and militant organizers to move into shop and industrial unions, attracted ideological radicals, and convinced some unionists that force coupled with disabling strikes were not only necessary and reasonable but ideologically justified and morally sanctioned. The disputes that resulted from these attitudes provoked a like response in owners, investors, managers, and businessmen, and led to unmanaged social conflict.

The classic confrontation of 1934 came in May, July, and August during strikes directed by Minneapolis Teamster Local 574. This union was ably led by three Trotskyite communists, the Dunne brothers (Grant, Miles and Vincent), all dedicated members of the Socialist Workers party. Their organizing successes were substantial: in February the coal drivers and in May the general drivers. Sensing erosion of its heretofore undisputed hegemony, the Citizens Alliance mobilized for a showdown. The alliance was determined not to negotiate or arbitrate and, unwisely, the businessmen in late May decided that they were an even physical match for the burly teamsters. After two days of bloodletting in the streets, Olson sent in 4,000 national guardsmen to restore order, and temporary—but not permanent—agreements were worked out.

A priest and a federal mediator had failed in May to arrange a settlement; Olson in June and early July met with no more success. Business refused any written agreement. In retaliation, Local 574 called a general drivers strike in mid-July, pickets began roaming streets, and commercial transportation was effectively shut down. This time the Republican city administration of Mayor A. G. Bainbridge ordered police chief Mike ("Bloody Mike") Johannes to terminate the strike which had created near street anarchy in some areas. Once again Olson found himself in the middle. To call in the national guard, in effect, meant to break the strike even if it was only intended to protect life and property. Olson sympathized with the union's wish to gain collective-bargaining rights, but he publicly expressed neutrality when he mobilized several thousand national guardsmen. The first climax came July 20 when fifty police escorted a delivery truck which was seeking to breach a picket barricade. With little or no warning, the police opened a shotgun barrage; when order had been restored two had been killed, about sixty-seven were wounded, some having been shot in the back while fleeing.

Olson declared martial law and set up a permit system for deliveries, national guardsmen patrolled streets, and leaders of Local 574 condemned the governor as a strikebreaker. For a month the city was administered under martial law while negotiations continued and Olson pushed for a settlement generally favorable to workers and the principle of collective bargaining. But he also had to defend his martial law proclamation in federal court, which (as a lawyer) he personally argued; eventually he won a favorable if reluctant decision justifying his action.

Politically, however, the 1934 teamster strike was difficult to assess accurately. It hardly gained Farmer-Laborism new converts, and it reinforced some public fear that beyond the party yet within the environment of social and economic change there lurked radical forces prone to violence and revolution. Nevertheless, the strike diverted attention from the party's radical platform, and it demonstrated Olson's committment to restoring order and legal process and his willingness to use national guardsmen against mass, violent, perhaps Marxist-led strikes. His action also served as a future warning to Trotskyite adventurousness.

More important in the long run, this strike reinforced moderates' understanding of third-party vulnerability and the continued advantages, indeed the necessity, of working with a national Democratic administration. During the second week in August, when Roosevelt visited Minnesota, Olson conferred privately with him and won a reassuring promise: the president agreed to exert pressure for a strike settlement on Minnesota banks and businesses by working through the Reconstruction Finance Corporation (RFC). Thus, while Olson locally attempted to get an agreement, the National Labor Relations Board called for a bargaining election, and the RFC threatened banks and businesses with a cutoff of loan funds unless the trucking owners and their allies capitulated. On August 21, after four months of acrimonious conflict, the Minneapolis business alliance agreed to a settlement, the strike ended, and the open-shop policy came to an end.[76]

The Fall Farmer-Labor Campaign

Olson's campaign this year proved to be his most difficult. Beginning first with his convention speech, then the platform, and finally the teamster ordeal, he spent a great amount of time on the defensive, reacting to the stresses and disorder. When the time came for campaigning, he returned to the all-party format and what Day labeled the "Roosevelt line" of strategy.[77]

Olson's approach met with no favor among most Farmer-Labor socialists, but to Olson and the state ticket it seemed the only sensible means to victory. Olson fought chain stores, banks, the steel industry and monopoly, and Republicanism and reactionary response to crisis while the thousands of copies of his platform interpretations were mailed throughout the state. He did talk about a vague Cooperative Commonwealth, but in his fall campaign keynote speech and those that followed he firmly secured Farmer-Laborism to Roosevelt's New Deal and emphasized progressive nonradical political alternatives leading to gradual change. His turnabout from March so embittered Howard Y. Williams that the FLPF organizer charged the state Farmer-Labor movement had been abandoned by its own office seekers. Symbolically enough, FLPF finances were just as depressed, and Williams was forced to live on $100 each month, a mere fraction of what he had been promised.

Olson's public rhetoric had to be measured against his private conversations and actions. During the depression Olson acted primarily as a manager of social conflict rather than as a catalyst or party theoretician advancing rapid fundamental social change. His speeches, although designed to recruit personal and party support, also had the objective of disarming advocates of direct action and radical change which could heighten conflict. His private acts and communications pursued similar objectives. Six weeks before the election he demonstrated another attitude about governance which during the upheavals of the 1930s made him into a political craftsman. Out of public ear-

shot he told the Minnesota insurance industry that he was "not therefore . . . bound by the platform of my party," and he assured the
industry that, aside from old-age pensions (the Social Security system
had not yet been enacted), "mother's pension," maternity allowances,
and the like, he generally opposed the state of Minnesota's entry into
the insurance business.[78] By no means did businesses and corporations
consider Olson an economic and social ally, and they continued to
curse increased corporate taxes, regulations, unionization, and Farmer-
Labor and Democratic reforms. Nonetheless, more astute businessmen
and industry sources considered Olson a friendly and usually trust-
worthy adversary whose rhetoric often exceeded his adminstration's
practices and whose policies were, under the circumstances, reasonable
rather than radical. They distinguished him from the socialists and
were much more charitable and less suspicious than they would be with
the next, and last, Farmer-Labor administration.

Olson and other Farmer-Labor candidates faced a difficult campaign.
Badly in need of Democratic votes, the governor praised Roosevelt
and claimed the president and he both worked for the same goals. A
major challenge was the renewal of enthusiasm for Democrats. Olson
pictured Regan as being out of step with the Democratic New Deal,
yet Olson and Day worried about keeping Regan sufficiently active in
the campaign so that he would retain conservative Democratic votes
and otherwise prevent defection to the Republican Martin Nelson.
Once more Olson's all-party style drew scorn from the left wing, and
he was attacked by the independent-filing A. C. Townley, who charged
Olson with masterminding a 1936 plan to lead Farmer-Laborism into
the Democratic party.[79] To Howard Williams such behavior was simply
expressive of a "turncoat attitude."[80]

In the final two weeks of the campaign Olson gained the political up-
perhand, helped in part by left-wing criticism which made him appear
moderate. Republicans charged Olson with driving jobs away from Minnesota and contributing to the unemployment problem. Olson came
out in favor of the merit civil service system and in the last days ignored
Regan and Nelson and concentrated his attacks upon the Citizens Alliance and two Minneapolis papers, the *Journal* and the *Tribune*.[81]

As usual, Henrik Shipstead waged a shrewd campaign. The senator
always avoided radical linkups and controversy, had no role in the disastrous March convention, and the fact that he once again (for the last
time) agreed to run on the Farmer-Labor label seemed additional proof
that party candidates were not ideologues but safe moderates. Shipstead faced a much weaker Republican opponent in N. J. Holmberg

but a stronger one in Democratic congressman Einar Hoidale, and he remained typically aloof and independent of the regular Farmer-Labor organization. Indirectly, however, Shipstead's presence helped Olson and the entire Farmer-Labor state ticket. Olson and Shipstead were on the threshhold of new victories, and Farmer-Laborism owed some of its success in regaining lost ground to their joint presence on the ticket; but measured against the high expectations of the previous winter, the outcome still had to be counted a setback.

Election Results

Farmer-Laborism appeared far from doomed as its modified campaign won five of eight state offices, Olson and Shipstead were reelected, three of its nine congressional candidates were victorious, and John T. Lyons (Farmer-Labor candidate for state auditor) was only 649 votes from defeating Stafford King. Farmer-Labor percentages ranged between 34 and 47, but Democrats were an ominous presence as they carried between 16 and 28 percent of the vote, led by Hoidale, and this cut sharply into the Farmer-Labor margins. No state candidate won half the vote cast, not even Shipstead (47.3 percent), and Olson's plurality (44 percent) dropped to a new low, 72,000. The worst setback came in the nonpartisan legislature, where Republican/conservatives regained control.

Although Republicans had not rebounded everywhere, there were signs of a comeback. They controlled the mayorships in Minneapolis (they would lose this in 1935) and St. Paul, reelected the state auditor and secretary of state, and elected five Republican congressmen: August Andresen (first district), Melvin Maas (fourth), Theodore Christianson (fifth), Harold Knutson (sixth), and William Pittenger (eighth). That is why the partial strengthening of state Democrats loomed so threateningly. Conservative Democratic Elmer Ryan won in the Second Congressional District, in two of nine congressional districts Democrats outpolled Farmer-Laborites, in the seventh they provided the only opposition (41 percent) to Paul Kvale, and in four more congressional districts Democrats polled over 20 percent. If Democrats continued such competitiveness and if their state and congressional campaign was tied to a popular Democratic presidential incumbent, the threat to Farmer-Laborism seemed certain to grow. Farmer-Laborites were now faced with ideological and strategic political choices, particularly between the New Deal and public ownership, and between pursuing independence and reaching agreements with an increasingly stronger Democratic competitor.

RESULTS OF THE 1934 MINNESOTA GENERAL ELECTION

(Candidate, No. of Votes, and Percentage of Total Vote)

OFFICE	REPUBLICAN	DEMOCRATIC	FARMER-LABOR	SOCIALIST	INDEPENDENT	COMMUNIST
Senator	N. J. Holmberg 200,083 (18.8%)	Einar Hoidale 294,757 (27.7%)	Henrik Shipstead 503,379 (47.3%)	Morris Kaplan 5,618 (.5%)		Alfred Tiala 5,620 (.5%)
Governor	Martin Nelson 396,359 (37.2%)	John Regan 176,928 (16.6%)	Floyd B. Olson 468,812 (44.0%)		A. C. Townley 4,454 (.4%)	S. K. Davis 4,334 (.4%)
Lieutenant governor	Franklin Ellsworth 331,747 (31.1%)	Arthur Reynolds 222,144 (20.9%)	Hjalmar Petersen 428,897 (40.3%)			
Attorney general	Oscar Youngdahl 345,372 (32.5%)	Alrie Anderson 190,049 (17.9%)	Harry Peterson 436,140 (40.9%)			Robert Turner 5,791 (.5%)
Secretary of state	Mike Holm 477,573 (44.9%)	H. T. Kennedy 170,545 (16.0%)	K. K. Solberg 359,322 (33.8%)			
Treasurer	Julius Schmahl 394,228 (37.0%)	Maynard Bartley 201,608 (18.9%)	A. H. Kleffman 377,742 (35.5%)			
Auditor	Stafford King 380,302 (35.7%)	Patrick Delaney 221,221 (20.8%)	John Lyons 379,654 (35.7%)			
Railroad and warehouse commissioner	Christian J. Laurisch 337,061 (31.7%)	Robert S. Close 197,264 (18.5%)	Charles Munn 420,117 (39.5%)			
Clerk of the supreme court	Grace K. Davis 336,479 (31.6%)	Clarence Smith 230,457 (21.7%)	Russell Gunderson 382,148 (35.9%)	Oscar Hawkins 5,751 (.5%)		

Note: The total percentage for each office is less than 100 because some voters cast blank ballots and some ballots were spoiled.

Minnesota Farmer-Laborism, by Millard L. Gieske, © 1979 by the University of Minnesota.

Day had become ambivalent about the 1934 platform. Forgetting his midyear anxiety, he told Olson the radical platform had "saved" the party in the sense that it distinguished Farmer-Laborism from other parties, but he worried about the cost in declining small business and farmer support. He also told Olson, "Hjalmar Petersen is the best available candidate in the Party to succeed you as Governor."[82] The just-elected lieutenant governor had reciprocal advice for Day. "That platform nearly broke the camel's back and if ever the Farmer-Laborites learned a lesson that should be it."[83]

CHAPTER 8

The Search
for Olson's Successor

Farmer-Laborism stumbled in disagreement over the real lessons to be learned from the 1934 election, with the result that internal ideological antagonism was unresolved as the time approached for a second generation of leaders to take over. At the same time, apart from its own tactical and strategic errors, Farmer-Laborism was increasingly at the mercy of factors over which it had little or no influence: violent labor organizational strikes, international relations, the United Front strategy and changed Communist tactics, the popularity of the national Democratic administration, and the struggle for power among those who wanted to control the post-Olson governorship.

The Farmer-Labor left continued to insist that much more had been gained than lost by the radical shift in the party's programmatic policy. Howard Williams argued that the platform had saved the party from being like the Democratic party, a contention denied by Farmer-Labor moderates who believed disaster had been averted only by a midcampaign switch in tactics. The dropping of the radical platform, the substitution of interpretations, and subsequent candidate avoidance of even these modifications made socialists more determined than ever to stay their course and defend "production for use" as an alternative to production for profits.

In early December 1934 the LIPA/FLPF sponsored a Mid-West Legislative Conference at St. Paul's Hotel Frederic to help in "creat[ing] a new economic order." Williams's vision was a doomsday choice; either the state and nation chose the Cooperative Commonwealth or it took another dialectical step toward capitalism's next stage, state capitalism or Fascism, as it existed in Germany and Italy.[1] To avoid this calamity Williams, New York publisher Alfred Bingham, economist Paul Douglas, and Wisconsin Progressive Thomas Amlie were determined to unveil a new national third party, which they were sure would receive labor support and generate between 5 and 10 million presidential votes in 1936. To Farmer-Labor moderates, this was pitiful political nonsence. Emil Regnier, the state Farmer-Labor campaign manager in 1932, publicly criticized it and urged Farmer-Labor legislators to boycott Williams's conference.[2]

In Minnesota three major political strategies were set in motion during 1935-36. Republicans hoped to reassemble an effective political coalition and to concentrate on exposing the Farmer-Labor drift toward a more socialized economy. Democrats, if united, would champion New Deal reforms and tie state candidates to Roosevelt; unfortunately for them severe differences divided the conservative John Regan/Joseph Moonan faction from the Joseph Wolf-John Meighen moderates allied with the Roosevelt New Deal. Farmer-Laborites set three goals: to elect Olson U. S. senator, to replace Olson with another Farmer-Labor governor, and to recapture control of the lower house.

OLSON'S 1935 LEGISLATIVE GAMBLE

For over forty years no Minnesota governor had succeeded in becoming a U. S. Senator. Mindful of this, Olson patterned a controversial legislative package which was certain to draw public attention though not necessarily popular approval. Olson could not expect the most controversial proposals to be approved by the current hostile legislature—in the house a renamed Republican/conservative caucus, the Independent Progressives, held a commanding 77 to 53 margin over the liberals. Nonetheless, he called for enactment of a comprehensive program which, rather surprisingly, returned him to a position much closer to the collectivists than the moderates. His 1935 legislative proposals, doomed to be rejected, were threefold:

A broadened *state new deal*, including liberalized old-age pensions, extension of the Mortgage Moratorium Act to May 1937, state enabling legislation for REA to electrify Minnesota farms (88 percent were still without electricity), and authorization for the Rural Credits Bureau to accept payment in crops (rather than cash) for purchased of state-owned land.

Tax reform through reduced homestead taxes, increased chain store and gross earnings utilities taxes, greater reliance on the income tax with "substantially increased" rates in the higher brackets, sharply graduated inheritance tax rates rising to 60 percent for estates valued at $1 million, and exemption of cooperative property from taxation on the basis that co-ops would equitably distribute wealth and income and eventually lead the way toward a Cooperative Commonwealth.

Finally, *public ownership*, beginning with a constitutional amendment authorizing the state to engage in the business of electric production and distribution, public utilities, packing plants, and "other key industries." Olson hoped that munitions manufacture would be nationalized (the desire for profits, it was assumed, caused the munitions industry to be a war monger), and he proposed, if this should happen, that the state mine and sell iron ore directly to the national government on the (mistaken) assumption that the state would sell at cost rather than for profit. Last, he again proposed a state central bank of deposit which would function as banker for government funds.

How radical was Olson becoming? Unquestionably he had moved far from the positions he had taken in 1931 and 1932. But his program for socialization did include a referendum to let the people express a preference either for private business activity or for public ownership of productive property; if voters rejected public ownership, he certainly was capable of declaring the public will to have been expressed. By moving leftward Olson helped reestablish his standing with the left, which had been badly damaged by his rejection of the 1934 platform.

The opposition took a different view. In fact, most of the proposals had no chance of being approved by the present legislature, and, not unexpectedly, the session ended in stalemate, causing Olson to call a short special December session to consider a state pension plan.[3] During and after the regular session legislative leaders were determined not only to defeat Olson's program but to cause him political embarrassment and undermine his expected campaign for the Senate. One device for accomplishing this was the legislative investigation, and the opposition settled on a Farmer-Labor trouble spot, patronage. Under the chairmanship of state senator James A. Carley, a Plainview Democrat, the welfare and highway departments were investigated for Farmer-Labor administrative irregularities; among the objectives of the study was that of discrediting Olson's management of state government.

The blame for so unproductive a legislative year had to be shared by all three parties, but Olson committed a major fault when he insisted on basic economic change instead of making a more limited attempt to bring about an expanded welfare state.

THE STRUGGLE TO SUCCEED OLSON

Olson's desire for the senatorship presented the Farmer-Labor movement with a new set of difficulties. First, his opponent was to be incumbent senator Thomas Schall, who would assuredly wage a dirty campaign. Schall rarely permitted principles to interfere with campaign tactics, and his speeches were likely to show the handiwork of disgruntled journalist Walter Liggett who seemed prepared to muckrake his way into Olson's private life (see pages 209-10).

The second and far worse disruption was over Olson's Farmer-Labor successor. Actually no available Farmer-Laborite could match the governor's political skills and consequently dominate the selection process. So the movement fell to quarreling between factions and over ideology. One of the most openly critical candidates of the outgoing administration was state director of personnel I. C. Strout who had led badgering attacks until Olson finally opened up patronage to the control of the Farmer-Labor Association. A Brainerd railway telegrapher who had entered the movement in the twenties but still maintained his Socialist party membership, Strout was liked by many in the left wing but his candidacy met a quick demise. Olson and Day strongly opposed it and for a long time wanted him removed as personnel director, though they put it off, fearing the antagonism of the association. However, following the exposures by Carley's special senate investigation and after the close of the legislative session, Strout was dismissed, replaced by moderate Emil Regnier.[4] Strout's supporters protested, but the dismissal ended his patronage power, undermined his association influence, and as a result stopped any chance he had for endorsement.

A second, more formidable candidate was state banking commissioner Elmer A. Benson. In light of later Farmer-Labor history, there is irony in Benson's early reputation. Correctly or not, some leftists believed he belonged to the association's moderate wing. As banking commissioner he handled his duties rather conventionally. When in 1935 Benson expressed reservations about some features of the 1934 platform, Howard Williams privately criticized him for lack of faith and incorrectly judged him weak and timid. During the two years he served as commissioner Benson built a state following through local contact, and, importantly, he attracted the attention of Abe Harris and other editorial board members of the association's *Minnesota Leader*, which in the summer of 1935 began a systematic buildup which excluded other potential candidates. Benson's advantage served to further weaken party solidarity, and it provoked charges that a small brain trust in the association was attempting to perpetuate its control and dictate the nomination. Demands were made upon *Leader* editor Henry Teigan to drop the paper's "Benson policy,"[5] but the insiders refused.

Other potential candidates included attorney general Harry Peterson, former congressman and senator Magnus Johnson, representatives Ernest Lundeen and Paul J. Kvale, and lieutenant governor Hjalmar Petersen. The most popular were Lundeen and Petersen, Lundeen because he had cultivated a stronger following with the left (though he also was distrusted for being opportunistic rather than principled).

Petersen was Benson's major competition. He had sponsored Olson's 1933 income tax bill when he was a state representative; he was popular with many rank and file; and some thought he was more liberal than Benson. Petersen considered running either against sixth-district congressman Harold Knutson or for the Railroad and Warehouse Commission. But by mid-July he had set his sights on the governorship and sought to encourage a movement to "draft" him for governor. Whenever others urged him on, he sent a carbon copy of his response to *Minneapolis Journal* reporter Charles Cheney,[6] and though not yet well known he tried to overcome this by relying upon fellow small-town editors and publishers for publicity. Petersen was no radical, but in 1935 he (and Lundeen) enjoyed a much closer working relationship with the Farmer-Labor Political Federation and the national Farmer-Labor movement than Benson did.

THE CREATION OF THE AMERICAN COMMONWEALTH FEDERATION

The national third-party movement itself had not decided on a campaign strategy for 1936. When the League for Independent Political Action began in 1929, the consensus was that widespread third-party success could be expected in 1936; in 1933 the newly created Farmer-Labor Political Federation held this belief too. Those who carried the message for these movements condemned private capitalism, and in magazines like *Common Sense, Social Frontier, Modern Monthly,* and *American Mercury* they called for deliverance from evil through the mechanism of a new national party.[7] Nevertheless, in early 1935 there was little or no evidence that such a prophecy was any closer to reality than it had been in 1929. LIPA's budget had fallen to $12,000, its membership had declined to between 4,000 and 5,000 with new withdrawals each month,[8] and a special appeal had to be made in order to print the April issue of the *Farmer-Labor Progressive.* LIPA's vision of having Floyd Olson serve as the third party's prophet and preacher had been scrapped, and Howard Williams in his more bitter moments had taken to calling Olson a demogugue who ranked in the same company as Louisiana's Huey Long and the Detroit radio priest Father Charles Coughlin. After Olson declined an invitation to address the Farm Holiday Association convention the LIPA leadership suspected the governor of having capitulated to pressure from Roosevelt and the White House.[9]

To revive the 1936 third-party movement once more, Congressman Thomas Amlie (Wisconsin), the national FLPF chairman, began discussions in April 1935 with a small bloc of liberal congressmen and senators which included Senator Robert La Follette (Wisconsin) and Senator Bronson M. Cutting (New Mexico), Congressmen Vito Marcantonio (New York), Byron Scott (California), Knute Hill (Washington), four other Wisconsin congressmen, and a few interested spokesmen for the railroad brotherhoods (such as Bryle Whitnew), hosiery workers, amalgamated clothing workers, united textile workers, and observers from the Norman Thomas socialists. The group discussed plans for a new "production for use" party.[10] At a second meeting in early May, which no senators and only half the congressmen attended, the decision was made to send a call for a national convention, which would convene in Chicago July 5-7.[11]

The call was signed by Amlie, Lundeen, Marcantonio, and Rep. George Schneider (Wisconsin), and was sent to 400 potential delegates. It declared, "the old order is breaking down and must be replaced . . . the present national leadership of the old parties offers no hope to the people . . . any action must be based upon a fundamental program, striking at the roots of the profit system." Accepting the invitation were 200 delegates who represented a variety of protest groups and interests: Farmers Union, Farm Holiday Association, the Grange, some AFL unions, the Wisconsin Progressive party, the Washington and New York Commonwealth federations, the California EPIC (End Poverty in California) movement, Farmer-Labor parties in Minnesota, Iowa, and Michigan, Technocracy, and (as an observer only) the Socialist party. Floyd Olson assured Williams that he continued to support "production for use," but claimed that a commitment to speak at Elbow Lake, Minnesota prevented him from attending. Amlie and Williams believed the real reason for Olson's absence was a desire not to antagonize Roosevelt and the Democrats.[12]

With Paul Douglas presiding, one more attempt was made to convince the delegates to create, if not a party, at least the framework out of which one might grow. But ideological differences prevented agreement, and this decision was delayed. In its place an accord was reached to create still another sponsoring organization, though once more a fight erupted, over its name. Williams, Amlie, and the midwesterners wanted "Farmer-Labor" in the name, but Alfred Bingham and the easterners rejected it. The convention finally settled on American Commonwealth Federation (ACF).

A more emotional disrupture occurred over the issue of whether to admit Communists into the ACF. Stepping down from his presiding chairman's duties, Douglas led a successful floor fight to bar Communists and admit only those who accepted "democratic process." Under resolutions chairman Vito Marcantonio a platform emerged which called for world peace, a generous welfare state, steeply progressive income and inheritance taxes, federal ownership of banks, mines, transportation, utilities, and munitions, and a government-owned trading corporation through which all foreign commerce would pass.

Now the third-party movement had three organizations marketing the new-party idea, and three separate headquarters. In New York Alfred Bingham ran the *Common Sense* publishing offices; in St. Paul Howard Williams oversaw the midwestern and western operations; and in Washington at the new national ACF office was Nathan Fine, recruited from the Rand School of Social Research. Fine's first priority was to undertake a $25,000 fund drive to finance ACF's state and national 1936 conventions. Although feature stories about the ACF appeared in *Colliers,* the *Progressive, The Nation,* and *The New Republic,* its treasury remained nearly bare, Williams and Bingham fell to arguing about whether the FLPF was a division within the ACF or vice versa, and by fall 1935 payment of Williams's salary was months behind.[13] Against such a chronically underfinanced challenge the Democratic party felt reasonably secure as it recruited its critics to patronage offices and work in newly created or expanded federal agencies. Financially and politically, pennies were hardly a match against millions of federal dollars.

To this disadvantage had to be added the irksome practice of local Communist infiltration into the ACF/FLPF as the CP:USA expanded its United Front campaign. This brought bitter complaints from Congressman Tom Amlie about Vito Marcantonio's association with Communists and about how their presence in the ACF damaged relations with most of organized labor.[14]

OLSON CHALLENGES THE PATRONAGE SYSTEM

Meanwhile the patronage snarl in Minnesota seemed to be developing into the major volatile element influencing the choice of Floyd

Olson's successor. Vince Day pined for the day when a permanent civil service law would end patronage meddling by the association,[15] and Olson was increasingly aware of the damage it was doing to the Farmer-Labor reputation. But because Olson was constantly pestered by county units of the association to reappoint Strout to another term as budget and personnel commissioner, the governor kept putting off the final decision to fire Strout. When Strout realized he would not receive another term, he submitted (on August 18) a letter of resignation, an action which bitterly angered association leaders and resulted in an emergency session of the central committee. Ironically, state commissioner of purchases Carl R. Erickson and Strout himself (by $126.60!) were delinquent in paying their monthly assessments[16] — all state employees were required to pay a 10-percent assessment to the association — and Olson's decision to discharge Strout was popular with most state employees who resented the forced assessments and who faced discharge if they refused to pay. Determined to eradicate the public black eye of patronage, Olson went further and forced the association to withdraw its job offer to the departing Strout.

These challenges to the Farmer-Labor Association brought on a counterattack through a special Association Committee of Fourteen which purported to exonerate Strout's conduct as personnel director. The committee report claimed (or complained) that only 22 percent of all new state employees were recruited from the association, whereas 78 percent were Republicans, Democrats, or independents, and concluded that Olson was injuring the movement by his style and tone of administration, his method of campaigning, and his use of all-partyism which the committee charged was a threat to the association and undermined its ability to control Olson or any other Farmer-Labor administration.[17]

After Olson had successfully defied the association on the Strout matter its leaders were even more determined to play a dominant role in selecting the next Farmer-Labor candidate for governor.

THE LIGGETT ATTACKS AGAINST OLSON

Another source of attacks upon Olson, this time coming from outside the movement, was the series of the poison pen articles by sensationalist journalist Walter Liggett. Liggett once had been active in the Nonpartisan League and after a ten-year absence he returned to Minnesota in 1933, serving for a while as editor of the (Bemidji) *Northland Times;* then in Red Wing he helped reestablish the *Organized*

Farmer. In late 1933 representatives of the Olson administration asked him to serve as editor of the *Austin American,* a new pro-union paper which it was hoped would help offset the highly Republican local press in southern Minnesota.

Trouble began when Liggett was forced out of Austin following frequent hassles with a new union, the Independent Union of All Workers. Claiming a promotional loss of $2,642, Liggett sued the union and Olson. To quiet him, an out-of-court settlement of $490 was reached in August while Henry Teigan, Roger Rutchick, and Billy Friedell co-signed a $1,000 note to help Liggett establish a Rochester newspaper,[18] the *Midwest American.* Now, however, Liggett began writing scathing denunciations of Olson and the state administration, even alleging irregularities in the governor's personal living habits, and he expanded some of these articles into campaign pamphlets. Farmer-Laborites suspected Liggett of defecting to Thomas Schall, particularly when they learned he had moved into a Minneapolis house owned, they believed, by Schall.[19]

As a political thorn Liggett was irritating but small, yet he added to the growing accumulation of criticisms against the governor. Vince Day was now sufficiently worried so that he sought to have Liggett exposed in a national magazine, *Modern Monthly,* as a journalist for sale.[20] Olson, it was to be remembered, had pledged in 1930 to restore the principles of sound governmental administration in the state. The patronage boondoggle and the growing number of suspected abuses appeared to contrast with this pledge.

THE PROBLEM OF ORGANIZATIONAL STRIKES AND COMMUNISTS

In the meantime, the highly visible role of local communists in some parts of the Twin City labor movement was becoming a growing liability for Farmer-Laborism. They played a major part in the militant organizational strikes of 1934, 1935, and 1936. The success of General Drivers (teamster) local 574 in 1934 did bring an organizational victory, but at a price of growing schism in local and national unions and in Farmer-Laborism. The leaders of 574 were Trotskyite (Socialist Workers party) communists who were bitter enemies of teamster national president Daniel J. Tobin and who otherwise were distrusted by the conservative AFL craft unions. In addition, the Trotskyites were sworn blood enemies of Stalinite Communists (CP:USA) who pledged loyalty to the USSR.[21]

In 1935 a series of bitter organizational strikes erupted in Minneapolis. In July a violent outburst at the Flour City Ornamental Iron

Works escalated into a clash between police and union pickets, despite the fact that the new Minneapolis Mayor, Thomas Latimer, was a Farmer-Laborite and former member of the Socialist party. While this dispute smoldered unsettled, hosiery workers struck the Minneapolis Strutwear Knitting Mills. The Strutwear strike was even more economically harmful, violent, and threatening to property; it lasted longer; and it caused Latimer to appeal to Olson for help from the national guard. Olson sent in troops but did so without declaring martial law. This brought a challenge in federal court under a claim that he had exceeded gubernatorial authority. Olson reluctantly withdrew the troops,[22] but by now both sides had agreed to a negotiated settlement.

The Communist issue was further compounded in May 1935 by a Communist party, USA, central committee decision — "Let Us Penetrate Deeper Into the Rural Areas"—announcing a new membership guideline. Communist party members now were encouraged to join rather than prevented from entering the Farmer-Labor party. One reason for the change in party line was growing communist fear of Adolph Hitler and the National Socialists (Nazi) party. Another was the communist belief that the Farmer-Labor movement was potentially a major third party in the United States, and the CP:USA warned its members that third-partyism would "find fertile field unless stopped by us."[23]

Until now the Communists had been among Olson's militant critics and their change of tactics went largely unnoticed at first. Upon entering the Farmer-Labor party, they gained new influence, sided usually with the left, and by March 1936 they could boast of seating forty convention delegates while claiming an additional one hundred fellow travelers who "firmly adhered to a Left position on all questions of principle."[24] The price for Farmer-Laborism would be considerable, though the impact came largely after 1936.

THE GENESIS OF THE SCHISM IN THE FARMER-LABOR PARTY

By year's end, it was apparent that a major confrontation within Farmer-Laborism was coming. Although the ultimate clash did not occur in 1936 but was postponed to 1937 and 1938, the originating source of tension was the decision in late 1935 by lieutenant governor Hjalmar Petersen to seek the governorship and work against association insiders determined to give the nomination to banking commissioner Elmer Benson.

Petersen first became angry when *Minnesota Leader* columnist Abe Harris ("Capitol News") began a nine-month campaign which publicized Benson in weekly stories about party and administration activities. Although Petersen excused Benson from personal responsibility for the buildup, he believed himself to be the more logical successor to Olson by virtue of experience, reputation, and popularity among the rank and file. Petersen had some basis for his claim, and among his original supporters he counted Howard Y. Williams, Brainerd Farmer-Laborite Charles Halsted (a member of the state house in 1937-45 and 1953-65 and a candidate for governor in 1948), and *Minnesota Union Advocate* editor A. F. Lockhart. When his drive failed, he pointed an accusing finger at a conspiratorial brain trust and the governor,[25] and he vowed vengeance.

THE DEATHS OF LIGGETT AND SCHALL

Two unexpected and violent deaths would have a profound effect on the 1936 campaign. They hinted darkly of conspiracy, both political and criminal. First, in early December 1935 muckraking Walter Liggett was gunned down on the street. Liggett also had been exposing the city's liquor syndicates, and the generally accepted murder hypothesis was that the Minneapolis underworld had silenced an irritating critic. Nevertheless, in *Modern Monthly* ("Who Killed Walter Liggett?") a personal letter written by Liggett three days before his murder predicted Olson might arrange his death. (Ironically, Liggett had been a friend of J. M. Near, a scandal writer of the twenties, whom Olson as Hennepin County Attorney had prosecuted under Minnesota's Gag Law which the United States Supreme Court declared unconstitutional in the famous *Near v. Minnesota* prior censorship case.)

Liggett's murder was a political setback since it refocused attention on his attacks against Farmer-Laborism. Such bad publicity worried the state administration, and even Farmer-Laborites speculated about who had arranged the Liggett murder. Howard Williams thought maybe it came at the hand of Charles A. Ward, president of Brown and Bigelow in St. Paul, since Liggett portrayed the rehabilitated Ward as a former drug pusher and procurer of prostitutes.[26] The truth was never uncovered, but it increased some people's apprehension about Farmer-Laborism's possible connections with urban crime.

By far the greater political shock came December 21 when blind Senator Thomas Schall was killed in Washington, D.C. in a hit-and-run automobile accident. Few connected Shall's and Liggett's deaths. But the outcome removed an incumbent from Olson's path to the

Senate. The major concern, however, was over who would be appointed to fill the unexpired term. Olson considered resigning and taking the appointment himself, which threw the Benson brain trust into a panic because this would elevate Hjalmar Petersen to governor and make it extremely difficult to dislodge him from the party nomination. But Olson ultimately decided to appoint a loyal stand-in whom he could trust to step aside later. Candidates considered for this role included Vince Day, Willmar publisher and state senator Victor Lawson who was a veteran agrarian spokesman, former congressman and lieutenant governor Henry Arens of Jordan, and Elmer Benson. Although the governor was under extreme pressure from Abe Harris, George Griffith, Joseph Poirier, and Roger Rutchick to appoint Benson in order to strengthen his bid for the governorship, he held back. To force Olson's hand, the Harris group planned a simple conspiracy: print an exclusive story in the *Minnesota Leader* officially announcing Benson's appointment. Although Olson had been denied the opportunity to announce his own decision, when the story broke in late December it was accepted by most Farmer-Laborites as the normal course of events. Olson's biographer lends additional testimony to the conspiracy doctrine.[27] Yet it also is true that Vince Day, in a December 23 memo to Olson, gave a warm endorsement to Benson as a selection which "would meet with [Party] approval," and he added that Benson was "one of the few in the Party that you can absolutely rely upon for full and complete cooperation."[28]

By now Hjalmar Petersen was angered beyond reason, and circumstances would soon not only increase his distrust of the association hierarchy but also set the stage for a major Farmer-Labor showdown.

OLSON'S ILLNESS AND TRANSFER OF LEADERSHIP

The final stroke of Farmer-Labor misfortune came in late December shortly after Olson had belatedly seconded Benson's Senate appointment. Perpetually suffering from intestinal ailments, Olson was scheduled for exploratory surgery at the Mayo Clinic very late in December. The surgeons discovered abdominal cancer of the pancreas in an advanced stage of development; the disease was diagnosed as inoperable and incurable. Olson was dying and had but seven and one-half months of life remaining. Transfer of Olson's gubernatorial influence was certain to ignite an internal Farmer-Labor struggle for control over the Minnesota movement.

A major question to be settled was whether any person in the party was sufficiently able to bridge the gap between workers and farmers, moderates and radicals. Even Olson himself had lost some of his early effectiveness as party mediator. A month before the announcement of Benson's appointment, Petersen had begun to complain broadly about Olson, and he confided to *Journal* reporter Charles Cheney that the move to advance Benson in the party "will only put so much more blood on the teeth of my friends for the convention next March."[29] While Olson recuperated, Petersen went about the task of seeking convention delegates and stopping Benson, speculating as he did that Ernest Lundeen might challenge Olson in the Senate primary. Although Petersen was mistaken about Benson's overall strength among the rank and file, he was accurate in foreseeing a sharp fissure in Farmer-Laborism.

By now Olson was much too weak to command or widely influence party affairs, though he still expected to campaign for the Senate. To the extent he could, Olson sought to tame the furies. From his Mayo hospital bed he wrote Benson, praising him for the prestige and good publicity he brought to both Benson and the state. Olson also advised him to push hard for iron-clad neutrality legislation by keeping absolute control in congressional hands with "no discretion in the executive." Personally, Olson declared, "I wouldn't trade the life of one youth for the whole damned 'freedom of the seas,' " and he warned that Roosevelt's and the Democratic party's neutrality legislation was an unacceptable compromise which peace advocates should reject.[30] Olson thus expressed the classic sentiment of Farmer-Labor isolationism which had emerged in 1917-1918 and had grown into almost an ideological principle in the 1920s. Benson was very moved by the advice.

Olson appeared much less certain how to deal with Petersen and how to keep him from further rupturing party ranks. The governor made three or four requests that the two meet in secret and confidential conference, and Petersen finally accepted a January 30 meeting date in Rochester. Olson bluntly told Petersen that Benson was far ahead in the quest for delegates, and he warned his lieutenant governor that he had only an outside chance for convention endorsement. But Petersen also believed, perhaps incorrectly, that he had extracted a promise from Olson to work for a joint convention endorsement of Petersen and Benson, with the nomination issue to be settled in an open primary.[31]

Benson meanwhile worked through a well-disciplined campaign organization, relying on Abe Harris for public relations, George Griffith's (patronage) oil inspectors, and his own bank field examiners to make contact with local Farmer-Labor clubs. Petersen relied largely on his personal appeal, he avoided making appearances before local association conventions, and he fashioned broadside attacks against what he called "Mexican generals" and party "fixers." In an Owatonna speech he charged that tax money and savers' deposits in banks closed by the state were being used to finance part of the Benson campaign. These self-righteous attacks worried the left and the association hierarchy, and to quiet Peterson it was suggested he run for Congress or another state office. His growing carelessness with words inevitably brought harsh rejoinder, but he refused to recant the charges.[32]

Petersen was among the first Farmer-Laborites to know the truth about Olson's real illness and the even higher stakes involved in the nomination outcomes. But the major import of his campaign was that he turned increasingly toward the political right while Benson moved left. The shift both in Petersen's thinking and in his political base of support was ironic. He still praised the national third-party movement in 1936; however, his support from Farmer-Labor socialists had dwindled and he substituted for it an appeal to moderates and old-line progressive reformers. He charged that left-wingers who were responsible for the disastrous 1934 radical platform were organizing for Benson. Although Petersen personally was not guilty of it, some of his backers were anti-Semitic racists who slandered Jewish Benson strategists like Abe Harris. Labor conservatives also rallied behind Petersen. The Duluth Central Labor Union's Political Committee, for example, sent a strong protest to association state secretary Irene Welby challenging the sending of five St. Louis County Communists to the state convention, and others protested the sharply increasing numbers of state civil service employees being selected as convention delegates.[33]

THE STATE FARMER-LABOR CONVENTION

As the time for the state Farmer-Labor convention drew near, it was obvious that the movement lacked a commanding personality (Olson had been out of public contact since January) and was split over the Benson/Petersen nomination as well as over the forthcoming attendance of Communist delegates. In mid-February, right before Olson departed for Tucson, Arizona, to convalesce for three weeks, he told a news conference that he was staying neutral regarding Benson and Peterson and he asked the convention to remain neutral as well. However, the governor took no steps to ensure neutrality, and this left Petersen feeling betrayed once more. Benson's mounting lead in delegate strength did not bring increased unity. Veteran Farmer-Laborite Magnus Johnson, a one-term congressman and for twenty months a senator, pledged firm public opposition to Benson and a fight in the primary.

Howard Williams and his LIPA-FLPF-ACF political collage hoped to steer the Minnesota convention toward issuing a call for a national third-party presidential convention, and to this end he worked with a group which included John Bosch, depute attorney general Roger Rutchick, Marian Le Sueur, Mrs. Charles Lundquist, and mostly anti-Roosevelt and anti-New Deal left-wingers sympathetic to the idea. However, sensing insufficient support for the idea, Williams quietly attempted to work with Minnesota Communists who would be attending the Farmer-Labor convention. This put him in conflict with the Duluth and St. Paul labor assemblies as well as with his own leadership; Tom Amlie, Alfred Bingham, Nathan Fine, and George Schneider were unalterably opposed to any Communist agreements with or participation in the third-party movement, and they forewarned Abe Harris about it when he visited them in Washington.[34] Williams argued long distance with Nathan Fine over the presence of Communist delegates, justifying it by claiming that Farmer-Labor clubs were allowing Communists as members and that whenever they demonstrated ability they were taken "for what they are."[35]

The Communist issue already was volatile in Hennepin County, and, rather strangely, almost no attention was given to Adolph Hitler's German reoccupation of the demilitarized Rhineland which took place two weeks before the state convention. In mid-March at the Hennepin convention, which stood solidly for Benson, the bitterest moments came when a resolution was offered to strip Minneapolis Farmer-Labor mayor Thomas Latimer of his association membership because he had used police and had called for state militia assistance in maintaining order and protecting property during the violent Strutwear strike. Offered by the left wing, the resolution carried, but not before Latimer had shouted a denunciation which would be repeated hundreds of times in 1937 and 1938. The mayor condemned the replacement of "old-time Farmer-Laborites" by Communist infiltrators who, he charged, took orders from Moscow or from the Trotskyite Dunne brothers who controlled the Teamster General Drivers Local 574.

Farmer-Laborism now had still another growing internal disorder to manage. In the 13th Minneapolis ward Farmer-Labor club a call was sounded to bar Communists from the club and from the state convention, and an expulsion resolution was debated in a closed state central committee session.[36] The issue simmered on.

Floyd Olson's last convention appearance, before the opening session of the state convention on March 27, was an exhibition in personal courage. Although Olson had lost fifty pounds, he delivered a two-hour, twenty-page valedictory to his five administrative years, attacked Republicans, the status quo, the "system," and the U.S. Supreme Court for overturning progressive congressional legislation.

On foreign policy Olson was extremely isolationist. Recognizing Hitler's militant ambitions, he nevertheless called for strict American neutrality and an absolute trade embargo with all combatants. For guidance Olson looked backward to the 1917-18 experience, the "illegal" British blockade and retaliations by German submarines, and he issued a stern prophetic warning. Predicting war between Germany and England was "now imminent," he declared it most important that America remain at peace. Recalling the loss of American lives in 1917-18 and the $100 billion cost of the war, he concluded, "Even the price of complete isolation is a small price to pay compared to that."[37] Olson sounded like Henrik Shipstead; as always, the man most touched by his reasoning was Elmer Benson.

Isolationism was integral to Olson's major concern, *An Economy of Abundance*. The climax of his convention address was a call for fundamental change in the American political and economic system. This "system has shown clearly that it cannot and will not provide a decent standard of living for the American people." Much of the change he had seen taking place was "mere reform," was inadequate, and Olson declared that the men in charge of running the country's economy were unwilling to provide "an economy of abundance." As a result he concluded capitalism had to be discarded, replaced with "a system of collective ownership," and lastly "a system of government ownership and operation" when corporate size became massive and complex. With his usual warning about peaceful and lawful transition, Olson proposed a national *Human Rights Amendment* granting Congress the power to regulate industry and the authority to own, manage, and operate business, mining, manufacturing, industry, commerce, and banking enterprises. Olson's conversion to collectivism now neared completion. Abandoning his usual party cautiousness, Olson encouraged Farmer-Laborites to assist other states in developing Farmer-Labor, Liberal, or radical parties, though he made no recommendation on the "question of becoming a national party." Delegates had to decide this for themselves. His preference

was to run Farmer-Labor candidates for state and congressional office; but he stopped short, apparently deliberately, of including the
presidency! Clearly, Olson did not believe it wise or possible to jetti-
son Democratic assistance even in Minnesota, and this itself was evidence of third-partyism's overall structural weakness as it faced the
rival New Deal Democrats.

In both its direction and composition the 1936 Farmer-Labor convention was a study in contrast and conflict. Olson had come closer
to representing the ideological economic aspirations of the left, but
it was by no means certain that Farmer-Labor voters had been radicalized nor was Olson necessarily in step with general public attitudes
about ownership and production. Equally serious was the association's inability to come to grips with the Communist issue, and for
this a heavy price would be paid in 1937-38. The credentials committee seated radical antagonists: General Drivers Local 574 delegates, including Grant Dunne and William S. Brown, were allowed in,
and both denied being Communists, which technically was true since
they were Trotskyites; five Stalinite Communist (CP:USA) delegates
from St. Louis County were also admitted. Communist district organ
organizer Joseph Moreland was pleased by CP:USA success and
claimed forty delegates overall (which was close to Howard Williams's
estimates), and to them could be added about 100 more fellow travelers, or a voting bloc of approximately 140 in a convention of 667.
Tranquility could not last long in any organization where Trotskyites and Stalinites mixed freely.

The platform had been considerably lightened after the burdensome 1934 adventure. Public ownership no longer was a state responsibility but was made a national issue, and the more strident 1934
concepts were replaced with Planned Plenty. "Ultimately" economic
security was to be achieved by collective ownership of natural resources and monopoly industry. The long-term goal was the Welfare
State, but the immediate objective came to be issues that currently
appealed to workers and farmers. The perceived virtue of the 1936
platform was that it kept the socialist faith intact but did not saddle
candidates or a new Farmer-Labor administration with programs
which threatened or were unpopular with small independent and
moderate-sized businesses.

The national third-party issue was skirted in a similar fashion. Although professing support for the general principle of a national
(i.e., presidential) third party, the delegates studiously avoided any
1936 endorsement of it. Instead, a special Farmer-Labor committee

was to study it, and Howard Y. Williams's plan to issue a call for a special national convention met with defeat.

Exactly how socialist had 1936 Farmer-Laborism become? This remained unclear. Left-wingers chafed under the platform's imprecise language and challenged the value of "ultimate" socialization of the economy. But when Grant and Miles Dunne offered a floor amendment for state governmental operation of idle factories, which the 1934 platform had endorsed, it suffered an overwhelming defeat. So too did a socialist proposal for government ownership of non-agricultural basic industry.

Hjalmar Petersen, who for months had threatened to be a convention lion, went out like a March lamb. Benson had a six-to-one delegate margin, and Petersen accepted the inevitable though he later claimed to have had nearly 40 percent of the delegates. A resolution for joint endorsement of Petersen and Benson was defeated 555 to 95, and at midnight Petersen took the floor and announced he and good Farmer-Laborites would elect Benson governor.[38] For his timely about-faced, Petersen gained endorsement for railroad and warehouse commissioner, which was taken away from eighth-district left-winger John T. Bernard by labor conservatives. Bernard would be a surprise congressional victor in November.

At 2 A.M. delegates were introduced to Benson, whom very few really knew. His political style, economic philosophy, and personality were almost unknown. And Benson began by being more cautious than Olson. He too called for "substantial economic change by national action," a national third party "some time or other," fundamental change in ownership of wealth, and he ridiculed "fake red charges" which had been unjustly heaped upon Farmer-Laborism in the past. Benson would come to be the symbol of left-wing Farmer-Laborism, but at this time he was hardly considered that. Indeed, Howard Y. Williams had such a reputation; for this reason he was rejected as the front-running candidate for lieutenant governor, and the place was given to Gottfried Lindsten, a legislative spokesman for the Minnesota railroad brotherhoods. Once more, as with Petersen, conservative labor delegates headed by St. Paul unionist Frank Starkey led the fight against Williams and the campaign for Lindsten. Williams again was embittered, grumbled privately about "Mexican generals," and advised Wisconsin governor Phillip La Follette that Benson was "a very poor campaigner."[39]

A substantial core of Farmer-Laborites were dissatisfied with what took place at the convention. *Union Advocate* labor editor A. F.

Lockhart stayed critical of Olson (a "man less worthy of public trust than" Thomas Schall) and suspicious of Benson for being involved in the "tricks used to pack that convention. . . ." He advised Petersen to maintain a safe distance from Benson and to remember that Petersen's endorsement for commissioner was insisted upon by labor people and not the Benson followers.[40] And old Magnus Johnson kept his pledge to challenge Benson in the primary.

BREAKING THE NATIONAL THIRD-PARTY MOVEMENT

Olson's and Minnesota Farmer-Laborism's apparent shift to the left had to be discounted against prevailing political realities. If socialization was a congressional responsibility and if Democrats were not about to nationalize industry, then Farmer-Labor advocacy of national public ownership policies carried little meaning. And if Farmer-Laborites rejected the creation of a national party, it was unlikely that the ideal goals enunciated in the 1936 platform would ever be realized.

After the convention Howard Williams and his allies in the Farmer-Labor party continued to press for a national convention. During the second week of April Williams addressed a postconvention Farmer-Labor committee reviewing the subject. What occurred left little doubt about Olson's real intentions: Williams had just launched into a discussion of convention publicity (10,000 delegates would rally!) when Olson strode unexpectedly into the meeting, interrupting it with a blunt declaration of his complete opposition to any third-party presidential campaign in 1936. Once more Olson's brief embrace at the state convention of regional and possibly national Farmer-Laborism had to be questioned. As governor and now as candidate for senator, Olson was not about to forget what got him this far in politics. He, and Farmer-Laborites, needed Democratic help and votes. Lest there be any doubt, Olson soon after appeared as an honored guest at the Minnesota Democratic party's Jefferson Day dinner, planned this year by the Wolf-Meighen faction, Olson's old allies.

A crushed Williams told ACF's Nathan Fine that Olson's latest treachery showed "the kind of political trader you have to deal with in Governor Olson," whom Williams accused of being "out for himself to build his own personal machine and win elections regardless of movements or principles." "I get so thoroughly disgusted with him at times that I wish we could push him entirely out of the picture."[41]

Each day there seemed less likelihood of a new party emerging which would draw five to ten million votes, win forty congressional seats, and gain the presidency in 1940, which were Williams's original goals.[42] Norman Thomas had soured on Minnesota Farmer-Laborism, considered it populist not socialist, and deplored the "watered-down" Farmer-Labor platform. Thomas himself expected to be a presidential candidate after his party faction won decisive control of the New York Socialist party following its primary. Nathan Fine and Alfred Bingham advised Williams to cancel a planning conference scheduled for May 30 in Chicago, and after a ten-day California trip Paul Douglas concluded that prospects for a third party were nil in that state.[43]

Williams and his six-member Farmer-Labor committee were increasingly isolated. The group was chaired by Hennepin's Selma Seestrom and included Marian Le Sueur, Rudolph Rautio, I. C. Strout, Paul Harris, and H. O. Peterson, most of whom were and would be identified with the left wing of the movement. In search of allies, they found that few rallied to the cause except Communists. Clarence Hathaway, Communist *Daily Worker* editor in New York, expressed interest,[44] and when invitations were sent out for the May conference Hathaway and Earl Browder were both invited as Communist representatives. Ironically, however, the Communist party was having problems with its own party rank and file now that they had been encouraged to penetrate the Minnesota Farmer-Labor party by becoming members. Some Communists were too quick in acknowledging past errors in their behavior toward Farmer-Laborism, and Hathaway was critical of them for announcing support of the Farmer-Labor platform, Olson, and Benson before the CP:USA central committee had decided the party line! Olson still was suspect for his "antiparty behavior," his cooperation with Roosevelt and the New Deal, and for his seizing of teamster records in the 1934 strike.[45]

By spring, as the American Commonwealth Federation abandoned its aspirations for a national party in 1936, it was clear that those in command of the Minnesota Farmer-Labor party and the state administration would sabotage any plan that used Farmer-Laborism as a stalking horse for a national third-party adventure. Indeed, Vince Day (who was now a municipal judge) had advised Olson immediately before the state convention to undercut Williams, Hjalmar Petersen (mistakenly still suspected of being left-wing), John Bosch, and Emil Youngdahl, and to prevent Carl Erickson, George Creel, and Marian Le Sueur from gaining control of the *Minnesota Leader.*[46]

Nevertheless, Williams and Seestrom plunged ahead with their plans for the May conference. Angered by this defiance, Bingham and Fine charged Williams with self-deception and repetition of William Mahoney's blunder of 1924, and Fine complained bitterly that he could learn about Williams's activities only through reading the Communist *Daily Worker*. Williams remained adamant, cautioned Seestrom to exercise more care to prevent Communist domination, but reassured her, "I am not opposed to having Browder and Hathaway" participate.[47]

The episode underscored the sharp disagreement generated by the entire Communist issue. Abe Harris, for example, discounted the likelihood of "injury to the movement" from Communist participation, and he argued with Amlie and Bingham that Communists had mended their ways after realizing their past errors.[48] (It would be several years before Harris changed his mind.) Paul Douglas, however, was highly critical of Williams's activities, argued that Communists were ideologically incompatible with the American third-party movement, and rebuked Williams for telling the *New York Times* that Amlie would preside in Chicago as a way of forcing that role upon the Wisconsin congressman.[49] Williams held firm, attributed news leaks appearing in the *Communist Daily Worker* to Roger Rutchick ("Rutchick is close to the Communist party"), and admitted that Rutchick had accepted delegate recommendations from Clarence Hathaway of the *Worker*.[50]

Rudolph Rautio presided May 30 before eighty-one delegates and eleven visitors from twenty-two states. Olson sent tepid greetings to the delegates, mentioning the possibility of a national Farmer-Labor party. Other greetings came from David Dubinsky of the International Ladies Garment Workers Union, Sidney Hillman of the Amalgamated Clothing Workers Union (ACWU), the rail brotherhoods, and the League Against War and Fascism. Abe Harris handled conference publicity. But the net result of the conference was an anticlimactic resolution, offered by J. B. S. Hardman, asking the Minnesota Farmer-Labor Association to launch a national third party and to coordinate its campaign through a twenty-five-member Advisory Council chaired by Minnesotan Sander Genis of the ACWU; Williams was to be council secretary. However, the absence of ACF and labor support belatedly brought the admission that there would be no new 1936 presidential party, and the decision was made to support, where possible, third-party congressional candidates.[51] The national third-party movement was about where it had been in 1929-30.

THE 1936 CAMPAIGN AND ELECTION

In terms of the economic outlook, the year 1936 did not show great promise for Republicans, and with ideological turmoil, Olson sick and dying, and near insurrection over the governorship, Farmer-Laborism seemed more vulnerable than ever. The party that should have gained the most from these circumstances was the Democratic. But although Roosevelt and the New Deal provided a powerful national symbol, the state Democratic party lacked a commanding leader, a personality around which to rally, and a strong state campaign tied loyally to the president.

Republican Rebuilding

This year Republicans were more realistic about the kind of appeal needed to recapture a public following. Less defeatist than in recent years, they returned to more progressive themes. At the state convention on April 18, though still talking about efficiency and economy in government, overspending in Washington, and waste in the Farmer-state administration, Republicans actually designed a platform which seemed to borrow rather heavily from the 1930 and 1932 Farmer-Labor documents: support for the St. Lawrence Seaway, abolishment of tax-exempt securities, aid to cooperatives, consumer loan protection, party designation for the legislature, and higher import tariffs to protect agriculture. And sensing the growing unpopularity of Farmer-Labor patronage chicanery, they pledged enactment of a merit system for state employment.

On foreign policy, Republicans sounded like old-line Farmer-Labor isolationists. Profits should be taken out of war, both men and material should be drafted, and they said unequivocally: "We are implacably opposed to participation in European entanglements. . . ." What separated them from Farmer-Laborism? Apparently a pledge for more effective administration of law and order during labor violence and, of course, staunch Republican opposition to Farmer-Laborism's socialist wish for greater government take-over of traditional industry.[52] The party also unveiled several new faces. One was the state leader for the Alf Landon 1936 presidential campaign, legislative representative (1925-30, 1933-61) Roy Dunn of Pelican Rapids, who was elected national committeeman, and twenty-nine-year-old Young Republican state chairman Harold E. Stassen of South St. Paul, also a delegate to the national convention.

Democratic Dissension

If ever there was a time for Democrats to put away fratricidal hostilities, it was the year 1936. All the party needed was a small element of luck, some good candidates, self-confidence, able direction, and a strong campaign. Although they had a popular president who was a masterful politician and a source of inspiration, Minnesota Democrats would fail miserably in doing the things critical for victory.

Part of the blame rested with Democratic national chairman James A. Farley who not only miscalculated the election but was willing to sacrifice these hinterland Democrats unnecessarily. In Minnesota responsibility for the 1936 disaster had to be shared equally by the two main factional antagonists, the Wolf-Meighen New Deal liberals and the Moonan-Regan-Ryan conservatives. The first group always seemed willing, even eager, to reach some one-sided agreements with Farmer-Laborites by which they sacrificed immediate opportunity in the hope of gaining some future advantage which never seemed to materialize. The expectation always was eventual absorption of Farmer-Laborites into the Democratic party. Conservatives, by contrast, never seemed to understand that the balance of party power in Minnesota rested largely with German and Scandinavian voters, candidates, and party officers. The Moonan-Regan-Ryan group treated the party as though it was a Minnesota version of ward ethnic politics in Irish Boston.

As a result, the Democratic factions went their separate ways, each planning its own state convention. The Moonan group first assembled in Mankato on February 1, endorsed Roosevelt, and designated second-district congressman (1935-41) Elmer J. Ryan of South St. Paul to be the next national committeeman and a replacement for incumbent Joseph Wolf. Two days before, the Wolf faction announced it had stripped state chairman Joseph Moonan of his party office; it discharged his state committee; and it scheduled a April 20 Jefferson Day Dinner which effectively excluded conservatives, brought in Senator Burton K. Wheeler (Montana) as special speaker, and welcomed Floyd Olson as its honored guest. Wheeler told the gathering that Olson "really is a Democrat" and all but swore him in as the next senator. The following day the Wolf group assembled a mass convention of several thousand delegates in the St. Paul auditorium and endorsed its own set of candidates, among them Patrick Delaney who was to run for U.S. senator but who found time to praise Olson for bringing Farmer-Labor votes to Roosevelt.

There was little left for the Moonan Democrats now other than to reconvene their convention in Minneapolis on May 2, adopt a platform (which was similar to the Republican's), and endorse a second slate of candidates. Before adjourning, the conservatives announced they would refuse compromises with the Wolf group on candidates and delegates to the national convention.[53]

A suicidal tendency to fight among themselves rather than to campaign for victory plagued the Democrats until 1943, an ironic situation in an ideological sense because Democratic differences were narrower and less basic than those found within the Farmer-Labor movement. And the results of the June 15 primary election indicated that Democrats were potentially stronger and that Minnesota's political realignment was yet incomplete. Each party had a sufficient number of state and congressional contests to discourage malevolent crossover voting. Magnus Johnson (26 percent) filed and campaigned unsuccessfully against Benson. Theodore Christianson won the Republican nomination from the widow of Thomas D. Schall. The Wolf Democrats captured nearly all state nominations, with the exception of that for railroad and warehouse commissioner. And Ernest Lundeen rewon nomination in the Third Congressional District, Howard Williams gained a close victory in the fourth, and John T. Bernard was nominated in the eighth. The 534,309 primary voters gave no hint that a party landslide was in the making:

Party	No. of Votes	Percentage of Total Vote
Democratic	129,272	24.2%
Farmer-Labor	195,527	36.6%
Republican	209,510	39.2%

The November outcome still appeared undecided.

The Farmer-Labor Campaign

Summer brought with it little or no Farmer-Labor harmony, and internal dissension actually increased after the primary. Physically Olson was rapidly declining, but he struggled to keep up the appearance of preparing for a Senate campaign. On June 25 and 29 he delivered his last two speeches, at Brainerd and Minneapolis, though he could barely swallow and scarcely stand.[54] The rest of the time he spent at Gull Lake (his summer home) or at the Mayo clinic, out of public sight.

By July party leaders all recognized that Olson was near death, and this reignited Hjalmar Petersen's anger. In mid-July his allies A. F. Lockhart, Victor Lawson, and the Grand Rapids state senator, Dr. J. Lawrence McLeod, urged him to attempt to gain the nomination for governor, but since Benson was the lawful nominee and the party had first to agree on that. Benson refused to take the Senate nomination, primarily because Benson's backers and the patronage machine still did not want Petersen as governor.

For a brief time Petersen considered taking over Olson's nomination, if he could, but he gave up this possibility quickly. Instead he contended that the natural course was for Benson to run for the Senate. To Vivian Thorp, political reporter at the *Minneapolis Journal,* Petersen privately declared that he would have defeated Benson in a primary campaign had he chosen to do so, and he faulted Magnus Johnson's unsuccessful opposition, saying the immigrant Kimble dirt farmer's major accomplishment was handshaking and cow milking. The hot summer with its record July heat and drought — there were several 114° F. days — contributed to Petersen's irritability. Increasingly contemptuous of Olson (the "crown prince"), he bluntly told Abe Harris, whom he had come to hate, that "three jolts on the chin" from Mexican generals was enough and warned that if he received another "somebody would be hurt."[55]

After July 9 Olson stayed almost exclusively at the Mayo Clinic in Rochester. He returned briefly to Gull Lake on August 8, and the final week of his life was spent in Rochester. By this time Petersen could no longer contain his frustration. On August 13, nine days before Olson's death, the lieutenant governor wrote a venomous letter, telling Olson the time had come to "square the account." Never a confidant to Olson, Petersen declared crudely, "nor shall I ever suck around anyone to be [one]," though in the letter's final version he changed the offensive words to "cater to." Claiming he sacrificed himself at the convention and saved Benson from looking "like thirty cents," he asked Olson to withdraw from the Senate race and designate Benson the replacement candidate.

> If you are unable to go through with the campaign on account of illness and you resign from the candidacy to the senate as well as your position as governor, you have the opportunity to square the account with me. You can arrange it so that Elmer becomes the candidate for the Senate and that I become the candidate for Governor.[56]

Olson, of course, did not answer, and the letter likely was never read to him. The governor's final political will and testament was a brief penciled note to personal secretary Herman Aufderheide. In it he ordered an end to the 10-percent assessment practice "against janitors, scrubwomen, etc." which the machine required as a Farmer-Labor tithe for the privilege of state employment. Complaining about the "mess [made] out of campaign contributions," he declared, "I am really getting angry about this" since voluntary funds were sufficient to run campaigns.[57] On the morning of August 22 he died, a mere shell of his once 200-pound self.

The impact of Olson's death on Farmer-Laborism was salutory, and his stoic suffering seemed to temporarily increase his value to the party. Now a patron saint of Minnesota politics, he belonged to memory and legend. Masses of people viewed his body lying in state inside the capitol rotunda. Fifty thousand turned out for the funeral at the Minneapolis auditorium where Governor Philip La Follette of Wisconsin delivered the funeral oration. Even Governor Hjalmar Petersen seemed becalmed; in spite of pressure from Howard Williams to remove Olson administrators and some of the machine's Benson supporters, Petersen refused.[58]

The adjustment in the Farmer-Labor ticket was achieved by having congressman Ernest Lundeen file for the vacated Senate nomination and by replacing Lundeen with state senator Henry G. Teigan. Lundeen still was relatively close to Petersen, and the two cosigned an LIPA letter of September 10 publicly endorsing "production for use,"[59] a concept which Olson had shied from during campaigns. Benson, too, carried forward a much more cautious campaign than later history would expect from him.

The Democratic Blunder

The major move of the campaign, however, did not come from the Farmer-Labor camp. Rather, Democrats, in their most colossal blunder in state history, were about to give Farmer-Laborites a victory with no strings attached. Once more, inept Minnesota New Deal Democrats masterminded themselves into giving away nearly everything but the party name. This outcome was strange in view of national Democratic chairman James A. Farley's earlier success in bringing the two state factions into closer, if short-lived, cooperation. J. F. D. Meighen now served as state chairman, and the conservative group was pacified by the appointment of John P. Erickson as national committeeman. The truce ended and fratricide recurred when Farley put the Minnesota Roosevelt campaign in the hands of Meighen[60] and the liberals commenced to suspect some Moonanites and especially Congressman Elmar Ryan (a law partner of Harold Stassen) of secretly working for Republican gubernatorial nominee Martin Nelson and other Republicans.

Democrats always underplayed their Minnesota resources, and Meighen ensured that the 1936 campaign would be no exception.

Actually, many Farmer-Laborites were looking for help and some probably were capable of interparty exchanges. No less a figure than Howard Williams sought a personal endorsement from Father Coughlin's National Union for Social Justice on the pragmatic grounds that it would provide him vital Catholic votes in St. Paul! In the third district Henry Teigan similarly compromised his principles.[61] But Farmer-Laborites were always tough bargainers. During August and before Olson's death Meighen Democrats had suggested to Farmer-Laborites that Benson run for the Senate, and Meighen proposed to withdraw Patrick Delaney as the Democratic Senate candidate and have him endorse Benson. In return, Farmer-Laborites were to leave the vacated gubernatorial nomination unfilled and instead support Democratic nominee Fred Curtis. Both parties were to campaign jointly for Roosevelt.[62] Farmer-Laborites refused the offer.

In September panic seized the Democrats, largely because James A. Farley began believing the weekly *Literary Digest* polls. When Meighen called at Democratic national campaign headquarters in midmonth, Farley painted a gloomy picture of William Lemke's Union party cutting deeply into the Minnesota Roosevelt vote, and Farley speculated the national outcome could well depend on the Minnesota presidential vote. Farley asked for swift action by Meighen, who immediately returned to Minnesota and prepared now to sacrifice both Curtis and Delaney in return for a Farmer-Labor endorsement of Roosevelt![63] Farmer-Laborites found the offer too good to turn down. Democrats overlooked or forgot that Olson and many Benson supporters had fought efforts to run a third-party candidate against the president and that Williams's LIPA-FLPF campaign had been stopped.

Curtis obediently endorsed Benson, and Delaney announced his withdrawal, saying simply that he did it to help Roosevelt.[64] Anguished cries were emitted by Republicans, and a chorus of charges was issued by Moonan-Regan-Ryan Democrats who declared Meighen's act a betrayal of his earlier pledge to rebuild the Minnesota party. In retaliation, some of the disgruntled formed a Democrats-for-Nelson club, and the state party was split badly for the next half-dozen years.

Three days later White House presidential aide Marvin McIntyre wired congratulations to the parties for uniting in a common cause. The next day it was announced that Roosevelt would begin a Midwest whistle-stop tour from Minnesota. On October 9, after meeting with Democratic and Farmer-Labor leaders, Roosevelt was introduced by Benson and Shipstead, and in an address at the state capitol the president praised cooperatives and the New Deal benefits of the Agricultural Adjustment Act, rural electricity (REA), reciprocal (flexible tariffs) trade policy, and political harmony between Democrats and Farmer-Laborites.[65]

After the withdrawals and Roosevelt's visit the Minnesota campaign turned anticlimactic, the outcome largely misread by the Farmer-Labor movement.

Understanding the Election

The 1936 campaign ended in a jubilant Farmer-Labor victory, its greatest ever (and last). Not only were Benson (58 percent of the vote) and Lundeen (57 percent) treated to landslide victories (winning by a quarter-million votes), but they were joined by six other statewide candidates and five Farmer-Labor congressmen: Henry Teigan (third district), Dewey W. Johnson (fifth), Paul J. Kvale (seventh), John T. Bernard (eighth), and Richard T. Buckler (ninth). Howard Williams came within 360 votes of winning in the fourth district. Such success tempted some Farmer-Laborites into believing that the future of their movement was secure and that Farmer-Laborism was certain to expand into other states. And in Bernard and Teigan the movement had a genuine radical and a bona fide socialist in major public office. The left wing and the new governor saw the outcome as evidence that a sharp new third-party realignment was under way.

Republicans had suffered another setback. Benson turned out to be a rather difficult political target in 1936, in part because he campaigned as a moderate, not a radical; he opposed a sales tax and criticized chain stores, big business, the steel trust, and the Republican press. Rarely had he lost his temper during the campaign. Perhaps the worst incident was when he called the *St. Paul Pioneer Press* "just a bunch of cheap, racketeering, business newspaper politicans," but he otherwise avoided radical words, themes, and phraseology.[66] After the withdrawals of Curtis and Delaney, the national Roosevelt campaign helped the Farmer-Laborites as Roosevelt neutralized much of the state and local Republican effort, ("the party of Hoover"). However, Republicans did win victories for three congressmen — August Andresen (first district), Melvin J. Maas (fourth), and Harold Knutson (sixth), all incumbents — and secretary of state Mike Holm plus control of the conservative state senate.

Democrats were the major casualties in 1936; the unwise withdrawals of Curtis and Delaney appeared to cut deeply into the state

RESULTS OF THE 1936 MINNESOTA GENERAL ELECTION
(Candidate, No. of Votes, and Percentage of Total Vote)

OFFICE	REPUBLICAN	DEMOCRATIC	FARMER-LABOR	SOCIALIST	INDUSTRIAL	UNION	COMMUNIST
President	Alf Landon 350,461 (30.1%)	Franklin Roosevelt 698,811 (60.0%)		Norman Thomas 2,872 (.2%)	John W. Aiken 961 (.1%)	William Lemke 74,296 (6.4%)	Earl Browder 2,574 (.2%)
Senator	Theodore Christianson 402,404 (34.6%)		Ernest Lundeen 663,363 (57.0%)				
Governor	Martin A. Nelson 431,841 (37.1%)		Elmer A. Benson 680,342 (58.4%)		Earl Stewart 7,996 (.7%)		
Lieutenant governor	Arthur E. Nelson 403,412 (34.6%)	A. C. Knudson 153,357 (13.1%)	Gottfried Lindsten 502,856 (43.2%)				
Attorney general	Oscar F. Youngdahl 382,846 (32.8%)	Thomas Gallagher 156,018 (13.4%)	Harry H. Peterson 530,815 (45.6%)				
Secretary of state	Mike Holm 545,965 (46.9%)	Carl Hennemann 113,217 (9.7%)	Paul C. Hartig 426,668 (36.6%)	Vincent R. Dunne 3,722 (.3%)			
Treasurer	Julius A. Schmahl 451,179 (38.8%)	Ray M. Lang 150,524 (12.9%)	C. A. Halvorsen 468,713 (40.3%)				
Railroad and warehouse commissioner	Frank W. Matson 359,959 (30.9%)	Arthur N. Cosgrove 138,386 (11.9%)	Hjalmer Petersen 557,619 (47.9%)				

Note: The total percentage for each office is less than 100 because some voters cast blank ballots and some ballots were spoiled.

Minnesota Farmer-Laborism, by Millard L. Gieske, © 1979 by the University of Minnesota.

party's vote. Ironically, these turned out to be unnecessary, since Roosevelt, besides nearly carrying every state in the nation, led all Minnesota candidates at 60 percent and 700,000 votes, a tally which came in spite of third-party opposition from Norman Thomas (Socialist) and North Dakotan William Lemke (Union). (In contrast, Benson and Lundeen faced only Republican opponents.) Democrats in Minnesota had returned to the hard times of the past. In 1934 the state party vote had averaged 23 percent; in the June 1936 primary it had been 24 percent; but in November 1936, it fell to 12 percent. Even so, when Democratic opponents stayed in the contest, the Farmer-Labor state vote fell to an average of 43 percent. In three party contests the highest Farmer-Labor winner was Hjalmar Petersen with 48 percent.

The one exception to the Democratic disaster was conservative congressman Elmer J. Ryan, a withdrawal critic, who was reelected. To accurately calculate the impact that a united Democratic party campaign might have had if it had marched resolutely behind Roosevelt from beginning to end is impossible. Withdrawals fractured the party. Moonan-Regan-Ryan conservatives, as they worked for Republican Martin Nelson, literally argued that they were attempting to save their party from self-destruction and Farmer-Laborism,[67] one reason why the yet-to-come 1938 realignment was Republican rather than Democratic.

The outcome left Hjalmar Petersen extremely bitter. As he prepared to give up his four and one-half month stint as governor, he blamed George Griffith, I. C. Strout, and Abe Harris for the "patronage mess" and for manipulating the direction in which the party was moving. At the end of the year Petersen quickly condemned the machine and the Department of Conservation in particular. Abe Harris, who had edited the *Minnesota Leader* (the association paper) and now served as editor of the state-published *Conservation Volunteer*, was Petersen's intended target. Not only did Harris take offense at the governor's comments, but he made the mistake of writing a poisonous letter accusing Petersen of disgracing the governorship and of being a "dirty, filthy coward" whom he advised to "submit at once to a lunacy examination by a commission of alienists" because there are "many unhappy people confined in the St. Peter institution who are far more sane than you are."

> If you think that I am going to take this lying down, you are under the wrong impression. You may be governor to some people, but you are ten

degrees lower than a rodent to me. If it is a fight that you crave, you can have it.[68]

Elmer Benson thus was saddled with a new burden before he even had been sworn into office, and the die was unmistakably cast for what would follow.

CHAPTER 9

Benson Takes Command

[The majority of citizens are] no longer content to suffer at the hands of a system which, during periods of so-called prosperity, gives them nothing more than a mere existence and, during periods of depression, inflicts upon them misery, hunger, and want.

Private industry has given ample proof of its inability to supply even our most elemental social and economic needs.

ELMER BENSON, *message to the Minnesota legislature January 6, 1937*

It is commonly said that Elmer Benson was miscast in the role of governor and as a result Farmer-Laborism was brought to near ruin. Benson undoubtedly contributed to his party's problems, but he also inherited from Olson a movement full of contradictions and disturbances over which he had little control.

Aside from Knute Nelson, who was almost his direct political opposite, Benson held the most agrarian values and outlook of any Minnesota governor since 1890. Of Norwegian heritage, Benson continued to live (and in 1979 still does) in the Appleton home where he was born. He spent a year in law school, then served in World War I, after which he returned to Appleton. There he worked as secretary to a cooperative elevator and livestock association, and was cashier in a local bank. Sympathetic to the temperance movement through the influence of his mother and as a result of family experience, he joined the Nonpartisan League and later the Farmer-Labor party. For a lifetime he held firmly to the prairie populists' suspicions not only of economic oligarchies but also of city-oriented politics. Although he became a loyal supporter of organized labor, he always harbored the agrarian's distrust of what he too frequently saw as labor union "racketeering." (In this general sense he was a Jeffersonian.) In sum, Benson's background strengthened his appeal as a Farmer-Labor leader.

Yet his personality was a very real political liability. It was nothing like Olson's. Whereas Olson could get on well with such disparate groups as workers and businessmen (one hour he might be rhetorical radical, the next he would be on good terms with Farmer-Labor economic adversaries, men like St. Paul banker Richard Lilly and industrialist Charles Ward), Benson lacked the gubernatorial temperament: he was grim, strained, serious, often apolitical, and seldom easygoing and relaxed. When Benson spoke out against special interests and monopolies after becoming governor, his adversaries were convinced not only that he criticized a "system" (which through compromise and bargaining might be improved) but that he had them personally in mind as individual wrongdoers. Indeed, when he discoursed on injustices, which he did frequently, too often he would intemperately single out for attack those who were best left undisturbed. He once told a mutual acquaintance of St. Paul's Catholic archbishop that the prelate could "go to hell," a remark which always made Benson chuckle when he remembered it but which hardly was a good way of soliciting St. Paul's Catholic vote. However, this was Benson's style — direct, stubborn, outspoken, sometimes profound, occasionally profane — and the Farmer-Labor movement had to live with it for better or worse.

Benson was also handicapped by the fact that the political environment was now much more inhospitable to Farmer-Laborism than it had been in 1931, when Olson took office. First, there were serious ruptures in organized labor and a growing schism within the American Federation of Labor and its Committee (soon-to-be Congress) of Industrial Organizations (CIO) which was unionizing industries like automobiles and mining. Second, Democrats emerged as the basic party of change and realignment, and in Minnesota this fact finally began to register once the Roosevelt vote and the national trend were observed. Third, those opposing patronage and machine control of the Farmer-Labor party saw Benson as the symbolic and titular head, whereas Olson had often appeared to be separated from and independent of the association. Fourth, in 1935-36 feuding Stalinists and Trotskyites had entered the association, giving the movement ideological elements which were bound to become volatile and disruptive when thrown together or when mixed with social- ists, refugee progressive Republicans, and old-time Nonpartisan Leaguers. Fifth, the third-party movement, regionally and through- out the nation, was rapidly weakening and near collapse, a victim of the Roosevelt New Deal.

When Benson began his administration, he did not realize how politically threatening Communists would be to the Farmer-Labor movement. He incorrectly assumed that "Red scare" campaigns were a thing of the past, were no longer effective, or that the public had become disinterested in radical activities. Sometimes deliberately, sometimes compulsively, Benson boldly stood up for principles when opponents and "reactionaries" attacked. The most formidable of these opponents was former governor Hjalmar Petersen.

THE BENSON-PETERSEN FEUD

Benson was the first Minnesota governor to have a party rival, in the state administration, already actively beginning a campaign to unseat him by the time he took office. Petersen's short four-month term coincided with the 1936 election, and he plainly enjoyed his role as chief executive. Rather steadfastly Petersen maintained he did not hold Benson personally responsible for the state machine's grasp for power; his animosity was primarily directed toward the left-wing group surrounding Benson. Peterson had not always been an econo- mic and political antagonist of the left, and as late as September 1936 he more than Benson had spoken like the collectivist. Never- theless, his ideological thinking was undergoing a change. What helped trigger it, and what in its own right was a major cause of his growing dispute with association leaders, were clashes over patron- age.

While governor, Petersen angered the association by making several administrative appointments without consulting and getting the ap- proval of the association leadership. The most provocative instance occurred in October 1936 following the death of veteran Farmer- Laborite Knud Wefald, a member of the Railroad and Warehouse Commission. Petersen deliberately ignored the Farmer-Labor Asso- ciation when he sought advice about a possible successor to Wefald and, probably unwisely, relied in part for counsel upon Fred Ossanna, a Minneapolis attorney of sometimes dubious reputation. Petersen's choice for the interim appointment was former Winona state representative (1925-33) Harold R. Atwood, a selection which the left found completely unacceptable. One reason was ideological: Atwood had repudidated the radical Farmer-Labor platform of 1934. And it was suspected that Atwood would feel obligated to Petersen once the latter took his seat on the RRW commission. Critics introduced affidavits before the Hennepin County Farmer-Labor Association and the association state committee charging that Atwood had signed an undated letter of resignation which would force him to vote for Petersen as commission chairman and which would ensure his supporting the appointment of Oliver Ossanna (brother to Fred) as commission secretary.[1] Another expressed fear was that Atwood would follow Petersen's lead in commission decisions and policy making.

No letter of resignation was ever produced, but the charges were a source of embarrassment to Petersen. In November he made an emotional defense of Atwood before a tumultuous session of the state committee where he engaged in a heated exchange with Selma Seestrom and Marian Le Sueur, two outspoken leftists who were largely responsible for the charges, though the Ossannas more than Petersen seemed their primary target. Part of their antagonism toward Fred Ossanna was moral indignation, but some of it appeared to be ideological: as a labor attorney he worked with the Trotskyite Dunne brothers of teamster local 574, whereas Seestrom and Le Sueur tended to align with American Communists (the Stalinist CP:USA). Ossanna also was suspected of maintaining connections with the murky underworld of Minneapolis labor racketeers. Petersen categorically denied taking or demanding any type of loyalty pledge from Atwood,[2] and from his perspective this was but one more effort by the state association machine to discredit him politically. The episode added to his growing antipathy toward the association and his emerging ideological distrust of Communist sympathizers whom he now was coming to identify as the core of his opposition. He soon started to lump Communists, fellow travelers, the machine, party job seekers, and the incoming administration as partners in political crimes against him.

Near the end of Petersen's gubernatorial term he decided to fill several other administrative vacancies rather than leave them for Benson. In December he even attempted to remove Conservation Commission chairman E. V. Willard. The Conservation Department was one of those units honeycombed with patronage appointees ever since the association had insisted upon the dismissal of non-Farmer-Laborite game wardens and of one division head, Erling Swenson, a Farmer-Laborite not favorable to the association. Willard was victimized in large measure because he headed a department where Petersen's blood enemy, Abe Harris, served as director of publicity. Petersen suspected Harris of being Conservation's phantom director, and at Willard's dismissal hearing — which voted three to two in favor of retaining him — Petersen referred to Harris as a former "swivel chair artist and propaganda expert,"[3] leaving little doubt about who was Petersen's real target.

Other incidents contributed to Petersen's dissatisfaction with the party regulars. He and recently reelected attorney general Harry H. Peterson, whom Petersen appointed to the state supreme court in December, were not invited to the Benson inaugural reception. On Benson's first day in office the state governmental hierarchy and the party were dividing into pro- and anti-Benson factions.[4] At the same time the association central committee ended the practice of sharing editorial control of the *Minnesota Leader* with the Farmer-Labor Sustaining Fund Committee,[5] the practical effect of which was to lessen the influence of Sustaining Fund outsiders and, more directly, to promote Abe Harris to general editor of the *Leader* as Henry Teigan's replacement. Petersen saw all these things as an ever tightening ring of control by a disciplined state machine. By January 1937 he — and his supporters — believed his mission in political life was to reopen the party, to cast out ideological undesirables, and consequently to defeat Elmer Benson in 1938.

BENSON'S EARLY DAYS IN OFFICE

With Benson's maverick personality, there was little chance that he would enjoy a political honeymoon during his early days in office. District court judge Vince Day instinctively sensed Benson's weakness. In an effort to help the new administration and ward off trouble, Day counseled Benson to make all personnel changes the first two weeks ("The sooner they are made the sooner they will be forgotten), to adopt some informal civil service plan, to "select your campaign manager" for 1938 immediately, to "keep the Democrats divided," and to maintain "your contacts with the Scandinavians and the Germans." Last of all, Day warned, "control your anger," possibly by seeking relaxation outside the office as Olson had done.[6] For Benson the latter would be most difficult. Olson had pursued very worldly interests, like whiskey, women, and resort clubs which played honky-tonk music; these were hardly appealing to the more puritanical and sober Benson.

Benson's personnel appointments brought on a nasty controversy. Shortly after the election he had indicated a willingness to let party leaders bear the major responsibility for filling administrative vacancies, but when he proposed to appoint Paul Rasmussen state personnel director,[7] Selma Seestrom and the left wing in Hennepin County descended upon him in outrage. Like his two immediate predecessors, Benson was charged with keeping some holdover Republicans in the highway department and with reneging on a promise to make room for more Farmer-Laborites.[8] Soon moderates and conservatives in the American Federation of Labor accused him of siding with the Committee of Industrial Organization (CIO) and of being unduly influenced by Sander Genis (of the Amalgamated Clothing Workers Union) and Roger Rutchick.[9]

It was not known what Benson's relationship with the legislature would be. A brief special session which convened in December to enact social security legislation offered no clue. The state senate was still controlled by the conservative caucus, and in January Harold Barker of Elbow Lake was elected speaker of the house over Edward J. Chilgren of Little Fork. Barker was a liberal but no radical, and had bolted the Republican party in 1928 never to return. In the senate the liberal caucus was ably led by moderate George Lommen of Eveleth. The legislature was not sympathetic to public ownership proposals.

BENSON'S 1937 LEGISLATIVE PROGRAM

Benson and his advisers put together a comprehensive legislative program, an omnibus undertaking which was an outline for a beginning state social welfare system. Although it included a few public ownership proposals (liquor dispensary, cement plant, electric power), they were relatively modest, and many of the reforms Benson sought were to be associated with liberalized state government for the next three decades. Declaring that government no longer was a "mere huge policeman" to protect property rights, he said it was time to make government "the great guarantor of social and economic justice and security for all the people."[10] To this end he ambitiously proposed a long list of needed legislation:

reorganization of the Conservation Commission
state-owned liquor dispensary
state-owned cement plant

state-owned electric power system by constitutional amendment
extension of the mortgage moratorium
graduated tax on chain farming
tax on butter substitutes
establishment of a consumer research bureau
expansion of the system of cooperative enterprise
compulsory workmen's compensation
full crew and train length maximums
state civil service system
sharply progressive chain store tax
fair trade laws
expanded state aid for schools
free school bus transportation
teacher tenure law
ban on the use of strike breakers
liberalized payments to the aged and unemployed
liberalized state employee benefits
homestead property tax reform
imposition of mining company income taxes
expanded vocational education and adult education
work relief program
repeal of the criminal syndicalism law
expansion of the Bureau of Criminal Apprehension
lowered interest rates (from 6 percent to 4 percent)
party designation of legislators
creation of a state planning board
sharp progressive increases in income tax rates.

Costs for the overall program had to be met in two ways: through higher taxes and by higher prices set by "fair trade" laws (price fixing). The objective was redistributive in that Benson expected the wealthy to bear the tax burden. (He looked to workers, farmers, teachers, governmental employees, and small businessmen for support.) Within two weeks seventy-five bills were introduced to carry out the program, while the chairman of the house tax committee, Edward Hagen of Milan, introduced the administration's tax bill.

Benson's "soak the rich" state income tax proposal excluded 95 percent of all Minnesota taxpayers and began at $5,000 annual income where the tax rate was 5 percent, ending at 12.5 percent at the highest levels. (Under the 1933 state income tax act the maximum rate was 5 percent.[11]) The corporate rate ranged from 5 percent to 16.5 percent. These proposed changes were not radical, but the daily metropolitan newspapers usually treated them as though they were. By comparison, in the 1970s the individual income tax provides about 50 percent of all Minnesota *state* revenue, and most full-time employees pay it!

This program was very ambitious for any single bienniel session, and it required a governor of consummate skills who could persuade, negotiate, rally public support, and work in close harmony with legislative leaders. Benson was not such a man. Getting him into political trouble were his impatience, personality, ill-chosen words, and occasionally his allies. In addition, his preamble — like some of Floyd Olson's speeches before the association in 1934 and 1936 — made it clear that he looked for capitalism's eventual replacement. Believing this to be only the beginning, Benson's political and economic enemies asked, What is next?

Predictably, the legislative session became deadlocked. Critics began to blame Benson for political ineptness, poor timing, and narrow partisanship even though his long-term goals were sound. AFL *Union Advocate* editor A. F. Lockhart said Benson's inability to work with key legislators was the main reason why civil service reform and protective legislation against loan sharks were defeated. "If you can intercede with God and the Virgin Mary to do something for Elmer," Lockhart told Congressman Henry Teigan, "you will be doing a real service for the party."[12] Veteran Farmer-Labor legislator S. A. Stockwell (a socialist) and Hjalmar Petersen declared Benson had doomed civil service reform with the questionable insistence that the act take effect one year after passage, or in sufficient time to "grandfather in" as many Farmer-Labor replacements as possible.[13]

During the regular session the legislature did pass Farmer-Labor proposals, including reorganization of the Conservation Department, fair trade legislation, extension of the mortgage moratorium, workmen's compensation, aid to dependent children, continuing contracts for teachers, and reduced farm loan interest rates of 4 percent. But an antilobbying bill, the state liquor dispensary, the proposed state electric power constitutional amendment, party designation of legislators, a state Wagner act (guaranteeing the right to organize and bargain collectively), civil service reform, the loan shark bill, most welfare legislation, and all state ownership proposals were either rejected or hopelessly tied up in committee. Spectacular controversies surrounded the relief bill, increased iron mining taxes, homestead property tax relief, and the bill to increase individual and corporate income taxes, overshadowing the credit Benson received for ending a bitter Albert Lea machine strike.

Benson's patience had worn thin after only three months in office, and as the ninety-day legislative session neared an end he grew increasingly truculent. In a general sense the governor's overall program was already a compromise because it fell far short of what the public ownership wing of the party really wanted; nevertheless, Benson was stubborn and refused to negotiate and bargain with the legislature. Worse, he became bellicose even with some members of his own caucus.

Some senate liberals resented the governor's mood and method. One of them was Grand Rapids physician J. L. McLeod, a moderate who in an April 1 radio address criticized the administration tax program as a "monostrosity based on politics." Benson further injured himself when, in discussing with the liberals some bills bottled up in committee, he testily reacted to a question by exclaiming, "I will not be cross-examined."[14]

THE CATASTROPHIC PEOPLE'S LOBBY RALLY

A major blunder was now in the making. Some of Benson's political and ideological sympathizers were determined to come to his aid; they ended by doing him and Farmer-Laborism irretrievable harm. John Bosch, the militant head of the state Farm Holiday Association (FHA), also served as leader of the state People's Lobby, and he often took a radical's view of the political process. Although Bosch was no revolutionary, he sometimes found merit in an occasional display of popular might, and what better way was there to rattle legislative cages than to stage a protest march that ended at the capitol steps when the legislature was still in session? Bosch recruited marchers from Farmer-Labor clubs, the Workers Alliance, FHA, and the People's Lobby, gathering somewhere between 1,500 and 5,000 marchers on April 4, 1937, for the walk to the capitol.

Benson gave the marchers a send-off speech in which he faulted "reactionary legislators," called them the "most dangerous element in government and society today," and in defending his tax program offered the opinion that it would be passed "if you apply the pressure." Carelessly Benson added, "It's all right to be a little rough once in a while." Such words could be interpreted two ways and were rather typical of the governor's sometimes belligerent rhetoric. Yet they rather contrasted with Floyd Olson's usual admonitions about peaceful progress in a democratic society. Other speakers were moderate, such as Appleton mayor A. T. Forsberg and socially democratic and even pacifistic Susie Stageberg, whereas others came from the militant left: Chester Watson of the Workers Alliance, A. H. Urtubees of the Minneapolis Central Labor Union, and Fred Lequier of the state Timber Workers Union.

For most of the day little of consequence occurred, and the deportment of the demonstrators seemed hardly newsworthy. Unfortunately, as ranks thinned in late afternoon radicals like Communist Harry Mayville, John G. Soltis, Harold Bean, Sam Davis, Chester Watson, and Robert Cheska became increasingly prominent. Suddenly and with no warning they rushed into the capitol, burst through a locked door, and inundated the room where the senate tax committee was in session, thereby putting some senators in fear for their physical well-being. Turning on stalwart conservative A. J. Rockne — a longtime antagonist of Farmer-Laborism, Floyd Olson, and now Elmer Benson — Mayville called him "an exploiter and a leech." The committee was quickly gaveled into adjournment, and at about 5:00 P.M. 200 demonstrators laid siege to the senate chamber, commandeering it into an overnight hostelry. Not until 9:30 A.M. the following morning, after a personal appeal from Benson, did they vacate. Once again the governor proved careless with words, remarking that the demonstrators had "done a good job."[15]

Benson and state Farmer-Laborism never recovered from this illconceived display, and if posterity demands a date to mark the movement's decline and fall, April 4, 1937, would be the most appropriate. The People's Lobby take-over appeared to most legislators an uncalled-for kind of intimidation, and the severest critics labeled it a capitol "riot." A few discussed impeaching the governor. Compromise with Benson was now out of the question. Liberal after liberal arose on the senate floor to express condemnation and apology, and they included veteran legislators Victor Lawson, Harry Bridgeman, and Gerald Mullin, and of course McLeod. Although George Lommen defended Benson and did not hold him responsible for the unlawful behavior, nearly everyone was embarrassed. The Ramsey County attorney considered prosecuting six demonstrators.[16] Politically, Benson now headed a crippled administration.

When a special May session was called to complete unfinished business, seventeen house independents who had caucused liberal in January now defected, though Harold Barker retained his speakership.[17] The stalemated session dragged inconclusively into July, and a compromise tax schedule became law without Benson's signature. Thirtyyear-old Harold E. Stassen, the outgoing chairman of the Young Republican Federation, quickly expressed a theme which became the rallying cry of Republican moderates over the next year and one-

half: progressive Minnesota legislative reform was now being sabo-
taged by an unholy alliance of intrenched reactionaries and dangerous radicals.[18] A new political alignment was under way.

FARMER-LABOR DESTABILIZATION

Destabilization within Farmer-Laborism went far beyond Benson's
tongue and Petersen's insurgency. Basically, it was institutional more
than personal, and Floyd Olson in his prime likely could not have
staved it off. Unlike Republicans and Democrats, a third party
cannot lose its political territory and expect to regain it at a later
time, nor can it call in regional and national reserves when disaster
strikes. Congressman Henry Teigan sensed the party dilemma shortly
after the election when he observed it was "expand or disintegrate."[19]

Decline of the National Movement

Howard Williams thought one way of expanding was to bring Minnesota Farmer-Laborism and Wisconsin Progressivism into closer
cooperation. In mid-December 1936 he, congressman Tom Amlie,
Milwaukee mayor Daniel W. Hoan (a socialist), and a few Minnesota
leftists including Charles Egley, Marian Le Sueur, Selma Seestrom,
and others met in St. Paul, but nothing of substance happened.[20]
Richard Scammon, a native Minnesotan, son of the medical school
dean at the University of Minnesota, activist in the 1934 teamster
strike, and now a postgraduate political scientist, sought to export
the movement to Michigan,[21] with little success.

Between April 1936 and January 1937 membership in the Farmer-
Labor Association increased by 14,522, or 41 percent, and the *Minnesota Leader* in late 1936 claimed a paid circulation of 44,000,
though each month its operating losses ranged between $1,000 and
$3,500.[22] In June 1937 Howard Williams was still arguing that
Farmer-Laborism's strength was increasing in thirty states, and he
expressed confidence that the movement had finally crushed the old
parties in Minnesota and Wisconsin.[23] This attitude seemed in part
validated by a national Gallup poll of February and August 1937,
which showed 21 percent of the voters (9.5 million) interested in a
1940 Farmer-Labor presidential party.[24] But astute observers like
Dale Kramer of the Farmers Union knew it was dying for a variety
of reasons.[25]

Williams may have had his own doubts about regional and national
third-partyism, for in the spring of 1937, after overlooking his pre-

vious distrust of Benson, he appealed to the governor for a state job and in October was appointed director of state veterans affairs.[26]

In New York Alfred Bingham, one of the founders of the League for Independent Political Action in 1929 and a longtime ally of Williams, told delegates to the socialist League for Industrial Democracy on June 19, 1937, that both the socialist and communist movements were incapable of generating popular support. Bingham had revised his thinking about Roosevelt, whom he now saw as undermining Fascism and bringing on some socialist reforms. Minnesota Farmer-Laborism, Bingham added, was much too narrow in its economic and political appeal to be copied elsewhere because it could not gain and keep the support of the American middle class.[27]

In Wisconsin Tom Amlie largely agreed with Bingham. Although Amlie had toiled faithfully for the third-party movement, he credited Roosevelt with carrying a score of progressive congressmen to victory, among them Voorhis, Allen, Coffee, Hill, Magnusson, O'Connel, Scott, and a dozen or so more Democrats. Citing Minnesota, Wisconsin, and possibly Oregon as exceptions, Amlie pronounced third-partyism almost dead and said he was prepared to support Roosevelt in 1940. "If Roosevelt is renominated" (for a third term), Amlie concluded, "we shall have to support him."[28] Henry Teigan, a lifelong socialist, had reached a similar judgment and admitted that Roosevelt was the best president he had witnessed in a life devoted to political action.[29]

Factional Disturbances in Minnesota

Between the November election and the new year, party infighting appeared to be on the increase. In St. Paul AFL labor moderates gained control of the Trades and Labor Assembly, and in Ramsey County Farmer-Labor moderates ousted Paul Tingle, a leftist, as chairman of the local association central committee. Across the state, efforts were under way to wrest association power from the followers of I. C. Strout, Carl Erickson, Marian Le Sueur, and the Hennepin County radicals. Usually these struggles were along ideological lines. A. F. Lockhart of the *Minnesota Union Advocate* applauded the changes, and so did Henry Teigan ("more than I can tell you").[30]

At the 1937 association state convention in late January, Benson appeared to misunderstand the reason for his 57-percent victory, and he told the delegates, "we need no longer fear red scare campaigns. . . ." Aware of growing unrest in the movement, Benson pleaded with the delegates "not to permit the spirit of disharmony to enter our ranks."[31] Nevertheless, opponents moved quickly to depose Strout as association secretary, charging him with being dictatorial, and they accused Marian Le Sueur of fomenting internal antagonism. She in turn denounced state oil inspector George Griffith for running an "invisible government" within the association. Harold L. Peterson of Willmar easily defeated Strout (615 to 205); house tax committee chairman Ed Hagen of Milan defeated Selma Seestrom of Minneapolis for vice-chairman; and Paul Harris was re-elected state chairman.

The association was thrown into increasing disarray. Although the convention endorsed a merit system of civil service — to take effect one year after passage (as Benson proposed) — it fought the Sustaining Fund Committee and in general disagreed over who should be in command. To make matters worse, late in the session Hjalmar Petersen insisted upon making a speech in defense of his brief tenure as governor.[32] Peace and calm settled briefly over the delegates only when a KSTP recording replayed an old Floyd Olson speech, which provoked the always irreligious A. F. Lockhart to comment, "I guess a lot of the yokels thought Floyd had been pulled from cold storage for the occasion. But I am sure it's just a phonograph record. I may be wrong however."[33]

Signs of political decay, some of ominous character, were increasing, and anti-Semitic references to Abe Harris became more common and started to show up in letters-to-the-editor columns.[34] Meanwhile, Democrats had moved a comfortable distance away from Farmer-Laborites. In April Hjalmar Petersen was invited to the Democratic party's Jefferson dinner, and although he gave no indication of his newly discovered interest in merger, speakers at the dinner talked about remaking the state Democratic party into a publicly acceptable alternative to what they now called a radical Farmer-Labor state administration.[35] Increasingly, Farmer-Laborism was being isolated politically and ideologically.

The Minneapolis City Election

To the national disintegration of the movement and the disarray at the state convention had to be added the disastrous 1937 Minneapolis city election which swept from power a Farmer-Labor mayor and city council. The outcome was an ominous warning about what might occur in 1938.

The February 1937 Minneapolis Farmer-Labor convention made the previous month's state convention appear peaceful and serene.

At the center of the controversy was Mayor Thomas Latimer, a lawyer of relatively mild socialist leanings who deserved a better fate at the hands of his own party. But the backwash from the violent 1935 Flour City Ornamental Iron strike, in which he had requested and Olson had sent national guardsmen to maintain public order, brought upon Latimer a wrathful left-wing reaction and led to the charge of police intervention and strikebreaking because he had permitted nonstrikers to pass harmlessly through massed picket lines. In 1936 Hennepin leftists had sought to expel Latimer from the association and now they were determined to thwart his reelection. Latimer's difficulties were compounded further by the ideological split between Stalinists and Trotskyites. He had joined the Minnesota unit of the American Committee For the Defense of Leon Trotsky, which automatically invoked the CP:USA charge of renegadism. In the Minneapolis Central Labor Union A. H. Urtubees led the labor opposition, and the emerging CIO was still another of his antagonists. Fearing a disaster in Minneapolis and the impact it would have on state Farmer-Laborism, Elmer Benson urged the two ideological factions to accept a two-week adjournment during which time, the governor hoped, saner minds might bring about a compromise. However, the Latimer forces calculated that the truce would gain them nothing, and their decision was to call a rump convention.

The basic line of attack of the Latimerites was developed by Allen Sollie, Violet Johnson, Patrick J. Corcoran, and Trotskyite Miles Dunne and was dominated by the charge that Stalin Communists had infiltrated the Farmer-Labor party (i.e., Association) in a subversive attempt to gain control. At the rump convention speaker after speaker arose with a laundry list of Red charges which made the campaign oratory of Republicans J. A. A. Burnquist and J. A. O. Preus in 1918 and 1920 seem almost restrained. Yet these were Farmer-Laborites declaring that members of their own party were Communists or Communist sympathizers! Owen Cunningham warned, "The people must decide between Communism on the one hand and Americanism on the other." Miles Dunne of teamster local 544 declared, "Roger Rutchick, Selma Seestrom, A. H. Urtubees and Lendert Boerebach are Communist stooges." And a resolution carried which charged Communists and Communist sympathizers such as John Soltis, Sam Davis, Harry Mayville, Nat Ross, Clarence Hathaway, and others[36] with dominating the Hennepin County Farmer-Labor Association.

The resulting division of forces tended to put the AFL, the Farmer-Labor moderates, and the Trotskyites on the side of Latimer, whereas the CIO, the Farmer-Labor left, and the Communists became his unyielding opposition. Once more, the increasingly vulnerable Benson attempted to intercede, this time by dispatching Guy Alexander, Sander Genis, and Steve C. Lush on an unsuccessful peacekeeping mission. Neither side would budge, and the left-wing regulars endorsed former university football All-American Kenneth Haycraft, the director of the state old-age pension board, as its candidate for mayor. They labeled Latimer a renegade and traitor, accused his followers of Red-baiting, and lost a court skirmish that sought to deny the mayor the use of the name "Farmer-Labor" in his campaign.[37]

The spreading waves of vitriolic denunciation rolled into a May 1-2 meeting of the association's state central committee, where they split this body into two bitter factions. Fred Miller, a labor associate of A. F. Lockhart, offered an antileft resolution that asked the association to keep out of the Minneapolis free-for-all; it was defeated with a vote of ten to eight. Then Valeria Pappenfus and Koscie Marsh proposed that the state committee "go on record opposing the Communist party and declare we do not desire their support in the future"; Selma Seestrom and Hilliard Smith succeeded in tabling that resolution.[38]

Thus seesawed the primary campaign. Although Haycraft won a 236-vote victory over Latimer, the ideological battle took a heavy toll. Latimer and Haycraft together barely outpolled the former four-term Republican mayor George Leach, whose 50,861 ballots were solid evidence he was benefiting from antiradical sentiment, just as he had in the 1920s. Leach was about to become the first (and only) five-term Minneapolis mayor.

Too late did Farmer-Laborites realize their error. Leach's victory failed to budge Farmer-Labor left-wingers controlling the Hennepin association. After the June general election they defiantly announced a refusal to expel Communists and instead claimed (erroneously) that Farmer-Laborism's decline in the midtwenties had come about because the movement had resorted to "red-baiting and expulsion of Communists or [Communist] sympathizers." Instead, the left wing congratulated itself for defeating Latimer and looked forward to "victory in 1938 with Benson for Governor."[39]

But Henry Teigan, for one, admitted he should have endorsed Latimer rather than Haycraft.[40] And Kenny Haycraft, whom the left had used, offered a realistic appraisal: he foresaw a rapid dwindling of Farmer-Labor support and warned Teigan that drastic action was necessary to halt the precipitous decline in Farmer-Labor popularity.[41]

Party Crisis over Foreign Policy

State Farmer-Laborism now was hardly in a position to absorb any more divisive struggles and still hope to survive the 1938 campaign, which was expected to be bitter. Unfortunately, one more issue not only intruded but undermined an area of agreement which had hitherto united nearly all Farmer-Laborites.

Historically isolationist, Farmer-Laborism had been bonded by its foreign policy, which had made common allies out of socialists, liberals, progressives, Nonpartisans, farmers, workers, Marxists, and Minnesota's dominant northern European ethnics (Norwegians, Swedes, Germans, plus the Irish). After 1918 these groups welcomed the retreat into isolationism as Farmer-Labor leaders clung to this standard. Shipstead, Olson, the Kvales, Carrs, Petersen, Benson, Williams all attacked imperialism, Wall Street, and the profiteering war and defense industry, even though they might disagree on other economic and ideological issues. Shipstead and Olson had spoken in common opposition to America's defense preparedness, its meddling in European politics, and its defending the international interests of Great Britain. Olson passed on to Elmer Benson the belief that the United States best served itself and mankind by remaining neutral and not wasting its resources and manpower on military spending. Benson took the advice readily and in mid-1936 rhetorically asked on the senate floor, "if we are not spending that money for the purpose of aggression, why are we spending it?"[42]

Isolationism up to 1936 was nearly an automatic response of conservatives, moderates, and leftists. In near unison they would chant "keep the profits out of war," and then tear into Wall Street, the business search for international markets, and higher defense spending which they believed would lead to intervention in foreign affairs. The one exception was their willingness to dump agricultural surpluses into international trade.

Suddenly this policy began to change, first with the rise of European Fascism but particularly with the outbreak of the Spanish Civil War. The war itself pitted an embryonic Republican regime (called the Loyalists), which seemed to be steadily moving toward constitutional democracy, against the Falangist (Fascist) military dictatorship of General Francisco Franco. Coincident with the war was the about-face of Soviet foreign policy and the Comintern's decision to pursue a Popular Front strategy in common opposition to Fascism, especially German Nazism which the Russians feared most from a strategic point of view. Hitler and Mussolini sided with their fascist ally Franco, armed him, and then tested their military weapons and tactics on the Spanish battlefront while the Soviet Communists rallied to the support of the Spanish Loyalists.

Fundamental destabilization in European power politics quickly telescoped into Minnesota Farmer-Laborism. Disciplined Communists in its association immediately espoused the new Communist party line, and they were joined by the fellow travelers and many (but not all) Farmer-Labor leftists. However, traditional Farmer-Labor isolationists other than the radicals continued to adhere to a noninterventionist foreign policy, and they probably spoke for the vast majority of the Farmer-Labor rank and file as well as the party's supporting voters.

As European political conditions changed rapidly, a difficult problem developed for Farmer-Labor congressmen, state officeholders, and the movement in general. The left wing continued to distrust high American military budgets (because they believed the armed services and Wall Street were both aggressively imperialist), but the more militant left saw virtue in sending American war material to the Spanish Loyalists, and they encouraged American volunteers in paramilitary organizations like the Abraham Lincoln Brigade to serve on the Spanish front. This put them in conflict with the mood of Roosevelt and the Democratic congress (and Republicans) between 1936 and 1938 when the initial national reaction was to retreat to or at least renew isolationism by passing strict neutrality legislation which forbade contraband sales and arms shipments to foreign combatants.

The two congressmen most caught up in the dilemma were Henry Teigan (third district) and John T. Bernard (eighth). Privately, Teigan was candid about his preference, which was to abandon traditional Farmer-Labor isolationism. "It [the Spanish War] may be a fight between Fascism and Communism but if so, yours truly will go with the latter," Teigan told an acquaintance in January 1937. "I am death on the damned Fascists."[43] In April Teigan released a statement declaring workers and farmers had an obligation to rally to the defense of their international brothers wherever a repressive and reactionary government threatened their common cause.[44]

Teigan's changing foreign policy attitudes reflected his new naive romanticism toward the Soviet Union, perhaps coming about through his recent contact with Farmer-Labor Communists and through reading the rather glowing descriptions about the Soviet experiment written by British socialists like Sidney and Beatrice Webb. "The fact remains that democracy is developing steadily and fairly rapidly" in Russia, Teigan told a Norwegian author, and he predicted that in ten years "the Russian people will enjoy greater political democracy than do those in any other lands, including Scandinavia." Although he was not so blind as to fail to see the existence of a Soviet proletarian dictatorship, he dismissed it as temporary and excused it because, he said, at the time of the 1917 revolution the Russian people were too illiterate for democracy. In October Teigan told a Russian editor of *Soviet Union Today* that "no true liberal can deny that the change from Czarist to democratic rule in the USSR" had in just twenty years brought far-reaching benefits to Soviet citizens, and that he hoped through expanded prosperity "the democracy inherent in the Soviet system may be extended."[45]

The major difference between Teigan and Bernard was how and to whom they expressed their opinions on Spain and foreign policy. Teigan was much more likely to express himself privately, but Bernard, because he was more radical and less cautious, made public speeches in support of the Loyalists. In one crucial congressional vote, Bernard cast the only vote against an arms embargo, and the effect of it was to allow a munitions ship bound for Spain to reach international waters where it could not be stopped by the U.S. Coast Guard. Bernard's internationalism closely paralleled that of the Comintern, and moderate Farmer-Laborites immediately, and within a few years even some of the Farmer-Labor left, suspected him of following the Communist line on foreign policy.

The impact of the Spanish crisis compounded the mounting political problems of Elmer Benson. The governor was about to be politically victimized again by a controversial issue over which as governor he had little control and not much direct responsibility. It would have made good sense for Benson to remain silent on foreign policy and to limit his speeches to domestic issues. But it was not in his nature to remain silent, and when he did speak out, he linked domestic and international politics and was injured by both. Disappointment over legislative defeats and a growing belief that Roosevelt was not going far enough in his reforms and that the remedies of the New Deal were largely stopgap measures embittered the governor and altered his perspective.

In August Benson agreed to participate in a New York rally of the American League Against War and Fascism. Addressing 10,000 demonstrators, Benson charged that after eight years of depression the lesson to be learned was of big business continuing to erect barriers against workers, and he warned that corporations were becoming the partners of an increasingly dangerous American Fascist movement. Although he endorsed Roosevelt for a third term, he also predicted that a strong national third party would emerge in 1940 while the world struggle intensified between the forces of democracy and fascism.[46] Apparently he numbered Communists among the defenders of political freedom.

Throughout 1937 and into 1938 controversy over foreign policy accelerated the rupture in Farmer-Laborism. Not only did moderates remain isolationist, but growing disagreement over the Spanish question brought an increased demand that Communists and radicals be expelled from the association. The Minnesota left, however, continued to work with them. Howard Williams succinctly summed up its attitude when he said, "Put the cards on the table" when dealing with Communists, and he urged Communists to calm down lest they injure the movement.[47]

Outside the Farmer-Labor arena the Mnnnesota right wing served warning that radicalism and the Communist issue were ripe for exploitation. Senate conservative leader A. J. Rockne privately told Williams that Farmer-Laborites were fussing around with political problems about which they knew little, and "we all out here in the country know you as a near Communist or near Socialist or something of that kind."[48]

THE 1938 PRIMARY CAMPAIGN AND ELECTION

Although ideological confrontations and changing conditions had a great impact on Minnesota Farmer-Laborism, the party's 1938 campaign struggle revolved about the personalities of the two main combatants, Hjalmar Petersen and Elmer Benson. Petersen had waited three tense years for this gubernatorial campaign, and Benson's time in office had intensified his social criticism. Neither seemed willing to back away from the stands they took, nor would their supporters allow them.

Benson had finished little over three months in office when the unofficial Petersen campaign was begun by Farmer-Labor state senator J. Lawrence McLeod, the Grand Rapids physician who served as minority caucus chairman. Using the People's Lobby fiasco and the Benson tax program as his reasons for attacking the governor and arguing that the political trend was away from Benson and toward the middle-of-the-road, McLeod in May urged Petersen to begin a regular schedule of speechmaking.[49]

Petersen needed very little encouragement. Although he claimed to like his new regulatory duties[50] and felt secure in his six-year term, he had a strong drive to regain the governorship. As a small newspaper publisher (the *Askov American*) he knew not only how to generate news but how to disseminate it statewide. His early attacks on Benson came in the form of broadsides against the Farmer-Labor machine, which he claimed was subverting the democratic process.[51] Some state Democrats sought to get national chairman James A. Farley to intercede on Petersen's behalf in order to encourage him.[52] Although Petersen saw himself as the moderate alternative to the radical faction, it was not until after George Leach had decisively defeated Kenny Haycraft that he realized the political value of adding an anti-Communist crusade to his campaign.[53]

By summer 1937 Petersen already was attracting broad attention, his early campaign being indirectly aided by senate conservatives (like Senator Donald O. Wright) who assailed Benson for creating turmoil, hatred, and disruption.[54] Nationally known author-news commentator Elmer Davis predicted in *Colliers* (a weekly magazine) that Benson was in danger of being defeated and that Petersen was a possible new man of Minnesota political destiny.[55] Even those who attempted balanced analysis, like Vivian Thorp of the *Minneapolis Journal,* and acknowledged Benson's commitment to the underprivileged, found him ill-tempered, lacking in political wisdom, and concluded that state governmental effectiveness was seriously impeded as a result.[56]

As Petersen's attacks drew growing attention, they were censured by the Benson majority on the Farmer-Labor central committee,[57] and in a searing follow-up the first week of August Petersen condemned the propaganda and partisanship of the *Minnesota Leader* and "the warped views of its editor Abe Harris."[58] This careless diatribe drew a rebuke from McLeod and a warning to Petersen against intemperate outbursts.[59] More significant were the changes in Petersen's thinking and speeches about economics. During a midsummer tour in conservative southern Minnesota Petersen began to say that socialism had swung too far to the left and that there was wisdom to be rediscovered in Jefferson's admonition that the best government did the least governing.[60]

When Petersen persisted in his steady barrage, the Farmer-Labor state central committee demanded he appear before it for questioning, and in an unyielding two-and-one-half-hour session on September 9 Petersen charged the *Leader* with being one-sided and narrow-minded, setting class against class, and being commanded by those whose personal self-interests it served.[61] A committee of three was appointed to investigate, but the outcome was never in doubt and only one member bothered to examine what Petersen claimed to be evidence supporting his contentions. Before a December report exonerated the *Leader's* management,[62] Petersen reminded Abe Harris he had not forgotten Harris's testy vendetta of the year previous.

Impact of Anti-Semitism and Labor Violence on Benson's Campaign

Coincident with the early Petersen campaign was a wave of growing anti-Semitism. Although there is no evidence that it was encouraged by Petersen, it did serve to benefit him at the expense of Benson and he took no positive action to stop it. With increased frequency slurs were directed against the "Jewish *Leader,*" and some small newspapers and rural Farmer-Laborites urged Petersen to join the tirade (which he did not). "Hjalmer's love (sic) for the Mexican Generals and the Jewish Triumvirate (Abe Harris, Arthur Jacobs, and Ruger Rutchick)," wrote the *Murray County Herald*, "had not subsided, and once he opens his campaign, the people of the state can expect to hear some startling statements and see some scalps fly."[63]

In addition to anti-Semitism, Benson was injured by a series of incendiary labor disturbances. In the spring of 1937 the governor interceded in a tense confrontation between armed farmers and picketing timber workers.[64] Then late in the year Norman Thomas Socialists and Trotskyites clashed in the Farmer-Labor Association after the Workers party (Trotskyites) had infiltrated and taken command of the Minnesota Socialist party (SP) in an effort to remake the SP into a more revolutionary Marxist movement.[65]

More hurtful yet to the overall political environment was the cold-blooded murder of an official of teamster local 544, Patrick J. Corcoran. A moderately conservative AFL official and a vice-president of the Minnesota Federation of Labor, Corcoran had come to local 574 as part of a peacemaking compromise which national AFL president William Green had reached with the Trotskyite Dunne brothers and their 574 union, which now was renumbered 544. Corcoran served as chairman of the North Central District (teamster) Drivers Council, and the reorganization evolved out of growing tension between the AFL and the CIO and represented an AFL attempt to undermine the independent industrial union movement.

Benson and the state administration had neither direct nor substantial indirect involvement in these vicious union power struggles, though politically Benson was very sympathetic to the CIO and its organizers. But the Farmer-Labor name still associated Benson and the state administration with union hooliganism in the minds of a sizable sector of the voters. There was more popular intrigue than usual because ten days before the murder *Minneapolis Tribune* gossip columnist Cedric Adams had written that Corcoran was "ticketed for elimination." The AFL blamed the murder on CIO hoodlums, though neither a police investigation nor a Hennepin County grand jury could solve the case. The Hennepin County CIO industrial council denounced Green, teamster international president Dan Tobin and the local Trotskyites, the Dunnes, William Brown, and Farrell Dobbs who, the CIO declared, were resorting to a labor union reign of terror. To further complicate the matter, Communists usually coalesced around or were active in CIO unions rather than in the AFL or the teamsters union. The political connection in these sordid struggles came in local CIO leaders' denunciations of Green, Tobin, the Dunnes, and 544 for what was alleged to be an antiunion alliance against Elmer Benson; it was simultaneously claimed that the same group stood behind Petersen's campaign, which in turn supposedly had as its real objective the return of Minnesota Republicans to power.[66]

Steady Farmer-Labor disintegration, the dissolving of the old coalition, and Benson's mounting disabilities not only encouraged Petersen but also brought him a steady stream of unsolicited advice. Some thought he should become a Democrat, others said a Republican, and A. J. Rockne suggested he campaign as a fusion Republican-Democratic-Independent universally endorsed by the safe-and-sane elements in Minnesota politics.[67] By year's end, however, Petersen had decided to fight for his nomination through the Farmer-Labor primary.

A week before Hjalmar Petersen's mid-January candidacy announcement, the Farmer-Labor Association state committee adopted, ten to eight, a resolution of censure declaring him guilty of giving comfort to the enemies of Benson and Farmer-Laborism while aiding the forces of political reaction.[68] That there were eight dissenters demonstrated how deep the division within the movement had become. For example, house speaker Harold W. Barker demanded before the Minneapolis Fifth Ward Farmer-Labor club that Peterson be expelled from the association.[69] But in January conservative labor forces friendly to Petersen and led by William Brennan easily won control of the St. Paul Trades and Labor Assembly, soundly defeating a slate of pro-Benson candidates.

Petersen and the Communist Issue

Petersen delivered a statewide radio announcement on January 17 which had a devastating impact upon Benson and the state administration. With his brother-in-law and J. Lawrence McLeod as advisers,

Petersen had gone through four revisions of the speech, and they wondered whether the final version somewhat overplayed the Communist issue.[70] Petersen opened with a pledge to replace harassment of business with encouragement of industry, to stop wasteful misuse of public funds, and to eliminate party disunity. ("I am not bringing dissension into the Farmer-Labor party. Existing dissension is due to the disruptive leadership now in control.")

The real savageness of the Petersen attack came when he talked about Communist penetration. "We must decide whether we are going to adhere to Farmer-Labor and good American principles or surrender our party to Communist influences," Petersen warned, adding that Communist leaders were "welcomed with open arms" by the Benson state administration. In so doing, Benson and his administration were said to ignore and override the association's constitution, which denied membership to those advocating the overthrow of government by force. And Benson was accused of subverting Floyd Olson's long practice of active anti-Communism. Recalling how Communists "damned and cursed Governor Olson," Petersen declared they now were "enthusiastically accepted by our present Governor" and as a reward for Communist party service Benson put them on the state payroll!

Petersen's second pledge, therefore, was to end what he called Communist influence in the Farmer-Labor party. He predicted that voters would expel the Communists from state government just as they had in 1937 eliminated them from Minneapolis local government. Denying that this was old-time Red-baiting and that he was making these serious charges for personal gain, Petersen contrasted the past with the present. "What evidence of communism can we find in the public career of Knud Wefald, Magnus Johnson and Floyd Olson?" he asked rhetorically, and then added: "But I charge that the present Governor has taken prominent Communist leaders into his fold, and used his high office to further their Program." He named none, however. But moralizing further (and either overlooking or forgetting how some anti-Semitics had rallied to him), Petersen said he would rather be defeated than depend for victory upon un-American support. He pledged to eliminate Communists from the party and the state administration if elected. Let the people decide![71]

The aftershocks of the announcement pleased Petersen; by his own count thirty-nine editorials were favorable, twelve neutral, and seven critical. McLeod too considered it an excellent beginning. The theme of the counterattack against Petersen appeared within a week in the *Minnesota Leader* where Abe Harris described Petersen as a

political Charlie McCarthy (the then popular radio dummy) who
served as a mouthpiece for Republicans Roy Dunn, Martin Nelson,
and Harold Stassen. Petersen was said to have finally revealed what
many had long suspected: that he was a reactionary on ideological
and social issues; that on a personal level he was a vain, jealous politician who hated Benson primarily because he (not Petersen) was
governor; and that he resorted in desparation to Red-baiting only
after other attempts at political slander had failed.[72]

Petersen would become a much more formidable opponent than
the Benson wing first anticipated largely because his support came
from both the rural areas and segments of organized labor, especially
the AFL and the teamsters. Nor was Petersen alone in airing the
Communist issue. For example, the January 27 edition of the (teamster) *Northwest Organizer* echoed his charge by declaring it was
"well known" that the Communist party exercised excessive influence in the Farmer-Labor party and that Abe Harris used "Stalinist
methods" to stifle and repress the opposition.[73] Indeed, in a private
warning to Benson three years later, Harris would substantially agree
and admit that some Farmer-Laborites were guilty of following the
Communist lead, especially on foreign policy.

It was clear the Benson forces were genuinely concerned about the
issue and believed it made the governor vulnerable to criticism from a
portion of organized labor which should have been his natural ally.
In an effort to relieve some of the labor pressure Frank Starkey, Carl
Carlgren, and Roger Rutchick (who was Benson's personal secretary)
met with the *Minnesota Union Advocate*'s publishing board to dis-
suade it from continuing the editorial policy that Benson was "soft"
on the Communist issue.[74] But attempts like these were constantly
undermined by the Communists themselves, this time by a Communist public announcement endorsing Benson's reelection because he
was the best labor governor in the United States.[75]

Eventually Benson and his administration became cautious, and by
the time of the state convention they had verbally shifted more toward the political center. During a mid-February Benson-apprecia-
tion dinner, at which Wisconsin's progressive governor Philip La
Follette served as a featured speaker, Benson delivered a spirited
defense of his Farmer-Labor program, called for higher teacher salaries, deplored the intrusion of anti-semitism into 1938 politics,
condemned violence, and pledged not to use national guard troops
to break strikes. But he still refused — as he would in future decades
— to acknowledge any Communist problem, instead calling it a

pseudoissue and a mask used by exploiters to shield their ulterior motives.[76]

Ideological Turmoil within the Farmer-Labor Organization

One reason for Benson's continuing self-confidence was the sheer size of the Farmer-Labor Association membership. By December 1937 subscribers to the *Minnesota Leader* neared 100,000, and the Benson wing believed this represented sympathetic support and an insurmountable lead which Petersen could not overcome.[77] (Petersen really did not have any comparable organization but relied largely on a personal following and whatever labor support he could muster.) However, the Farmer-Labor Association would soon be weakened by a growing ideological schism between moderates and left-wingers, and the ideological issue above all others would be the single greatest influence in the 1938 election.

An ideological battle occurred in February at the Fifth District Conference of the Farmer-Labor Women's Federation (FLWF) when Mrs. Charles Lundquist, the FLWF state president, strongly objected to the activities of an "invading" group, led by Selma Seestrom, which interrupted the proceedings. Lundquist, a Petersen supporter and Benson critic, charged the Seestrom "intruders" with being "Communistic."[78]

In early March a similar disturbance erupted at a meeting of the St. Paul Tenth Ward Farmer-Labor club when consulting engineer Steven Gadler, seeking endorsement for the legislature, demanded the expulsion of club trustee Rose Tillotson on the grounds that she was the Communist committee chairwoman of Ramsey County. Speaking against the Gadler resolution was Howard Y. Williams, who argued against launching a purge of Farmer-Labor membership.[79]

At the convention in the Third Congressional District a coalition of moderates and antiradicals gained control, but they did not deny Henry Teigan or Benson reelection endorsement (though state representative John H. Nordin later decided to file in the primary against Teigan).[80]

A different situation prevailed in Hennepin County, where the dominant left wing demanded the expulsion of any member or unit found to be working against the Farmer-Labor program, its constitution, or its endorsed candidates.[81] Not only were Petersen and his followers the intended victims, but this was also an attack on all-party activity which Floyd Olson had used so effectively in the past.

In such manner the ideological civil war seesawed until the March state convention. At a tempestuous three-hour session of the Ramsey County Farmer-Labor central committee, and not withstanding his defense by Farmer-Labor founder William Mahoney, Gadler's membership in the party was revoked and he was denied his delegate seat to the state convention because he had "injected discord" and "disregarded desires of the majority" in his controversial attacks upon Farmer-Labor Communists. Then, defying logic, the committee by a vote of 130 to 18 stripped three Communists — Tillotson, Leon S. Cuthill, and chairman Wilbur Broms of the Minnesota Young Communist League — of their Farmer-Labor membership. Gadler apparently was removed primarily because he was believed to be a Petersen supporter.[82]

An even more severe rupture occurred March 23 at the Farmer-Labor Women's Federation state convention in Duluth, attended by 1,200 delegates. Led by outgoing seven-year president Mrs. Charles Lundquist and her successor, Mrs. Josephine Tomai of St. Paul, moderates were in firm command. Factional discord greeted one issue after another in this most bitter of all FLWF conventions, and not until late in the convention day did civility return and then only after respected Susie W. Stageberg pacified the women by admonishing their unruly and discourteous behavior.[83] Three anti-Communist resolutions were approved in spite of heavy left-wing resistance.

The Farmer-Labor Association State Convention

Months of internal ideological discord and Hjalmar Petersen's bid to capture the Farmer-Labor nomination for governor finally cast upon Benson and his managers the somber realization that not only was the governor's future uncertain, but Farmer-Laborism itself was at a turning point. Suddenly apprehensive, Benson and convention leaders now retreated from public ownership issues and moved toward a position much more compatible with Floyd Olson's 1930 and 1932 campaigns and the conventions which preceded them.

However, factional discord could not evaporate overnight. For one thing, the left-wing Hennepin group offered a resolution to expel what it called the "disloyal" elements. Convention strategists successfully bottled it up in the constitution committee. A right-wing Farmer-Labor demand to expel Communists was also kept out of convention debate, and a bloody floor fight was avoided when anti-Communist resolutions were expediently buried in the platform and resolutions committee where they were not acted upon.

At the outset Benson sought to deny endorsement to interim railroad and warehouse commissioner Harold Atwood (whom Petersen had appointed) and suggested St. Paul AFL leader William Wright as a replacement, but when the AFL and the rail brotherhoods resisted dropping Atwood, Benson backed down though Atwood was made to publicly pledge support for Benson's reelection. Otherwise the governor exhibited a much milder side of his personality and political beliefs, sought to avoid controversial confrontation, and the tactics he and his supporters now pursued were intended to present Petersen as the political odd-man-out in Farmer-Laborism.

Benson's relatively moderate demeanor and the care he exercised in preparing himself and Farmer-Laborism for the 1938 campaign were major surprises at the convention. Muting radical sloganeering, Benson instead appealed for an economic democracy and a "society in which war, unemployment and poverty must be banished." Although he may still have been thinking in terms of socialism, he avoided its more politically dangerous references. Like Franklin D. Roosevelt, he said that great corporations and Wall Street sought to extend their dominance through the mechanism of the Republican party. Reviving the old Farmer-Labor principle of international nonintervention, Benson (unlike Roosevelt) attacked military preparedness legislation and "big navy bills," demanded government control of the munitions industry, and warned against an industrial mobilization bill which he said placed economic control in the hands of a few super industrialists. Equally important, Benson resolutely adhered to strict isolationism, and unlike Farmer-Labor leftists he did not advocate American intervention on the side of the Spanish Loyalists, though ideologically he certainly supported them.

The Communist issue was the most threatening to him, and he felt very sensitive about it. As he had done so frequently, Benson pleaded for a rejection of Red-baiting, declaring "intelligent people know the Farmer-Labor party is not a Communist party and that it does not have a Communist program." Finding the source of these attacks to be "special privilege," Benson also warned of dangerous false liberal prophets who disseminated "vile falsehoods and defamations." About their motivation he said, "They are not trying to save the state from Communism, but to restore the rule of plunder." He professed he would rather lose the election "than defend that which is wrong."[84]

Nevertheless, Benson and his state administration, his defenders, and the Farmer-Labor left continued to be injured by the Communists themselves. Hardly did the Communists conceal their presence nor did they try to go unnoticed, for during the convention they distributed handbills to delegates, pledged loyal support to the association, approved the platform even before it was announced, endorsed the Farmer-Labor slate of candidates before they were chosen, and expressed warm special praise for congressmen Henry Teigan and John Bernard![85]

The 1938 association platform took on a conservative tone when compared with those of 1934 and 1936, a fact which drew immediate attention and comment from the metropolitan press. Gone were references to a dawning new social order, and public ownership proposals had been mysteriously stripped away; even a plank for socialized medical care was surgically removed in committee. At one point a lonely voice was heard to call out from the floor for a resolution embracing "production for use," but the presiding chairman ignored the words as though they were an ideological profanity. Was this modern Farmer-Laborism? Old-timers like William Mahoney, anti-Communist but socialist, scarcely could believe what they were hearing. Mahoney offered an amendment to place idle factories under government operation. It lost overwhelmingly! Another veteran socialist, Duluth attorney Sigmund Slonin, speculated that the change represented an unexpected turn to the extreme right.[86] The strongest language the platform writers could bring themselves to use was declaratory and mild: an economic crisis still existed, one third of the nation was ill-fed, unemployment was too high, and "fundamental changes in our social system" were needed to solve social and economic problems. But the platform offered no explicit programs to change these conditions beyond those offered by the New Deal. In short, the generalizations were commonly expressed a quarter-century later by Democratic presidential candidates without fear of radicalizing their party.

The Farmer-Labor ticket was equally unobtrusive. Benson almost alone stood as a symbol of the left, and now he apparently strived to change this image. John J. Kinzer, a moderate state representative from the German brewery town of Cold Spring in conservative Stearns County, won endorsement for lieutenant governor. State treasurer C. A. Halvorson was reendorsed, and another moderate, John T. Lyons of Le Center, again served as candidate for auditor. William S. Irwin, who became an appointed attorney general after the 1936 electee was appointed by Petersen to the supreme court, also gained endorsement. The left's success was limited to I. C. Strout's victory in the contest for clerk of the supreme court.

At 5:05 A.M. on the morning of March 27 a weary convention adjourned, and temporarily some Farmer-Laborites believed the serious party breaches had been skillfully closed. Henry Teigan called it the best convention in twenty years.[87] However, the true test of this claim could not be made until June and November. It was not the party's perception of itself and Benson which counted most, but Petersen's and, more important, the public's.

Petersen supporters were unimpressed; to them the changes were cosmetic and further proof of deception. State senator Harry A. Bridgeman of Bemidji, a legislator for sixteen years, had urged the association to take an open anti-Communist stand. When it did not, he concluded it refused because Communists had infiltrated Benson's state administration. He told Petersen, "If something is not done to eliminate the gang we will not have any Farmer-Labor party." Petersen of course agreed: "The communists are here and they are getting stronger every day in our party. They are boring from within and are not with us to do us any good." When Olson became ill, Petersen said, he was too weak to resist the manipulators who first put Benson in office and then let in Communists and their sympathizers; now "the present state administration is in so deep with the communists that they cannot shake them."[88] On this theme Petersen prepared to contest Benson in the primary.

Courting the Democrats

Although the fortunes of the Minnesota Democrats would not rebound in 1938, the civil war within Farmer-Laborism did alter Democratic thinking. For years liberal Democrats had more or less considered the Farmer-Labor movement a surrogate to Democratic success while awaiting the unknown time when they could absorb Farmer-Laborism. In past agreements, Farmer-Laborites had shortchanged Democrats, a fact that nearly all Democrats belatedly realized.[89] Democrats now sensed their growing political equality with Farmer-Laborites and the declining vitality of the Farmer-Labor movement. And many Democrats were disturbed and even frightened by Benson's unpredictable and maverick style and his sympathy for the political left. St. Paul attorney Francis M. Smith (in 1944 one of the principal legal advisers on merging the two parties) concluded, as many Democrats now did, that "the Reds are actually dominating the Farmer-Labor Party."[90]

The ill-conceived Democratic withdrawals were not to be repeated. Farmer-Laborites sensed the new attitude, which pervaded even the

White House. These subtle changes sufficiently alarmed Henry Teigan into asking White House staff about them; he came away feeling reassured that "the big chief" was "strong for Elmer" and "the rest of us."[91] Benson, however, disbelieved that all was well.

Indeed, significant changes were occurring. Lacking their former confidence, Farmer-Laborites now were asking Democrats for assistance or volunteering help in the hope of securing future Democratic favors. Meanwhile, Democrats acted more confident and independent. The attitudinal change was evident in the 1938 St. Paul city election. In the spring Democrat John J. McDonough barely lost the mayoral election to Republican William H. Fallon. McDonough's followers were convinced that he did so well (he would win in 1940) because he won the support of the many Catholic Democratic voters, and they discounted the local impact of both Benson's and the Farmer-Labor party's of endorsement of McDonough.[92] They were also mindful of Farmer-Laborism's sharp setback in the 1937 Minneapolis election.

Stassen and the New Republicanism

To change the political alignment of Minnesota voters, Republicans had to overcome their minority status and their image (given them by Democrats and Farmer-Laborites) of being reactionary representatives of major business enterprise and narrow economic self-interest. Rising to the Republican challenge was young, ambitious thirty-one-year-old Harold E. Stassen, the Dakota County Attorney, who waged his own campaign against the party old guard and its traditional organizational establishment. Stassen promised a new Republicansim pledged to progressive reforms, a socially sensitive party capable of meeting depression's lingering problems, and an administration that would use New Deal reforms and some of its own without hesitation. Stassen claimed these goals were attainable through orderly and peaceful means, which contrasted with the divisive, dangerous, and unnecessary radical alternatives demanded by Benson and militant Farmer-Laborism.

But Stassen first had to gain the gubernatorial nomination by defeating Martin Nelson, who twice had lost his bid for the post, and Minneapolis mayor George Leach, who for years had wanted to be governor. Stassen was not the choice of the regular organization, a fact which actually strengthened his appeal in the fall since he appeared to represent a younger more responsive Republicanism.

The Bitter April-June Primary Battle between Benson and Petersen

Hjalmar Petersen's position in the Farmer-Labor party was sometimes parallel to Stassen's in the Republican party. Petersen, too, fought the party organization, but, unlike Stassen, he had a weak campaign organization and relied primarily upon personal appeal and individual endorsements. Actually, Petersen's endorsements came from a rather wide segment of Farmer-Laborism: former Minneapolis mayor William A. Anderson, Brooten dentist S. C. Shipstead (brother of the senator), the son of Magnus Johnson, a score of legislators, the Democratic chairman of the Sixth Congressional District, Mrs. Knud Wefald, Mrs. Charles Lundquist, R. A. Trovatten, and scores of old-time Farmer-Laborites who came out of the Nonpartisan League.[93] Secretary-treasurer of his volunteer committee was J. Lawrence McLeod. Even the mayor of Benson's hometown, A. T. Forsberg of Appleton, announced for Petersen.

Petersen hammered at bossism, the party and its administration machine, and the Communists, whom he charged with wrecking the traditional Farmer-Labor party. Soon he made a shambles of the apparent calm and unity of the Farmer-Labor Association's state convention. When he faced weekly disappointments as party regulars defected to Benson, Petersen attempted to use them as evidence of party machine duress. Charles Munn and Harold Atwood of the Railroad and Warehouse Commission, attorney general William Ervin, and supreme court justice Harry H. Peterson he claimed were his natural supporters, and their defections he described as forced capitulations brought on by "dictatorial nitwits" of the Benson administration who "connive, shakedown, and racketeer" until even good men are under such tremendous machine pressure that they are forced to yield.[94] He argued the crisis was statewide and appealed to Republicans, Democrats, Farmer-Laborites, and independents. In speech after speech he promised to drive out machine misrule and wasteful administration, to expel Communists, and simultaneously to oppose Fascism.

At first the Benson campaign ignored Petersen in the mistaken belief that he was a minor threat unworthy of attention. By mid-May, however, unmistakable signs indicated to Benson strategists that they had seriously underestimated the effect of Petersen's slashing attacks upon Benson. "We are up against a tough battle and we must not leave any stone unturned that can win us votes," Benson's former personal secretary C. D. Johnston confessed to Henry Teigan.[95] The Benson counterattack then turned upon Petersen. Tom Davis, who in years past had run against Floyd Olson and campaigned for Senator Thomas Schall, delivered a tough radio speech against Petersen by quoting from Petersen's last bitter letter to Olson in which he asked the dying governor to balance the account. "Can any friend of Floyd B. Olson vote for a man like that . . .?" Davis asked WCCO and KROC listeners, answering that no true Christian was justified in voting for Petersen.[96]

Benson attempted to focus public attention upon his liberal legislative proposals, his program of economic security, and his administrative pursuit of the larger public interest. At another time or in the hands of another campaigner this might have worked better. But Benson too often ill-timed his other activities and misanswered questions. For several months, while under pressure from the association, he sought the removal of state WPA administrator Victor Christgau, a former two-term congressman from the first district whom left-wingers ideologically mistrusted and accused of opposing the unionization of WPA workers. Although Christgau ultimately was discharged, Benson's action angered many moderate Democrats and alienated them from the governor. Another setback for Benson occurred when rumors circulated about possible administration scandal in connection with purchases and construction at Bemidji State Teachers College. And some religious fundamentalists took up Benson Red-baiting. Revealing "The Sinister Menace of Communism to Christianity," Riverlake Gospel Tabernacle evangelist Luke Rader literally led prayers for a Petersen victory.[97] Benson likewise suspected the Catholic Church hierarchy of quietly working against him.[98]

Benson never was a politically patient man, and such attacks and criticisms took their toll. A fortnight before the primary balloting, in addressing about one hundred clergy and their wives, Benson appeared more angered than usual, and among other things the governor lumped together war, the press, his political opponents, and the Minnesota senate, charging them with having a corrupting moral influence upon the state. Luckily, he had not included the clergymen, but notwithstanding this oversight someone asked the inevitable question: Was he a Communist? Benson exploded. The issue, he shouted, was "fake," and those who raised it knew less about it than he did and he knew absolutely nothing. The *Minneapolis Star* honored his expressive candor with an appropriate headline: "BENSON DENIES HE IS ATHEIST OR COMMUNIST."[99]

The Primary Election and Its Aftermath

Thus was waged the most bitter Minnesota primary election in the twentieth century. On June 20 over three-quarters of a million primary voters cast ballots, nearly two-thirds the number who would vote in November. This was almost a quarter-million (235,067) more primary voters than had turned out in 1936, a 44-percent increase. Farmer-Labor votes more than doubled, up 117 percent; Republican votes increased 25 percent; but Democrats suffered a 37-percent decline, or a drop of nearly 50,000 votes. The election results indicated that the public had grown increasingly dissatisfied with the trend in Minnesota politics.

Party	1938 Votes	1938 Percentages	1936 Percentages
Farmer-Labor	424,308	55.2%	36.2%
Republican	263,473	34.2%	39.2%
Democratic	81,595	10.6%	24.2%

Benson survived this factional civil war with a narrow 51.4-percent victory over Petersen, but his reelection chances were severely, even fatally damaged. Benson's 16,030 plurality (218,235 to 202,205) fell far short of the 50,000-vote margin predicted by some of his optimistic supporters, and he owed his victory to the three most populous counties of Hennepin, Ramsey, and St. Louis which combined provided the governor with a 27,181-vote plurality and 45 percent of his total vote. St. Louis County alone, which included the Iron Range and Duluth, gave him 17,414 more votes than Petersen (30,300 to 12,886) and reflected the leftward thrust of iron miners and their militant new union organizers who worked vigorously for Benson. Nevertheless, this kind of active political support, and that of the left-wing industrial unions in Minneapolis and St. Paul, proved to be a limiting factor which seriously narrowed Benson's base of appeal and worked against the conscientious effort to make him appear more moderate. Petersen actually carried fifty-one of eighty-seven counties (or 59 percent), fifteen more than Benson.

Meanwhile, Stassen, winning with 47 percent of the Republican vote, had performed rather impressively considering that he ran against well-known Martin Nelson and George Leach and a third candidate. The Democratic gubernatorial nomination went to Thomas D. Gallagher of Minneapolis, but the party otherwise slipped badly, the 1936 withdrawals apparently turning dissatisfied voters toward a realignment with young Republicans and Stassen.

Benson and Farmer-Laborism's chance for recovery rested to a large degree on the attitude of Hjalmar Petersen and his campaign workers. Petersen's narrow defeat or near victory was organized on a $6,800 shoestring,[100] a mere fraction of what the Stassen and Benson operations had at their disposal. Some Petersen supporters were so mistrust-

ful of the state administration that they believed an honest count of
votes might even have given him victory, though no proof of voting
irregularities was offered. But Jean W. Wittich, who had headed Floyd
B. Olson's All-Party Volunteer Committee in 1930 and later served in
his administration, still speculated that balloting irregularities took
victory away from Petersen.[101]

Benson and his organization were shaken by the close race, and they
attempted to overcome its effect by accommodating Petersen and his
followers. Petersen was very slow to react. Ten days after the election
he dryly commented, "Let the people rule,"[102] and his campaign
manager, J. Lawrence McLeod, urged him to stay away from the Ben-
sonites. McLeod soon defected from Farmer-Laborism, joined the
Stassen campaign, and advised Petersen that in the event of a Stassen
victory "his organization would undoubtedly take it upon themselves
to assure your re-election . . . as long as you wanted it."[103]

Not all of Petersen's supporters were so reluctant to make peace
with Benson. Editor A. F. Lockhart of the *Minnestoa Union Advocate*
considered Stassen to be as bad as Floyd Olson and wondered whether
Benson was the lesser of the 1938 evils.[104] New men were added to
the Benson campaign staff in an effort to broaden his more moderate
appeal. St. Paul Democrat Lewis E. (Scoop) Lohmann was designated
campaign chairman, the secretary to moderate ninth-district Farmer-
Labor congressman Richard T. Buckler, Harold C. Hagen (who later
succeeded Buckler as congressman and switched to the Republican
party), became campaign secretary, and Petersen backers David Lundeen (nephew of the senator) and John H. Nordin joined the reelection
staff.[105]

By mid-August both Stassen and Benson organizers intensified efforts to recruit Petersen volunteers. One group, led by Rev. John Flint,
met at the Dyckman Hotel and pledged to support Benson. But another
not only ridiculed Benson's new moderate image but preferred a party
realignment to a continuation of the current Farmer-Labor administration. This group, during a meeting at the old West Hotel in Minneapolis,
renamed itself the Independent Progressive Voters of Minnesota (IPV)
and announced it would continue to fight the "sinister forces" that
brought machine rule and corrupt politics into the state. McLeod and
Mrs. Charles Lundquist were elected IPV chairman and secretary. Invited to address the IPV, Petersen fell short of endorsing its action,
but he told the group the "capitol hill machine" was doomed and he
declared it senseless to condemn private enterprise and then turn loose
"connivers, chislers, and incompetents" in state government. The IPV
organizers voted 41 to 5 to endorse Stassen's election.[106]

IPV's spontaneity appeared partly staged and Stassen organizers apparently were well aware of what was being done, but then too this group was hardly different from Floyd Olson's carefully orchestrated All-Party volunteers of 1930 and 1932. In fact, Stassen was building an almost identical All-Party campaign organization as he sought to advance himself and rebuild the Republican party.

In spite of these setbacks, Benson organizers were not to be faulted for their efforts to win an endorsement from Petersen. In late August Lohmann and attorney John Hougan spent a futile hour and one-half urging Petersen to forget past differences with Benson, but McLeod continued to press him to stay neutral.[107] A month later, on September 19, A. T. Forsberg and attorney Frank E. Wright pleaded with Petersen for three hours and urged him to come to Benson's fall keynote speech in Appleton. Petersen again refused. The following day Minneapolis Democrat John P. Devaney, a former state supreme court justice (1933-37), asked Petersen to meet personally with Benson and consider grounds for reconciliation. Whether in good faith or not, Petersen finally agreed and was driven to Benson's home where he, the governor, Devaney, and Wright discussed grievances. Petersen made one inflexible demand: that there be a public retraction by Abe Harris and the *Minnesota Leader* of what he said were bogus charges, abuses, and misrepresentations to which he had been subjected over the past several years. Either Benson could not do this, or Harris refused. No accommodation was reached and no endorsement was forthcoming, though Devaney continued to urge Petersen to join Benson.[108]

Word of these meetings leaked out, and rumors quickly circulated about a pending political deal between the two enemies.[109] Petersen's brother and newspaper partner Svend cried, "For God's sake stand pat; and tell them all to go to Hell!" Then state senate arch conservative A. J. Rockne tantalized Petersen with the possibility of succeeding Shipstead in 1940, implying that a Benson endorsement would likely rule this out.[110] After a week of silence Petersen on September 27 released a statement of nonalignment. He pledged to continue working "to keep the Farmer-Labor party true to its best tradition and ideals," admitted "I was up to bat and struck out," and said it was now time for others to "go to bat and let Minnesota voters — the umpire — cast ballots in accordance with their best judgment."[111] Although Petersen's metaphor was poor, his evasion was clear enough. He had not endorsed Benson.

Petersen's decision helped Stassen and hurt Benson, just as it was intended to do. He doubted that Benson personally wanted his support and suspected that the governor was only following the expedient advice of campaign managers. McLeod, now working with the Stassen All-Party volunteers, reinforced Petersen's decision by telling the commissioner that Scoop Lohmann while intoxicated had bragged about how he had successfully double-crossed the beguiled Petersen.[112] However, Petersen also was leery of Stassen for the same general reason he disliked Benson—both men blocked his path to the governorship.

THE 1938 FALL CAMPAIGN

Farmer-Laborites Wage a "New Deal" Campaign

In 1938 Benson and his party faced political issues they could not control and changing times which put their movement increasingly outside the mainstream of public concerns. So during the summer and fall a major effort was made to pull Farmer-Laborism back into the circle of political moderation from which it had been removed, sometimes by its own doing. Benson and his fellow Farmer-Labor candidates now repeated New Deal slogans and attempted to reidentify with the Roosevelt economic and Democratic political recovery. With this new strategy they sought to rejoin the moderates in their party and to win in November.

Left-wing Farmer-Labor candidates were also caught in the nasty web of rapidly altered foreign policy relationships which caused a backlash in American politics. Congressman Henry Teigan was one of those who sought to bury his pro-Spanish Loyalist attachments when he realized the Catholic Church identified Communists and their sympathizers with the Loyalists and was making political war in 1938 upon politicians who were believed guilty of wrongful fraternization. Suddenly, Teigan fell deliberately silent on foreign policy in the hope that this would end the Church's opposition to his reelection.[113]

Equally damaging to Minnesota Farmer-Laborism was the newly exhibited coolness of the White House toward Benson. Teigan believed that one reason for this was Roosevelt and presidential adviser Harry Hopkins's assessment that Benson was a growing political liability, and, as Hopkins prepared plans for Roosevelt's controversial third term, he feared antagonizing Minnesota Democrats, a growing number of whom opposed Benson's reelection.[114] Politically, Farmer-Laborism found that Democrats had the upper hand, and Teigan attempted to convince the national leadership that Benson was loyal to the New Deal and exceedingly supportive of Roosevelt! To prove it, Teigan sent Roosevelt counsel Tommy Corcoran a pro-New Deal speech of Benson's with the comment that the White House would surely appreciate the support it was receiving from Benson.[115]

Benson's rediscovered enthusiasm for the New Deal was most evident at his campaign kickoff speech delivered September 20 in Appleton. Introduced by Democrat John Devaney (who owed his state supreme court appointment to the patronage powers of Floyd Olson!), Benson avoided any mention of public ownership and production for use. He attacked Republicanism and big business, warned the public against believing that Roy Dunn (a conservative legislative leader) and Republicans had been converted to progressive politics, and praised a Minnesota Plan for helping agriculture. In every way possible Benson sought to erase his former radical image. He favored tax reform, opposed the sales tax, applauded pay-as-you-go state financing, and told of the encouragement he gave the Board of Regents in getting it to admit its error in the 1917 dismissal of Professor William A. Schaper. Nearly every phrase praised moderation and New Deal reform. When he talked about his own state programs, he apologetically and almost pathetically added, "this in no way disparages what has been done by the New Deal," or he said there was "no Hoover in the presidential chair today."

Benson went out of his way to escape entrapment on the Communist issue and to dodge the repeated attempts to label him a Communist sympathizer. Communism was a dictatorial movement, he said, and "there is no room in our party for anyone who believes in dictatorship of any form." His statement on foreign policy cut across the Communist issue because, unlike the CP and some left-wing Farmer-Laborites, Benson remained staunchly isolationist and pledged continuing opposition to American involvement in European power politics. As he spoke the Czechoslovakian Sudetenland situation was becoming a crisis; millions of troops were being reported as massed for war in the event Nazi Germany annexed the Sudetenland. But Benson was firm in urging the United States to mobilize for peace, and he declared, "never again must we send our boys across the seas to die on foreign soil."

Benson, for the duration of the campaign, was attempting to return left-wing Farmer-Laborism to the positions always taken by moderate Farmer-Laborites. Radical rhetoric which had cropped up during 1934, 1935, 1936, and 1937 went into hiding. Benson liberally wrapped himself and the party in New Deal bunting. The central campaign issue was said to be the prevention of the Hoovers and Landons from taking control of the state. Farmer-Laborism was the New Deal. Minnesota must stay in the New Deal column. "The Farmer-Labor party has supported Roosevelt and the New Deal," Benson argued, adding, "The Farmer-Labor party brought the New Deal to Minnesota."[116]

The Republican Campaign

The case Republicans made against Benson and Farmer-Laborism was neither startling nor original. Almost every denouncement of the governor had already been uttered scores of times by Hjalmer Peterson and other Farmer-Laborites determined to defeat Benson and his state administration, eliminate radicals and Communists from party and government, and return the movement to more moderate objectives.

Republicans largely conducted an effective cleanup campaign. They too promised continued reform, attacked bossism, condemned political machines and job selling, and pledged to introduce the merit system of civil service. Contracts for purchases and construction were to be let only after competitive open bidding; "sweetheart" arrangements with favored businesses would end; Farmer-Labor waste would be replaced by Republican administrative efficiency. And like Floyd Olson before him, Stassen built his campaign around the All-Party volunteer committee, staffing it with the familiar names of former Farmer-Laborites and Democrats like R. A. Trovatten, J. Lawrence McLeod, Mrs. Charles Lundquist, Mrs. John Lind, Magnus Johnson Jr., and Young Republicans Edward J. Thye and Richard Golling.

The Republican campaign at times was brutal. Former Republican state auditor and one-term congressman Ray P. Chase led the worst of the attacks with his campaign book *Are They Communists or Catspaws?* for which Abe Harris filed a libel suit against him. (It was settled out of court several years later.) Virulent anti-Semitism erupted, and racial slurs were heaped upon Benson advisers like Harris, Arthur Jacobs, and Roger Rutchick; coming as they did during the rise of the Nazi movement, worried Jewish state leaders hurriedly created the Minnesota Jewish Council as a vehicle for civil rights protection.[117]

The Failure of Benson's Strategy

Because time has dulled our memories of the Farmer-Labor past, Elmer Benson's 1938 campaign has often been misrepresented. Apologists occasionally describe Benson as preferring principle to victory and defeat to compromise. This romantic notion may better express his later attitude, particularly Benson's prominent role in Henry Wallace's 1948 presidential campaign. But it is an oversight to ignore how hard Benson worked to be reelected and how far he was willing to go in playing the role of a liberal defender of Roosevelt and the New Deal who just happened to be a member of the Farmer-Labor party.

Liberal or radical, which version would be believed? Try as Benson might in 1938, he never succeeded in altering the popular majority perception that he headed a left-wing state administration which was out of step with the times and which sometimes was guilty of administrative malpractices. Although scuttling the left-wing Farmer-Labor call for public ownership and production for use, Benson was partly done in by the refusals of Communists and radicals to leave him alone.

Since becoming governor Benson was held in special high esteem by the Communist party, USA. Its national party secretary Earl Browder, an occasional social and personal acquaintance of Congressman Henry Teigan, once told Teigan and a small gathering of friends that Benson was easily the finest governor in the country because he was a man "of courage and good sense."[118] In a September 1938 issue of *New Masses*, Meridel Le Sueur forthrightly declared, "The Communist Party of Minnesota, without selfish political aims, fights the pro-fascist Stassen, the tory in liberal disguise, and stands solidly and powerfully behind Elmer Benson."[119] Eighth-district congressman John T. Bernard was another Farmer-Laborite whose radical embraces hurt the party. An active and enthusiastic backer of the new militant CIO industrial unions and the United Auto Workers, Bernard as a result lost further standing with the more moderate Minnesota State Federation of Labor, which in 1937 had rejected Bernard's request to speak before the state federation convention and continued attacking his radicalism right up to the eve of the 1938 election.[120]

Benson's campaign was further damaged in mid- and late October when the Dies Committee in Washington received testimony from ten Minnesotans, including Steve Gadler, Mrs. Charles Lundquist, Violet Johnson, Rasmus Borgen, Albert Lundquist, Herman Husman, and Andrew G. Cooper, who all described Communist activities in the Minnesota Farmer-Labor party. Borgen testified as a confessed CP member until 1937; Gadler named thirty-five individuals he claimed were Communists; and Mrs. Lundquist talked of CP activities in the Farmer-Labor Women's Federation. Some on Gadler's list were fairly well-known left-wing or radical Farmer-Laborites: Minneapolis alderman Herbert G. Finseth, Chester Watson of the Workers Alliance, *Minnesota Leader* business manager Clint Lovely and editorial writer Steve Adams, Lem Harris of the Farm Holiday Association, Charles Rowaldt, John Soltis, "Maribell" [sic Meridel] Le Sueur, and various CIO organizers.

For Benson such testimony was the kiss of political death. Lewis Lohmann, his campaign manager, branded it false and misleading, and Clint Lovely denied being a Communist. But Mrs. Lundquist attempted rebuttal by declaring that those who denied it were lying. In desperation a telegram was sent to Dies inviting him to hear Benson praise

Roosevelt and the New Deal at a state campaign rally, but the conservative Texas Democrat not only refused to attend but further injured Benson by charging the governor and his followers with using deceptive Communist tactics.[121]

To make matters worse for Benson, damaging anti-Communist campaign flyers were now being circulated. One included a photograph allegedly showing him riding in a Communist parade. Bryle A. Whitney, a national officer of the brotherhood of railway trainmen, came to Minnesota and over WCCO radio defended Benson and declared the photo a fake.[122] Republicans then released a statement from the photographer certifying its authenticity, with a citation from the *New York Herald Tribune* upholding the story.

A few liberal Democrats still spoke out for Benson. Joseph Wolf, arguing that Thomas Gallagher had no chance of winning, again endorsed Benson. In the First Congressional District the Farmer-Labor candidate withdrew, and Benson endorsed conservative Democrat Joseph Moonan who was running for Congress! Despite Wolf's efforts and the presence on the Benson reelection campaign staff of Lohmann and John P. Devaney, Benson had lost major Democratic assistance. John Regan of Mankato, always an opponent of Farmer-Laborism, made a statewide radio broadcast urging Democrats to stay with their own party candidates. And as was to be expected, Benson periodically lost the battle to control his temper, once engaging in a bitter public exchange with the daughter of Charles Lindbergh Sr. and a group of Lutheran clergymen.[123]

By now Benson's charge that Stassen was owned "lock, stock, and barrel" by the railroads and the steel trust had little political sting. The third-party experiment was failing, and Minnesota was taking another step toward classic two-party competition.

Voter Realignment in the November Election

A massive shift in voter alignment in November swept Benson and the Farmer-Laborites out of power. The Farmer-Labor gubernatorial vote, which had brought a landslide 58-percent victory in 1936, fell to 34 percent in 1938, a drop of nearly 300,000 votes. The outcome was no off-year fluke, for 1,144,926 votes were cast, only 19,000 fewer than two years before. Of eighty-seven counties, Benson carried only six (Clearwater, Koochiching, Lake of the Woods, Pennington, Roseau, and St. Louis), all of which were in the far north central or northwest portion of Minnesota, mostly along the Canadian border. He won in St. Louis County by only 1,296 votes of 98,000 cast; in Pennington by only 13; and he lost in Swift, his home county, by 231.

RESULTS OF THE 1938 MINNESOTA GENERAL ELECTION
(Candidate, No. of Votes, and Percentage of Total Vote)

OFFICE	REPUBLICAN	DEMOCRATIC	FARMER-LABOR	INDUSTRIAL
Governor	Harold E. Stassen 678,839 (59.3%)	Thomas Gallagher 65,875 (5.9%)	Elmer A. Benson 387,263 (33.8%)	John W. Castle 899 (.8%)
Lieutenant governor	C. Elmer Anderson 590,404 (51.6%)	Ray M. Lang 113,483 (9.9%)	John J. Kinzer 374,577 (32.7%)	
Attorney general	J. A. A. Burnquist 530,971 (46.4%)	John D. Sullivan 154,799 (13.5%)	William S. Ervin 378,385 (33.0%)	
Secretary of state	Mike Holm 690,312 (60.3%)	Hugh T. Kennedy 83,298 (7.3%)	Paul A. Rasmussen 328,474 (28.7%)	
Treasurer	Julius Schmahl 603,029 (52.7%)	Len Suel 91,156 (8.0%)	C. A. Halvorson 378,160 (33.0%)	
Auditor	Stafford King 616,145 (53.8%)	J. B. Bonner 92,320 (8.1%)	John T. Lyons 364,636 (31.8%)	
Railroad and warehouse commissioner	Frank W. Matson 546,345 (47.7%)	Arthur N. Cosgrove 110,484 (9.6%)	Harold Atwood 395,493 (34.5%)	
Clerk of the supreme court	Grace K. Davis 537,629 (47.0%)	Francis M. Smith 137,064 (12.0%)	I. C. Strout 364,988 (31.9%)	

Note: The total percentage for each office is less than 100 because some voters cast blank ballots and some ballots were spoiled.

Minnesota Farmer-Laborism, by Millard L. Gieske, © 1979 by the University of Minnesota.

The only significant Farmer-Laborite to escape defeat was ninth-district congressman Richard T. Buckler. Henry Teigan lost in the third district by 2,937 votes; veteran representative J. Paul Kvale was defeated in the seventh by 6,822; John Bernard lost in the eighth by 13,579; and Howard Y. Williams, who came within 360 votes of winning in the fourth district in 1936, now lost by 19,694. Everywhere Farmer-Laborites were hurt by the presence of active Democratic candidates, and conservative Democrat Elmer J. Ryan was reelected in the second district.

However, Farmer-Laborism's collapse did not immediately serve to revive Minnesota Democrats. Statewide they usually ran between 6 and 10 percent, their strongest candidate receiving only 13.5 percent. And in four congressional contests Democrats captured 35, 44 (Elmer Ryan), 17, and 19 percent.

The realignment resulted, therefore, in a massive shift of power to Republicans, who won eight congressional seats, all state offices, and control of the legislature. Stassen's astounding 59-percent triumph immediately drew national attention. And the 1938 party realignment was taken by a growing number of liberals and Democrats to be a sign that the third-party experiment had run its course and was now a luxury too politically expensive to be tolerated much longer.

In a general sense, of course, it was true that Republicans made a sizable comeback everywhere as they began to recover from their overwhelming 1936 nationwide defeat. In the Congress Republican House membership increased by 75 seats to 164 (or 38 percent) and 7 new Senate Republicans were added. The Republican upsurge was even stronger within the Midwest. In the 1936 elections in the twelve-state Middle West (Illinois, Indiana, Iowa, Kansas, Michigan, Minnesota, Missouri, Nebraska, North Dakota, Ohio, South Dakota, and Wisconsin) plus Montana, Republicans had won only a single governorship (South Dakota), Democrats had won nine, Farmer-Laborites one, Progressives one (Wisconsin) and Independents one (North Dakota). Two years later when nine of these states held gubernatorial elections, Republicans won seven, and in 1940 three more switched.

Nevertheless, the regional Republican upswing was only one factor contributing to Minnesota Farmer-Laborism's collapse, which likely would have come even in the absence of a major Republican trend outside the state. The third party was being pushed aside, as in Wisconsin where the Progressive party's Governor Philip La Follette was defeated in 1938. Not only were ideological and foreign policy issues undermining the Farmer-Labor foundation and accelerating defections in the party apparatus, but as a third party it had almost no effective reserves outside the state to call upon for help when political trends returned to more normal patterns.

And even in defeat Democrats had been strengthened, since they now could deal with Farmer-Laborites on terms far more advantageous than before.

CHAPTER 10

The Debate over Merger

THE AFTERMATH OF DEFEAT

"It came as a shocking surprise to most of us," Henry Teigan lamented, "we had not expected the election to go the way it did."[1] Third-partyism had been staggered, the small liberal third-party bloc in Congress two-thirds decimated as its charter members Teigan, Bernard, Amlie, Boileau, O'Connell, and Scott were defeated. For Minnesota Farmer-Laborism the 1938 election was no mere setback but a disaster of yet undetermined dimension. Almost immediately it led to a severe cut in association membership, the ending of state employee "contributions," and the stopping of recruitment efforts. Two general attitudes emerged. The left-wing Farmer-Laborites, the movement's socialists of one kind or another, argued that the party should continue and resist merger with or absorption by the Democratic party. By contrast, increasing numbers of right-wingers and moderates now tended to explore ways of uniting with Democrats or of defecting to the Republican party.

Defeat, however, increased the price state Democrats could impose upon Farmer-Laborites in merger considerations. Although weaker at the polls, Democrats still had access to federal patronage, whereas Farmer-Laborites were out of power and much less popular than before. And the Meighan liberal Democratic faction, disillusioned by the Benson administration, agreed the one-sided agreements with Farmer-Laborites were a thing of the past.[2]

Explaining the Disaster

Farmer-Laborites agonized over who and what had caused the massive setback. Nearly every Farmer-Laborite had an opinion about this. The right wing demanded a purge of Communists which, if carried out, was certain to be bitter and disruptive. In a postelection statement Hjalmar Petersen called for critical self-appraisal, Charles Halsted of Brainerd asked for a housecleaning, and Vince Day told the president that Benson's political ineptitude had brought on defeat. "I can't understand it myself," Howard Y. Williams admitted, "but it is a fact and we must accept it," though he tended to acuse the "silent vote" of switching to the Republicans for continued progressive change. Elmer Benson put the blame on a two-year newspaper "hate campaign" that exploited Farmer-Labor disharmony and allowed state conservatives to manipulate this issue into victory. Wisconsin Progressive governor Philip La Follette, who also suffered defeat, saw a "gradual but unmistakable drift of public opinion" to Republicans, who wisely chose to accept progressive social programs rather than attack them.[3] Abe Harris, now permanently leaving Minnesota politics, praised Benson as a great governor "but the world's worst politician."[4] Ironically, Benson had returned to Appleton, entered the speculative business of land investment and farm real estate, a capitalistic venture which was beginning to make him a wealthy man!

Only a few Farmer-Labor office holders remained—representative Richard Buckler, Senators Ernest Lundeen and Henrik Shipstead, and railroad and warehouse commissioner Hjalmer Petersen being the most important. Several were unsure about their party ties, and an air crash would claim Lundeen's life in 1940.

Petersen's Republican Temptation

For a time Hjalmar Petersen was tempted by the prospect of reaching political agreement with Harold Stassen, and J. Lawrence McLeod repeatedly urged him to leave the Farmer-Labor party. Stassen played political cat-and-mouse with Petersen; three days before the election he asked Petersen whether he wanted to become United States senator, and while on a postelection vacation he sent him vague wires of greeting. At a mid-November conference the governor-elect talked variously about high appointment, asked Petersen to abandon the Farmer-Labor party, and invited him to join Stassen in rebuilding the Republican party into a progressive Minnesota coalition. Tentative palns were even made to have Petersen accompany Stassen to Madison for a conference with Philip La Follette.[5] In December the two met for the last time, but by now Stassen's ardor had cooled, he did little else than listen politely, and Petersen sensed that Stassen had changed his mind about inviting him into Republican ranks. Cordial relations between the two soon ended.

In January 1939 Petersen was further alienated when Stassen cut the biennial budget of the Railroad and Warehouse Commission, a move Petersen interpreted as an attack upon the regulatory function as well as a personal affront to a potential 1940 gubernatorial rival. It drove Petersen back into the Farmer-Labor party, where he stayed another six years. By February Petersen turned sour on the Independent Progressive Voters of Minnesota, which had worked for Stassen, and declined an invitation from McLeod, Mrs. Charles Lundquist, and Jean Wittich to join its ranks. Petersen now expressed criticism of Stassen's patronage policies, accusing the governor of firing Farmer-Laborite job-holders in a way reminiscent of the old Benson machine.[6] Politically, the impact of Petersen's falling out with Stassen helped extend Farmer-Laborism's lifespan because the left wing, traditionally an opponent of merger, and Petersen now had a common enemy in Stassen.

Shipstead Switches Parties

Petersen, however, spoke for only part of non-left Farmer-Laborism. Another element inched closer to Democrats, and the most prominent remaining Farmer-Laborite, Henrik Shipstead, finally moved over to the Republican party.

Shipstead had long been a major source of irritation to the left wing. Ideologically, he was progressive but not collectivist; he rarely worked for or cooperated with the association; and for years the party social-ists had wanted to dump him. But not only was Shipstead politically shrewder than his critics; he always could win more votes than any other Farmer-Labor candidate.

In 1938 the senator conveniently avoided direct or indirect involve-ment in both the Benson-Petersen primary and the Stassen-Benson fall campaign. Although rumors had long circulated about his switching parties—he always sat on the Republican right side of the Senate—in name alone Farmer-Laborites still needed him badly, and even Henry Teigan misjudged that the "S.O.B." would stay with his old party.[7] By 1939 Shipstead severed his Farmer-Labor ties, which extended all the way back to 1918. It was another loss the party could ill afford.

The Farmer-Labor Association's Schism over the Communist Issue

What contributed significantly to Shipstead's departure and the growing number of defections of other Farmer-Laborites was an unyielding party schism over the Communist issue. Believing radicals were the major reason for the party's ouster from power, moderates and right-wingers on the Farmer-Labor state committee wasted little time in demanding a purge. At a December 3 state committee meeting state senator George Lommen of Eveleth, lame duck fifth-district congressman Dewey W. Johnson, state representative Edward Hagen of Milan, and Walter Turnquist of St. Paul succeeded in passing a resolution calling for expulsion of all known Communists from the association.[8]

Labeling this action a repressive witch-hunt, the staunch leftists in control of the Hennepin County Farmer-Labor Association angrily branded Lommen, the other purge sponsors, and a host of others (including Paul Rasmussen, Ernest Lundeen, George Griffith, the Trotsky-ite Dunne brothers, and labor leaders Jack Carrier and Steve Lush) "Jew baiters, red baiters, and Minnesota Tammany politicians" who brought unwelcome turmoil and who, if not stopped, "will completely wreck the Farmer-Labor party." Lommen, Johnson, Carrier, Lush, and John Kinzer (recently defeated for lieutenant governor) retaliated with a joint letter to state Farmer-Laborites blaming the "spectre of Communism and other influences" for defeat, and whether the fear was real or distorted, Lommen warned, "the fact remains that thousands of sincere Christian people in Minnesota believed it was. . . ."[9]

Ideological warfare was carried to the floor of the December 18 meeting of the Hennepin County Farmer-Labor Association. Lush, Carrier, David Lundeen, and Archie Ogg demanded immediate enforcement of the state purge, but when Lundeen tested it by resolving to expel John Soltis he first was booed and then his resolution was tabled. With a two to one majority, the left dominated the local convention, elected Ralph Ahlstrom chairman over Lush, 225 to 115, and renamed Selma Seestrom secretary after her opponent withdrew with the caustic comment that she refused to be an officer "for a bunch like this." Moreover, the left's answer to the purge movement was to argue that Comminist expulsion violated the Farmer-Labor Association's state constitution![10]

The same ideological antagonism erupted in late January 1939[11] at the state convention, but now the left, speaking through Walter Frank, started its own offensive by demanding expulsion of all known Petersen supporters. The right-wing coalition, however, immediately countered by accusing fifty-seven Farmer-Labor radicals of being either Communists or Communist-sympathizers and demanded they not be seated at the convention. St. Paul AFL leaders Harry O'Connell and Ray Wentz carried the attempted purge to the credentials committee where the list was trimmed. O'Connell said the practical test of delegate eligibility was whether a Farmer-Laborite had signed a 1936 petition placing Communist Earl Browder on the Minnesota ballot as a presidential candidate. This whittled the list of accused to fourteen. The proposal passed the committee eight to four and was approved by a 319½ to 209½ floor vote. Thirteen of the expelled were from Minneapolis or other parts of Hennepin County, and they included Oscar and Madge Hawkins, Steven Adams, and Walter Harju. When Frank again proposed, "Let's forget the Communist question," he was booed and the convention voted to declare Farmer-Labor membership closed to Communists and Fascists.[12]

Emerging now was a significant new alignment in Farmer-Laborism whereby St. Paul labor leaders were the spearhead of opposition to the Hennepin left wing. At a January 31 meeting of the Hennepin central committee the expulsions again drew bitter denouncement, this time from Seestrom, who accused Myrtle Harris, Blanch McIntosh, and Lush of witch-hunting and who condemned the releasing of purged names to the newspapers.[13] So volatile was the situation between the left and right Hennepin factions that in late March association state chairman Harold Peterson attempted to mediate differences.

To air grievances, each group was given a separate one-hour hearing. The right-wing faction, with Seestrom and Leendert Boerebach present as "observers," met first. David Lundeen testified, "If the policy is to be in favor of those who pride themselves in being Communists, then something is wrong," and he argued that the 1938 disaster could have been predicted since some Farmer-Labor candidates had run with open Communist support and since Communist and Farmer-Labor campaign literature had been distributed side-by-side. Lundeen said the left party faction had to realize that when it flirted with Communists the price of such radical association was to destroy public confidence in Farmer-Laborism. And organized labor, Lundeen added, lost confidence in the Farmer-Labor party "because they were sick and tired of the Harold Beens and other Communists running the show while old-time Farmer-Laborites couldn't even get into the Governor's office."

Blanche McIntosh followed with a charge that "it seems that one has to be either a Communist or at least in sympathy with them" to be elected a delegate, and she specifically accused Selma Seestrom of protecting infiltrating Communists and simultaneously stifling their Farmer-Labor opposition whenever it conflicted with left-wing ideology or policy. The effect was said to be steady withdrawal of non-Communists from the association, and McIntosh described her

Fourth-Ward Farmer-Labor club as being predominantly Communist now. The only salvation was to strip prominent leftists like Orville Olson of their influence and power, McIntosh bleakly concluded, and "Unless [Seestrom], and Mr. Boerebach with her are removed from the Farmer-Labor Association the movement in Hennepin is dead."

Given a résumé of the charges, left-wing faction leaders denied there was any significant connection between Communist affiliation in the association and the 1938 reversal, claiming instead that the Republican comeback was probably the result of Benson's proposal for a state-owned liquor dispensary system. Although this had been at best a marginal issue in the campaign, liquor wholesale and retail distributors had strongly resisted it. Walter Frank claimed that biased reporting by the *Minneapolis Tribune* and *Journal* — they had branded him a "Red" — had provided a ready campaign issue which he said Republicans had unscrupulously exploited. Former municipal judge Arthur LeSueur, a pioneer in the Nonpartisan League and then the Farmer-Labor movement, also denied the validity of the Communist issue and its connection with the 1938 defeat; instead, he speculated that the voting public's worry about a possible tie between racketeering elements and some Farmer-Laborites and the patronage controversy were leading causes of the party's political downfall. And political scientist Richard Scammon (who was much more moderate in his later life) declared the university Farmer-Labor club had reached the consensus that if any group was to be expelled it should be divisive right-wing critics who he said were the minority.[14]

Differences of such ideological magnitude could be neither compromised nor settled, and the bitter controversy lingered on, not just for months but for years to come during times of peace and war.

THE NEW MOLD OF MINNESOTA POLITICS

Hastened by Farmer-Labor ideological division, a newly forming Minnesota political environment was beginning to alter the party system substantially. Although a half-dozen years were to pass before formal changes would be completed, unmistakable patterns were emerging which would make the 1940s much different from the 1930s.

Stassen and the Republican Buildup

The first major difference was the impact Harold Stassen had upon the Republican party and its opposition. With Farmer-Laborites locked in schismatic confrontation, Stassen enjoyed a much freer hand in dealing with the 1939 legislative session than had been the

case with the 1937 session. The young governor succeeded in eliminating much of the bitter wrangling between the executive and legislative branches of government, a marked contrast to the bitter fights
of the Olson and Benson years.

Stassen proposed and got civil service reform, and though there
were some changeovers from Farmer-Laborite to Republican employees before the civil service law went into effect, these were relatively
few and nothing like the scale of discharges which the Farmer-Labor
Association had sought during the bitter days of the depression.
Stassen reorganized state government, combined the old powerful
"Big Three" departments of budget, personnel, and purchasing into
a new Department of Administration, created a state labor concilia-
tion service, helped push through the legislature a controversial old-
age homestead lien act to help finance old-age assistance (long criticized, it was repealed thirty-four years later), accepted a token iron
mining tax increase, and claimed a $2-million reduction in state
spending over that of the previous Benson budget and some $19 mil-
lion less than that proposed by Paul Rasmussen, departing Farmer-
Labor budget director.

With relative harmony replacing the acrimony of the three previous regular sessions, Stassen could maintain that these modest gains
were the result of his effective leadership. But his accomplishments
were enthusiastically inflated by the Cowles newspapers (the *Tribune*
and the merging *Star-Journal*) as well as by the Ridder family's
Northwest Publications (*St. Paul Pioneer Press, Dispatch,* and *Duluth
News-Tribune*). Noncritical evaluations appeared in which Stassen's
accomplishments were described as at long last channeling the state's
energies toward constructive social purposes, and his journalistic
send-off has been unmatched in modern Minnesota history.[15] This
was very different from the frequent cataloguing of controversies
during the Farmer-Labor years.

During the nascent stage of Stassen's Minnesota popularity he
keenly appreciated his high standing in Gallup polls and confidently
looked toward reelection in 1940. Having mastered relatively easily
his Farmer-Labor and Democratic opposition, the governor found
some of his most entrenched resistance coming from old-guard Republican and economic interests who found his populism hard to accept. Somewhat like Olson, Stassen received his first sharp criticism
from his own party's flanks and vocal right-wingers like George N.
Briggs, who published a business-oriented conservative newsletter
("Information") which rarely praised him and frequently complained
about "do-gooder" reforms and expensive "Big Government" public

services. Stassen's heresy was further compounded by the suspicion that he favored liberal New York Republican governor Thomas E. Dewey for the 1940 presidential nomination.[16] However, Stassen later surprised the right wing by working for Wendell L. Willkie (a converted Democratic businessman), an irregularity which was considered an even greater transgression, for Republican mossbacks were attracted to Ohio Republican senator Robert A. Taft.

Prospecting for Democratic and Farmer-Labor Cooperation

Outside the Republican party the Stassen opposition was just beginning to explore ways of mobilizing against him. The Democratic strategy was to do two things: first recruit prominent Farmer-Laborites into their ranks and then build a solid base from which they could permanently fuse the two parties through a formal legal merger. After 1938 Democrats decided to absorb Farmer-Laborites in a way that blended the two parties but otherwise kept the Democratic party intact, while submerging the Farmer-Labor name and organization.

St. Cloud Times publisher Fred Schilplin, who was a moderate voice of the dominant, usually conservative Catholic Democrats in Stearns and adjoining counties, first invited Hjalmar Petersen to join Democrats in January 1939, and he repeated the offer after the 1940 general election.[17] Petersen was leery in part because he wanted to make certain that such an action would further his own political ambition (which remained the governorship). As a result he vacillated between leaving the Farmer-Labor party and staying in it. In March 1939 Petersen urged Missouri Democratic senator Champ Clark to become an anti-third term presidential candidate, journeying to Washington where he met with Clark, Lundeen, Shipstead, and James A. Farley, who by now was another opponent of the three-term presidency. Petersen sought to prevent any forced 1940 Democratic and Farmer-Labor coalition against conservatives and reactionaries,[18] though he avoided committing himself to the Farmer-Labor, Democratic, or new fused party. His reasons for opposing Roosevelt remained largely mysterious and seemed to relate to the assistance the president had given Benson in 1936 and a possible judgment that without it Benson might have been defeated earlier.

These early discussions between the two parties were expanded in mid-April at the Nicollet Hotel where nearly 200 Democrats and moderate-to-conservative Farmer-Laborites gathered for a dinner conference. The Democratic party was broadly represented, and Farmer-Laborites present included Petersen, John T. Lyons, and Charles Munn. A major topic of discussion was a possible two-party

1940 coalition which divided candidacies for state office evenly between the parties. Munn, whose term on the Railroad and Warehouse Commission was ending, led another discussion about the legal complications of merger, but he also urged Democrats to help elect popular Farmer-Laborites. To further explore means to cooperation, an eighteen-member committee, nine from each party, was created, with representation drawn from each congressional district.[19] The very fact that Democrats and Farmer-Laborites could meet openly signified an important change in thinking about the relationships between the two parties and demonstrated that within both there existed many individuals willing not only to join in a common campaign but also to explore the basic question of formal unification.

Contributing to the pro-fusion mood was the fact that Farmer-Laborism was in decline in Minnesota and elsewhere. In Minneapolis in 1939 Republican George Leach won an unprecedented fifth term as mayor, and his victory was in part due to the Farmer-Labor right wing's refusal to work with leftists. After the election the Farmer-Labor Association sponsored a rally in an effort to rekindle depressed spirits. Unfortunately, Tom Amlie, Elmer Benson, Harold Peterson, and Henry Teigan could find little to say that would cheer the group, although Benson did deliver, as he would many times, an emotional rebuke to Stassen and political reactionaries.[20] Benson's presence as national chairman of the moribund League for Independent Political Action (Howard Williams was national director) had not rallied that organization either. LIPA's goals were now much more limited: keeping the nation out of war, supporting the New Deal and programs like the Tennessee Valley Authority's electric generating and regional development policies, defeating reactionary Republican state administrations, and working for the nomination of a New Deal Democrat in 1940.[21]

Farmer-Labor survivors now were being encouraged by Democrats to join them in a party fellowship, the invitations coming from often unexpected sources. There was little surprise when Democrats in the Ninth Congressional District asked local Farmer-Laborites to meet for joint discussions, but the change of heart affecting state Democratic chairman Joseph Moonan of Waseca was a new departure. Moonan previously had been an arch opponent of fusion; now he welcomed Farmer-Laborites, promising them healthy coexistence in the Democratic party where as liberals they could continue working for the New Deal. Even Mankato conservative John Regan said kinder things about Farmer-Laborites. Under this relaxed Democratic atmosphere defections of spirit if not of actual membership began to occur as individuals like Josephine Tomai, president of the Farmer-Labor Women's Federation, and Paul Rasmussen became very comfortable with the flexible arrangements being made to accommodate them. Thus, as Stassen's strength increased and his ambitions expanded, a growing number of members in the two opposition parties were drawn into closer organizational fellowship.[22]

THE TWO VOICES OF FARMER-LABORISM

To slow down Harold Stassen's rise in popularity, let alone defeat him, was a major undertaking, and 1940 was a poor year for it. A fall 1939 Gallup Poll showed stable public support for the young governor, and a winter 1940 survey by the local Midwest Research Reports projected 45 percent approval, 32 percent disapproval, and 23 percent undecided.[23] Highly organized and well financed, Stassen was sufficiently strong, and politically skillful enough, so that only the combined efforts of Democrats and Farmer-Laborites seemed capable of defeating him.

By contrast, the Farmer-Labor organization was a shell of its once robust self. Association membership had fallen from 20,000 in 1938 to only 3,000 in 1940,[24] evidence that many state employees had been coerced into joining the association and were no longer threatened under the current Republican administration, especially under the new civil service system.

Hjalmar Petersen briefly considered becoming a Senate candidate if Shipstead chose not to run.[25] Then he again set his sights upon the gubernatorial nomination and sought to end his feud with Elmer Benson by approaching the former Farmer-Labor governor through Appleton attorney Frank E. Wright, who agreed with him that selfish former associates of Benson were largely responsible for their split.[26] At a minimum Petersen believed Benson was obligated to remain silent during the campaign, and the commissioner was urged by a few former Benson supporters and some Democrats to make the gubernatorial campaign.[27]

The Farmer-Labor schism, however, went much deeper than the feelings of a handful of its best-known leaders. In Hennepin County the Farmer-Labor Association, under continued left-wing control, remained adamantly opposed to fusion or cooperation with Democrats, and its central committee denounced efforts to expel "Reds" from the association.[28] At a badly split third-district convention a 33 to 17 vote admitted four Hennepin delegates who had been denied seats at the 1939 state convention. The decision so angered the minority moderates, who charged it with being in violation of explicit instructions from the state chairman, that fourteen members bolted the convention and sent a rival slate of delegates to the state convention.[29]

Nearly an identical division occurred at the St. Louis County and the eighth-district conventions. At the district convention in Virginia, John T. Bernard, Herman Griffith, Frank Puglisi, and their radical followers were in tight command, and an anti-Communist Farmer-Labor faction bolted, set up a rival convention at Hibbing, and sent a warning to state chairman Harold Peterson that it was "time to divorce ourselves from this undesirable element" and that moderate Farmer-Laborites "don't care to have this un-American element in our party any longer nor are we going to tolerate their dictating to us."[30] Farmer-Labor state senator (1935-63) Homer M. Carr of Proctor told the state chairman the party had better have "the guts" to throw out the radicals and take a "stand on the issue of Communism" or he and many others would leave the party and go their independent way.[31]

A Shattered State Convention

Farmer-Labor ideological segregation nevertheless was tempered by the political reality of Republican rebirth and Stassen's growing presence in Minnesota politics. Since confrontation injured victor and victim alike, the moderates in visible control of the March 8-9 state convention were reluctant to overextend their numerical advantage while the left was sufficiently practical to hope for its own comeback. Consequently, the mood was one of restraint and of objectives held in check. Keynote speaker Philip La Follette, the former Progressive Wisconsin governor, reinforced this feeling and warned against working with any national third-party against New Deal Democrats.

Despite these cautions there was little if any narrowing of real factional differences. The autonomous Farmer-Labor Women's Federation continued its attacks upon the Farmer-Labor left wing, Mrs. Charles Lundquist lauded Hjalmar Petersen and Charles Munn for their service on the Railroad and Warehouse Commission, and the federation demanded that the state convention deny seats to Selma Seestrom and seven other delegates. Meanwhile, Elmer Benson wound up being the unwitting catalyst in an explosion that shattered the temporary calm.

Invited to address delegates attending an evening dinner, the former governor was treated to a standing ovation which some leftists took as solid evidence of his continuing popularity among the rank and file. Later at the convention John T. Bernard requested that Benson be invited to deliver an unscheduled address. By itself this was cause for neither alarm nor open opposition. But Bernard shattered the ideological truce with another request: that the association elect Benson its new state chairman. To the astonished right wing this maneuver was seen as a bold attempt to shift power from the moderate Farmer-Laborites back toward the left. Bounding to his feet, state representative George Hagen condemned the proposal as a divisive shift and demanded instead the election of Edward Hagen. Benson, stung by such intense displays of feeling, withdrew his name and denounced those who he said were guilty of wrecking the party, shouting "We have stool pigeons in this convention."[32]

Because passions flamed again and the old bitterness had returned, convention managers saw little reason to continue, and a decision was made to adjourn proceedings for a three-month cooling-off period and to reassemble delegates in Brainerd on June 21.

The St. Paul City Election

In the meantime, a significant shift in political alignment was taking effect in St. Paul, giving Democrats an expanded base of support and with it new political influence and governmental control. The 1940 city election reforged a 1932 coalition of generally moderate forces in the Trades and Labor Assembly, the right-wing Farmer-Labor movement, and a number of Catholic Democrats from St. Paul; together they formed, under the effective political umbrella of the Labor-Progressive Association, largely a campaign organization.[33] Uniting behind the mayoral candidacy of Irish Democrat John J. McDonough, who had once served in the legislature (1925-33), the coalition won an impressive victory and four-to-three control of the city council.

This election heralded the second stage of Democratic recovery in Minnesota and was politically important for several reasons. It revived an important local Democratic power base, it stood in marked contrast to the political rejection of Minneapolis's left-wing Farmer-Laborites, and it represented a successful attempt at building bona fide cooperation between Democratic and moderate Farmer-Labor forces. McDonough, who would be one of the leaders in the 1944 merger movement, had appointed Farmer-Laborite Harry T. O'Connell as his campaign manager, and O'Connell in 1939 had been the leader of organized labor's moderate forces when they had sought to expel radicals from the Farmer-Labor Association.

McDonough quickly was identified as a Democratic labor mayor and was cited as proof that local Democratic fortunes in Minnesota were steadily improving.[34]

The Reconvened Convention

The three-month convention hiatus allowed Farmer-Laborites to work out a limited compromise, or at least to accept a cease-fire in the ideological warfare. But rapid changes in foreign relations and the course of the European war actually widened differences more than ever. Hitler's sudden blitzkrieg overran France, British survivors were evacuated at Dunkirk, and the French resistance collapsed with the dictated Nazi armistice. As western military resistance ended and Great Britain became the last western representative democracy to remain in the war, there developed a significant change in the attitude of Farmer-Labor moderates and even some socialists who identified with French and other western European Social Democrats. Moderates, including some longtime Farmer-Labor isolationists, supported the western allies against the Nazis even though they opposed direct American armed intervention. Midwest and Minnesota isolationism was being modified. In the Farmer-Labor platform committee socialist William Mahoney (the chairman) and George Hagen pushed a preparedness plank but also pledged to keep American troops out of Europe, a policy not very different from Franklin Roosevelt's.

Radical Farmer-Laborites, however, stoutly resisted these changes, continued to label war a root problem connected with Wall Street, capitalism, and imperialism, and championed a foreign policy similar to that advocated by the Soviet Union and the CP:USA, positions which all seemed logical to the left following the infamous Hitler-Stalin nonaggression pact of August 1939. Communists and most of their Farmer-Labor fellow travelers denounced the foreign policy preferences of the moderates. Elmer Benson likewise condemned the shift toward preparedness as war hysteria, and pledged to resist it even if he ended up being the last voice of opposition in the state. Not all the Farmer-Labor left wing was as adamant. Howard Y. Williams sounded increasingly ambivalent and wavered between advocating limited American military preparedness and condemning the "machinations of Wall Street and international bankers to get us into war."[35] Williams was now beginning to undergo a change in his political attitudes, and after the war he would emerge as a defender of the Truman-Marshall-Atcheson cold war policy, as would his LIPA colleague Paul H. Douglas.

Economic issues likewise split the left and the right wings. State senator George Lommen, the minority legislative leader, led the right in defeating (300 to 173) a left-wing proposal for the state of Minnesota to assume operation of iron mines as well as a one-dollar increase in the royalty tax on state-owned iron ore. The right tolerated a general statement in the 1940 association platform that natural resources and monopoly industries, including banks, munitions, and public utilities, should "ultimately be collectively owned." But the moderates were quite unenthusiastic about such endorsements, which were more a political convenience than an agreement on the substance of policy.

More popular immediate issues concerned endorsement of the Townsend plan's $200 monthly retirement program, repeal of Stassen's old-age lien law, reduction of the 36-percent interest rate on small loans, and increases in state income tax rates and iron mining taxes. When the convention ended, moderate Farmer-Laborites went away believing they had successfully checked the power of the radicals and the Hennepin left wing,[36] and now they seemed ready to cease their ideological bickering for the duration of the campaign. The Minnesota press generally greeted the platform as the most moderate in nearly a decade.[37] One other significant difference had developed. For the first time since 1924 there were no convention endorsements, and party nominations were to be settled in an open Farmer-Labor primary!

Rival Slates of Candidates

Left and right factions went their separate ways in organizing for the primary. Left-wing delegates assembled July 28 in Minneapolis to form a "progressive" slate of candidates, made up of Elmer Benson (senator), Charles Egley (governor), Howard Y. Williams (lieutenant governor), Selma Seestrom (secretary of state), Carl Flodquist (railroad and warehouse commissioner), and congressional candidates Chester Watson (fourth district) and John T. Bernard (eighth district). The right united behind George Lommen (senator), Hjalmar Petersen (governor), Harold Barker (lieutenant governor), James Heller (secretary of state), and Charles Munn (railroad and warehouse commissioner). Petersen was the most aggressively optimistic of the candidates; he talked boldly of defeating Stassen and even traveled to the Democratic national convention to solicit Democratic support.[38]

Leftists quietly buried the majority of their collectivist preferences, and the most commonly expressed fear among radicals was that the Lommen-Petersen forces were likely to cooperate with Democrats and possibly even sacrifice the third party by fusing it into a new Democratic-Farmer-Labor party.[39] The major source of factional discord continued to be the Communist issue. When William Mahoney assumed editorship of the *Minnesota Leader* his editorials quickly took the form of a warning to the left that Communist penetration in the movement would not be tolerated, four weeks before the primary election a stern editorial announced that the association was under no obligation to support a Farmer-Labor nominee,[40] a threat directed particularly at gubernatorial candidate Charles Egley (a left-wing official of the Farmers Union) as well as at Selma Seestrom, Carl Flodquist, and Chester Watson. And George Lommen, bitterly angry about the unexpected filing of Benson for the Senate, accused the former governor of breaking a pledge at Rochester not to become a candidate for any public office.[41]

The Primary Election

On September 9, the half million primary voters, in picking seven nominees for each party, had to be bewildered in selecting from among a total of sixteen Farmer-Labor, twenty Democratic, and thirty Republican candidates. Republican popular appeal still appeared strong; 59 percent voted Republican, 23 percent Farmer-Labor, and 17 percent Democrat. Two years before 55 percent had been attracted to the intense Farmer-Labor struggle.

Party	No. of Votes	Percentage of Total Vote
Republican	340,772	59.4%
Farmer-Labor	133,548	23.3%
Democratic	99,084	17.3%

Farmer-Laborism experienced further setbacks. Henrik Shipstead had filed in the Republican primary, though in the spring a few Farmer-Laborites hoped to see him retire from politics, apparently because his defection appeared to symbolize a trend to the Republican party at the expense of both Farmer-Laborites and Democrats.[42] Although Shipstead faced Republicans Ray P. Chase, Martin A. Nelson, five other candidates, and the opposition of national committeeman Roy Dunn,[43] he won an impressive 50 percent of the vote, and his closest challenger, Nelson, fell far behind (29 percent). Injured by Shipstead's switch, Farmer-Laborites suffered another unexpected blow when Senator Ernest Lundeen was killed in a Virginia airplane crash ten days before the election while returning to Minnesota to attend a Townsend rally.

Democratic recovery, so obvious locally in the St. Paul city election, hardly looked impressive in the primary. Nevertheless, the outcome would produce another important change in the party. For years there had existed a split between the two Democratic factions of Regan-Moonan and Wolf-Meighen. Now there emerged a third faction connected with the gubernatorial nomination of former St. Paul assistant attorney Edward Murphy, who was an ally of small-town banker Elmer Kelm of Chanhassen. Although Kelm eventually played a leading role in merger negotiations during 1943-44, his emergence in Democratic ranks initially drove one more wedge between Farmer-Laborites and Democrats. George Hagen and Hjalmar Petersen distrusted Murphy and Kelm because they suspected them of having some kind of dubious connection with Harold Stassen and of being infiltrators into the Democratic party, for the purpose of sabotaging joint Democratic and Farmer-Labor efforts to defeat Stassen.[44] Although no evidence sustained such a privately held animosity, Petersen always remained highly skeptical about Kelm's motivations, and Elmer Benson too distrusted Kelm for largely the same reason.

THE FALL CAMPAIGN AND ELECTION

There would be no dramatic breakthrough in Democratic and Farmer-Labor cooperation in 1940, and any progress in this area was connected with the presidential campaign. After the primary there was some closing of Farmer-Labor ranks, but ideological differences ruled out any basic agreement. Susie Stageberg, a twenty-year veteran of Farmer-Laborism, urged Petersen to wage a common campaign with Benson and Charles Egley, the manager of the Farmer's Union Livestock Commission Company in South St. Paul, and in offering Petersen congratulations she also observed that there could not be economic abundance until "public ownership and extension of cooperatives" had become the common method of producing and distributing wealth. Petersen disagreed. "If we had government ownership of practically everything," he responded, "I feel we would have a solution something like that in Russia—a Communist dictatorship."[45]

During the duration of the campaign Petersen was publicly more charitable toward the left than he had been in 1938 for the logical reason that this now was in his self-interest. But others among the moderate-to-right faction remained decidedly antagonistic toward the left. Under state law, party officers were selected by the nominated candidates and were completely independent of the Farmer-Labor Association and its officers. Yet when Petersen asked Herman Aufderheide

of New Ulm to become chairman of the Farmer-Labor central committee, Aufderheide adamantly refused out of strong personal dislike of
Benson. "I conscientiously cannot support Elmer Benson as long as
he travels with the communistic crowd that caused our downfall two
years ago," Aufderheide declared, adding pessimistically that Benson's
presence on the ballot made it nearly impossible for other Farmer-
Labor candidates to win.[46] State representative George Hagen of
Crookston for similar reasons declined to sit on the state committee
and warned Petersen to stay away from Benson, lieutenant governor
candidate Howard Y. Williams, and congressional nominee John T.
Bernard.[47]

The Democratic and Republican Campaigns

When Democratic nominees voted ten to five to make Elmer Kelm
the new state Democratic chairman, both Wolf and Moonan partisans
lost their influence in the party. Kelm pledged to work for all nominated Democrats, and though a welcome new face in Democratic cir-
cles, he was not well received by liberal Democrats. Some believed he
was friendly with congressman Elmer Ryan, a vigorous opponent of
the three-term presidency, and they questioned whether Kelm would
work enthusiastically for Roosevelt's reelection. State Young Democratic chairman John B. McGrath was more outspoken, charging Kelm
with planning to turn the party over to Republicans.[48]

Continuing uncertainty about where Kelm's real political loyalties
rested made it difficult to bring Democrats and Farmer-Labor moderates together in common support of Roosevelt, and during a Farmer-
Labor state committee debate on the presidential campaign the left
wing proposed to place on the November ballot a rival set of Farmer-
Labor presidential electors pledged to Roosevelt. Not only did the left,
too, distrust Kelm, but it also wished to protect Farmer-Labor autono-
my and otherwise resist any steps that could lead toward two-party
merger. Kelm correctly denounced the plan as a risk that jeopardized
Roosevelt's chances of carrying the state, calling it treacherous political blackmail. The proposal was finally killed by Petersen, St. Paul
labor spokesman John Findlan, and right-wing Farmer-Laborites.[49]

But Petersen by no means was pleased with Kelm's rise to power,
and at the start of his own campaign he publicly accused the new Democratic chairman of being linked with an alleged Stassen Republican
takeover of the Minnesota Democratic party. Kelm's retaliation was
simple: there would be no agreements with Farmer-Laborites in
1940.[50] The two opposition parties thus remained distant and there
was no followup to the discussions that had begun in 1939.

Although merger sentiment suffered, this did not entirely end the slow Democratic process of recruiting individual Farmer-Laborites to the state Roosevelt campaign, and it accordingly served to strengthen the organizational hand of the Democrats. There were four rather distinct Democratic groups—Kelm, McDonough, Meighen, Moonan (and their respective allies)—competing to take command of the state Roosevelt campaign, and national leaders of Roosevelt's third-term drive again sought to tie Democrats and Farmer-Laborites into some organizational confluence in order to ensure that the president would win the state electoral vote. In a rebuff of Kelm, the direction of the state party's presidential campaign was once more placed in the hands of John F. D. Meighen,[51] who held the dubious distinction of having engineered the ill-considered 1936 Democratic withdrawals. Simultaneously, however, Farmer-Laborite Paul A. Rasmussen and former supreme court justice John P. Devaney were made cochairman of the Minnesota affiliate of the National Committee of Independent Voters for Roosevelt and Wallace. The selection was additional evidence of the national administration's determination to bring some Democrats and Farmer-Laborites into closer political affiliation.

Stassen, a supporter of Republican presidential candidate Wendell Willkie and the 1940 national Republican keynote speaker in July, was subjected to a strong Farmer-Labor attack during the final campaign month and was criticized for the old-age lien law, alleged mismanagement of Anoka County's tornado relief funds, and the 36-percent small loan ("loan shark") act. The lien law was especially unpopular with many senior voters since persons who accepted old-age assistance payments had a state lien placed upon their real property equal to the value of the payments. Unpopular with recipients and heirs alike, the lien law "taxed" those who owned homes while giving the same assistance "free" to those without property.

But these were Stassen times in Minnesota, and in mid-October the governor announced the appointment of thirty-four-year-old Joseph H. Ball, political reporter for the *St. Paul Pioneer Press* and *Dispatch*, as interim United States senator. The appointment of Ball, an internationalist, was widely praised by the major newspapers (one of which had been his employer) as an example of Stassen's "nonpolitical" sense of sound judgment. A whistle-stop swing by Willkie through the solidly Republican counties between Winona and St. Paul, the public's preoccupation with national issues, the debate over the third term, and the trend of international events tended to obscure the more local issues and controversies. As a result the 1940 Minnesota election would bring no dramatic political shift, no Farmer-Labor comeback, and only a slight gain in Democratic appeal.

A "Reinforcing" Election

The 1940 election reinforced the realignment of 1938 and demonstrated that Stassen and the state Republicans could maintain politicol preeminence and withstand the pressure of a presidential campaign in which national issues competed with or transcended the controversial themes so prevalent in 1938. And for those impatient to wage a united rather than a divided campaign against Republicans and Stassen, the results provided strong empirical evidence that merger was imperative and that the emergence of a two-party system was only a matter of time.

Roosevelt's performance in Minnesota had plunged from a landslide victory in 1936 to 49.5 percent of the total state vote and a 48,000-vote plurality over Willkie (45.8 percent) in 1940. The erosion of support was a major reason why the national administration began to expedite efforts to bring about merger in time for the 1944 election. The president had carried Minnesota four years earlier with a 350,000-vote victory (60 percent of the total vote), but he now was outpolled by Stassen and two other Republican state candidates. It is hazardous to try to generalize about what these election trends signified, since personal judgments about candidates sometimes transcended issues. For example, Shipstead, an isolationist, won easy reelection (49.3 percent), and although he had switched to the Republicans he still won a plurality in 84 of 87 counties; Roosevelt, leaning more and more toward assisting England and Churchill in their lonely war against Nazi Germany, carried the state with a total vote nearly identical to the senator's; and Stassen the emerging internationalist did slightly better.

Farmer-Laborism was receding. Five of its seven state candidates had votes ranging between 22 and 25 percent, and Petersen, leading the ticket with 35 percent, still was outpolled by close to 200,000 votes. Henry Teigan, Dewey Johnson, and John T. Bernard failed badly in comeback attempts. The lone survivor, and barely, was ninth-district congressman Richard T. Buckler (43.4 percent), a narrow 675-vote victor. The legislature remained solidly conservative (or Republican), though the nonpartisan ballot offered better protection for a surviving remnant of the farmers' movement. Farmer-Labor strength was now concentrated in the Northwest prairie counties, the northernmost tier of counties, the Iron Range, and St. Louis and Ramsey counties.

The most bitter of the defeated candidates was Hjalmar Petersen. He blamed the Ridder publications (its publishers and editors including Bernard H. Ridder, James Russell Wiggins, and Herbert [Lewis]

RESULTS OF THE 1940 MINNESOTA GENERAL ELECTION

(Candidate, No. of Votes, and Percentage of Total Vote)

OFFICE	REPUBLICAN	DEMOCRATIC	FARMER-LABOR	SOCIALIST	INDUSTRIAL	COMMUNIST	WORKER'S
President	Wendell Willkie 596,274 (45.8%)	Franklin Roosevelt 644,196 (49.5%)		Norman Thomas 5,454 (.4%)	John W. Aiken 2,533 (.2%)	Earl Browder 2,711 (.2%)	
Senator	Henrik Shipstead 641,049 (49.3%)	John E. Regan 248,658 (19.1%)	Elmer A. Benson 310,875 (23.9%)				Grace H. Carlson 8,761 (.7%)
Governor	Harold E. Stassen 654,686 (50.3%)	Edward Murphy 140,021 (10.8%)	Hjalmar Petersen 459,609 (35.3%)		John W. Castle 3,175 (.2%)		
Lieutenant governor	C. Elmer Anderson 598,369 (46.0%)	Frank Ryan 265,793 (20.4%)	Howard Y. Williams 305,418 (23.5%)				
Attorney	J. A. A. Burnquist 604,763 (46.5%)	John D. Sullivan 278,750 (21.4%)	David J. Erickson 284,337 (21.8%)				
Secretary of state	Mike Holm 800,754 (61.5%)	Austin T. Haley 176,195 (13.5%)	James I. Heller 230,148 (17.7%)				
Treasurer	Julius Schmahl 649,581 (49.9%)	Richard M. Fitzgerald 228,179 (17.5%)	C. A. Halvorson 296,477 (22.8%)				
Railroad and warehouse commissioner	N. J. Holmberg 577,691 (44.4%)	Arthur N. Cosgrove 232,997 (17.9%)	Charles Munn 329,180 (25.3%)				

Note: The total percentage after each office is less than 100 because some voters cast blank vallots and some ballots were spoiled.

Minnesota Farmer-Laborism, by Millard L. Gieske, © 1979 by the University of Minnesota

Lefkovitz) for one-sided pro-Stassen reporting, lodged a similar complaint with Charles Cheney of the *Minneapolis Star-Journal,* and accused George Gallup of unethically using his American Institute of Public Opinion polls to influence the election.[52]

For the Democratic party there was modest recovery to be found in a marginal gain in votes, but this was accompanied by a new determination to no longer put Farmer-Labor electoral interests ahead of its own. Regan outpolled Benson in forty-four counties and, excluding Minneapolis, St. Paul, Duluth, and St. Louis Counties, actually had more combined votes than Benson in eighty-four counties. State and congressional Democratic candidates would win no elections when their votes ran between 15 and 20 percent, yet these performances were encroaching upon Farmer-Labor strength and it seemed that the Democratic party was on the verge of overtaking the third party. The defeat of second-district Democratic congressman Elmer Ryan caused ambivalent feelings and brought relief to some because he finally was trapped by his own political dalliance: never warm toward Roosevelt and often appearing to be an outsider in his own party, Ryan was opposed to the third term and even publicly courted endorsements from Shipstead and Willkie. When he ran against Irish Republican Joseph P. O'Hara, Ryan could find few Democratic party regulars who were willing to tolerate him, and many worked behind-the-scenes to defeat him rather than suffer any longer because of his infidelity.[53]

The Democratic effort was further burdened by its narrow ethnic base. Six of seven nominees for state office and six of nine congressional candidates carried Irish surnames: two Murphys, two Ryans, and a Fitzgerald, Haley, Hogan, Moran, O'Brien, O'Connor, Regan, and Sullivan. Such a concentration was appropriate for Boston politics, but it had severe limitations in Minnesota. The party badly needed a linkup with Scandinavians.

EXPLORING WAYS OF MERGING THE FARMER-LABOR AND DEMOCRATIC PARTIES, 1941-42

This latest election defeat convinced more Democrats and Farmer-Laborites that they should seriously explore ways of merging their strength or combining their parties. The process was to be difficult and sometimes painful, both psychologically and legally. No quick, easy solution existed, but the subject could no longer be suppressed.

St. Cloud newspaper publisher Fred Schilplin, long an influential leader in the sixth district, had a plan, and in December 1940 he shared it with Hjalmar Petersen, William Mahoney, Harold Peterson, David Lundeen, Charles Munn, and labor leaders William Gydesen and Robley (Red) Cramer. State senator Homer Carr also pressed the issue and talked about eliminating left-wing influence in order to make merger possible. The Minneapolis Jefferson Club pursued a similar interest and invited Petersen to discuss the merger issue. In spite of such inducements Petersen held back, because he was plagued by an imaginery vision of Republicans infiltrating Democratic ranks and because he distrusted some national Democratic leaders like chairman Edward J. Flynn.[54] As a result, Petersen played no positive role in the merger effort.

Meanwhile, some Farmer-Laborites were moving into Democratic ranks. Crookston state representative George Hagen and most of the officers of the Polk County Farmer-Labor Association announced they were abandoning their party and joining the Democrats. A former FBI agent, Hagen said his old party "had served a useful purpose" but conditions were such that its continuance was no longer required.[55] At the same time Judge John F. D. Meighen began to work on the legal problem of modifying the Democratic party structure so that it could formally accommodate Farmer-Laborites moving, not as individuals but as a body, into Democratic ranks.[56] This side of the fusion question, so poorly understood over the years by some who later claimed credit for merger, was a basic reason why merger took nearly three years to be completed.

Other equally important issues delayed the process of merger. One was ideology. Democrats, especially conservatives, were highly skeptical about allowing radicals into their party and worried about the damage they could cause. Most of the Farmer-Labor left wing offered uncompromising resistance to merger, and while they controlled the association the chances for changing that policy remained slim. This was another reason why Farmer-Labor moderates now wanted to purge the leftists.

Foreign policy represented still another stumbling block. Bitterly opposing Roosevelt's international foreign policy, the left considered it an unthinkable deviation from the Farmer-Labor principle of opposing "capitalistic wars" of imperialism among western European powers. The left steadfastly refused to distinguish between western representative democracies and Nazi Germany and Fascist Italy. After the Hitler-Stalin nonaggression pact of August 24, 1939, the Communist line switched to strict opposition to American intervention in European affairs. Fellow travelers in the Farmer-Labor movement, and Communist infiltrators, echoed these sentiments almost without exception.

The Foreign Policy Dilemma

Traditionally, Farmer-Laborites were isolationists, but after the European war broke out in 1939 the left and the right isolationists began to split sharply. No longer could they be united by the 1917-18 cry to take profits out of war and conscript wealth along with draftees. This was because the Farmer-Labor right largely sided with western democracies, even though it opposed direct armed American intervention, while the left in late August 1939 took the position that active opposition to Hitler should cease since he and Stalin had reached a nonaggression peace pact. Oscar Hawkins, one of the expelled Hennepin delegates at the January 1939 association convention, was representative of this point of view, and he defended the agreement by asserting that the Soviet Union had "consistently stood for peace and against wars."[57]

Farmer-Laborism's next severe break over foreign policy came with the outbreak of the Russo-Finnish war in late 1939. Most northern Minnesota Finns reacted antagonistically to the Soviet invasion of Finland, and this contributed to the strong feelings in St. Louis and Itasca counties and the entire eighth district to purge Communists and fellow travelers from the Farmer-Labor Association. Again, Oscar Hawkins typified the Farmer-Labor left when he defended the Soviets: he parroted the Communist line by saying that Russians were forced to intervene because British and American dollars dominated Finnish affairs and because Great Britain was using Finland as a base "in her long-term planning for future attack on socialist Soviet Russia."[58] A dialectic was at work, according to Hawkins, and neither the Nazi nor the Allies deserved victory. He speculated that a stalemate between Nazi and British-French forces might even lead to improvement for humankind if it created conditions that would bring on a revolution to end the imperialist era and usher in a new "era of World Citizenship, brotherhood, and cooperation."[59]

These fundamental differences had the effect of further weakening moderates' ties to Farmer-Laborism. This might have hastened the merger movement had the right wing not suffered a setback at the January 1941 association state convention. On the second ballot for state chairman, Elmer Benson was elected over the moderate Charles Munn, 256 to 252, and the former governor's victory came primarily from the nearly unanimous support he gained from the solidly left-wing Hennepin delegation. Next Paul Rasmussen, now a member of a newly formed Democratic-Farmer-Labor *ad hoc* committee, was denounced as a "renegade Farmer-Laborite." Benson attempted to play down his ideological differences with the moderates

("I am not half as radical as you think I am."), Munn was elected vice-chairman in a display of reconciliation and he praised Benson for his leadership, but the peace between factions was short-lived. Resolutions of opposition were adopted that condemned Roosevelt's proposed Lend Lease aid program for the Allies and that attacked Democratic-Farmer-Labor fusion.[60]

Three weeks later William Mahoney publicly announced his resignation from the Farmer-Labor state committee, giving as his reason the resumption of efforts by Communists and fellow travelers to "pervert [the Farmer-Labor Association] into extremist channels."[61] Duluth's socialist attorney Sigmond Slonin said he would wait one more year before resigning to see if fellow travelers would be purged.[62]

Petersen and the America First Movement. Alienated from the leftists and suspicious of Democrats and about merger, Hjalmar Petersen, like some right-wing isolationist Farmer-Laborites, next joined the American First movement which now was attracting critics of Roosevelt's foreign policy like Henrik Shipstead, congressman Harold Knutson, Republican isolationists, and Charles Lindbergh, whose father had been active in early Farmer-Laborism.

Early in March 1941 Petersen addressed a WCCO radio audience, warning against entangling European alliances, the folly of seeking to export democracy, and stressing the necessity of strengthening American military capacity, but for the singular purpose of defense, not intervention.[63] By fall Petersen was working with the America First Committee, and as an advocate of Fortress America, he, Knutson, and Shipstead were regulars on the America First speaking circuit in Minnesota and occasionally elsewhere.

The foreign policy schism cut obliquely across all three parties. Mindful of the political opportunity that could be gained from America First activity,[64] Petersen for a time considered becoming a 1942 isolationist Republican candidate for governor.[65] Harold Stassen spoke in open support of Roosevelt's Lend Lease program. Farmer-Labor state senate minority leader George Lommen of Eveleth, like some moderate Farmer-Laborites, defended Lend Lease and Roosevelt's interventionist assistance to the British.[66] And Elmer Benson was in the most untenable position of all.

Benson's Dilemma, June 1941. Not every leftist in Elmer Benson's controversial former administration shared the ex-governor's isolationist sentiments about the proper American role in the European conflict. Abe Harris was one who vigorously disagreed with it. A victim of 1938 anti-Semitism, Harris had joined the ranks of Washington's liberal journalists and now was suffering from progressive heart disease. Unlike Benson, Harris had dramatically shifted his position on foreign policy, Communists, and Roosevelt's policy toward the British and French, and he attempted to convince Benson that he too should change his thinking. The major event responsible for the Harris shift was the Hitler-Stalin pact, and Harris minced no words in arguing with Benson about it. The worst imaginable situation, Harris wrote, would result from a Hitler victory. The "great mistake that many liberals and radicals were making today" was to describe Hitler as a mere Fascist manifestation of the highest form of capitalism. He bluntly told Benson the Farmer-Labor party "must steer clear of the Communist line."[67] By now Howard Y. Williams had similarly concluded that Benson was fundamentally wrong on foreign policy.

Stubborn as always and impossibly inflexible about foreign policy, Benson refused to budge. But his position suddenly became politically untenable when, on 22 June, Hitler launched a massive surprise invasion into the Soviet Union. Overnight American Communists were converted from unyielding neutralists to advocates of a worldwide crusade against Nazi imperialism. A depressed Harris told Benson that now he would have to live with his mistake and remain an isolationist. To change, Harris pointed out, would make it appear that "your line changed because the Communist line changed." The one-time University of Minnesota boxer (Floyd Olson had served as Harris's student manager) declared that Minnesota Communists had gained too much influence in the Farmer-Labor party. His indictment was stinging:

> I am satisfied that it was mainly the work of the Communists at the last State Convention that brought about opposition to the Lend-Lease bill and other measures that the liberals and independent radicals of this country almost universally supported, and gave the Farmer-Labor Party the reputation in Washington and throughout the country as Communist controlled — a charge not altogether without some merit. The Farmer-Labor line paralleled the Communist line almost without a flaw. There has been no difference whatever in the editorial policy of the Minnesota Leader and the Daily Worker. I know, because I have examined this. The same American Peace Mobilization crap, and the rest of the gutter organizations, that I call them. I call them gutter, because I think that intellectually they went into the gutter.

As a former editor of the *Minnesota Leader,* Harris' sounded as though the Farmer-Labor party's mission had run its course and

Farmer-Laborism's fate was subordinate to the larger purpose of defeating Hitler and Nazism. He found proof of Farmer-Labor impotence in the third consecutive election setback of Minneapolis Farmer-Laborites and the 1941 defeat of its mayoral candidate Al Hansen, who was soundly thrashed by a Republican newcomer, Marvin J. Kline. To Harris, this demonstrated the Communists' continuing influence in Hennepin County and the price Farmer-Laborism paid for it.[68]

Weakly, Benson attempted to defend his isolationism, and he vividly recalled Floyd Olson's warning letter of February 1936 when Olson so eloquently argued against European entanglements. Harris responded that times had changed, that isolationism was a pre-Nazi search for principles, and he reminded Benson that Olson was, above all else, a practical man who adjusted political policies to suit altered times and circumstances.[69]

In August, as Benson weighed an invitation to speak at a New York rally of the American Labor Party, the former governor insisted that although he hoped to see Hitler defeated his basic attitudes on foreign policy remained unchanged. Asking Harris what he recommended, Harris answered: Don't attend. "I am sure [it] is controlled by the Communists," and if Benson desired to announce a change in position on foreign policy, there had to be a better place than this to reveal it.[70] Benson stayed away.

Harris indeed was correct about the sudden shift in position of the *Minnesota Leader,* whose editorial advisory board consisted of Bernard Simmer, Viena Johnson, Selma Seestrom, and Frank Puglisi. Before the June 1941 invasion the *Leader* had frequently featured antiwar cartoons and antiinterventionist editorials. Suddenly in July all this ended, and the paper began to print patriotic governmental advertisements that urged Americans to "Buy Defense Bonds." An October editorial was candidly forthright: "Since Russia has become the active partner in the war against Hitler the entire foreign policy picture has changed."[71] Changes like these did not go unnoticed. Howard Y. Williams told his wife that Viena Johnson, the secretary-treasurer of the Farmer-Labor Association, "must take her orders from the Communists," and the former LIPA third-party organizer added, "It is strange how Communists can work their way into places."[72]

The Continuing Disintegration of Farmer-Laborism

War and the Communist issue, often in contradictory ways, had a bearing on the merger issue and helped weaken individual ties to an independent Farmer-Laborism. The sedition trial in 1941 of Minnesota Trotskyites (Socialist Workers Party) under the newly enacted federal Smith Act hurt Farmer-Laborism because the Dunne brothers were involved; Vince Dunne was convicted, Miles Dunne acquitted, and shortly afterward Grant Dunne took his own life.[73] Stalinist Communists, whom the Justice Department did not prosecute, seemed pleased by the turn of events against the Trotskyites.

Other events cut into Farmer-Labor ranks. After a front page *Leader* assault upon Hjalmar Petersen in response to an editorial in his *Askov American,* Charles Munn resigned in protest as association vice-chairman in March 1941 and sixth-district Farmer-Labor chairman Charles Halsted of Brainerd announced his resignation.[74] Although Howard Williams was now a severe critic of the Communists, he suffered from suspected guilt by association and lost his job in the Federal Security Agency on the basis of a false charge of being a Communist or Communist sympathizer. He was later cleared of the charges by the Civil Service Board, but federal employment still eluded him.[75]

The Democratic Advisory Council and Merger

Farmer-Labor weakness encouraged Democrats to develop a scheme for fusion which could take effect as early as 1942 — too optimistic a schedule as it turned out. Planned largely by Judge John F. D. Meighen of Albert Lea, former supreme court justice John P. Devaney, and Thomas Gallagher, it originally sought to create a dues-paying Democratic organization, and they were willing to compromise on the name — Democratic-Farmer-Labor — to coax individual Farmer-Laborites into the organization. Those who did not voluntarily join they hoped to enlist through formal merger later on. Already the Democrats counted upon the services of Paul Rasmussen, George Hagen (who might be their gubernatorial candidate), and Charles Halsted.

The most serious problem facing Democrats was state law. Minnesota statutes prohibited candidates and party workers from switching to another party unless they could legally pledge they had supported a majority of that party's candidates in the previous election. Therefore, delegates to a fused convention and candidates for public office faced potential legal challenges from any of several sources: opponents of merger, losers in endorsement contests, losers in a primary, and Republicans seeking to disrupt or prohibit merger.

The search for a successful strategy drew the attention of the White House and the Democratic National Committee (DNC), thus further weakening the opposition of antimerger Democrats. The first step came in 1941 when the DNC created a Democratic Advisory Council for Minnesota (DAC), making John P. Devaney its chairman. When Devaney unexpectedly died that September the chairmanship was passed to former state representative (1935-39) Theodore Slen of Madison after assistant national chairman Oscar E. Ewing was satisfied that Slen would work effectively for merger. By spring 1942 the DAC under Slen's direction had a nucleus of Democratic and Farmer-Labor fusionists: national Democratic committeewoman Ida McCabe Kayser, state chairman Elmer Kelm, Margaret Dripps, John Erickson, Thomas Gallagher, James Landy, Fred Schilplin, former Farmer-Labor state administrator Carl R. Carlgren, George Hagen, Charles Halsted, and Carl Eastvold.[76]

The major barrier, however, was Elmer Benson and the Farmer-Labor left, whose resistance would rule out merger before 1944. Still suspicious of Roosevelt and believing the New Deal inadequate, Benson before December 1941 argued that Roosevelt gave insufficient relief to American farmers, consistently displayed greater sympathy for urban workers and organized labor, and had not redeemed his 1936 pledges nor alleviated the stressful conditions of the 1930s.[77] Complaining to Roosevelt about farm policy, Benson was not reassured by the president's insistence that conditions for farmers were improving, and he dismissed the assertion as "mostly the bunk."[78] By fall 1941 Benson complained that farmers were treated as though they were American peasants. As events increasingly alienated him, Benson was critical of "reactionary" labor leaders while accusing Communists and the extreme Farmer-Labor left wing of being nearly as opportunistic as the extreme right. For a time he considered resigning as association chairman.[79]

Meanwhile, Democrats had finally discovered what they believed could be the legal key to unlock the merger mechanism. Devaney and Meighen thought it was a written party constitution. Up to 1939, state statutes had largely dictated party structure and method of choosing party officers, and no allowance had been made for party constitutions. Fortunately, the 1939 legislature had authorized political parties to adopt party constitutions to provide for internal governance, party structure, and decision making. Written more to benefit Republicans, the law was to be the means by which Democrats merged Farmer-Laborites into their party.

The idea of a Democratic state party constitution had first been advanced in 1938 by St. Paul lawyer Francis M. Smith, but it never reached floor debate at the state convention that year. Meighen began reworking the Smith plan in late 1940.[80] Under it Democrats and Farmer-Laborites were each expected to issue a convention call for a common date and common place of assembly; independently both parties were to adopt identical constitutions. Merger was to come about through this action. The constitution plan was connected to the activities of the Devaney-Slen Democratic Advisory Committee, and by March 1942 Meighen had drafted a rudimentary constitution, patterned after Smith's 1938 outline, which he presented to the Jefferson Club of Minneapolis, at work on its own version. Copies of these documents were circulated to Kelm, Slen, and the DAC.[81]

Legal refinements and a left-wing change of heart were necessary before fusion could occur. The American declaration of war following the Japanese attack at Pearl Harbor on December 7, 1941, only slowly began to dissolve the left wing's resistance, and fusion thus was out of the question for 1942. Nevertheless, the Meighen version of a constitutional party merger was printed by *St. Cloud Times* publisher Fred Schilplin in his paper on July 15.[82] One more election was to pass before Benson and the left accepted what many moderate Farmer-Laborites and Democrats had agreed upon in principle as early as 1939-40.

The Last Hurrah

Farmer-Laborism had declined but not collapsed despite Democratic preparations to assume major responsibility for opposing Stassen and Minnesota Republicanism. The third party had survived largely because Hjalmar Petersen had doggedly pursued the governorship and because the Farmer-Labor left had unrelentingly resisted fusion with Democrats. One more solid defeat and the impact of the war on Benson and the radicals would bring a critical shift in their attitude.

For twenty years and longer, state Democrats had too patiently awaited the Farmer-Labor demise. By 1942, however, such a passive strategy made excellent political sense. In the spring St. Paul city election, through a common campaign that combined Democrats, Farmer-Laborites, and organized labor, Democratic Mayor John J. McDonough and the liberals on the city commission won an impressive reelection victory. By now Democrats were following two fundamental tactics toward Farmer-Laborites: recruiting individual Farmer-Laborites while working to merge the Farmer-Labor party into the Democratic party, and withholding support to Farmer-Labor candidates as a means of hastening the collapse of the third party.[1] And the state Democratic Advisory Council (DAC) urged party factions to avoid disruptive primary campaigning and preprimary endorsements.

Stassen was an unwitting ally of the Democrats: his popularity and the left wing's (as well as Petersen's) hatred of him were strong inducements for combining political forces to prevent his further advancement, either to the Senate or to the presidency. And Democrats used him in still another way: as a defensive barrier against Farmer-Labor revival. Stassen served to block Petersen's pathway at a time when Democrats were not yet strong enough to dislodge Farmer-Laborites, and the White House opposed Petersen for his isolationism and record of opposition to Roosevelt's international policies.

THE 1942 GUBERNATORIAL CONTEST
BETWEEN STASSEN AND PETERSEN

An unexplained anomoly of Minnesota's 1942 campaign was that Stassen announced he would run for a three-month term of office, after which he was to resign to go on active duty as a lieutenant commander in the Navy. The arrangement seemed weighted by political consideration. For the White House staff and state Democrats, there were accrued advantages in keeping Stassen in office through 1942 and into 1943. Stassen recognized his own advantage in such an arrangement since it allowed him to continue influencing and shaping the basic outline of Minnesota Republicanism.

Stassen's 1942 campaign helped draw closer men as different as Hjalmar Petersen and Elmer Benson. Among conservatives within the Republican party there was growing resentment of Stassen and Republican liberals. Roy Dunn of Pelican Rapids, the Republican national committeeman, denounced him for being a divisive influence in the Republican party.[2] Conservatives sometimes disliked him for his opposition to the presidential ambitions of Ohio senator Robert A. Taft. Some business spokesmen like George Briggs denounced him for being too friendly toward unions and a bigger "spender" than Elmer Benson.[3] By the end of the 1941 legislative session, senate minority leader George Lommen, when bitterly attacking Stassen's proposed state budget, charged the governor with deceiving the public about overall spending. In a speech denouncing Stassen which WCCO cancelled, Lommen praised A. J. Rockne (a conservative), Charles Orr (a Republican), and James Carley (a Democrat) as men who had forgotten more about state finances than Stassen would ever know.[4] Taken together these incidents were growing evidence of a tendency among anti-Stassen groups to coalesce in order to maximize their strength. And by themselves the old non-Communist liberal-left bloc remained much too weak to be effective against Stassen or any one else. The national third-party movement of the 1930s also had faded, replaced in May 1941 by a new anti-Communist liberal organization called the Union for Democratic Action (UDA), an early forerunner of the postwar Americans for Democratic Action. Reinhold Nieburh was UDA chairman, Tom Amlie the Washington, D.C. director, and Howard Williams, who began working for the UDA in 1942, the midwestern director. Unlike LIPA's goals in the 1930s, UDA's goals were limited to the election of liberals, which usually meant Democrats.[5]

Farmer-Laborism's inability to recruit new political talent forced it to rely again on political veterans like Petersen and Benson, who had failed it in the past. Abandoning now his seat on the Railroad and Warehouse Commission, Petersen as the last state officeholding Farmer-Laborite wanted to run again for the governorship, his fourth attempt in four elections (and it would not be his last). Because Petersen was active in the America First movement up to Pearl Harbor and only mildly involved in Farmer-Labor activities during the first four months of 1942, there was speculation that he might challenge Stassen in the September Republican primary.[6] Some Republicans, like conservative congressman August H. Andresen, encouraged Petersen to run, and Petersen believed he held the key to Stassen's defeat.[7] Stassen, having failed in an attempt to force the resignation of national committeeman Roy Dunn, had enough problems with the Republican conservatives not to want Petersen as a Republican mucking up matters even more.

Badly wanting the governorship, Petersen might have switched parties had it been feasible and to his advantage. But George Hagen urged him not to go with the Republicans, and state Democratic chairman Elmer Kelm was hostile toward him ever since Petersen accused Kelm of being a Republican masquerading as a Democrat.[8] Petersen therefore limited himself to making attacks upon Stassen. In mid-March he released a public letter asking Stassen to help Minnesota servicemen obtain the right to vote while away on military duty; Stassen wrote back, telling him to quit playing politics.[9] On April 1 he denounced Stassen's announced intention of seeking reelection only for the purpose of serving a three-month term before going on active duty in the Navy as a lieutenant commander.[10]

Wartime politics thus impinged on both Stassen's career and the merger movement. Stassen's announcement about naval duty helped quiet whatever criticism there was of him for not joining the war effort as a serviceman. And the governor's continued presence in Minnesota politics through the election and into 1943 served to block Petersen's chances of election, either as a Farmer-Laborite or as a converted Republican. The near one-year deferment of active duty smacked strongly of White House intercession or encouragement; Petersen was no admirer of Roosevelt and supported the war as an isolationist rather than an internationalist, and if in Stassen's absence Petersen was elected he remained a likely source of resistance to Farmer-Labor merger.

FARMER-LABOR PARTY VERSUS FARMER-LABOR ASSOCIATION

When in January 1941 the Benson left-wing faction narrowly gained control of the Farmer-Labor Association, moderates and right-wing Farmer-Laborites looked for a way of neutralizing the radicals. Some moderates wanted to continue as a third party, whereas others sought control for the purpose of working out a merger agreement with Democrats. Consequently, one right-wing plan was to organize the legal machinery of the Farmer-Labor party into a rival organization to oppose the left-dominated Farmer-Labor Association.[11]

Leading the Farmer-Labor *party movement* were St. Paul labor leaders John Findlan and Adolph Karlsson and members of the liberal bloc in the legislature. They gathered February 1 at the St. Francis Hotel to discuss the party reorganization plan as a means of rebuilding the movement "along lines entirely divorced from any possible suggestion of connection with the Communist element." This meant, at the minimum, a new attempted purge of Farmer-Labor radicals, and though the right had not yet advocated fusion it refused to rule out the possibility of merging its party with the Democratic party.

Worried by defections, the activities of the DAC, and the renewed determination of the "party group" to purge Farmer-Laborism, the left wing sponsored a mid-February "unity" conference at the Minapolis Dyckman Hotel. About 500 Farmer-Laborites showed up. and though moderates and right-wingers were underrepresented, both George Lommen and Charles Munn pleasantly surprised Benson by delivering rather conciliatory addresses.[12] As had been the case for years, Benson and the left's major fears were that the right intended to splinter the movement in 1942 and, even more frightening, that Farmer-Laborism might succumb to merger fever.

Feeding this anxiety were the plans of Lommen, Findlan, and the party group to call a state conference for May, at which time the Farmer-Labor future was to be discussed. Benson had requested, as a compromise, that the letter of invitation be signed jointly by the party group (Findlan, legally, was the state party chairman) and the association,[13] but St. Paul labor leaders rejected it and insisted the letter carry only the signatures of Findlan and Lommen. The left was made more uneasy in mid-April when Lommen told the association state committee that one topic certain to come up for discussion in May was whether the Farmer-Labor party should be merged into the Democratic party.[14] In past years such a heretical disclosure would have immediately brought on vehement condemnation by the left, but in the present weakened state of the movement the leftists did not wish to do anything that might provoke the right into defecting and joining the Democrats or, even worse, merging the two parties. Selma Seestrom and state senator John Blatnik of Chisholm therefore urged reconciliation, and only a radical firebrand like Frank Puglisi spoke out against the "sinister intentions" of the coming conference.[15]

Continuing Schism of Left and Right

Through spring and into summer the party group and the association group remained chronically divided over organization, candidates, ideology, and relations with Democrats. The heralded May 28 conference, which was to discuss the Farmer-Labor future, in no way came to grips with basic Farmer-Labor problems, internal controversy, or ways of mending differences between factions. In a general way it was a minor victory for the left since merger had not been given encouragement. But neither had there been any agreements on candidates or candid discussions about what really divided the party and the association. Instead, conferees listened to Washington Democratic congressman John M. Coffee (a sympathizer of third-partyism in the 1930s), Elmer Benson, Hjalmar Petersen, Harold Hagen, Howard Williams, and Paul Rasmussen attack Stassen, Senator Joseph H. Ball, Wendell Willkie, "Toryism," and the state Republican administration for declining iron ore revenues, the old-age lien law, and the 36-percent small loan interest rate.[16]

Howard Williams accurately described the conference as bankrupt.[17] Petersen and the party faction were as committed as ever to waging a campaign free of appeals for public ownership and candidates aligned with it.[18] Radicals and left-wing Hennepin County Farmer-Labor Association continued to denounce Petersen and the "party group," CIO-United Electrical Workers organizer William Mauseth accused Petersen of being an "appeaser," and Selma Seestrom belabored George Hagen for being an opponent of the Loyalist forces during the Spanish civil war.[19]

In May the two Farmer-Labor factions started jousting for candidates. Herman Aufderheide (Floyd Olson's former secretary) urged Petersen to run for governor again, and so did Paul Rasmussen; Rasmussen also asked supreme court justice Harry H. Peterson to become a candidate for United States senator.[20] Minnesota politics in 1942 was starting to take the air of a Gilbert and Sullivan opera as alliances shifted back and forth to accommodate experdiency, ambition, and, occasionally, ideology and/or principle. To stop Petersen's nomination, Howard Williams began organizing an opposition by working through the association central committee and the Central Labor Union of Minneapolis. However, lacking a Farmer-Labor candidate powerful enough to strongly challenge Petersen in the primary, the left was forced into risky strategy which partly undermined its own antimerger philosophy. Williams was commissioned to negotiate with Democratic national committeeman and DAC chairman Theodore S. Slen of Madison and to offer him the Farmer-Labor gubernatorial nomination! If Slen accepted the candidacy, several Farmer-Labor congressional candidates were to be withdrawn in order to help the Democrats.[21] Nevertheless, on the eve of the association state convention, Slen declined the offer[22] and ran instead as seventh-district Democratic candidate for Congress.

On June 27 the association state convention searched in vain for unity but discovered mainly disagreement. Petersen boycotted it entirely, though he still had some support among the minority. However, the left had no candidate to run against him. Benson firmly turned down a plea that he oppose Petersen. Then an offer was extended to Williams, but AFL delegates reacted hotly against that and instead proposed Paul Rasmussen. So bitter did the debate become — since Rasmussen was considered not only a moderate but an apologist who was too friendly with Democrats and the DAC — that convention managers temporarily adjourned the delegates to quiet the disorder. During the interim fifty delegates met in closed session to seek a more orderly way of compromising. Meanwhile, Rasmussen found new allies, so that Williams decided to withdraw; as a reward Williams was anointed for the lieutenant governor endorsement.

When Rasmussen and Williams were introduced to the convention as a campaign team, spokesmen for the AFL, CIO, and farm groups testified at the rostrum that differences had been put aside in the name of Farmer-Labor harmony, though radical William Mauseth still grumbled that Rasmussen was an "appeaser." Then Harry H. Peterson was endorsed for senator and another moderate, David Erickson, for attorney general; Benson and Viena Johnson were retained in their posts of state chairman and secretary-treasurer. The platform sought to combine modest government ownership with the welfare state. The old-age lien law and the 36-percent small loan rate were to be repealed; iron ore taxes were to be increased; farmers were to be subsidized by selling them credit at cost; farm rent was to be frozen at 1940 levels; and 100-percent taxation was proposed for all annual income in excess of $25,000. Finally, the association asked for public ownership of utilities and government ownership and operation of all war plants.[23]

To make certain the association had not forgotten him, Hjalmar Petersen sent a curt telegram announcing he would file for governor as a Farmer-Laborite.[24]

After the convention and into fall the public was bewildered whenever it attempted to discover which policies, ideology, and candidates best represented Minnesota Farmer-Laborism. Was the third party moderate or radical? Was it still serving a useful political purpose? Editor Robley (Red) Cramer of the *Minneapolis Labor Review,* for example, was still calling for a system of public ownership,[25] while William Mahoney, now a St. Paul Farmer-Labor congressional candidate, was denouncing the association for being Communist-dominated. In a published letter of resignation ("Communist control of the association impels me to withdraw from the association."), which he inserted in the *Minnesota Union Advocate,* Mahoney charged that history was repeating itself, that extremists in Hennepin and Ramsey counties were about to "poison and destroy . . . the Farmer-Labor party," and he refused to be "a party to such betrayal."[26] That was an opinion with which Hjalmar Petersen had long agreed, though he was much more guarded than Mahoney in what he said in public.

The left suffered another severe jolt in late July. Harry H. Peterson had given no indication whether he would run for senator, though the association central committee expected him to file. Two days before the filing deadline Peterson released a scathing denunciation of Paul Rasmussen and the Farmer-Labor Association, charging Rasmussen with double-crossing Hjalmar Petersen and the association with being autocratically ruled by a trouble-making left-wing consortium. Rasmussen in turn declared Peterson was "cowardly," and the association released a statement claiming it was relieved to be rid of Peterson because it had discovered he was an "appeaser."[27]

The "unified" Farmer-labor movement now had left and right slates. Running with Petersen were Henry Arens (former legislator, lieutenant governor, and congressman) for senator, St. Paul labor leader Juls Anderson for lieutenant governor, Charles J. Johnson for treasurer, and Charles Smeltzer for secretary of state. To Rasmussen and Williams the left added Elmer Benson for senator, Carl Flodquist for treasurer, Daniel Collins for secretary of state, and George Olson for railroad and warehouse commissioner.

THE STASSEN SUCCESSION

Farmer-Laborites were not alone in failing to avoid factional division. As Stassen prepared to leave Minnesota he brought new tension to

the Republican party by attempting to pick as gubernatorial successor a reliable moderate who could retain public confidence and who
otherwise might aid his postwar return to politics whether that led
to the Senate or a presidential campaign. For two terms Stassen had
tolerated a colorless and inarticulate lieutenant governor, C. Elmer
Anderson of Brainerd; now Stassen and other party leaders close to
the governor prepared to dump Anderson. Stassen's choice for lieutenant governor was deputy state commissioner of agriculture Edward J. Thye who had strong credentials as an agricultural spokesman: a Northfield farmer and former tractor salesman, Thye had
served as a director of the Minnesota Farmer Bureau and the Twin
City Milk Producers Association. In terms of long-range political
judgment Stassen was not to be faulted, for he set in motion a chain
of events which ultimately brought Thye to the Senate (1947-58),
resulted in progressive Luther Youngdahl's becoming governor (1947-
51), and kept alive for two more decades the public impression of
Minnesota Republicanism as a moderate alternative. During this
period the state had evenly balanced two-party competition.

Nevertheless, C. Elmer Anderson, highly resentful of what to him
seemed a cavalier and ungracious dismissal, decided to challenge it by
running against Thye in the primary, and the old guard once more
backed Martin Nelson against Stassen even though Nelson had run unsuccessfully for governor in every election since 1934. In a year when
thirty-eight candidates filed for eight offices in the statewide Republican primary, internationalist senator Joseph W. Ball was opposed by
three others, of whom the leading was New Ulm editor Walter Mickelson, a onetime secretary to Senator Henrik Shipstead. In the general
election, Nelson petitioned to be a candidate against Ball.

THE IMPACT OF THE WAR ON THE FARMER-LABOR CAMPAIGN

Under different circumstances Republican factionalism might have
assisted in rebuilding Farmer-Laborism, but 1942 was not a year
when the third party could capitalize on it. War news remained grim.
The 1942 third-party campaign was in part a repetition of the anti-
Communist 1938 crusade, yet it also altered some traditional behavior among old Farmer-Laborites. Howard Y. Williams, for example,
thought it was the time to make war on isolationists in all three
parties, and as a result he led an effort to give quiet assistance to
China medical missionary (1925-31, 1934-38) Dr. Walter Judd, who
had begun in 1939-40 to carry on a nationwide speaking campaign

against Japanese militarism in the Far East and now sought to take the nomination away from isolationist fifth-district Republican congressman Oscar Youngdahl.[28] And Farmer-Laborites withheld putting their isolationist congressional candidates into the field in the first and sixth districts in order to help Democrats against Republicans.[29]

Thus the war contributed to the Farmer-Labor ideological schism by further weakening the party and making it more vulnerable to merger or collapse. Mrs. John T. Lyons, whose husband was a candidate for a seven-week term as senator on the right-wing slate, informed the Farmer-Labor state committee she would not support Rasmussen, whereas Josephine Tomai reaffirmed her personal endorsement of Petersen.[30] In this context leftist Paul R. Tinge, recording secretary of the St. Paul Milk Drivers union, rebuked the right-wing slate for being "Munich-Chamberlain appeasers," "pro-Hitlerites," and "obstructionists," condemned Petersen and his followers for being America Firsters who were disloyal to the war effort, and charged the Farmer-Labor right-wing faction with being party intruders.[31]

The rightist response to Tinge and the left was brutally swift and showed how wide and permanent Farmer-Labor division was. Written by William Mahoney and delivered over WCCO radio by Henry Arens, it charged Benson with pursuing a pro-Communist foreign policy. ". . . when Hitler [and the Germans] attacked their friend, Joe Stalin, the Communists, overnight became war-minded," Arens explained, asking: "Do you really think Elmer, that you are going to appease the German people of this state, and get their votes by bleating over the radio that you love their music and their cooking?"[32]

PRIMARY RETURNS

The best indication of the relative health of the three Minnesota parties was found in the total votes cast in the September 8 primary: 424,000 votes, or 78 percent, were Republican and only 117,000, or 22 percent, went to Farmer-Laborites, with the Democrats not filing any state candidates in the primary. Farmer-Laborites tallied little more in the November election. Stassen, meanwhile, had won his third nomination (51.5 percent) as Nelson (33.6 percent) fell 76,000 votes behind the governor. Equally important, Edward Thye (41 percent) held a comfortable 50,000-vote margin over C. Elmer Anderson (29 percent), the closest of six challengers.

The Farmer-Labor schism continued into fall. The right wing won four of six primary contests, but Benson easily defeated Arens and Mrs. Ernest Lundeen, widow of the former senator. Petersen (56 percent) avoided heavy campaigning before the primary, hoping to let die some of the left's antagonism. Nevertheless, there was no mellowing of attitudes at the official meeting of the nominated candidates on September 17 to elect *party* officers. The right wing held a narrow eight to seven advantage, and five days later at a second meeting John Findlan was elected state chairman over the left-backed A. I. Johnson, a moderate legislator (1941-57) from Benson and future DFL house speaker. When, in the vote for party secretary, Josephine Tomai was selected over the left's Viena Johnson, Benson exploded, threatening to withdraw from the race and to campaign against right-wing candidates. Reluctantly the right agreed to rescind the vote and Viena Johnson was named secretary, but not until after Juls Anderson protested that Johnson was *persona non grata* with St. Paul labor groups who, he said, would refuse to make campaign contributions if she remained a party officer.[33]

THE FALL CAMPAIGN

Elmer Benson had neither forgotten nor forgiven Hjalmar Petersen's past actions, and in recalling privately Petersen's 1936 letter to the dying Floyd Olson, Benson spoke scornfully of "the most evil, wicked forces in our society" which he associated with Petersen's hidden but real political supporters.[34] Nor had Petersen altered his thinking about Benson and the radicals he believed were so loyal to the former governor. However, despite these underlying differences, during the final six weeks of the last Farmer-Labor campaign the two men called a truce and toward the end they actually made joint appearances at Farmer-Labor rallies.

Ideologically the two Farmer-Labor sides were still far apart. For example, at a September 20 meeting of the Farmer-Labor Association state committee Viena Johnson proposed that support be given only to those nominees who agreed to be bound by the collectivist platform, whereas fifth-district candidate Joseph B. Gilbert, who a quarter century earlier had helped organize the Nonpartisan League, declared the association might as well support Stassen as so ideologically timid a candidate as Petersen. It was not the party faction alone which strongly objected to such exclusion, however; both Howard Williams and Elmer Benson attacked it as shortsighted. No one in his or her right mind, Benson warned, could support "political fakirs" like Ball and Stassen.[35]

Petersen understandably went out of his way to avoid criticizing Benson publicly, and Benson's new caution was quickened by Martin Nelson's filing by petition to run as an independent opposing Joseph Ball. Benson sensed the possibility of a major political upset, and Petersen gained confidence from it because he believed Benson supporters now would abandon efforts to defeat him and instead work to elect Benson.[36] Late in October appeals went out to David Dubinsky and the national labor left to help Benson win,[37] and Petersen plunged enthusiastically into anti-Stassen attacks, condemning his iron ore taxation policy, excessive state spending, and alleged sympathy for Wall Street and the Steel Trust.[38] And both Benson and Petersen demanded parity income for farmers.

Nevertheless, for both men it was an uphill fight, politically and financially. Petersen won support from most of the railroad brotherhoods, but Stassen was endorsed by the Minnesota CIO. Some veteran Farmer-Laborites, like district judge Vince Day, contributed money to Benson *and* Petersen,[39] but the Stassen-Republican campaign was again far better funded. Farmer-Laborites had to beg and borrow and otherwise rely upon the sometimes mysterious fundraising activities of Clarence Fisher, who operated under aliases like "C. Fish" and received a 40-percent commission on every dollar he was able to account for![40]

It was more difficult to assess both the intent and the impact of the 1942 Democratic campaign in Minnesota. If the goal for Democrats was to win state and congressional offices, it would be difficult to discover a less imaginative and more ineffective appeal, since the party seemed neither enthusiastic nor prepared to finally push aside Farmer-Laborites as the main Republican opposition. During the primary only one congressional district cast more than 2,000 Democratic votes, and there were no statewide nomination contests. Worse, in a state where German- and Scandinavian-surnamed candidates had long dominated politics, Democrats seemed relentless in their pursuit of the Irish vote as two of every three candidates carried that ethnic imprimatur: Burke, Delaney, Fitzgerald, Gallagher, Haley, Kelley, Murphy, two O'Brien's, O'Rourke, Ryan, and Sullivan.

Whether or not such a Democratic strategy had merit, in one particular the party had acted wisely and in its long-term self-interest. This was in its determination to do nothing that could lead to giving assistance to the Farmer-Labor party, its candidates, or otherwise extending Farmer-Labor life beyond 1942. As in 1940, so now the Minnesota Democratic party was marking time, awaiting the final breakup of Farmer-Laborism. The election was more like an Irish wake whose mourners live in anticipation of a still better tomorrow.

ELECTION RESULTS

By November 3 it was evident that public interest in a wartime election had fallen dramatically, for tens of thousands either were away on military duty or were more concerned with their jobs and overtime wages. In any case, it was not a time of economic and social protest which could reawaken a Farmer-Labor following. The turnout, 817,511, was the smallest since 1926 and had dropped 37 percent, or nearly a half-million votes, below 1940. This benefited Republicans and incumbents as the old party swept every state office and eight of nine congressional seats, and conservatives won overwhelming control of both legislative houses.

Among Farmer-Laborites Petersen (at 37 percent) retained creditable but hardly impressive public support; he outpolled Benson (26 percent) by nearly 86,000 votes. Jules Anderson was the only other Farmer-Labor candidate who exceeded 30 percent. Consolation was hard to find and was largely limited to Farmer-Laborites outpolling Democrats two- or sometimes three-to-one and the 604-vote reelection of ninth-district congressman Harold Hagen, who in fact successfully switched to the Republican party in 1944 and retained his office until January 1957.

Although the state Democratic appeal fell below the Farmer-Labor performance, often by 100,000 votes, Democrats offered candidates for every state office including auditor (where no Farmer-Laborite ran), in two congressional districts Democrats were the only Republican opposition, and in two other congressional campaigns Democrats outpolled Farmer-Laborites.

In spite of the Republican triumph, the 1942 election suggested that voter realignment was turning Minnesota into a potentially competitive two-party state and showed that the only way of defeating the Republicans was through joint Democratic-Farmer-Labor opposition. Ball, Stassen, and Thye did not command unbeatable majorities with voter support of 43.6, 50.1, and 51 percent respectively. Nelson won 100,000 votes (13.4 percent) and cut into Ball's margin of victory, and though popular Stassen actually ran behind five of nine Republicans on the state ticket. Thus there was a growing realization among pragmatic Democrats, Farmer-Laborites, and those

RESULTS OF THE 1942 MINNESOTA GENERAL ELECTION

(Candidate, No. of Votes, and Percentage of Total Vote)

OFFICE	REPUBLICAN	DEMOCRATIC	FARMER-LABOR	INDEPENDENT PROGRESSIVE	INDUSTRIAL GOVERNMENT	COMMUNIST
Senator	Joseph Ball 356,297 (43.6%)	Edward Murphy 78,959 (9.7)	Elmer Benson 213,965 (26.2%)	Martin Nelson 109,226 (13.4%)		
Governor	Harold Stassen 409,800 (50.1%)	John Sullivan 75,151 (9.2%)	Hjalmar Petersen 299,917 (36.7%)		Harris Brandborg 4,278 (.5%)	Martin Mackie 5,082 (.6%)
Lieutenant governor	Edward Thye 417,008 (51.0%)	Joseph Kowalkowski 81,911 (10.0%)	Juls Anderson 250,410 (30.6%)			
Attorney general	J. A. A. Burnquist 432,695 (52.9%)	Patrick Burke 114,385 (14.0%)	David Erickson 187,074 (22.9%)			
Secretary of state	Mike Holm 555,918 (68.0%)	Austin Haley 67,222 (8.2%)	Daniel Collins 146,825 (18.0%)			
Treasurer	Julius Schmahl 453,110 (55.4%)	Richard Fitzgerald 103,850 (12.7%)	Charles Johnson 183,458 (22.4%)			
Auditor	Stafford King 483,416 (59.1%)		W. L. Kelly 211,250 (25.8%)			
Railroad and warehouse commissioner	W. I. Nolan 382,586 (46.8%)	Arthur Cosgrove 104,448 (12.8%)	Charles Johnson 209,509 (25.6%)			Robert Kelly 18,777 (2.3%)
Clerk of the supreme court	Grace Davis 362,760 (44.4%)	Eugene O'Brien 154,376 (18.9%)	Katherine Amundson 185,742 (22.7%)			

Note: The total percentage for each office is less than 100 because some voters cast blank ballots and some ballots were spoiled.

Minnesota Farmer-Laborism, by Millard L. Gieske, © 1979 by the University of Minnesota economic interests which did not identify with the Republican coalition, that the time for mergered party realignment was overdue if electoral victory was the objective of a competitive plebiscary political process.

COPING WITH A BITTER FARMER-LABOR DEFEAT

Many Farmer-Laborites left and right took this last defeat especially hard, and in the aftermath Farmer-Labor cohesion disintegrated further. By now it was increasingly evident that whichever faction controlled the association or the party brought a feeling of alienation to the other faction and with it a tendency to abandon the movement. Each side likewise placed a large share of the blame for defeat on the other.

Initially Hjalmar Petersen thought it time to quit politics. He traced the state CIO support of Stassen to Communists and fellow travelers who, he said, preferred to defeat Petersen rather than be concerned about a Stassen victory, and privately he blamed his defeat on the left wing's refusal to reciprocate the goodwill he and other moderates had extended to Benson.[41] Petersen philosophized that Farmer-Laborism's end was near, telling his 1938 primary campaign manager J. L. McLeod that third parties usually survived twenty years and disappeared.[42] He neither confirmed nor denied rumors he would switch parties and become a Republican.

Among radicals and the left there was no agreement either in interpreting the defeat or in planning what to do next. Following a district-by-district résumé of the election at a December meeting of the association state committee, Walter J. Kennedy pointed to the 1892 Populist party platform as the classic example of anticipating future reform in public policy, and he concluded, "whether we like it or not, it appears to be the role of the third-party movement to pave the way for others." Carl Flodquist said that Farmer-Laborites could derive satisfaction from the defeat of Hjalmar Petersen, but Benson sharply rebuked such thinking by retorting that the election "was a fatal blunder" because Stassen was a worse choice for the state than Petersen.[43] No one offered constructive thought on what Farmer-Laborism's next move should be, except there was nearly unanimous left-wing agreement to continue opposing merger with Democrats.

The events of the fall left Benson feeling moody and depressed. In October shortly before the election his old adviser Abe Harris had died; Benson took defeat hard and felt a sense of shame for having been temporarily beguiled by the hope of victory. Benson had gained the backing of Minnesota's Townsend Clubs, and with a campaign theme, "Everything to Win the People's War," he had expected to do much better. Now he was liberal in distributing blame for the defeat; those he held most responsible were corrupt and stupid labor leaders,[44] organized labor, rank-and-file workers, indifferent voters, churches—and the national Democratic administration.

Toward Roosevelt, Benson had become downright antagonistic. He concluded it was a tactical error not to have attacked the national administration, telling Viena Johnson, "Fascist minded people" who had been placed in power now were scuttling the New Deal. Three days after the election he sent a temperamental letter to Roosevelt and charged the national administration with giving aid to Minnesota Republican candidates for governor and senator ever since 1938.[45] He remained extremely bitter through early winter. "You can't name one person in our National Administration in a key responsible position," Benson complained, "who is not a dyed-in-the-wool reactionary and consciously or unconsciously [an] American [Fascist]."[46]

Mavericks, social critics, and protest movements in general had a hard time in 1942. In Nebraska George W. Norris, veteran Republican progressive senator, was defeated by conservative Kenneth W. Wherry. Although it was a liberal anti-Communist organization, the Union for Democratic Action[47] came under attack by the Dies House Un-American Activities Committee. The UDA Washington and New York offices were closed when rent money ran out; Tom Amlie's salary was unpaid from May to October; and Howard Williams had no success with the UDA in the Midwest, though its few remaining members hoped to see Henry Wallace groomed as Roosevelt's successor.[48]

By 1943 the important political question in Minnesota was less whether Farmer-Laborism would merge and more a matter of which Farmer-Labor faction would be in a position to negotiate with Democrats and receive some of the spoils of party and office. Even Elmer Benson's attitudes were about to be mellowed by wartime unity, and they may have been modified, or at least made more ambiguous, by his life outside politics. Benson's private interests were becoming, ironically, somewhat capitalistic even though publicly he continued to play the role of the anticapitalist. In Appleton he had become the business partner of Republican A. J. Kaufman, who helped provide investment capital and restore his entrepreneural skills. The two partners were owners and managers of thousands of acres of farmland which they had obtained through the acquisition of forfeited assets of defunct banks closed by the depression.[49] Thus the radical Benson was on the road (and in time in a Cadillac automobile) to becoming a legitimate petty-bourgeois millionaire. Both personally and politically Benson in wartime was coming to feel less need for Farmer-Laborism than ever before.

By early spring rather dramatic changes served to increase merger's appeal to Farmer-Laborites. First, the overall trend of the war against Nazi Germany began the process of disarming the Farmer-Labor left's traditional opposition to merger. After British and American forces pushed the German Afrika Korps out of North Africa, they captured Sicily, invaded Italy, and forced Mussolini from office, and the Western Allies appeared to be more equal partners with the Soviets in pressing the war against Hitler. In January 1943 at the Casablanca conference Roosevelt spontaneously announced the doctrine of unconditional surrender for Axis powers. These events went far in changing the mood of the Farmer-Labor left. By November, when merger discussions were well under way, the Teheran meeting of Churchill, Roosevelt, and Stalin was taken as additional proof that war had brought the ideological antagonists into more harmonious relationship.

True, serious barriers still had to be overcome both within the Democratic and Farmer-Labor parties and between the two. Democrats had their own factional disorders, and an enlarged party, expanded to accommodate Farmer-Laborites, was certain to result in a loss of personal power by Minnesota's Irish Democrats. Then too there were clashes between individuals, as between Democratic state chairman Elmer Kelm and St. Paul attorney Francis M. Smith who barely tolerated one another; yet both were crucial to merger planning. St. Paul Democrats never got along particularly well with their Minneapolis counterparts. And in early 1943 Democrats, as they began to lay out a merger strategy, did not know whether they should approach the two major Farmer-Labor factions simultaneously or attempt to work almost exclusively with the more sympathetic right-wing group.

Fortunately for the Democrats, the political climate was becoming more favorable to merger. Not the least important change was the wartime removal of Hjalmar Petersen from political activity. Petersen obtained employment at Federal Cartridge Corporation, and after he lost favor with its president, Charles Horn, he landed a federal civil service job in the Office of Defense Transportation, a position which effectively silenced his opposition. Vice-President Henry A. Wallace, long one of the few favored Democrats among left-wing Farmer-Laborites, likewise served as an important psychological link between the parties. The left, in fact, requested that Wallace deliver the keynote address at the February 1943 Farmer-Labor state convention,[50] and when this proved impossible, Howard Williams asked White House aide Eugene Casey to assist in bringing California Democratic congressman Jerry Voorhis (an advocate of cooperatives) to the convention.[51] Slowly the psychological barriers were being lowered.

A Right-Wing Coup for Merger

After the February 21-22 convention the left remained in command of the association and Benson and Viena Johnson were reelected to their state offices. However, the left-right factional gulf had widened beyond repair, and speakers and resolutions once again bitterly condemned "party group" attempts to destroy the association.[52] What lay beneath the left's rhetoric were right-wing plans to call a 1943 Farmer-Labor *party* convention for late March.

As announed by Juls Anderson, John Findlan, and William Mahoney in mid-February, it was a call for writing a Farmer-Labor *party* constitution. Although this was legal under state law, to the left-wingers in control of the association it represented political heresy of the worst sort. Left-wing members of the party central committee, claiming party meeting notices were late in arriving, strenuously objected, and in protest Viena Johnson and Victor Lapakko walked out in boycott. Nevertheless, a February 25 call was sent announcing March 15 as Farmer-Labor caucus day, to be followed by a state convention on March 27-28. The stakes in this gamble were high, for whoever controlled the legal machinery of the party convention commanded the party, and the supreme fear of the left was that this maneuver was the first step toward merger with Democrats.[53]

The left had no choice but to compete at the caucuses for control of the party. Mobilizing quickly, the association executive committee dispatched letters to all association members, urging them to turn out March 15 and grimly warning that the "party group" was seeking to change the name of the party "and hand it over to a new third party organization to give support to American Fascists in the next election."[54] In reality, this reexpressed the left's adamant opposition to Democratic and Farmer-Labor merger. But within a year that in fact was the general legal process followed in the two-party merger.

Beginning at the county level, right-wing Farmer-Laborites placed friendly colleagues into newly created posts as county chairmen. They were a mixture of old and new political and legislative faces, and many would become active in the DFL, men like Gordon C. Peterson, George Vikingstad, Frank Yetka, E. L. Prestemoen, Charles Halsted, C. F. Gaarenstrom, Ray Hemingway, Edward Chilgren, Paul Harris, K. K. Solberg, and Curtis Olson. To ensure control of the credentials committee, party chairman John S. Findlan appointed reliable moderates including

Harold Atwood (who had just run for Congress as a Democrat), Charles Munn, Minneapolis labor leader Gene Larson, Harry O'Connell of St. Paul, and longtime Willmar publisher Victor Lawson.[55]

Simultaneously with these occurrences, the national administration and the Democratic National Committee initiated discussions with state Democratic and Farmer-Labor leaders, and during these talks a pessimistic assessment was given about the coming 1944 presidential campaign and the crucial need to plan for it early. Also of concern was the rise in Stassen's national popularity, especially if he became part of the national Republican ticket, since a March Gallup poll ranked him the third most popular Republican in the United States, behind Thomas E. Dewey and Wendell Willkie.[56]

It was no accident that, on the eve of the Farmer-Labor caucuses, Postmaster General Frank Walker and DNC Vice-Chairman Ambrose O'Connell came to Minnesota. Upon Elmer Kelm, John Findlan, other leaders of the two parties, and labor officials the two national Democrats pressed the urgency of merger. Walker's preference was party unification, and he relied heavily upon Findlan, Mayor John J. McDonough, and St. Paul labor leaders for encouragement. Kelm did not stand in opposition to merger, but he did insist that fusion would be considered only when Farmer-Laborites literally abandoned their party and were absorbed into the existing machinery of the Democratic party.[57] In coming months an established pattern of visits between Washington and Minnesota became common, though often they were made under cover of "discussing the war effort and postwar readjustment."

Victory for the Left

The fate of merger was now in the hands of some 230 delegates at the March 27 party convention, but this was no friendly competition between two otherwise compatible coalitions. A near riot broke out when the credentials committee denied seats to some contested delegates who at one point in the proceedings attempted to forcefully break through a door and seat themselves. Outside Hennepin County the moderates, or "party faction," held a comfortable margin, but Hennepin was almost solidly in the hands of leftists and radicals. Armed with this 55 to 5 advantage, the left was able to muster a majority vote of 126 to 105, and leftist Paul R. Tinge was elected party chairman. The right then walked out,[58] leaving the left wing in sole control of the party as well as the association. When a party constitution was adopted, its declaration of principles declared that an end to "conflict of economic interests in our present society" would come only in the "supplanting of private monopoly by government ownership and control of all such monopolies."[59]

Democrats now faced a difficult choice. Did they want to associate, let alone merge, with advocates of government ownership, and if they did, how could they convince leftists to stop opposing merger? The reaction of right-wing Farmer-Laborites varied. In an April 1 press release William Mahoney frightened conservative Democrats by announcing "the communist germ was now isolated in the Farmer-Labor party of Minnesota,"[60] and privately he told Hjalmar Petersen the "Communist take-over" was due to Findlan's stupidity.[61] Other rightists opposed to merger talked of creating another party, the "Independent Progressives," while some veteran Farmer-Laborites, including Charles Halsted and a group of legislative liberals, declared they were abandoning their old party to join the Democrats. To Viena Johnson this was good riddance, for she found Halsted and men like him to be capitalistic apologists who favored crumbs for the masses while opposing fundamental socioeconomic change, which she said was so different from leftist policies of standing "opposed to capitalism."[62]

During April, May, and June 1943, Democrats, moderate Farmer-Laborites, and White House advisers were unsure what to do next. Findlan talked vaguely about creating a Minnesota Liberal League; Roosevelt White House aide Eugene Casey traveled to Minnesota where he discussed problems with Findlan and McDonough, which supposedly related to the War Production Board; and a few days later McDonough returned to Washington on "public business."[63]

Three other at the time unrelated events took place, two of which would have a direct bearing upon merger. Harold Stassen resigned as governor in April to go on active duty. A newcomer to Minnesota politics was also introduced then, a thirty-one-year-old Hubert H. Humphrey, Jr., who soon made a dramatic first impression upon Minneapolis city politics and state Democratic leaders; after the June election Humphrey too became interested in merger once he learned about it. Ideologically speaking, however, the most significant event came out of Moscow with the May 1943 announcement that the Communist International (Comintern) had been dissolved. Whatever the connection, direct, indirect, or residual, there soon occurred a noticeable shift in attitude of the Minnesota left wing in the Farmer-Labor Association and party: opposition to Democratic and Farmer-Labor merger, for two decades one of the first pinciples of the left faction, was about to be discarded in mid-1943 as the bid to ensure Roosevelt's reelection took on a broader appeal.

The Introduction of Humphrey

The unveiling of Hubert H. Humphrey in Minnesota politics may have overshadowed the importance of the merger movement and even made it unnecessary and obsolete. Conceived in Minnesota and raised in South Dakota, Humphrey was a child of the depression, which made him an emotional believer in the Democratic New Deal. He lived in an extremely politically sensitive family with a small-town pharmacist father who was a disciple of William Jennings Bryan, Woodrow Wilson, and then Franklin D. Roosevelt. For a time Humphrey looked toward a university teaching career, but in 1940 rather than complete his doctoral requirements he went to work for the government at various positions in the Public Works Administration and later the War Manpower Administration. His education and career had been delayed, so that by 1943-44 he had pent up enthusiasm which exploded as he plunged into politics. Without doubt, Democrats had not uncovered so valuable a commodity since the days of Governor John Johnson in the first decade of the century.

As late as March 1943 Humphrey was unknown to the general public, though in the early forties he began introducing himself by speaking to literally hundreds of city groups and service organizations, by cultivating the friendships of labor leaders, and through contact with local newspapermen. Using his contacts and a rare ability to gain attention and coverage, he soon was the most exciting personality to appear in the 1943 Minneapolis campaign. After not much more than one month's effort he won the mayoral primary nomination and the right to oppose incumbent Marvin Kline. Eight years had passed since liberals (and radicals) had last won in Minneapolis, and for the first time he built a broad coalition of support among University of Minnesota intellectuals, the Central Labor Union, AFL and CIO local unions, moderate Republicans, the League of Women Voters, moderate Farmer-Laborites, and even some radicals.[64] Although Humphrey lost the election by 5,984 votes, he had attracted so much favorable attention by his multitude of proposals, press releases, energy, and seeming irrepressible enthusiasm that many liberals recognized him as a valuable resource around which to build Democratic fortunes in Minnesota.

Assuming that national events, the Cold War, and the Truman 1948 campaign were hardly, if at all, affected by the 1944 merger, there is reason to believe that even in the absence of fusion Humphrey's career would have still followed much the same pattern and would have been as successful. Humphrey was and remained a liberal Democrat; he provided his party with the dynamic and dominant personality it had lacked for decades; and allowing for marginal differences of outcome elsewhere in the party, there is strong reason to believe a Democratic revival would have taken place in Minnesota without formal merger.

Assessments of Humphrey's contribution to the Democratic and Farmer-Labor merger have tended to exaggerate his role. Humphrey was not the "father" of DFL merger; it likely would have occurred in his absence—most of the planning and legal research was not done by him and actually took place before he became active; and he was not in a position to substantially affect the left-wing shift of position from opponent to advocate of fusion. Fusion was about to occur because of an accumulation of events, defections, and inducements to unify which were increasingly evident over the previous two years and which actually went back to 1938, or more properly to as early as 1926 in the "round robin" proposal and the idea of a single liberal anti-Republican party. Nevertheless, Humphrey was prominent in the final months of negotiations and unquestionably made significant visible contributions then, particularly in his chosen role as mediator between Democrats and Farmer-Laborites and through enthusiastic encouragement he imparted to committee negotiators, in keeping with his unique political personality. The weight of evidence about merger hardly supports the later contention that Humphrey was the man who merged the two parties, a myth which understandably developed in the light of his later significance as one of the foremost politicians of his generation.

MERGER

Merger pieces large and small began to fit together. Financially, the Farmer-Labor Association had reached almost the level of insolvency,[65] and if merger was to occur eventually the left wing much preferred to be the faction participating in the negotiations on the assumption that it could push Democrats much farther toward progressive social reforms than would right-wing Farmer-Laborites.

Fusion activity increased in July. In midmonth St. Paul Mayor John McDonough went to Washington, supposedly to discuss with Roosevelt "hospital, airport and post-war housing construction," which seemed rather incredulous since he was accompanies to see the president by Postmaster General Frank Walker, who served as the chairman of the National Democratic party.[66] At the same time forty-year-old St. Paul attorney Francis M. Smith resumed legal research on technical questions relating to merger. In the first week of August Smith circulated a legal memorandum on merger for use by McDonough, deputy national Democratic chairman Oscar Ewing who now became the principle DNC liaison officer working on merger, and leftist attorney

Roger Rutchick who assumed the role of legal counsel to the Benson-left-wing merger advocates. Smith's comprehensive memorandum presented a brief history of the two parties, described the process that had led to fusion between Democrats and Populists in the late 1890s, anticipated possible legal complications, and set out the procedures necessary to merge Democrats and Farmer-Laborites.[67]

Somewhat strangely, Minnesota newsmen failed to discover the significance of these developments, yet beginning the first week in August a number of important national Democrats, all veterans of party organizing and past campaigns, filtered into Minnesota. The first to arrive was James A. Farley, who suitably (and deceptively) enough during wartime toured the Twin City Ordnance facility; but the real reason for his visit was to have a dinner conference with John Findlan, St. Paul labor leader William Wright, and Frank Starkey who often advised McDonough.[68] Coming to St. Paul three days later were Frank Walker and Oscar Ewing, whose purpose was to formally initiate merger discussions between leaders of the two parties. Walker and Ewing first met with Findlan, Wright, and St. Paul labor leaders Harry O'Connell, Martin and Gerald O'Donnell, William Brennen, Joe Prifrel, John Calgren, and James Russell. Then Humphrey brought before them a Minneapolis delegation that included Charles Munn, Douglas Hall, Vince Day, Guy Alexander, Ralph Dickman, and AFL and CIO spokesmen such as Reuben Latz, Roy Wier, Eugene Larson, Harold Seavey, Robley (Red) Cramer, and William Mauseth.[69]

From the left, right, conservative, liberal, and radical quarters merger sentiment gained wider support. Elmer Benson was "more than pleased with the attitude" he encountered in his discussions about merger, and he heaped praise upon Ewing and Walker "for the splendid manner in which you conducted conferences and negotiations."[70] Ewing and Walker now urged state Democratic chairman Elmer Kelm to appoint a merger committee to work out the problems. When Kelm reacted cautiously, Benson not only became irritated but appealed to Walker that "something be done promptly" to get Kelm to act more positively on merger.[71]

It was ironic that weary Kelm Democrats dragged their feet whereas left-wing Farmer-Laborites, for years merger's traditional opposition, were actually more swift and positive in taking action. For a September 26 meeting of the Farmer-Labor state central committee Viena Johnson outlined the choices: merger, cooperation but no merger, and an independent "no deals" Farmer-Labor campaign in 1944.[72] Not every Farmer-Laborite immediately warmed to the merger proposal; those who did not were won over by the leadership. Charles

Egley talked about the "desirablilty of entering the Democratic movement to give guidance to it from within."[73] After a resolution was passed empowering Benson to appoint a merger committee to plan for fusion of Minnesota liberal forces in time for the 1944 campaign, Benson chose to work with Egley, Carl Flodquist, and Viena Johnson.[74]

While Kelm dallied, other Democrats were less reticent. Former congressman Einar Hoidale urged merger action,[75] and to boost prospects while silencing a potential fusion critic, John McDonough appealed directly to Roosevelt for assistance in landing a federal job for Hjalmar Petersen.[76] Because Kelm still held back, Benson made another strong appeal to Walker and Ewing, warning them that Kelm was aligned with Democrats unfriendly to the Roosevelt administration and asking them to exert influence upon the Kelm-controlled state Democratic organization or face the prospect that the 1944 Minnesota national convention delegation "will be anti-administration unless the plan which we have discussed is carried through."[77] Kelm, however, was puzzled by the Benson-left reversal of position on merger and reluctant to share power with the left-wing Farmer-Laborites, though he continually reassured Walker and Ewing that he intended to appoint a merger committee as soon as he had lined up sufficient Democratic support.[78]

The Democratic Merger Invitation

At a joint meeting of the state committee of the Farmer-Labor Assocation and party in mid-November a formal vote of approval was taken to indicate receptivity to a merger offer from the Democrats. Ten days later, on November 26, Kelm finally issued an official Democratic invitation, one to Benson as association chairman, the other to Tinge as party chairman. Emphasizing the two-party tradition and inviting Farmer-Laborites "to join our ranks," Kelm said the purpose was to unite "the democratic and progressive forces" into a single party, and in the event fusion proved not possible, he asked for an integrated 1944 campaign against the Republicans.[79] Benson expressed pleasure over the invitation, telling newsmen that Kelm's letter was "extremely friendly," his sole qualification being that although he personally endorsed merger it had to be officially accepted by Farmer-Laborites.[80]

Four courtship months of negotiation had to pass before the marriage took place. The first week of December each party appointed five-member committees, which were to meet separately and jointly as needed, to draft the final plans and divide the spoils of party office between them. Democrat Francis M. Smith and Farmer-Laborite Roger Rutchick were entrusted with preparing the legal documentation for

for merger.[81] And to boost enthusiasm while ensuring there would be no retreat, AFL, CIO and rail bortherhood officials met again with the Farmer-Labor state committees and urged amalgamation. Some veteran Farmer-Laborites preferred to retain the Farmer-Labor Association as an "educational association,"[82] and a few held out for naming the new party Farmer-Labor-Democratic, but merger was to be on fundamentally Democratic terms, and these wishes had to be sacrificed.

One week into the merger year of 1944 Benson and Tinge gave Kelm another affirmative answer: "We are for it." Citing the need for political unity in prosecuting the war and expressing fear about the alleged power of Herbert Hoover, Alfred Landon, Thomas Dewey, Robert Taft, Arthur Vandenberg whom they lumped with publishers Col. Robert McCormick of the *Chicago Tribune* and William Randolph Hearst, Gerald L. K. Smith, and reactionaries in general, Benson and Tinge urged swift merger action and suggested the Special Democratic Committee and the Special Farmer-Labor Committee meet soon "to begin to work upon the practical details." Farmer-Laborism, they assured, stood ready to "rock the foundations" of Minnesota Republicanism.[83]

The Wallace Rally

Before the end of January Benson traveled to Washington, met with Roosevelt, suggested some farm proposals he wanted passed, and volunteered his services to the president in the forthcoming election.[84] Yet up to now a serious shortcoming of the merger movement was the lack of involvement of large blocs of the rank and file. To compensate for this and to give the final discussions a strong psychological sendoff, a mass rally was planned for February 14 in the Minneapolis Armory. Sponsored jointly by the two parties, the association, and local unions, the rally was designed to break through any emotional barriers separating the two sides. Fortunately, Vice-President Henry A. Wallace was on a Midwest speaking tour attempting to rekindle sentiment for the New Deal, and he was chosen as the climactic speaker of the event. And the arrangements general chairman was the upcoming Hubert H. Humphrey, who played a role that was made to order for his enthusiastic personality.

On the afternoon of rally day Democrats and Farmer-Laborites were beseeched to forget the past and work together for the future. Tinge presided and speaker upon speaker—Benson, Egley, Humphrey, McDonough, Slen—prepared party followers for the end of liberal division in Minnesota. Benson was, if not the most emotional, at least the most candid of the speakers. "We Farmer-Laborites haven't much choice," he admitted at one point. Declaring the choice now was between Roosevelt or a reactionary, Benson told why he was sacrificing the movement. "We can't have a Farmer-Labor president, we can't have a socialist president at this time. If we can have a socialist president in 20 years I'll be happy. . . ."[85]

Wisely, Democrats kept silent at the mention of such twenty-year goals, and in the afternoon a resolution carried urging the leadership to bring merger discussions to a successful conclusion. Nevertheless, an undercurrent of separatism seemed not far beneath the surface. Although Democrats and left-wing Farmer-Laborites might rally in good faith around a general call for peace, prosperity, security, and world rehabilitation, resolution language that condemned "defeatists, isolationists, believers in a negotiated peace [and] supporters of fascism at home and abroad," while not objectionable in the Democratic context of 1944, recalled a style of speech reminiscent of the Popular Front movement. Again, Democrats refrained from objecting publicly to resolution language that suggested merger had an impermanent quality to it: "a third party in Minnesota cannot function on a national scale and the times and conditions are not yet ripe for the organization of a National Third Party yet."[86] Democrats wanted merger, and as long as the Farmer-Labor practice was legally being put to an end they could well afford the cost of avoiding comment.

Humphrey introduced himself and the Vice-President to nearly 10,000 cheering voices, and Wallace did not disappoint those who hoped he would lead progressives out of the wilderness and into a bright new liberal fellowship. Around the theme of unity and meaningful political purpose, Wallace called on Farmer-Laborites to renew their political spirit in the Democratic party and to help in the search for liberal public policies. Looking idealistically forward to a hopeful and progressive postwar period, he appealed for a "people's peace," regional planning and development, and he reminded his audience that the government had a responsibility to better feed some ten million impoverished American families. To midwestern protest he was a modern Jeremiah, deploring the flow of farmers' cash to the Eastern seaboard where it rested, he said, as Wall Street deposits which corporate America used to manipulate public policy for the benefit of the few rather than the many.[87]

No Democratic leader could have better delivered a final prayer over Farmer-Laborism and a benediction of welcome to remnant third-party souls coming into the Democratic party. Already Wallace had a strong liberal and radical following in Minnesota, among Democrats and Farmer-Laborites, and it would be a source of unification at first but would become a cause of revived schism after the war was over.

Final Arrangements

A week later, on February 22, new national chairman Robert E. Hannegan and his vice-chairman Ambrose O'Connell came to Minnesota urging Democratic follow-through and agreement on merger. Their forum was a $25 Washington Day dinner whose toastmaster was the irrepressible Humphrey.[88]

Although history's judgment may show that merger was not critical to later Democratic party success in Minnesota, neither the state nor the national party in 1944 was in any position to know this and it was empirical fact that Roosevelt's 1936 plurality of 350,000 votes had plunged to less than 50,000 in 1940. Hannegan's message to Minnesota Democrats was a much more palliative variant of James Farley's 1936 withdrawal request: Roosevelt's leadership had to be retained, Minnesota was a key Midwest state to his reelection, and merger was imperative if the state was to stay in the Roosevelt column. And Humphrey, as he dreamed about his own future, saw personal advantage in fusion and feared that without it he could end up being just another liberal also-ran. In part assumed and in part assigned was Humphrey's role as "liaison" between merger's principal negotiators,[89] a fact which further explains the tendency in later years to overstress his importance and undervalue the work of others.

During the final six weeks the major unresolved issue was an equitable division of party offices between Democrats and left-wing Farmer-Laborites, a question which was made more serious for Democrats since, ideologically speaking, they would have much preferred to negotiate with the moderate Farmer-Labor wing and not the Benson faction. Meanwhile, Rutchick and Smith, having refined their legal research and preparation, were now convinced they had a challenge-proof strategy to change the party names which would withstand a court test.[90] Their brief was circulated the last week of February.

During the critical final stage of negotiation a short special session of the legislature was called to enact a wartime servicemen's voting act, and this brought on uneasiness growing from a fear that Republicans would create some unknown legal barrier that would scuttle fusion. In addition, a few Farmer-Laborites and Democrats continued to suspect Kelm of plotting to prevent final agreement.[91] Neither materialized.

Crucial procedural agreements were hammered out by merger conferees in marathon sessions between March 2 and 5. On Friday, March 3, the White House sent in Oscar Ewing to act as troubleshooter and facilitator. Finally, on Sunday, the Democratic central committee announced, at the Dyckman Hotel, the 1944 party call for caucuses and a state convention. In the St. Paul meeting hall of the Amalgamated Clothing Workers Union, the Farmer-Labor Association and the Farmer-Labor party each issued a statewide call for March 28 caucuses and a state convention.

The plan now set in motion was for the Farmer-Labor name to be dropped and in its place was to be substituted the name "Freedom party." Shortly afterward Democrats were to reincorporate as the Democratic-Farmer-Labor party of Minnesota, and delegates from the two conventions were to come together as a single united convention and party, adopt a new DFL party constitution,[92] appoint party officers, and select delegates to the 1944 Democratic national convention.

There were dissenters to the very end, and they came from nearly every political and ideological corner. The old Farmer-Labor right-wingers, at least those who had not already defected to the Democratic party, were stunned that Democrats could so cavalierly welcome Farmer-Labor leftists and radicals. One such right-winger was Hjalmar Petersen, who wondered how it was possible for what he called "the discredited people" in the movement—like Benson, the "patronage group," Communists, and fellow travelers—to be welcomed into the Democratic party.[93] William Mahoney issued another of his annual April 1 attacks upon Benson, Communists, and fellow travelers, this year charging them with responsibility for finally destroying the Farmer-Labor party.[94]

Opposition of the Farmer-Labor right was not so much to merger as it was in keeping with its decade-long battle against the left. In four years, when a purge of DFL leftists would occur the old Farmer-Labor moderates who refused to join in 1944 would join the new party. But through most of winter 1944 people like Mrs. Josephine Tomai, president of the Farmer-Labor Women's Political Federation, opposed merger. At the same time conservative Mankato Democrat John Regan, who in the 1930s had refused to help Farmer-Labor candidates, was blunt in declaring Henry Wallace's postwar economic program unacceptable.[95]

Opposition also developed within some labor ranks. National AFL president William Green worried about excessive CIO influence in the merged party. And Robley (Red) Cramer, longtime editor of the *Minneapolis Labor Review* and a left-wing Farmer-Laborite whose roots extended to the early 1920s, condemned merger as a tragedy and a hoax.[96] The person most upset was the grand old lady of temperance and Farmer-Laborism, Susie Stageberg, who resisted to the very end what she said was a "top-down" merger of "the dear old party that had meant so much to me and many other of our pioneer builders in Minnesota." Always moralistic, pietistic, and faithful to her Lord and party, she did not fault Benson, toward whom she felt "so dear." But she was distressed upon hearing a report that Roger Rutchick had been given $10,000 to, as she put it, "swing the deal."[97]

To Henry Wallace, however, merger was glory, laud, and honor. Minnesota liberals had touched him as much as he them. Urging Oscar Ewing to return to Minnesota for the final unification ceremonies, Wallace bestowed high praise upon Elmer Benson for "the important part which you have been playing in doing this job." When Benson reported to Roosevelt on the final preparations for merger, he happily assured the president everything was arranged to successfully merge the two parties, and he also urged the return of Ewing to Minnesota to see that negotiated promises were kept and that fusion was handled smoothly at the state conventions.[98]

When Ewing came back in mid-April, to the disgust of the temperate Benson, he "was drunk as the Lord." The two parties did become one in name, but ideologically speaking they had not been merged. To the future were left some serious postwar questions. Could wartime unity prevail in peacetime? Would the old Farmer-Labor divisions between ideological left and right reemerge in the new DFL? Were socialists and collectivists compatible with Democratic liberalism. What new issues would be debated in postwar foreign policy? Was it possible to find agreement among Farmer-Laborites and Democrats so different as Elmer Benson, Charles Halsted, John Regan, Elmer Kelm, and talented newcomers like Hubert Humphrey and his postwar allies? Would there be a struggle for power after 1944?

That, dear reader, is another story.

Notes

Notes

CHAPTER 1

1. Observers have long found it difficult to explain the presence or degree of absence of socialism in the NPL (or the Farmer-Labor party). See Robert L. Morlan, *Political Prairie Fire; The Nonpartisan League, 1915-1922* (Minneapolis, 1955), pp. 353-58. Edward C. Blackorby, in *Prairie Rebel; the Public Life of William Lemke* (Lincoln, 1963), p. 58, for example, argues that the NPL's socialist proposals were designed to save capitalism, especially small entrepreneurs like farmers. However, the subjects of league collectivism (banks, mines, utilities, etc.) were hardly as charitable in their assessment of the NPL program.

2. For a history of the Equity Cooperative Exchange, see Robert H. Bahmer, "The American Society of Equity," *Agricultural History*, 14 (Jan. 1940), 33-63; Theodore Saloutos and John D. Hicks, *Agricultural Discontent in the Middle West, 1900-1939* (Madison, 1951), chap. V, pp. 111-48; Benjamin Drake papers and James Manahan papers (Minnesota Historical Society). This section is based largely on these sources.

3. The Equity Cooperative Exchange, *Co-Operation in Marketing of Grain* (Minneapolis, n.d. [ca. 1912]), 48 pp; *The Equity Co-Operative Exchange* (St. Paul, n.d.), 14 pp.; Saloutos and Hicks, *Agricultural Discontent*, p. 137.

4. Morlan, *Political Prairie Fire*, pp. 20-21.

5. Minority Report, Senate Grain Exchange Investigation, 1912 Minnesota Legislature; Drake papers.

6. See the Manahan papers (Minnesota Historical Society). William J. Bryan to Manahan, May 13, 1907; Manahan to Bryan, Oct. 9, 1907. Manahan bolted to the Republican party in 1911.

7. Equity Cooperative Exchange, *Co-Operation in Marketing of Grain*, pp. 9-41, gives a brief history of Loftus's and Manahan's successes against "Big Business."

8. See the Drake and the Manahan papers, 1913.

9. Loftus to the *Minneapolis Daily News*, Dec. 20, 1913, in Drake papers.

10. House Resolution 424, 63rd Congress, 2nd session.

11. Theodore Saloutos, "Farmer Movements since 1902" (Ph.D. thesis, University of Wisconsin, 1940), pp. 90-94.

12. See W. E. Davis's articles in *The Northwest Agriculturist*, Oct. 4, 11, 18, 25, 1913, Collins's editorials for Oct. and Nov. 1913.

13. Equity Cooperative Exchange, *The Equity Cooperative Exchange is Truly Co-Operative* (St. Paul, n.d. [ca. 1915]), 8 pp; *The St. Paul Spirit* (St. Paul, n.d. [ca. 1914]), 3 pp; *Proposed Farmers Terminal Elevator, St. Paul, Minnesota* (St. Paul, n.d. [ca. 1914]); Charles E. Russell, "The Revolt of the Farmers. A Lesson in Constructive Radicalism," *Pearson's Magazine*, Apr. 1915, pp. 417-27. The Minneapolis Chamber of Commerce, for its part, continued to attack and propagandize against Equity: see its *The Chamber of Commerce of Minneapolis*, reprinted from *The Co-Operative Manager and Farmer* (the house organ of the chamber), 1914, pp. 35-66; the reprint was widely distributed in Minnesota and North Dakota and told of the "Square Deal" given by the chamber and the "Proof of Deception practiced on farmers and farmers' elevator" companies by Equity. The chamber even printed an attack upon Loftus made by Father O'Callaghan of Eden Valley.

14. See copy of original signed statement, Feb. 12, 1915, in which Equity was told that the Chamber of Commerce was "raising hell" with the firm of Frame, Dougherty and Co. for the Equity audit and threatened reprisals.

15. "Resolutions Adopted at the St. Paul Convention, Dec. 9, 1915."

16. Thatcher to Board of Directors, Nov. 1, 1917. Equity's working deficit was $123,689 on Nov. 1, 1917. The situation was bad, said Thatcher, and corrective action was necessary. "In many years auditing all kinds of business, never have I seen an institution turn its working margin so often as does your Corporation." Thatcher was president of Equitable Audit Company, Inc. See Drake papers.

17. Saloutos, "Farmer Movements," pp. 116-17.

18. See Christianson's editorial, "Open the Chamber of Commerce," in the *Dawson Sentinel*, Feb. 28, 1913.

19. Morlan, *Political Prairie Fire*, pp. 22-23; Saloutos and Hicks, *Agricultural Discontent*, pp. 152-57.

20. Saloutos and Hicks, *Agricultural Discontent*, pp. 164-70.

21. For a thorough discussion of the 1917 legislative session, see Morlan, *Political Prairie Fire*, pp. 92-108; Saloutos and Hicks, *Agricultural Discontent*, 176-77.

22. *The Western Comrade* (Llano, Calif.), Dec. 1917, pp. 9-10.

23. Morlan, *Political Prairie Fire*, pp. 353-54.

24. *Fargo Daily Courier-News*, May 21, 1916; which quoted from *The Iconoclast*.

Chapter 2

1. *Fargo Daily Courier News*, Nov. 2, 1916.

2. For the story of Johnson, see Winifred Helmes, *John A. Johnson* (Minneapolis, 1949).

3. Millard L. Gieske, "The Politics of Knute Nelson, 1912-20" (Ph.D. thesis, University of Minnesota, 1965), pp. 261-66.

4. *Ibid.*, p. 267.

5. *Ibid.*, pp. 272-76. Dunn was a newspaper publisher (*The Princeton Union*) and former candidate for governor in 1904; Fred Stevens had been a longtime congressman from St. Paul, Moos, who later became St. Paul postmaster, was an effective link with the German voters at least in 1916 (his son later became president of the University of Minnesota).

6. *Ibid.*, pp. 290-96, 299-301. The vote was Kellogg, 73,818; Eberhart, 54,890; Clapp, 27,668; and Lindbergh, 26,094.

7. *Minneapolis Tribune*, Jan. 3, 1917.

8. *Ibid.; Minneapolis Tribune*, Mar. 27, 28, 1917; Gieske, "Knute Nelson," pp. 375-77.

9. *Minneapolis Tribune*, Mar. 26, 1917; Theodore Saloutos and John D. Hicks, *Agricultural Discontent in the Midwest, 1900-1939* (Madison, 1951), pp. 177-78; William W. Folwell, *A History of Minnesota* (St. Paul, 1926), vol. III, p. 554.

10. Gieske, "Knute Nelson," pp. 361-64.

11. *Ibid.; Minneapolis Tribune*, Feb. 7, 1917; Gieske, "Knute Nelson," pp. 366-67. See also David Paul Nord, "Minneapolis and the Pragmatic Socialism of Thomas Van Lear," *Minnesota History*, 45 (1976), 2-10, which provides a broader analysis of Van Lear's political values and his 1916 campaign as a reform (not a radical) anticorruption candidate.

12. *Minneapolis Tribune*, Feb. 10, 1917. Rally speakers included Van Lear, S. A. Stockwell of the school board, University of Toledo professor Scott Nearing, and correspondent Peer Stromme.

13. *Minneapolis Tribune*, Feb. 9, 12, 1917; *Minneapolis Journal*, Feb. 12, 1917; Knute Nelson to Woodrow Wilson, Feb. 21, 1917, Nelson papers; see also Gieske, "Knute Nelson," pp. 368-70.

14. *Minneapolis Tribune*, Mar. 25, 1917. The editor was Rudolph Lee of the *Long Prairie Leader*; the Socialist was M. M. Randall.

15. *Minneapolis Journal*, Feb. 11, 1917; *Minneapolis Tribune*, Feb. 11, 1917; Gieske, "Knute Nelson," pp. 370-77.

16. *Minneapolis Tribune*, Apr. 1, 5, 1917; *St. Paul Pioneer Press*, Apr. 10, 1917. Gieske, "Knute Nelson," p. 378.

17. Gieske, "Knute Nelson," pp. 393-98.

18. Johnson to Nelson, Apr. 2, 1917, and Nelson to Johnson, April 7, 1917, Nelson Papers; Gieske, "Knute Nelson," pp. 407-9; Franklin F. Holbrook and Levia Appel, *Minnesota in the War with Germany* (St. Paul, 1932), vol. 2, p. 56. Charles W. Ames was president of West Publishing, Anton C. Weiss publisher of the *Herald*.

19. Gieske, "Knute Nelson," pp. 418-24.

20. Gieske, "Knute Nelson," pp. 411-16; Holbrook and Appel *Minnesota in the War*, pp. 41-42.

21. McGee to Nelson, Aug. 17, 1917, and Snyder to Nelson, Aug. 18, 1917, Nelson papers.

22. "Resolutions Adopted by the Nonpartisan League Conference," Sept. 18-20, 1917 (St. Paul), LeSueur papers.

23. *Minneapolis Tribune*, Sept. 20, 1917.

24. *Minneapolis Tribune*, Sept. 19, 1917; Gieske, "Knute Nelson," pp. 426-29.

25. *Minneapolis Tribune*, Sept. 21, 1917; Gieske, "Knute Nelson," pp. 430-31.

26. Gieske, "Knute Nelson," p. 432.

27. *Minneapolis Tribune*, Sept. 29, 30, 1917.

28. *Duluth News Tribune*, Oct. 8, 1917.

29. Gieske, "Knute Nelson," pp. 433-34.

Chapter 3

1. Minnesota Public Safety Commission, "History of Labor Difficulties with the Trainmen of the Twin Cities Lines in Minneapolis and St. Paul and the Strike which occurred as a result." See also Gieske, "The Politics of Knute Nelson" (Ph.D. thesis, University of Minnesota, 1965), pp. 451-55.

2. Burnquist to Ames, Dec. 4, 1917, Nelson papers.

3. Wilson to Nelson, Dec. 7, 1917; J. P. Tumulty to Nelson, Dec. 11, 1917; Wilson to Nelson, Dec. 19, 1917; all in the Nelson papers; Gieske, "Knute Nelson," pp. 456-68.

4. T. H. Walker to Joseph C. Doegan, Mar. 13, 1918 (circular letter), Nelson papers.

5. *Minneapolis Tribune*, Mar. 2, 1918.

6. Millard L. Gieske, "Knute Nelson," pp. 444-49.

7. Victor L. Stephenson to Nelson, Dec. 13, 1917, Nelson papers. *Minneapolis Tribune*, Jan. 1, 1918; Nelson to Judge W. H. Laman, Mar. 16, 1918, Nelson papers.

8. O. P. Briggs to Nelson, Mar. 18, 1918, Nelson papers.

9. *Duluth Labor World*, Jan. 19, 1918.

10. Robert L. Morlan, *Political Prairie Fire* (Minneapolis 1955), pp. 188-91.

11. "Platform and Declaration of Principles," Nonpartisan League, Mar. 19, 1918.

12. *Ibid.*

13. Morlan, *Political Prairie Fire*, pp. 191-93.

14. *Ibid.*, p. 198; Franklin F. Holbrook and Levia Appel, *Minnesota in the War with Germany* (St. Paul, 1932), vol. II, pp. 49-51.

15. *Minneapolis Tribune*, Apr. 5, 11, 12, 13, 14, 19; Gieske, "Knute Nelson," pp. 497-500. Peterson's offense was to claim that the "Wall Street press" was blocking peace and prolonging the war needlessly.

16. N. Grevstad to Will H. Hayes, Apr. 6, 1919, Nelson papers.

17. Teigan papers, from letters dated Apr. 26, 1918, and May 29, 1918.

18. Gieske, "Knute Nelson," pp. 516-20. The organizer was Edward E. Smith of Minneapolis, sometimes said to be one of the period's shrewd "bosses."

19. Holbrook and Appel, *Minnesota in the War*, p. 48; *Minneapolis Journal*, Mar.11, 1918.

20. Gieske, "Knute Nelson," pp. 524-25; *Legislative Manual*, 1919, pp. 250-53; *Minnesota Leader*, July 8, 1918.

21. William Leekley's interview with William Mahoney, July 26, 1940, Leekley papers.

22. *Minneapolis Tribune*, July 29, 1918.

23. "Manifesto Issued by the Working People's Political League," Aug. 25, 1918, 8 pp.; Farmer-Labor papers. A year later in New Ulm, labor took a decided turn to the left.

24. Undated speech, Mahoney papers; Fraser to Leekley, Mar. 30, 1940, Leekley papers; Gieske, "Knute Nelson," pp. 531-32, 537-40.

25. Gieske, "Knute Nelson," pp. 536-55.

26. Gieske, "Knute Nelson," pp. 569-70, 582-83.

27. *Ibid.*, pp. 635-37.

28. Gieske, "Knute Nelson," pp. 585-600. See *Brewing and Liquor Interests and German and Bolshevik Propaganda*. Report of the Subcommittee of the Judiciary of the United States Senate, June 1919. Senate Doc. 61, 66th Congress, 1st Session.

29. Jones to Nelson, Sept. 3, 1919, Nelson papers.

30. Townley and Gilbert were charged with conspiracy to teach sedition and discourage the draft. See *State v. A. C. Townley and Another*. 149 Minn. 5, 182 N. W. 773; Morlan, *Political Prairie Fire*, pp. 241-43, 256-61, 315-29; *St. Paul Pioneer Press*, Sept. 16, 1919. They were convicted on July 12, 1919, and sentenced in September. Nelson to Nicholay Grevstad, Mar. 7, 1919, July 19, 1919, and Nelson to McGee, Mar. 7, 1919, Nelson papers.

31. "Platform and Declaration of Principles," WPNPL, of the Labor Political Conference, New Ulm, July 20, 1919, Mahoney papers.

32. Lee Willcuts to Nelson, Oct. 2, 1919, Nelson papers.

33. Henry Teigan to Herbert Iverson, Dec. 8, 1919, NPL papers. Membership in North Dakota was approximately 40,000, total membership in all states 208,800.

34. John W. Nagle to Nelson, Dec. 8, 1919, Nelson papers; Gieske, "Knute Nelson," pp. 657-58.

35. "Minutes of the 1st Biennial Convention of the Working Peoples' League of Minnesota, St. Paul, March 24 and 25, 1920," in Teigan papers; Morlan, *Political Prairie Fire*, 279-83.

36. Willcuts to Nelson, July 28, 1919, and Nelson to I. A. Caswell, ca. Nov. 2, 1919, Nelson papers.

37. *Minneapolis Tribune*, May 8, 9, 1920.

38. Willcuts to Nelson, May 11, 1920, and Nelson to Preus, Apr. 28, 1920, Nelson papers.

39. Nelson to J. A. O. Preus, Jan. 9, 1919, and Nelson to Dr. Christian Johnson, Aug. 16, 1919, Nelson papers.

40. Morlan, *Political Prairie Fire*, pp. 280-81.

41. *Minneapolis Tribune*, June 3, 4, 7, 8, 10, 11, 13, 1920.

42. *Minneapolis Tribune*, May 4, 1920.

43. Gieske, "Knute Nelson," pp. 660-61, 668-71. On July 20 a state district court threw out the primary result on the grounds of Kvale's atheism charge against Volstead; however, the Minnesota supreme court refused to let Volstead be designated the Republican nominee on the ballot, so he ran as an independent and won in November.

44. Nelson to Willcuts, June 25, 1920, Nelson papers. It was commonly assumed, and probably correctly, that the additional candidates in the field were actually garnering regular Republican votes. Nelson considered it "outrageous for these men to remain in the field," and he said that the NPLers "will never be able to muster the votes that they did in this campaign and we have clearly got them on the run."

45. *Minneapolis Tribune*, July 2, 3, 1920.

46. *Ibid.*, July 8, 1920.

47. *Ibid.*, July 18, 19, 1920.

48. *Ibid.*, Aug. 7, 1920.

49. Morlan, *Political Prairie Fire*, p. 297.

50. Willcuts to Nelson, Oct. 2, 1920; Kellogg to Nelson, Oct. 25, 1920; Nelson to Walter H. Newton, Oct. 26, 1920; all in the Nelson papers.

Chapter 4

1. "As a Woman Sees It," undated original copy of column regularly appearing in the *Willmar Tribune*. Susie, whose husband Olaf had been a teacher or professor at the old Red Wing (Lutheran) Seminary, was a deeply religious Christian socialist. She ran as a Farmer-Laborite for secretary of state in 1922 and 1924, for Congress in 1932, and as a Progressive for lieutenant governor in 1950. She also was a strong temperance advocate. See the Stageberg papers.

2. Grace Keller to Stanley Rypins, June 25, 1920, Committee of 48 papers.

3. Organization Committee minutes, Feb. 6, 1920, Committee of 48 papers. University of Minnesota Professor Stanley Rypins was chairman and Professor Willus M. West national committeeman.

4. Stanley I. Rypins to Cora Marlow Kernes, Mar. 29, 1920, and Grace Keller to Eva Waterman, Apr. 22, 1920; Committee of 48 papers.

5. May 1, 1920, statement; Keller to F. A. Cloutier, May 7, 1920; "State Convention of the Committee of 48," June 12, 1920, transcript; Rypins to Keller, June 25, 28, 1920; "Minutes of the State Central Committee," July 22, 1920; Hopkins to Rypins, July 29, Aug. 2, 1920; Frank J. Esper to Rypins, Aug. 3, 1920; Keller to Hopkins, Aug. 11, 1920; "Special Meeting," Minnesota Committee of 48; Hopkins to Rypins, Aug. 25, 1920; Keller to Esper, Aug. 19, 1920; Keller to Hopkins, Aug. 27, 1920; Hopkins to Keller, Oct. 4, 1920; all in the Committee of 48 papers.

6. Asher Howard, ed. *The Leaders of the Nonpartisan League, Their Aims, Purposes, and Records Reproduced from Original Letters and Documents* (Minneapolis, c. 1920), 127 pp. Mailed anywhere in the state for three cents, it contained an open letter by Ole. O. Sageng, Frank E. Reed, and J. E. Haycraft, and purported to show the IWW and Socialist party affiliation of many NPL leaders.

7. Nov. 1920, pp. 193-200.

8. *The Nonpartisan League*, by Arthur LeSueur (pamphlet), in the LeSueur papers; *Minneapolis Daily News*, Jan. 3, 1921; *St. Paul Daily News*, Jan. 4, 1920; *Minot Daily News*, Dec. 29, 1920; *Fargo Courier-News*, Dec. 22, 1920; *St. Paul Daily News*; Dec. 23, 1920; *Minneapolis Daily News*, Dec. 23, 1920; *Fargo Forum*, Dec. 24, 1920. See also clippings, LeSueur papers.

9. *Kansas City Star*, Jan. 26, 1921.

10. *Ward County Independent*, Oct. 27, 1921 (vol. 20, no 29).

11. *Minneapolis Tribune*, Mar. 13, 14, 15, 16, 17, 1922; *Minneapolis Journal*, Mar. 13, 14, 15, 16, 17, 1922.

12. *Minneapolis Tribune*, Mar. 13, Apr. 1, 1922; *Minneapolis Journal*, Apr. 1, 2, 1922.

13. *The National Leader*, Mar. 20, 1922; *Minneapolis Tribune*, Mar. 18, 1922.

14. *The Leader*, Apr. 17, 1922; *Minneapolis Tribune*, Apr. 1, 2, 1922; *Minneapolis Journal*, Apr. 1, 2, 3, 1922. The remainder of the ticket was to include G. T. Lindsten of Minneapolis (an alderman) for lieutenant governor, Mrs. Eliza Evans Deming for auditor; Susie Stageberg for treasurer, Benjamin Drake for attorney general, Lily Anderson for secretary of state, Victoria McAlmon for clerk of the supreme court, and George Siegal for supreme court justice. However, by the first week in May the ticket had to be modified for not all agreed to run; Drake dropped out, and Siegel later announced his intent to run as a Democrat.

15. *Minnesota Star*, May 1, 11, 1922.

16. *Minneapolis Tribune*, Mar. 30, 1922.

17. *Ibid.*, June 9, 13, 1922.

18. *Ibid.*, Aug. 5, 9, 10, 11, 12, 1922.

19. *Ibid.*, Aug. 23, 24, 25, 27, 31, 1922.

20. *Ibid.*, Sept. 3, 9, 1922.

21. *Ibid.*, Sept. 12, 1922.

22. *Ibid.*, Sept. 24, 1922; *Minneapolis Journal*, Sept. 24, 1922; *Minnesota Star*, Sept. 24, 1922.

23. *Minneapolis Tribune*, Oct. 4, 5, 12, 1922.

24. *Ibid.*, Oct. 12, 1922.

25. *Ibid.*, Oct. 11, 14, 15, 1922.

26. *Ibid.*, Oct. 13, 20, 22, 1922.

27. *Ibid.*, Oct. 21, 1922.

28. *Ibid.*, Oct. 31, Nov. 2, 3, 4, 5, 1922; *Minnesota Star*, Nov. 1, 2, 3, 4, 1922.

29. *Farmer-Labor Advocate*, July 11, 1923.

30. *Minneapolis Journal*, Oct. 9, 1923 (quoted); Oct. 2, 7, 1923.

31. *Ibid.*, Sept. 30, Oct. 9, 1923, with editorials reprinted.

32. *Farmer-Labor Advocate*, Feb. 9, 1923.

33. *Ibid.*, Apr. 27, 1923.

34. *Minneapolis Journal*, Aug. 16, 18, Sept. 7, 8, 9, 1923.

35. *Minnesota Leader*, Oct. 1923; Cheney in the *Minneapolis Journal*, Oct. 12, 1923.

36. *Minnesota Union Advocate*, Jan. 1, 1925, reprints article from the *Daily Worker* by C. A. Hathaway, which explains the "majority" communist point of view on the June 17 (May 30) convention. At this time the line of the C. P. was anti-Farmer-Laborite.

37. Teigan to Hillquit, Jan. 4, 1924, Teigan papers.

38. Teigan to Fred E. Osborne, Jan. 3, 1924, Teigan papers.

39. *Minneapolis Journal*, Feb. 25, 1924; J. G. Brown, John Fitzpatrick, and Robert M. Buck to William Mahoney, Feb. 1924, with enclosed statement by Manley, Teigan papers.

40. Minutes of the St. Paul Conference, Mar. 10-11, 1924, Mahoney papers.

41. *Minneapolis Journal*, Mar. 12, 1924.

42. *Ibid.*, Mar. 12, 1924; *Minneapolis Tribune*, Mar. 13, 1924.

43. *Minneapolis Journal*, Mar. 14, 1924; *Minneapolis Tribune*, Mar. 15, 1924.

44. *Minneapolis Tribune*, Mar. 15, 1924.

45. Hopkins to Johnson wire, May 2, 1924, and Johnson to Hopkins, May 2, 1924, Teigan papers.

46. *Minneapolis Tribune*, May 2, 1924; *Minneapolis Journal*, May 2, 1924; Hopkins to Teigan, May 2, 1924, and I. G. Scott to Teigan, May 2, 1924, Teigan papers.

47. *Minneapolis Tribune*, Apr. 28, 1924.

48. For examples, see *Minneapolis Journal*, May 4, 15, 17, 25, 28, 29, June 8, 9, 11, 15, 1924.

49. *Minneapolis Journal*, May 28, 1924.

50. Teigan to Hopkins, May 28, 1924, Teigan papers.

51. Irving Howe and Lewis Coser, *The American Communist Party* (New York, 1962), pp. 133-38, 140.

52. Report of the National Farmer-Labor Progressive Convention, June 17, 1924, (16 pp.) in the Mahoney papers.

53. *Farmer-Labor Advocate*, Aug. 22, Sept. 3, 1924.

54. *Legislative Manual*, 1925, pp. 305-17.

55. *Farmer-Labor Advocate*, June 30, Sept. 3, 1924.

56. A. B. Gilbert to Farmer-Labor candidates, July 10, 1924, Teigan papers.

57. *Minneapolis Journal*, Aug. 14, 1924.

58. George H. Mayer, *The Political Career of Floyd B. Olson* (Minneapolis, 1951), pp. 30-36.

59. *Minneapolis Tribune*, Sept. 20, 1924.

60. *Minneapolis Journal*, Oct. 24, 1924.

61. *St. Paul Pioneer Press*, Oct. 26, 1924.

62. *Minneapolis Tribune*, Oct. 26, 1924; *Minneapolis Journal*, Oct. 25, 1924; *St Paul Dispatch*, Oct. 25, 1924.

63. Holmes to Teigan, Jan. 12, 1925, Teigan papers.

64. Pike to Gustav Erickson, Apr. 22, 1924, Strout papers.

CHAPTER 5

1. Teigan to Martin J. Teigan (brother), Nov. 17, 1924, and Teigan to J. Richard Brown, Jan. 17, 1925, Teigan papers. Brown lived in Spokane and was the contact through whom Teigan kept apace with his investment. See also Teigan to M. M. Samuelson, Sept. 21, 1925, Teigan papers. Ironically, Rev. O. J. Kvale, the Farmer-Labor congressman, was a serious and dedicated speculator in risk investments; see the Kvale papers.

2. Jacobs had charged that Magnus Johnson took a $25,000 bribe to support the World Court and that he stole farmers' money while serving as a director of the Equity Cooperative Exchange, all absurd charges. See Johnson to Teigan, Jan. 5, 1925; Teigan to Johnson, Jan. 6, 1925; Teigan to W. C. Brady, Jan. 14, 1925; mimeograph release by William A. Anderson, May 21, 1925; Elmer E. Adams to Johnson, June 17, 1925; Teigan to Johnson, June 27, 1925; Teigan to George B. Edgerton, July 21, 1925; Teigan to Linn A. E. Gale, Sept. 21, 1925; Edward Indrehus to Teigan, Sept. 22, 1925; Affidavit, March 3, 1926, by Gale A. Plagman; Plagman to Shipstead, Apr. 17, 1926. All are in the Teigan papers. The senate threw out the challenge in June 1926; *Minneapolis Tribune*, June 17, 1926.

3. Farmer-Labor Federation minutes, June 1, 1924, Leekley papers.

4. *Minneapolis Tribune*, Jan. 21, 1925, *Minneapolis Journal*, Jan. 20, 1925; *Farmer-Labor Advocate*, Jan. 14, 21, 1925.

5. Committee on Arrangements, call; press release, undated, Chase papers.

6. *Minneapolis Tribune*, Mar. 20, 21, 1925; *Minneapolis Journal*, Mar. 21, 1925; *Farmer-Labor Advocate*, Mar. 11, 15, 1925.

7. *Constitution of the Farmer-Labor Association of Minnesota*, adopted Mar. 20, 1925.

8. *Minneapolis Tribune*, Mar. 21, 1925.

9. Magnus Johnson to Albert Steinhauser, Apr. 9, 1925, Teigan papers.

10. Brekke to Teigan, May 15, 1925, June 19, 1925, and Teigan to Brekke, June 12, 1925, Teigan papers.

11. Teigan to C. F. Lowrie, Apr. 20, 1925, and Teigan to M. H. Hedges, May 6, 1925, Teigan papers.

12. *Minneapolis Journal*, Mar. 7, 25, 27, 28, 29, 1926; *Minneapolis Tribune*, Mar. 26, 27, 28, 1926.

13. *Minnesota Leader*, May 4, 1926.

14. C. E. Rutherberg, in the *Daily Worker*, May 29, 1926.

15. Thomas Canty to Teigan, May 29, 1926, and Teigan to Dear Bill, May 30, 1926, Teigan papers. The Canty article was not identified by author; see *Daily Worker*, June 7, 1926.

16. William V. Mahoney to Teigan, June 2, 1926, and Teigan to Mahoney, June 6, 1926, Teigan papers.

17. Thomason to Johnson, Mar. 31, 1926; Teigan to Thomason, May 22, 1926; Thomason to Teigan, May 26, 1926, all in the Teigan papers. Thomason was a former Socialist and early NPL organizer.

18. *Minneapolis Journal*, Sept. 6, 1926.

19. *Ibid.*, Sept. 9, 1926.

20. *Ibid.*, Sept. 29, 1926. The "keynote" speech was delivered at Fergus Falls.

21. *Farmer-Labor Advocate*, Sept. 1, 1926; reprints article from *Minnesota Union Advocate*.

22. *Minneapolis Journal*, Sept. 28, Oct 1, 4, 1926; Farmer-Labor Association papers, including copies of the letter; Quigley to Thomas Jackson, Sept. 10, 1926, and Elwood Mills to Victor E. Lawson, Oct. 6, 1926, Farmer-Labor Association papers. *Minnesota Leader*, Oct. 20, 1926.

23. *Farmer-Labor Advocate*, Oct. 1, 1926.

24. *Minneapolis Journal*, Oct. 4, 1926.

25. Teigan to L. A. Fritsche, Oct. 16, 1926, and Teigan to Carl E. Taylor, Oct. 5, 1926, Farmer-Labor Association papers.

26. Teigan to Lind, Sept. 15, 1926; Teigan to N. A. Mason, Oct. 4, 1926; Teigan to W. A. Oldfield, Oct. 4, 1926; all in the Farmer-Labor Association papers.

27. William McEwen to Canty, Oct. 2, 7, 1926; Canty to McEwen, Oct. 4, 1926; Canty to Teigan, Oct. 12, 1926; McEwen to Thompson, Oct. 13, 1926; Thompson to McEwen, Oct. 14, 1926; Thompson to Herman Wenzel, Oct. 30, 1926; Canty to McEwen, Oct. 30, 1926; all in The Farmer-Labor Association papers.

28. Emil Holmes to voters of Minnesota, Sept. 8, 1926, Teigan papers. *Legislative Manual*, 1927, pp. 185, 350-51.

29. *Minneapolis Journal*, Mar. 1, 6, April 3, May 4, 1927; *Minneapolis Tribune*, Mar. 1, April 2, 13, 1927.

30. See Dunne to Teigan, June 29, July 12, 1926, and Teigan to Dunne, July 8, July 31, 1926, Farmer-Labor Association papers.

31. Stageberg to Teigan, Dec. 10, 1926, Teigan papers.

32. "Need for a National Farmer-Labor Party," and "Why Farmer-Labor Movement Cannot Fuse or Combine," *Farmer-Labor Advocate*, Nov. 16, 1926.

33. Report of the Farmer-Labor state conference, Jan. 17-18, 1927, 17 pp., Farmer-Labor Association papers; minutes of the central committee, Farmer-Labor Association papers, Sept. 8, 1927; *Minneapolis Journal*, Jan. 18, 19, 1927.

34. (Chicago) *Daily Worker*, Jan. 21, 1927.

35. *St. Paul Pioneer Press*, July 12, 1927.

36. *Minneapolis Journal*, Feb. 17, Mar. 20, 23, 25, 1928.

37. *Minnesota Union Advocate*, Mar. 29, 1928; *Minneapolis Journal*, Mar. 28, 1928.

38. Farmer-Labor Press Service, April 2, 1928, release. The FLPS was really the creation of Henry Teigan, who not only prepared its material, but published much of it in the *Minnesota Union Advocate* under a FLPS byline. The seven states represented were Illinois, Iowa, Wisconsin, Colorado, Idaho, North Dakota, and Minnesota. The Minnesota Farmer-Labor Association state committee came as a delegation.

39. *Minneapolis Journal*, July 9, 12, 13, 1927, Jan. 29, February 11, 19, 1928. The factions were about equal in power and number, and neither seemed dominant in relation to overall control of the party. The fight over the chairmanship followed the death of state chairman C. A. Quist.

40. *Minneapolis Journal*, Mar. 16, 1928.

41. *Minneapolis Journal*, Apr. 12, 1928.

42. *Ibid.*, Apr. 21, 22, 27, 29, 1928.

43. Watkins release, Apr. 28, 1928. FLPS, Apr. 30, May 7, 1928, release (in Teigan papers).

44. Watkins release, Apr. 20, 1928, in the Teigan papers.

45. *Minneapolis Journal*, May 1, 3, 4, 6, 1928.

46. *Union Advocate*, May 24, 1928; *Minneapolis Journal*, June 1, 9, 1928.

47. June 14, 1928. The Socialist party did support Farmer-Labor candidates in 1928.

48. *Minnesota Union Advocate*, July 12, 19, 1928; *Minneapolis Journal*, July 9, 10, 12, 13, 1928.

49. *Legislative Manual*, 1929.

50. *Minneapolis Journal*, July 7, Aug. 9, 1928.

51. *Ibid.*, Aug. 21, 1928; *Minnesota Union Advocate*, August 23, 1928.

52. *Minneapolis Journal*, Aug. 25, 1928.

53. *Ibid.*, Sept. 6, 11, 18, 22, 1928.

54. *Ibid.*, Sept. 19, Oct. 25, 1928.

55. *Ibid.*, Sept. 28, Oct. 2, 6, 7, 1928.

56. *Ibid.*, Sept. 27, Oct. 3, 1928.

57. *Ibid.*, Sept. 24, 25, Oct. 11, 25, 1928; *Minnesota Union Advocate*, Oct. 18, 1928.

58. *Minneapolis Journal*, Oct. 19, 21, 22, 24, 1928.

59. *Ibid.*, Oct. 22, 24, 1928; *Isanti News*, Nov. 1, 1928; *Minneapolis Star*, Oct. 23, 1928.

60. *Minneapolis Journal*, Oct. 27, 28, 1928. *Minneapolis Tribune*, Oct. 21, 1928; *Minneapolis Journal*, Oct. 22, 1928.

61. Election returns are taken from the *Legislative Manual*, 1929; percentages are based on total votes cast in the election.

62. *Minneapolis Journal*, Nov. 13, 1928.

CHAPTER 6

1. Samuel Eliot Morison and Henry Steele Commager, *The Growth of the American Republic* (New York, 1962), vol. II, pp. 644-45.

2. Teigan, Farmer-Labor Press Service, May 20, 1929, release. A third Farmer-Labor candidate was unopposed.

3. *Askov American*, May 2, 1929; *Minneapolis Tribune*, Jan. 25, Feb. 5, 1929; *Minneapolis Journal*, Apr. 21, 1929.

4. Farmer-Labor Press Service, Oct. 21, 1929, release.

5. *Minneapolis Tribune*, May 5, 1929.

6. Minutes of Farmer-Labor Conference, St. Paul, Sept. 5, 1929.

7. The speech, in the *Congressional Record* Dec. 10, 1929, immediately drew strong attacks upon Schall. See Cheney, *Minneapolis Journal*, Dec. 26, 1929.

8. Constance Todd to Paul Douglas, Oct. 21, 1928, and Paul Douglas to Sherwood Eddy, Oct. 25, 1928, Howard Y. Williams papers.

9. The Call can be found in Howard Y. Williams papers.

10. Tentative Statement, LIPA, in Williams papers: John C. Bennett to Kirby Page, Dec. 23, 1928, Williams papers. For a discussion of the founding conference of the LIPA, see Donald R. McCoy, *Angry Voices; Left-of-Center Politics in the New Deal Era* (Lawrence, Kansas, 1958), pp. 4-39.

11. Kirby Page to Zona Gale, June 11, 1929, Williams papers.

12. John Dewey memo, Oct. 19, 1929, Williams papers.

13. A. B. Gilbert to Howard Y. Williams, Nov. 25, 1929, Williams papers.

14. Norman Thomas to Devere Allen, Nov. 30, 1929, Williams papers.

15. John Fitzpatrick to Williams, Dec. 6, 1929, Williams papers.

16. Ickes to Page, Apr. 18, 1929, Williams papers.

17. Frankfurter to Page, Apr. 24, 1929, Williams papers. Jane Addams to Page, Apr. 1, 1929, Williams papers.

18. Van Dusen to Page, Jan. 11, 1929, Williams papers.

19. Mahoney to Page, May 25, 1929, Apr. 16, 1929, Williams papers.

20. Teigan to Page, Apr. 11, 1929, Williams papers.

21. Document, Socialist party of Minnesota, circa June 1928, Strout papers.

22. *Minneapolis Journal,* June 13, 1930; *Minneapolis Tribune,* June 13, 1930.

23. *Farmer-Labor Leader,* Jan 15, 1930.

24. *Minneapolis Tribune,* Mar. 28, 29, 1930.

25. *Ibid.,* Mar. 29, 1930; *Minneapolis Journal,* Mar. 29, 1930.

26. *Farmer-Labor Leader,* Mar. 20, 1930.

27. *St. Paul Pioneer Press,* Mar. 31, 1930.

28. For example, see the *Minneapolis Labor Review,* July 4, 1930, and scores of issues of the Minnesota press, in Apr., May, June, July, 1930; see Shipstead papers and clippings.

29. Morison and Commager, *American Republic,* p. 646.

30. *Minneapolis Tribune,* Apr. 24, 1930.

31. *Minneapolis Journal,* Apr. 16, 17, 23, 1930; *Minneapolis Tribune,* Apr. 23, 1930.

32. *Minneapolis Journal,* Apr. 19, 1930.

33. *Ibid.,* Apr. 23, 1930.

34. *Ibid.,* June 4, 10, 1930; *Minneapolis Tribune,* June 4, 10, 1930.

35. Copy in Teigan and Shipstead papers.

36. *Minneapolis Journal,* June 13, 1930.

37. Charles Cheney, in the *Minneapolis Journal,* June 28, 1930.

38. August 15, 1930.

39. John Dewey to Herman Reel, Aug. 18, 1930, and Olson to Williams, Sept. 2, 1930, Williams papers.

40. Kvale to Williams, June 4, 1930, and Shipstead to Williams, June 2, 1930, Williams papers.

41. Activities of the LIPA, undated (ca. Mar. 25, 1931); George W. Jacobson to Williams, Sept. 27, 1930, Williams papers.

42. *Farmer-Labor Leader,* Oct. 15, 1930; Fred Tillquist to Strout, Oct. 6, 1930, Strout papers.

43. Williams to Shipstead, Sept. 18, 1930, Williams papers.

44. See *Owatonna Journal-Chronicle,* Oct. 24, 1930, for full page ad against Olson record.

45. Farmer-Labor Press Service, Nov. 17, 1930.

46. Teigan to James R. Bennett, Jr., Nov. 17, 1931, Teigan papers. Teigan argued that the value of gold, or probably any product, was determined by the amount of labor concealed

in its production and not by its supply or the demand for it; Marx, said Teigan, was correct; see Teigan to Tom Davis, Nov. 9, 1931, Teigan papers.

47. *Farmer-Labor Leader*, Dec. 17, 1930; Williams to Mrs. F W. Wittich, Nov. 26, 1930, Williams papers.

48. Williams to Murray E. King, Dec. 11, 1930, Williams papers.

49. *New York Times*, Nov. 7, 1930.

50. *Ibid.*, Nov. 16; *St. Paul Daily News, St. Paul Pioneer Press, Washington Star*, all Nov. 16, 1930.

51. *Minneapolis Tribune*, Dec. 28, 1930; *Washington Herald*, Jan. 18, 1931; *Congressional Record*, Jan. 15(5), 1931.

52. "A Brief Outline of Carl R. Erickson's Political History," in the Herman Aufderheide papers.

53. Strout to Elmer . . ., Feb. 2, 1931, and Strout to E. J. Hoffman, Feb. 4, 1931, Strout papers; *Montevideo News*, Nov. 30, 1931; *Minneapolis Journal*, Jan. 7, 1931; *Minneapolis Tribune*, Jan. 8, 1931.

54. Teigan to Charles L. Coy, Mar. 17, 1931, Teigan papers.

55. *Minnesota Union Advocate*, Feb. 26, 1931.

56. *Willmar Tribune*, Jan. 28, 1931; *St. Paul Dispatch*, Jan. 27, 1931.

57. *Willmar Tribune*, Jan. 28, 1931; *St. Paul Pioneer Press*, Jan. 28, 1931; *St. Paul Dispatch*, Jan. 27, 1931; *Minneapolis Journal*, Jan. 29, 1931; *St. Paul Pioneer Press*, Feb. 13, 1931; *Minneapolis Tribune*, Jan. 16, 1931; *Midwest Labor*, Feb. 17, 1931; *Minnesota Union Advocate*, Feb. 12, 26, 1931.

58. George H. Mayer, *The Political Career of Floyd B. Olson* (Minneapolis, 1951); for Olson's first legislative session, see pp. 57-77.

59. Mayer, *Floyd B. Olson*, pp. 70-76; *Minneapolis Journal*, Apr. 22, 23, 1923.

60. Mayer, *Floyd B. Olson*, pp. 78-92.

61. Teigan to William Lemke, Apr. 27, 1931; also, Teigan to Carl Lewis, Apr. 22, 1931; Teigan to Murray King, Mar. 18, 1931; Teigan to Norman W. Lemond, Mar. 30, 1931; all in the Teigan papers.

62. D. M. Frederickson to Williams, May 19, 1931, Williams papers.

63. Williams to Mahoney, June 2, 1931; Williams to national and executive committee, LIPA, June 30, 1931; Williams to William T. Evjue, Aug. 21, 1931; Williams to Shipstead, Sept. 4, 1931; Williams to Mahoney, Sept. 29, 1931; Williams to A. E. Smith, Oct. 1, 1931; all in the Williams papers.

64. Olson to Williams, Jan. 3, 1931, Williams papers.

65. Muste to Williams, Dec. 30, 1930, and Thomas to Executive Committee, LIPA, Mar. 6, 1931, Williams papers.

66. Undated, Williams papers.

67. Williams to Clarence Senior, May 5, 1931, Williams papers.

68. Thomas to Kirby Page, May 19, 1931, Williams papers.

69. Williams to Jesse H. Holmes, May 26, 1931, and see also Dewey to Minister Kolstad, May 27, 1931, Williams papers.

70. Morris Hillquit to Williams, Nov. 25, 1931, Williams papers.

CHAPTER 7

1. Henry Teigan to Martin Teigan, Feb. 2, 1932, Teigan papers.

2. Behrens to Williams, Jan. 15, 1932, Williams papers.

3. Fred Miller et al. to Frank Starkey, Apr. 2, 1932, Strout papers.

4. Teigan papers, Apr. 18, 1932.

5. *Minneapolis Journal*, Feb. 11, 16, 27, 1931.

6. *Ibid.*, Mar. 9, 10, 1932.

7. *Ibid.*, Mar. 13, 15, 1932.

8. *Ibid.*, Mar. 19, 20, 1932.

9. *Ibid.*, Mar. 14, 24, 1932.

10. *Ibid.*, Mar. 27, 28, 29, 30, 31, 1932.

11. Clarence Senior to Williams, Apr. 14, 1932, Williams papers.

12. Williams to Senior, May 4, 1932, Williams papers.

13. *Minneapolis Journal*, Apr. 5, 9, 10, 1932.

14. *Ibid.*, Apr. 4, 5, 17, 18, 19, 1932; George H. Mayer, *The Political Career of Floyd B. Olson* (Minneapolis, 1951), pp. 98-99; FLNS release, Apr. 18, 1932, Teigan papers.

15. *W. Yale Smiley v. Holm*, 285 U. S. 335 (1932).

16. *Minneapolis Journal*, May 14, 1932.

17. Muste to Williams, Dec. 30, 1930, and Thomas to executive committee, March 6, 1931, Williams papers.

18. Gitlow to Williams, January 5, 1932, Williams papers.

19. LIPA, News Bulletin, vol. I, no. 11, Feb.-Mar. 1932 (see Hawkins papers); Williams to Frederick Willis, Jan. 16, 1931, Williams papers.

20. Douglas to Williams, Jan. 25, 1932, Williams papers.

21. Williams to LIPA branch officers, Mar. 17, 1932, Williams papers.

22. Douglas to Williams, May 27, 1932, Williams papers.

23. Williams to Henry Gotliffe, May 1, 1932; Paul Douglas to Williams, May 27, 1932; F. H. LaGuardia to John Dewey, June 29, 1932; all in the Williams papers.

24. Lundeen to Williams, July 2, 1932; Darrow to John Dewey, July 3, 1932; Mahoney to Devere Allen, July 6, 1932; all in the Williams papers.

25. Williams to George H. Griffith, June 27, 1932; Oscar W. Behrens to Williams, July 25, 1932; Williams to P. A. A. Brient, August 2, 1932; Alvin Johnson to John W. Herring, Aug. 15, 1932; all in the Williams papers.

26. Vince Day memorandum to Olson, Aug. 26, 1932, Day papers; Mayer, *Floyd B. Olson*, pp. 103-7.

27. *Minneapolis Journal*, Oct. 28, 1932.

28. I. C. Strout to Jos. Poirier, Oct. 12, 1932, Strout papers.

29. *Minneapolis Journal*, Nov. 18, 25, 1932, Jan. 3, 4, 1933. The senate was controlled by the conservatives, 38 to 27. Day memorandum, Nov. 21, 1932, Day papers. Mayer, *Floyd B. Olson*, pp. 117-19.

30. Mayer, *Floyd B. Olson*, pp. 117-142 (chapter 8).

31. *Minneapolis Journal*, Jan. 4, 5, 8, 16, 1933.

32. Mayer, *Floyd B. Olson*, pp. 117-30.

33. Day to Olson memo, Feb. 10, 1933, Day papers.

34. Abe Harris to Vince Day, May 22, 1933, and Day memorandum to Olson, undated (ca. June 1933), Day papers.

35. Welch to Day, June 7, 1933, and H. L. Cushman to Olson, May 15, 1933, Day papers.

36. Mayer, *Floyd B. Olson*, pp. 145-48; see also Strout papers for data on patronage firings.

37. Villard to LIPA members, Nov. 23, 1932.

38. Williams to Olson, Nov. 25, 1932; Williams to the editor, *The Nation*, Dec. 21, 1932.

39. Douglas to John W. Herring, Feb. 23, 1932, and Williams to George Norris, Mar. 3, 1933, Williams papers. *New York Times*, Feb. 2, 1933.

40. Dewey to Harriet Boyd Hawes, Mar. 14, 1933, and Dewey to Lee, Mar. 27, 1933, Williams papers.

41. Lemke to Williams, May 26, 1933; La Follette to Williams, June 2, 1933; Williams to Senior, June 30, 1033; copy of call, July 1, 1933; Allen to Williams, Aug. 1, 1933; Holmes to Williams, Aug. 8, 1933; press release, Aug. 18, 1933; all in the Williams papers.

42. FLPF brochure, undated; see Oscar Hawkins papers.

43. Benjamin Mendal to Douglas, Sept. 5, 1933; Douglas to Williams, Sept. 9, 1933; Williams to Arnott Widstrand, Oct. 9, 1933; all in the Williams papers.

44. Williams to Bogue, Oct. 13, 1933, Williams papers.

45. Williams to Lockhart, Aug. 15, 1933, Williams papers.

46. Butler to Olson, Aug. 31, 1933, Olson papers.

47. Day memorandum to Olson, Aug. 22, 1933, Day papers.

48. The best single source is the Strout papers. See, for example, Strout to H. G. Creel (ed. *Farmer-Labor Leader*), May 27, 1933; Strout to Elmer Benson, Aug. 4, 1933, with a six-page list of employees to be fired; Strout to Oscar Widstrand, Mar. 1, 1935; memo of Feb. 27, 1935; Strout's card file; all in the Strout papers. See also the papers of Ray P. Chase.

49. Statement of Strout, Mar. 26, 1935, Strout papers.

50. Mayer, *Floyd B. Olson*, pp. 149-56.

51. *Ibid.*, p. 157.

52. *Ibid.*, p. 149.

53. Olson papers, Jan. 22, 1934.

54. Farmer-Labor Press Service, Sept. 19, 1933; Feb. 12, 24, 1934, in the Teigan papers. Mayer, *Floyd B. Olson*, pp. 166-69.

55. See Aufderheide papers, undated (ca. Mar. 1, 1934).

56. *Minneapolis Journal*, Mar. 4, 1934.

57. *Minneapolis Journal*, Mar. 11, 1934, and Mar. 12, 18; *Minneapolis Tribune*, Mar. 12, 1934.

58. *Minneapolis Tribune*, Mar. 13, 1934.

59. John S. McGrath and James J. Delmont, *Floyd Bjornsterne Olson: Minnesota's Greatest Liberal Governor* (St. Paul, 1937), pp. 246-48; *Minneapolis Tribune*, Mar. 28, 1934.

60. *Minneapolis Tribune*, Mar. 28, 1934.

61. *Minneapolis Journal*, Mar. 25, 26, 27, 28, 1934; *Minneapolis Tribune*, Mar. 25, 28, 29, 1934.

62. Day memorandums, Mar. 12, 1934, Oct. 17, 1934, Oct. 20, 1934, Nov. 15, 1934; all in the Day papers.

63. *Minneapolis Tribune*, Mar. 29, 1934.

64. Day memorandum, Apr. 4, 1934, Day papers.

65. *Ibid.*, May 2, 1934.

66. *Minneapolis Journal*, Apr. 13, 1934; *St. Paul Pioneer Press*, Apr. 13, 1934.

67. *Farmer-Labor Leader*, Apr. 15, 1934.

68. *Minneapolis Tribune*, Mar. 30, 1934; *Minneapolis Journal*, Mar. 29, 30, 1934; *St. Paul Pioneer Press*, Mar. 30, 1934.

69. April 12, 1934.

70. Williams to LIPA, May 25, 1934; in Aufderheide papers, Williams papers; Williams to Lundeen, Apr. 3, 1934, Williams papers.

71. Williams to Olson, May 23, 1934, Williams papers.

72. *St. Paul Pioneer Press*, Apr. 3, 4, 13, 14, 25, 1934. See Mayer, *Floyd B. Olson*, pp. 172-77, for a discussion of Olson's explanations.

73. Day memorandum, May 2, 1934, Day papers; Mayer, *Floyd B. Olson*, pp. 172-79.

74. Thomas R. Amlie to Alfred M. Bingham, May 21, 1934; Williams to Wisconsin LIPA, June 16, 1934; Williams to Amlie, July 3, 1934; Williams to Phil La Follette, July 9, 1934; Lemke to Williams, July 16, 1934, all in the Williams papers.

75. Oscar Hawkins to Norman Thomas, May 7, 1934, and Thomas to Hawkins, May 26, 1934, Hawkins papers.

76. Mayer, *Floyd B. Olson*, pp. 184-222, is a convenient and excellent source; see also *Minneapolis Journal, Minneapolis Tribune, St. Paul Pioneer Press*, May-Aug. 1934.

77. Day to Olson memorandum, July 18, 1934, Day papers.

78. Olson to Clyde Helm, state insurance federation, Sept. 25, 1934, Day papers.

79. Liggett to Williams, Oct. 9, 1934, Williams papers.

80. Bingham to Williams, Oct. 2, 1934, Williams papers.

81. Day memorandums to Olson, Nov. 1, 1934, Day papers.

82. Day memorandums to Olson, Nov. 9, 22, 28, 1934, Day papers.

83. Petersen to Day, Nov. 10, 1934, Petersen papers.

CHAPTER 8

1. Williams to LIPA, FLPF, Jan. 1935, Aufderheide papers.

2. James A. Hanson to Williams, Nov. 28, 1934, Williams papers.

3. See George H. Mayer, *The Political Career of Floyd B. Olson* (Minneapolis 1951), pp. 251-72.

4. Strout to Zelinko, Jan. 13, 1935; V. N. Johnson to Strout, Apr. 19, 1935; Fay Child to Olson, May 20, 1935; L. A. Gode to Woodie (Strout), June 26, 1935; all in the Strout papers.

5. Benson to Harold Hagen, May 23, 1935, Hagen papers; Behrens to Teigan, July 14, 1935, Teigan papers.

6. Petersen to George Strandvold, Nov. 10, 1934; Petersen to E. T. Ebbesen, May 18, 1935; Petersen to Charles Cheney, May 18, 1935; Petersen to Don Voight, July 17, 1935; all in the Petersen papers. The rail commissioner's $5,000 per-year salary and six-year term appealed to Petersen.

7. Rodman to Day, Jan. 17, 1935; Rodman to Day, Mar. 28, 1935, Apr. 13, 1935; Day to Rodman, Apr. 9, 1935; all in the Day papers.

8. Stockwell to Williams, Feb. 1, 1935, and Williams to Bingham, Mar. 21, 1935, Williams papers.

9. Alfred Bingham to Williams, Apr. 24, 1935, Williams papers.

10. Bingham to Williams, Apr. 7, 1935, Williams papers.

11. Bingham to Williams, May 2, 6, 1935, and Amlie to Williams, May 7, 1935, Williams papers.

12. Olson to Williams, June 17, 1935; Amlie to Williams, June 20, 1935; Olson to Amlie, June 28, 1935; all in the Williams papers.

13. *Minneapolis Tribune*, July 7, 1935; *Minneapolis Journal*, July 7, 1935; Bingham to Williams, July 13, 1935, July 18, 1935; Amlie to Williams, July 19, 1935; Fine to Williams, Sept. 20, 1935, all in the Williams papers.

14. Amlie to Williams, July 19, 1935, Williams papers.

15. Day to Olson, Aug. 23, 1935, Day papers.

16. E. T. Moeller to Strout, July 18; Willard Munger to Strout, July 20, 1935; Erickson to Moeller, July 24, 1935; Bernard to Strout, July 26, 1935; all in the Strout papers.

17. The report was released ca. Oct. 21, 1935; see "Meeting of Fourteen," a Farmer-Labor Association Investigation Report, 35 pp., in the Strout papers; also, The Committee to John T. Bernard, Oct. 21, 1935, in the Strout papers.

18. See brief, *Liggett v. Midwest Publishing Co., IUAW, Floyd Olson*, dated Aug. 2, 1934; release and settlement, Aug. 28, 1934. Liggett to Day, Aug. 6, 1934; Day to Olson memorandum, Aug. 20, 1934; Mitchell to Liggett, Aug. 24, 1934; all in the Day papers.

19. "Why I Resigned as Editor of the Austin *American*," by Walter W. Liggett, undated, 10 pp.; Frank Prochaska to Day, Apr. 17, 1934; Goldie to Day, June 8, 1934; all in the Day papers. Liggett to Williams, Nov. 28, 1934; Williams to Liggett, Nov. 30, 1934; Freda Kirchwey to Williams, Jan. 10, 1935; Williams to Kirchwey, Jan. 18, 1935; all in the Williams papers.

20. Rodman to Day, Apr. 13, 1935, Day papers. Rodman to Day, March 28, 1935, Day papers. Rodman originally entitled his article "Walter Liggett for Sale!"

21. Farrell Dobbs to Thomas L. Hughes, Oct. 20, 1934; Hughes to Dobbs, Apr. 12, 1935; Tobin to Emery C. Nelson (Mpls. CLU), Apr. 15, 1935; all in the Williams papers.

22. Mayer, *Floyd B. Olson*, pp. 273-78.

23. May 25, 27, 1935, report, printed in *The Communist*, 14, no. 7 (July 1935), 641-60.

24. Clarence Hathaway, "Problems in Our Farmer-Labor Party Activities," *The Communist*, 15, no. 5 (May 1936), 427-33.

25. Petersen to Prochaska, Aug. 3, 1935; Petersen to Charles Cheney, Aug. 13, 1935; Petersen to Cheney, Nov. 4, 1935; Voleny J. Stefflre to Petersen, Nov. 7, 1935; Petersen to Howard Frederickson, Nov. 26, 1935; Petersen to Cheney, Dec. 24, 1935; Petersen to Howard Williams, Dec. 26, 1935; all in the Petersen papers.

26. Williams to Philip Heiling, Dec. 13, 1935, Williams papers.

27. Mayer, *Floyd B. Olson*, pp. 282-88. *Minneapolis Journal* reporter Charles Cheney dug out the story and printed it March 10, 1936, two and one-half months after the coup.

28. Day memorandum to Olson, Dec. 23, 1935, Day papers.

29. Petersen to Cheney, Dec. 24, 1935; Petersen to E. J. Prochaska, Dec. 26, 1935; Petersen to Williams, Dec. 26, 1935; Petersen to Cheney, Dec. 26, 27, 1935; all in the Petersen papers.

30. Olson to Benson, Feb. 4, 1936, Benson papers.

31. Petersen to J. Lawrence McLeod, Feb. 10, 1936; Petersen asked that his confidential addendum be destroyed.

32. Petersen to Howard M. Frederickson, Feb. 25, 1936; Petersen to Medora Petersen, Feb. 27, 1936; Petersen to Dr. A. C. Bosel, Mar. 5, 1936; Petersen to Selma Seestrom, Mar. 5, 1936; all in the Petersen papers.

33. Spindler to Petersen, Mar. 14, 1936; and B. B. Hassenger to Irene Welby, Mar. 14, 1936, Petersen papers.

34. Williams to Erving Ingebrigtsen, Feb. 29, 1936; Williams to Edward Welsh, Mar. 3, 1936; Fine to Williams, Mar. 4, 1936; all in the Williams papers.

35. Williams to Fine, Mar. 11, 1936, Williams papers. Fine to Williams, Mar. 13, Williams papers.

36. *Minneapolis Journal*, Mar. 8, 9, 14, 1936.

37. *Minneapolis Journal*, Mar. 27, 1936, pp. 16-17 for full text.

38. *Ibid.*, Mar. 28, 29, 30, 1936.

39. Williams to Herbert A. Hard, Apr. 8, 1936, and Williams to La Follette, Apr. 2, 1936, Williams papers.

40. Lockhart to Petersen, Mar. 27, 1936, Petersen papers.

41. Williams to Fine, Apr. 13, 1936, Williams papers.

42. "Organized Labor Endorses New Party," news release, undated (ca. Oct. 1935), by Williams, in Herman Aufderheide papers.

43. Fine to Williams, Apr. 14, 1936, Williams papers.

44. Hathaway to Williams, Apr. 15, 1936, wire, Williams papers.

45. "Problems in Our Farmer-Labor Party Activities," *The Communist*, 15, no. 5 (May 1936), 427-33.

46. Undated Day memorandum to Olson shortly before the March 27-28 state convention; Day papers.

47. Williams to Amlie, May 12, 1936; Fine to Williams, May 16, 1936; Williams to Selma Seestrom, May 18, 1936; all in the Williams papers.

48. Harris to Bingham and Amlie, May 20, 1936; Williams papers. Bingham to Williams, May 22, 1936, Williams papers.

49. Douglas to Williams, June 15, 1936, Williams papers.

50. Williams to Douglas, June 18, 1936, Williams papers.

51. "Report of National Farmer-Labor Party Conference," in Farmer-Labor Association papers, undated.

52. *Minneapolis Journal*, Apr. 19, 1936.

53. *Ibid.*, Feb. 3, Apr. 21, 22, 30, May 1, 3, 1936.

54. Mayer, *Floyd B. Olson*, pp. 299-300.

55. Petersen to Clifford F. Hansen, July 15, 1936; Petersen to Vivian Thorp, July 31, 1936; Petersen to McLeod, Aug. 5, 1936; all in the Petersen papers.

56. Petersen to Olson, Aug. 13, 1936, original draft in Petersen papers.

57. Olson to Aufderheide, Aug. 15, 1936, Aufderheide papers.

58. Williams to Petersen, Aug. 28, 1936, Williams papers.

59. Lundeen and Petersen to LIPA members, Sept. 10, 1936, Williams papers.

60. Farley release backing Meighen, Aug. 14, 1936; Meighen to Erickson, July 7, 15, 1936; Erickson to Meighen, July 13, 1936; all in the Meighen papers.

61. Williams to John D. Sullivan, July 18, Aug. 3, 1936, and Caughlin to Williams, Aug. 5, 1936, Williams papers. Teigan to Frank Hopkins, Sept. 22, 1936, Teigan papers.

62. Meighen to William H. Dempsey, Aug. 26, 1936; Meighen papers.

63. Meighen to W. H. Dempsey, Oct. 9, 1936; Dempsey to Meighen, Oct. 5, 1936; Meighen diaries, Sept. 18, 29, Oct. 3, 1936; all in the Meighen papers.

64. *Minneapolis Journal*, Sept. 29, Oct. 1, 3, 4, 5, 6, 1936.

65. *Minneapolis Tribune*, Oct. 6, 7, 8, 9, 10, 1936.

66. *Minneapolis Journal*, Oct. 27, 28, 1936.

67. See *Minneapolis Journal* reference to Regan letter, Nov. 2, 1936.

68. Abe Harris to Petersen, Dec. 21, 1936, Petersen papers.

CHAPTER 9

1. Farmer-Labor Association state committee minutes, Nov. 28, 1936, 18 pp.

2. Petersen to H. E. Rasmussen, Apr. 5, 1938, Petersen papers.

3. *Minneapolis Journal*, Dec. 20, 1936.

4. Undated memorandum by Petersen, Petersen papers.

5. "A Statement of Facts," by the Farmer-Labor Association, undated (ca. Nov. 21, 1936), 4 pp., in Stageberg papers.

6. "Advice to Governor Benson when he took office by V. A. Day," memorandum in Day papers, undated.

7. *Minneapolis Journal*, Nov. 18, 1936; Selma Seestrom to Benson, Feb. 5, 1937, Stageberg papers.

8. John Allen to Teigan, June 15, 1937, Teigan papers.

9. A. F. Lockhart to Teigan, Mar. 19, 1937, Teigan papers.

10. *Minneapolis Journal*, Jan. 5, 1937, Teigan papers.

11. *Ibid.*, Jan. 21, 1937.

12. Lockhart to Teigan, Mar. 19, 1937, Teigan papers.

13. Petersen release, Mar. 13, 1937, Petersen papers.

14. *Minneapolis Journal*, Apr. 2, 3, 5, 6, 1937; *Minneapolis Tribune*, Apr. 5, 6, 1937.

15. *Minneapolis Journal*, Apr. 7, 8, 13, 1937.

16. *Ibid.*, Apr. 10, 11, 1937.

17. *Ibid.*, May 24, 25, 1937.

18. *Ibid.*, Apr. 24, 1937.

19. Teigan to Marian LeSueur, Dec. 18, 1936, Teigan papers.

20. Minutes of Minn.-Wisc. conference, Dec. 18, 1936, Teigan papers.

21. Scammon to Teigan, Jan. 5, 1937, Teigan papers.

22. Farmer-Labor Association papers, minutes, Nov. 21, 1936, Jan. 28, 1937.

23. *Farmer Labor Progressive*, vol. II, no. 1, June 1937.

24. See *Washington Post*, Aug. 22, 1937.

25. Dale Kramer to Williams, May 25, 1937, Williams papers.

26. Williams to Benson, Apr. 26, June 24, 1936; Roger Rutchick to Williams, Apr. 30, 1937; Benson to Williams, June 25, 1937; all in the Williams papers.

27. Bingham to Williams, June 29, 1937, with speech (5 pp) enclosed; Bingham to Williams, July 22, 1937; Williams to Bingham, July 19, 1937; all in the Williams papers.

28. Amlie to Williams, Aug. 30, 1937, Williams papers.

29. Williams to Verner Nelson, July 9, 1937; Bingham to Williams, Sept. 5, 1937; Jerome G. Locke to Williams, Sept. 23, 1937; all in the Williams papers; Teigan to O. B. Grimley, Dec. 9, 1937, Teigan papers.

30. Lockhart to Teigan, Jan. 14, 1937, and Teigan to Lockhart, Jan. 17, 1937, Teigan papers.

31. For Benson speech, see Farmer-Labor Association papers; also *Minneapolis Journal*, Jan. 29, 1937.

32. *Minneapolis Journal*, Jan. 20, 21, 1937; *St. Paul Pioneer Press*, Jan. 29, 30, 1937.

33. Lockhart to Teigan, Feb. 10, 1937, Teigan papers.

34. Lockhart to Petersen, Jan. 16, 19, 1937, and Harris to Petersen, Mar. 18, 1937, Petersen papers.

35. *Minneapolis Journal*, Apr. 14, 1937.

36. *Minneapolis Journal*, Feb. 27, 28, Mar. 13, 14, 15, 1937. Also Harry Levin, "Divided Front in Minnesota," *The Nation* (Oct. 2, 1937), 346-48.

37. See summons, petition, and order to show cause, dated Apr. 26, 1937, in Stageberg papers.

38. Farmer-Labor Association state committee minutes, May 1, 2, 1937.

39. Report of the Education Committee, Hennepin County Farmer-Labor Association, June 20, 1937, 5 pp. The report was signed by Hilliard Smith, Mrs. Alma Langseth, H. G. Finseth, Mrs. Alfred Carlson, Rubin Latz, Mrs. Al Joyner.

40. Teigan to Martin Teigan, June 30, 1937, Teigan papers.

41. Haycraft to Teigan, June 28, 1937, Teigan papers.

42. *Congressional Record*, May 8, 1936.

43. Teigan to Robert E. Gehan, Jan 23, 1937, Teigan papers.

44. Teigan statement, Apr. 3, 1937, Teigan papers.

45. Teigan to O. B. Grimley, Jan. 13, 1937, and Teigan to Jessica Smith, Oct. 10, 1937, Teigan papers.

46. *Minneapolis Journal*, Aug. 7, 8, 1937.

47. George F. Buresh to Williams, Jan. 6, 1937, and Williams to Buresh, Jan. 12, 1937, Williams papers.

48. Rockne to Williams, May 13, 1937, Williams papers.

49. McLeod to Petersen, May 13, 1937, Petersen papers.

50. Petersen to H. Z. Mitchell, June 5, 1937, Petersen papers.

51. Petersen to Dr. L. L. Sogge, June 1, 1937, Petersen papers.

52. James R. Bennett, Jr. to Farley, June 17, 1937, Petersen papers.

53. Bennett to John T. Lyons, June 19, 1937, and Bennett to Ernest Lundeen, June 19, 1937, Petersen papers.

54. *Minneapolis Star, St. Paul Daily News, Minneapolis Journal, St. Paul Dispatch*, all July 15, 1937. On their tax differences, see *St. Paul Pioneer Press, St. Paul Dispatch, St. Paul Daily News*, July 19, 20, 1937.

55. Elmer Davis, "Minnesota Worry-Go-Round," *Colliers* (June 24, 1937), 14-15, 41-42.

56. *Minneapolis Journal*, July 16, 1937.

57. State Committee minutes, Farmer-Labor Association, July 24, 1937, Stageberg papers.

58. Release, Aug. 3, 1937, in Petersen papers; see also *St. Paul Dispatch*, Aug. 3, 1937, and *Minneapolis Star*, Aug. 4, 1937.

59. McLeod to Petersen, Aug. 3, 1937, Petersen papers.

60. *Owatonna Journal-Chronicle*, July 6, 1937.

61. For Petersen's view of the September 9 meeting, see Petersen to Arthur M. Nelson, Oct. 9, 1937, and Petersen to Andrew Jensen, Nov. 1, 1937, Petersen papers. Also *Minneapolis Tribune*, Sept. 10, 1937; *Minneapolis Star*, Sept. 9, 10, 1937; *Minnesota Leader*, Sept. 18, 1937.

62. Petersen to the editor, *Minnesota Leader*, Sept. 20, 1937; Petersen to Harris, Sept. 20, 1937; Harris to Petersen, Sept. 23, 1937; all in the Petersen papers. *St. Paul Daily News*, Dec. 20, 1937; Petersen to Rev. John Flint, Dec. 23, 1937, and Flint to Petersen, Dec. 29, 1937, Petersen papers.

63. E. T. Ebbesen to Petersen, Dec. 24, 1937, Petersen papers. *Murray County Herald*, Dec. 30, 1937. For a more comprehensive analysis of anti-Semitism, see Hyman Berman, "Political Antisemitism in Minnesota during the Great Depression," *Jewish Social Studies*, 38 (1976), 247-64.

64. See Howard Y. Williams papers, Apr. 16, 1937.

65. Oscar F. Hawkins to Norman Thomas, Oct. 28, 1937, and Carl Pemble to Dear Friend (mimeo), Nov. 2, 1937, Hawkins papers.

66. *Minneapolis Journal*, Nov. 18, 19, 20, 22, Dec. 1, 8, 9, 1937. For a summary of the CIO charges against the AFL and the Dunnes, see the *CIO Industrial Unionist*, 1, no. 1 (Dec. 1, 1937).

67. Rockne to Petersen, Dec. 24, 1937, Petersen papers.

68. *Minneapolis Journal*, Jan. 9, 10, 12, 1938; the initial report gave only one dissenting vote, but this was corrected several days later.

69. *Minneapolis Star*, Jan. 14, 1938; *St. Paul Pioneer Press*, Jan. 29, 1938.

70. McLeod to Petersen, Jan. 5, 1937 [sic 1938], and George Strandvold to Petersen, Jan. 6, 1938, Petersen papers.

71. The original speech is in the Petersen papers, dated Jan. 18, 1938. See also *Minneapolis Journal, Minneapolis Star, St. Paul Daily News, St. Paul Dispatch*, Jan. 17, 1938; *Minneapolis Journal, Minneapolis Star, Minneapolis Tribune, St. Paul Pioneer Press, St. Paul Daily News*, Jan. 18, 1938.

72. *Minnesota Leader*, Jan. 23, 1938; McLeod to Petersen, Jan. 19, 1938, Petersen papers.

73. *Northwest Organizer*, Jan. 27, 1938.

74. *St. Paul Pioneer Press*, Jan. 30, 1938.

75. *Minneapolis Journal*, Feb. 6, 1938, *Northwest Communist*, 1, no. 1 (Feb. 1938).

76. *St. Paul Pioneer Press*, Feb. 13, 1938.

77. Clint W. Lovely to Teigan, Dec. 1, 1937, and Teigan to Abe Harris, Dec. 6, 1937, Teigan papers.

78. *Minneapolis Journal*, Feb. 21, 1938; Madge Hawkins to the *Journal*, Mrs. Charles Lundquist to the *Journal*, Mar. 7, 1938.

79. *St. Paul Pioneer Press*, Mar. 4, 1938; *Minneapolis Journal*, Mar. 4, 1938.

80. *Minneapolis Journal*, Mar. 7, 1938.

81. *Ibid.*, Feb. 28, Mar. 3, Mar. 14, 1938.

82. *St. Paul Pioneer Press*, Mar. 19, 1938.

83. *Minneapolis Journal*, Mar. 24, 1938; *St. Paul Pioneer Press*, Mar. 24, 1938.

84. *Minneapolis Journal*, Mar. 24, 1938, p. 8 for full text; *St. Paul Pioneer Press*, Mar. 25, 26, 1938.

85. *St. Paul Pioneer Press*, Mar. 26, 1938.

86. *Minneapolis Journal*, Mar. 27, 1938, p. 4, for text; *St. Paul Pioneer Press*, Mar. 27, 1938, p. 8 for text. *Minneapolis Tribune*, Mar. 27, 1938, p. 9 for platform.

87. Teigan to A. Stephen, Apr. 5, 1938, and Teigan to Arthur Jacobs, Apr. 6, 1938, Teigan papers.

88. Bridgeman to Petersen, Apr. 4, 1938, and Petersen to Bridgeman, Apr. 5, 1938, Petersen papers.

89. Meighen to W. A. Campbell, Feb. 26, 1938; Meighen to G. W. Comstock, Mar. 4, 1937; Meighen wire to James A. Farley, May 27, 1937; Meighen to Farley, May 23, 1937; all in the Meighen papers. Meighen to Francis M. Smith, Jan. 4, 1938, Smith papers.

90. Francis M. Smith to Joseph N. Moonan, Apr. 1, 1938, Smith papers.

91. For reports that Roosevelt was dropping support for Benson see *St. Paul Pioneer Press*, May 11, 1938; *St. Paul Dispatch*, May 11, 1938; *Minneapolis Journal*, May 11, 1938. Teigan to A. N. Jacobs, May 14, 1938, Teigan papers, disputes this. Benson has always maintained that Roosevelt also worked for his defeat, both before and after the primaries.

92. *St. Paul Pioneer Press*, Apr. 28, 1938.

93. James H. Murphy to Petersen, Apr. 7, 1938, Petersen papers.

94. Peterson to H. E. Rasmussen, Apr. 5, 1938, Petersen papers.

95. Johnston to Teigan, May 19, 1938, Teigan papers.

96. The Davis radio address was over WCCO, WEBC, KROC, May 24, 1938, copy in Petersen papers.

97. "The Sinister Menace of Communism to Christianity" by Luke Rader, undated; see Hawkins papers.

98. Benson interview with the author, Feb. 22, 1966.

99. *Minneapolis Tribune*, June 9, 1938; *Minneapolis Star*, June 10, 1938; see p. 6 for headline.

100. McLeod to Petersen, July 18, 1938, Petersen papers.

101. Wittich to Petersen, June 24, 1938, Petersen papers.

102. See July 1, 1938, statement in Petersen papers; also *Minneapolis Journal*, July 1, 1938.

103. McLeod to Petersen, July 14, 1938, Petersen papers.

104. Lockhart to Petersen, Aug. 11, 1938, Petersen papers.

105. *Minneapolis Journal*, July 26, 1938.

106. *St. Paul Pioneer Press*, Aug. 16, 1938; *Minneapolis Star*, Aug. 15, 1938.

107. Petersen to McLeod, Aug. 30, 1938, Petersen papers.

108. Petersen to McLeod, Sept. 19, 1938, Petersen papers.

109. *Minneapolis Journal*, Sept. 21, 1938.

110. Svend Petersen to Hjalmar Petersen, Sept. 22, 1938, and Rockne to Petersen, Sept. 23, 1938, Petersen papers.

111. Release in Petersen papers, Sept. 27, 1938; see also *Minneapolis Journal*, Sept. 27, 1938.

112. McLeod to Petersen, undated, Petersen papers.

113. Robert Greenberg to Teigan, June 1, 1938, Teigan papers.

114. Unsigned memorandum, July 28, 1938, Teigan papers.

115. Teigan to Corcoran, Aug. 12, 1938, Teigan papers.

116. For complete text, see *Minneapolis Journal*, Sept. 21, 1938, p. 10.

117. Samuel Scheiner to Elmer Benson, Dec. 27, 1943, Benson papers.

118. Henry Teigan to (Mrs.) Essie Teigan, Aug. 12, 1937, Teigan papers.

119. *New Masses*, Sept. 6, 1938, pp. 8-10, "Benson of Minnesota."

120. *Minneapolis Journal*, Oct. 10, 1938.

121. *Minneapolis Journal*, Oct. 17, 23, 24, 25, 1938.

122. Oscar Hawkins papers, Oct. 26, 1938.

123. *Minneapolis Journal*, Oct. 14, 1938.

CHAPTER 10

1. Teigan to William C. Lee, Nov. 14, 1938, Teigan papers.

2. W. H. Dempsey to J. F. D. Meighen, June 6, 1938; Meighen diary, May 13, 1938.

3. Halsted to Petersen, Nov. 28, 1938, Petersen papers; Petersen release, Nov. 9, 1938, Petersen papers; Day to Roosevelt, Jan. 18, 1939, Day papers; Williams to William Lauder, Nov. 10, 1938, and Williams to Ethel Clyde, Nov. 14, 1938, Williams papers. Philip La Follette, "Why We Lost," *The Nation*, Dec. 3, 1938.

4. A. I. Harris, "The Reviewing Stand," *Minnesota Leader*, Jan. 7, 1939.

5. "Harold" to Petersen, Nov. 15, 1938, Petersen papers. Also undated personal memorandum by Petersen (5 pp., 1939) and Petersen to Stassen, May 10, 1943 (but Petersen did not send the letter), Petersen papers.

6. Petersen to Magnus Johnson, Jr., Feb. 7, 1938, Petersen papers.

7. Teigan to Martin Teigan, Dec. 5, 1938, Teigan papers.

8. Farmer-Labor state committee minutes, Dec. 3, 1938.

9. Undated memorandum, (ca. Dec. 1938); also open letter to association members, Dec. 17, 1938; Lommen et al. to friends, Dec. 18, 1938; all in the Stageberg papers.

10. "Machine Politics and Tactics," 2 pp., in the Hawkins papers; and undated résumé in defense of the Hennepin left wing (ca. Feb. 1939). Minutes of the Hennepin county convention, Dec. 18, 1938, Stageberg papers; *Minneapolis Journal*, Dec. 19, 1938.

11. Teigan to Alfred M. Bingham, Jan. 31, 1939, Teigan papers.

12. *Minneapolis Journal*, Jan. 27, 28, 29, 1939. *Minneapolis Tribune*, Jan. 26, 27, 28, 29, 1939.

13. Stenographic record of the Jan. 31, 1939, meeting, 74 pp., in the Stageberg papers.

14. Stenographic record of the Hennepin Farmer-Labor Association meeting, Mar. 22, 1939, 34 pp., in the Stageberg papers.

15. For example, see the *Minneapolis Journal*, Apr. 16, 1939; Apr. 19, 1939 (p. 3 for the program).

16. "Information," Feb. 18, 1939, published by Minnesota Legislative Research Bureau, St. Paul; also Oct. 27, 1939, Nov. 10, 1939, and Nov. 17, 1939, in the Petersen papers.

17. Schilplin to Petersen, Jan. 25, 1939, Nov. 10, 1940, Petersen papers.

18. Petersen to Rev. John Flint, Mar. 30, 1939, and Petersen to McLeod, Mar. 31, 1939, Petersen papers; editorial in *Askov American*, Apr. 6, 1939.

19. *Minneapolis Journal*, Apr. 16, 1939.

20. *Ibid.*, June 19, 1939; *St. Paul Pioneer Press*, June 19, 1939.

21. Williams to LIPA members, Oct. 5, 1939.

22. Petersen to John R. Foley, July 22, 1939, and R. E. Casey to Petersen, Oct. 15, 1939, Petersen papers.

23. Midwest Research Reports, vol. 1, no. 1, Jan. 31, 1940, Feb. 5, 1940, in Petersen papers and Stageberg papers. Founded by Dr. C. R. Wasson, MRR served as a fledgling survey organization.

24. Farmer-Labor Association membership, 1937-38, see Farmer-Labor Association papers; "Report of membership . . .," Mar. 1, 1941, Farmer-Labor Association papers.

25. Petersen to Samuel B. Wilson, Dec. 27, 1940, Petersen papers.

26. Wright to Petersen, Jan. 25, 1940, and Petersen to Wright, Jan. 30, 1940, Petersen papers.

27. Barsness to Petersen, Feb. 9, 1940; Hagen to Petersen, Feb. 21, 1940; John R. Foley to Petersen, Feb. 28, 1940; in the Petersen papers.

28. Resolution, Hennepin County convention, Feb. 19, 1940; Hennepin County central committee minutes, Feb. 29, 1940; in the Stageberg papers.

29. Report of the credentials committee, state convention, Rochester, March, 1940, and Harold Peterson to Archie Ogg, Feb. 26, 1940, Farmer-Labor Association papers.

30. Frank Chelsoake to Harold Peterson, Mar. 3, 1940, Farmer-Labor Association papers.

31. Carr to Peterson, Mar. 5, 1940, Farmer-Labor Association papers.

32. *Minneapolis Star-Journal*, Mar. 8, 9, 1940; *Minneapolis Tribune*, Mar. 8, 9, 10, 1940.

33. *St. Paul Union Advocate*, May 23, 1940.

34. *Mankato Free Press, Austin Daily Herold*, June 17, 1940.

35. Minneapolis *Star-Journal*, June 22, 1940.

36. *St. Paul Pioneer Press*, June 23, 1940. Ogg to Peterson, Jan. 3, 1940, Farmer-Labor Association papers.

37. For general coverage, see *Minneapolis Tribune*, June 21, 22, 1940; *St. Paul Pioneer Press*, June 21, 22, 23, 1940; and *Minneapolis Star-Journal*, June 21, 22, 1940.

38. *Minnesota Leader*, June 15, July 15, July 30, Aug. 30, 1940.

39. See keynote address of A. E. Borchard on July 28, 1940, Stageberg papers.

40. *Minnesota Leader*, July 30, 1940 (actually printed in mid-August).

41. *Minneapolis Star-Journal*, Aug. 23, 1940.

42. Paul Rasmussen to Steve Lush, May 7, 1940, Shipstead papers.

43. *Ibid.*, Aug. 20, 1940, and Aug. 29, 1940.

44. George Hagen to Petersen, Sept. 26, 1940, Petersen papers.

45. Egley to Petersen, Sept. 16, 1940; Petersen to Egley, Sept. 23, 1940; Stageberg to Petersen, Sept. 16, 1940; all in the Petersen papers.

46. Aufderheide to Petersen, Sept. 21, 1940, Petersen papers.

47. Hagen to Petersen, Sept. 26, 1940, Petersen.

48. *St. Paul Pioneer Press*, Sept. 20, 1940; *Minneapolis Star-Journal*, Sept. 22, 25, 1940.

49. *St. Paul Pioneer Press*, Sept. 28, 30, Oct. 2, 1940; *Minnesota Leader*, Oct. 15, 1940; *Minneapolis Star-Journal*, Sept. 30, 1940.

50. *Minneapolis Star-Journal*, Oct. 4, 1940.

51. *St. Paul Pioneer Press*, Oct. 3, 1940; *Minneapolis Star-Journal*, Oct. 6, 1940.

52. Petersen radio address, WLOL, Nov. 11, 1940, Petersen to Gallup, Nov. 13, 1940. Petersen to Ridder, et al., Nov. 16, 1940; Ridder to Petersen, Nov. 18, 1940. Robert Allen to Petersen, Nov. 29, 1940; all in the Petersen papers.

53. *Minneapolis Star-Journal*, Oct. 20, 1940, for Willkie statement. Ryan to Shipstead, Oct. 2, 1940; Shipstead to Ryan, Oct. 5, 1940; wire (unsigned) to Shipstead, Oct. 17, 1940; all in the Shipstead papers.

54. Petersen to Philip F. La Follette, Dec. 24, 1940; Petersen to J. P. Coughlin, Dec. 30, 1940; Petersen to Geo. Hagen, Dec. 30, 1940, all in the Petersen papers.

55. Hagen to Petersen, Dec. 31, 1940, Petersen papers.

56. John F. D. Meighen to John P. Devaney, Nov. 14, 1940, Meighen papers.

57. Hawkins to Dear Folks, Sept. 7, 1939, Hawkins papers.

58. Hawkins to Dear Folks, Jan 19, 1940, Hawkins papers.

59. Hawkins to Dear Folks, Apr. 19, 1940, Hawkins papers.

60. *Minneapolis Tribune*, Feb. 1, 1941; *St. Paul Pioneer Press*, Feb. 1, 1941; *Minnesota Leader*, Feb. 1941. Farmer-Labor Association convention, minutes, Jan. 30, 31, 1941, Farmer-Labor Association papers.

61. Mahoney release, Feb. 24, 1941, Mahoney papers.

62. Slonin to Mahoney, Feb. 3, 1941, Mahoney papers.

63. Petersen address, WCCO, Mar. 9, 1941, Petersen papers.

64. America First Committee letter, Sept. 25, 1941; Knutson to Petersen, Oct. 17, 1941; Shipstead to Petersen, Oct. 18, 1941; all in the Petersen papers. For Petersen speeches, see Nov. 1941 Petersen papers.

65. Petersen to Marie T. Magree, Mar. 12, 1941, and Petersen to Walter Mickelson, Mar. 12, 1941, Petersen papers.

66. Undated *Minneapolis Tribune* clipping, by Orlin Folwick, in the Lommen papers.

67. Harris to Benson, Feb. 18, 1941, Benson papers.

68. Harris to Benson, July 15, 1941, Benson papers.

69. Harris to Benson, July 21, 1941, Benson papers.

70. Benson to Harris, Aug. 13, 1941; Harris to Benson, Aug. 18, 1941. Benson to Charles Yagoda, Aug. 23, 1941; all in the Benson papers.

71. *Minnesota Leader*, Oct. 1941, editorial.

72. Williams to Dear Jibby, Nov. 22, 1941, Williams papers.

73. See Dale Kramer, "The Dunne Boys of Minneapolis," *Harpers Magazine*, Mar. 1942, pp. 388-89.

74. Munn to Benson, Mar. 31, 1941; and Petersen to E. T. Ebbesen, Apr. 3, 1941, Petersen papers. *Minnesota Leader*, Mar. 1941.

75. Williams to Civil Service Commission, undated draft, 1941; Williams to Dear Ones, July 16, 1941; William C. Hull to Williams, Oct. 10, 1941; all in the Williams papers.

76. *Albert Lea Tribune*, Apr. 19, 1942; press release of Oscar R. Ewing, Feb. 25, 1942, Meighen papers.

77. Benson to Roosevelt, May 15, 1941, Benson papers.

78. Roosevelt to Benson, July 14, 1941, and Benson to Rutchick, July 18, 1941, Benson papers.

79. Benson to Williams, Oct. 30, 1941, Benson papers.

80. Meighen to Devaney, Nov. 16, 1940, Meighen papers.

81. Meighen address, Mar. 19, 1942; Henry Gallagher to Meighen, Mar. 23, 1942; Meighen to R. E. Sperry, Mar. 26, 1942; all in the Meighen papers.

82. *St. Cloud Daily Times*, July 15, 1942, p. 8; Meighen to Schilplin, July 6, 1942, Meighen papers.

CHAPTER 11

1. *St. Paul Pioneer Press*, July 23, 1942.

2. *St. Paul Pioneer Press*, Feb. 4, 1941.

3. *Information*, published by George N. Briggs, no. 54, Apr. 7, 1941, in Petersen papers; *Information*, no 55, Apr. 28, 1941, in Benson papers.

4. *Duluth Tribune*, Apr. 2, 1941; copy of Lommen speech in Shipstead papers, Teigan papers; *Caledonia Argus*, Apr. 11, 1941. For Stassen's answer, see Stassen to Lommen, Apr. 2, 1941, mimeo, Teigan papers.

5. Loeb to Williams, May 5, 1942, Williams papers. Amlie to Williams, Apr. 13, 1942; Amlie to Loeb, May 10, 1942; Amlie to Williams, May 23, 1942; Williams to Kingdon and Loeb, July 31, 1942; all in the Williams papers. See also *The New Republic*, May 18, 1942, a special issue prepared jointly by the UDA and the magazine.

6. *Minneapolis Star-Journal*, Apr. 22, 1942; also Dec. 6, 1941.

7. Petersen to Edward E. Barsness, Apr. 25, 1942, Petersen papers. *St. Paul Dispatch*, May 15, 1942.

8. *Mankato Free Press*, Apr. 22, 1942. Hagen to Petersen, May 14, 1942, Petersen papers. *Minneapolis Star-Journal*, Dec. 12, 1941.

9. Petersen to Stassen, Mar. 14, 1942, mimeo and Stassen to Petersen, Mar. 14, 1942, Petersen papers.

10. Mimeo copy of Apr. 1, 1942, broadcast, in Petersen papers. Andresen to Petersen, Apr. 6, 1942, Petersen papers.

11. Petersen to Dr. J. L. McLeod, Apr. 28, 1941, Petersen papers.

12. *Minneapolis Tribune*, Feb. 17, 1942; Benson to M. W. Thatcher, Feb. 18, 1942, Benson papers; *Tribune*, Feb. 22, 1942.

13. Lommen to Benson, Mar. 13, 1942, Benson papers.

14. Farmer-Labor Association state central committee minutes, Apr. 12, 1942, 12 pp., in Farmer-Labor Association papers and Stageberg papers.

15. Farmer-Labor Association central committee minutes, Apr. 12, 1942, in Farmer-Labor Association papers and Stageberg papers.

16. *Minneapolis Tribune*, May 27, 28, 29, 30, 1942; *St. Paul Pioneer Press*, May 27, 28, 29, 30, 31, 1942.

17. Williams to UDA, Frank Kingdon, James Loeb, May 31, 1942, Williams papers.

18. Elmer E. Adams to Petersen, June 3, 1942, Petersen papers.

19. *Minneapolis Tribune*, May 25, 1942.

20. Petersen to A. A. Kranhold, July 31, 1942; Petersen to Fay Cravens, August 13, 1942; Petersen to Harold Atwood, Aug. 15, 1942; all in the Petersen papers.

21. Williams to Kingdon and Loeb, June 15, 1942, Williams papers.

22. John F. D. Meighen diary, June 29, 1942, in Meighen papers.

23. *Minneapolis Tribune*, June 28, 29, 1942; *Minneapolis Star-Journal*, June 29, 1942; *St. Paul Pioneer Press*, June 28, 1942.

24. Williams to Kingdon and Loeb, July 7, 1942, Williams papers. Petersen wire to Lyons, June 28, 1942, Petersen papers.

25. *Minneapolis Labor Review*, July 3, 1942.

26. *Minnesota Union Advocate*, July 9, 1942; also *Minneapolis Tribune*, July 3, 1942.

27. *Minneapolis Tribune*, July 29, 30, 31, 1942; *Minneapolis Star-Journal*, July 29, 30, 31, 1942. Farmer-Labor Association central committee minutes, July 26, 1942; on this date the left still believed Peterson would run.

28. Williams to Kingdon and Loeb, July 31, 1942, Williams papers.

29. Williams to Kingdon and Loeb, Aug. 7, 21, 1942, Williams papers.

30. Farmer-Labor Association central committee minutes, July 26, 1942, Farmer-Labor Association papers.

31. For a copy of the Tinge speech, Sept. 4, 1942, see Petersen papers.

32. See Petersen papers, Sept. 5, 1942, for copy of speech; also Petersen to Arens, Sept. 15, 1942.

33. Minutes, Farmer-Labor party, Sept. 17, 22, 1942, Farmer-Labor Association papers. Petersen papers.

34. Benson to H. O. Berve, Sept. 17, 1942, Benson papers.

35. Farmer-Labor Association central committee minutes, Sept. 20, 1942, Farmer-Labor Association papers.

36. Henry Spindler to Petersen, Sept. 27, 1942, and Evelyn Petersen to Otto Baudler, Oct. 19, 1942, Petersen papers.

37. Paul R. Tinge to David Dubinsky, Oct. 24, 1942, Benson papers.

38. See Oct. 9, 17, 23, 31, Nov. 2, 1942, statewide radio address, in Petersen papers.

39. Vince Day to Petersen, Oct. 29, 1942, also Nov. 18, 1942, Petersen papers; Day to Benson, Oct. 29, 1942, Benson papers.

40. See Report on Finances, Farmer-Labor Association, 1942, and Secretary-Treasurer's Report, June 1942, Farmer-Labor Association papers.

41. Petersen to Art. W. Conaway, Nov. 9, 1942; Petersen to Henry Spindler, Nov. 10, 1942; Petersen to O. A. Kirtland, Nov. 21, 1942; Petersen to Edward A. Day, Dec. 3, 1942; Petersen to George Hagen, Dec. 12, 1942; all in the Petersen papers.

42. Harold C. Hagen, Dec. 18, 1942, and Petersen to J. L. McLeod, Dec. 22, 1942, Petersen papers.

43. Farmer-Labor Association central committee minutes, Dec. 6, 1942, Farmer-Labor Association papers.

44. Benson to Viena Johnson, Nov. 5, 6, 1942, Benson papers.

45. Benson to Roosevelt, Nov. 6, 1942, Benson papers.

46. Benson to National Federation for Constitutional Liberties, Dec. 29, 1942; see also Benson to Howard Williams, Dec. 5, 1942, Williams papers.

47. UDA suspicion of communist motives can be seen in the dissolution of the Comintern; see Loeb to Williams, May 29, 1943, Williams papers.

48. Amlie to Williams, Sept. 28, 1942; Loeb to Williams, Oct. 5, 12, 1942; Loeb to Williams, May 29, 1943; all in the Williams papers. Williams to Dear Ones, Nov. 23, 1942, Williams papers.

49. Benson to Charles Cheney, Mar. 11, 1942, and Cheney to Benson, Mar. 16, 1942, Benson papers.

50. Viena Johnson to Henry Wallace, Dec. 10, 1942; Viena Johnston to Erickson, Dec. 10, 1942; Wallace to Johnson, Dec. 17, 1942; John P. Erickson to Johnson, Feb. 12, 1943; all in the Farmer-Labor Association papers.

51. Williams to family, Feb. 10, 1943, Williams papers.

52. *Minneapolis Tribune*, Feb. 21, 22, 1943; convention minutes, 33 pp., Farmer-Labor Association papers.

53. Viena Johnson to Harold Hagen, Feb. 15, 1943; resolution, Feb. 21, 1943; Viena Johnson to state central committee, Feb. 16, 1943; all in the Farmer-Labor Association papers.

54. Executive Committee, Farmer-Labor Association to Dear Friend, Mar. 5, 1943, Hawkins papers. Committee of 50 to Dear Friend, Feb. 17, 1943, Farmer-Labor Association papers.

55. *Minneapolis Tribune*, Mar. 14, 1943.

56. *Ibid.*, Mar. 7, 1943 (Gallup Poll).

57. *St. Paul Pioneer Press*, Mar. 11, 1943.

58. *Ibid.*, Mar. 28, 1943; *Minneapolis Tribune*, Mar. 28, 30, 1943.

59. The Constitution of the Farmer-Labor party of Minnesota and Statement of Principles, dated Mar. 27, 1943, Francis M. Smith papers.

60. Copy in the Mahoney papers.

61. Mahoney to Petersen, May 27, 1943, Mahoney papers.

62. Viena Johnston to J. W. Huhtala, Apr. 27, 1943; Farmer-Labor Association papers; *Virginia Times-Tribune*, Apr. 21, 1943.

63. *St. Paul Pioneer Press*, May 9, 13, 14, 1943.

64. *Minneapolis Tribune*, May 2, 7, 9, 11, 1943; June 18, 1943. *Minneapolis Star-Journal*, June 10, 11, 12, 15, 1943.

65. Farmer-Labor Association state committee minutes, June 27, 1943; Viena Johnson letter to state committee, June 21, 1943, mimeo; Viena Johnson to Rudy Rautio, July 12, 1943; all in the Farmer-Labor Association papers.

66. *St. Paul Pioneer Press*, July 15, 16, 1943.

67. "Legal aspects in Minnesota of attempted political coalitions fusions or the merger of political parties and more especially of the changing of names of political parties and the assumption of a name by one political party relinquished by another." Aug. 5, 1943, Francis M. Smith papers.

68. *St. Paul Pioneer Press*, Aug. 8, 1943; *Minneapolis Tribune*, Aug. 8, 1943.

69. *St. Paul Pioneer Press*, Aug. 11, 1943.

70. Benson to Ewing, Aug. 26, 1943, and Benson to Walker, Aug. 26, 1943, Benson papers.

71. Walker to Benson, Sept. 4, 1943, Benson papers.

72. Viena Johnson to members of the Farmer-Labor Association state committee, undated, (Sept. 1943), Farmer-Labor Association papers. See also *Minneapolis Tribune*, Sept. 25, 1943.

73. Farmer-Labor Association state committee minutes, Sept. 26, 1943, Farmer-Labor Association papers; *Minneapolis Tribune*, Sept. 27, 1943.

74. See Viena Johnson press release, Oct. 6, 1943, Farmer-Labor Association papers; *Minneapolis Tribune*, Oct. 8, 1943.

75. Hoidale to Hjalmar Petersen, Sept. 4, 1943, Petersen papers.

76. McDonough to Franklin Roosevelt, Sept. 7, 1943, Petersen papers.

77. Walker to Benson, Nov. 5, 1943, and Ewing to Benson, Nov. 5, 1943, Benson papers.

78. Ewing to Benson, Nov. 29, 1943, Benson papers.

79. Kelm to Benson, Tinge, Nov. 26, 1943, Benson papers.

80. *Minneapolis Tribune*, Nov. 28, 1943.

81. Smith to Ewing, Dec. 4, 1943, Smith papers.

82. *Minneapolis Tribune*, Dec. 14, 1943; *Minneapolis Star-Journal*, Dec. 13, 1943.

83. Tinge and Benson to Kelm, Jan. 7, 1944, Benson papers.

84. Benson to Roosevelt, Feb. 5, 1944, Benson papers.

85. *Minneapolis Tribune*, Feb. 15, 1944; *Minneapolis Star-Journal*, Feb. 14, 15, 1944.

86. "Resolution for the Amalgamation of the Liberal Forces in Minnesota in a Farmer-Labor-Democratic Party to Win the War and the Peace," Feb. 14, 1944, Smith papers.

87. *Minneapolis Tribune*, Feb. 15, 1944.

88. *Ibid.*, Feb. 6, 22, 23, 1944; *Minneapolis Star-Journal*, Feb. 22, 1944.

89. *Minneapolis Star-Journal*, Feb. 14, 15, 1944; *Minneapolis Tribune*, Feb. 11, Mar. 1, 1944.

90. "Minnesota Legal Aspects of Proposed Change of Names of Farmer-Labor Party and of the Democratic Party," by Roger S. Rutchick and Francis M. Smith of the Minnesota bar," Feb. 21, 1944, Smith papers.

91. *Minneapolis Star-Journal*, Mar. 2, 1944.

92. *Minneapolis Tribune*, Mar. 6, 1944; *Minneapolis Star-Journal*, Mar. 6, 1944; *St. Paul Pioneer Press*, Mar. 6, 1944.

93. Petersen to Walter Mickelson, Feb. 16, 1944, Petersen papers.

94. Press release, Apr. 1, 1944, Mahoney papers.

95. *Minneapolis Tribune*, Feb. 20, 1944.

96. Quoted in the *St. Paul Pioneer Press*, Apr. 9, 1944.

97. Susie Stageberg to (probably) Viena Johnson, Mar. 7, 1944, Farmer-Labor Association papers.

98. Wallace to Benson, Mar. 14, 1944; Benson to Roosevelt, Mar. 8, 1944, Benson papers.

Bibliography and References

Selected Bibliography

Backstrom, Charles H. "The Progressive Party of Wisconsin, 1934-46." Ph.D. dissertation, University of Wisconsin, 1956.

Bahmer, Robert H. "The Economic and Political Background of the Nonpartisan League." Ph.D. dissertation, University of Minnesota, 1941.

Berger, Kenneth L. "A Rhetorical Analysis of the Public Speaking of Floyd B. Olson." Ph.D. dissertation, University of Minnesota, 1955.

Blackorby, Edward C. *Prairie Rebel; the Public Life of William Lemke*. Lincoln, 1963.

Blegen, Theodore. *Minnesota: A History of the State*. Minneapolis, 1975.

Burnham, Walter Dean. *Critical Elections and the Mainsprings of American Politics*. New York, 1970.

Chrislock, Carl H. "The Politics of Protest in Minnesota, 1890-1901, from Populism to Progressivism." Ph.D. dissertation, University of Minnesota, 1955.

————. *The Progressive Era in Minnesota, 1899-1918*. St. Paul, 1971.

Douglas, Paul H. *The Coming of a New Party*. New York and London, 1932.

Epstein, Leon D. *Politics in Wisconsin*. Madison, 1958.

Fenton, John H. *Midwest Politics*, New York, 1966.

Garlid, George W. "Politics In Minnesota and American Foreign Relations, 1921-1941." Ph.D. dissertation, University of Minnesota, 1976.

Gaston, Herbert E. *The Non-Partisan League*. New York, 1920.

Gieske, Millard L. "The Politics of Knute Nelson, 1912-1920." Ph.D. dissertation, University of Minnesota, 1965.

Haynes, John Earl. "Liberals, Communists, and the Popular Front in Minnesota: The Struggle to Control the Political Direction of the Labor Movement and Organized Liberalism, 1936-1950." Ph.D. dissertation, University of Minnesota, 1978.

Hicks, John D. *The Populist Revolt: A History of the Farmers' Alliance and the People's Party*. Minneapolis, 1931.

Hinderaker, Ivan H. "Harold Stassen and Developments in the Republican Party in Minnesota, 1937-1943." Ph.D. dissertation, University of Minnesota, 1949.

Holbrook, Franklin F., and Appel, Livia. *Minnesota in the War with Germany*. 2 vols. St. Paul, 1928-32.

Jenson, Carol E. "Agrarian Pioneer in Civil Liberties: The Nonpartisan League in Minnesota during World War I." Ph.D. dissertation, University of Minnesota, 1968.

La Follette, Belle Case, and La Follette, Fola. *Robert M. La Follette: June 14, 1855-June 18, 1925.* 2 vols. New York, 1953.

Larson, Bruce L. *Lindbergh of Minnesota. A Political Biography.* New York, 1973.

Lorentz, Sr. Mary Rene. "Henrik Shipstead: Minnesota Independent, 1923-1946." Ph.D. dissertation, Catholic University of America, 1963.

McCoy, Donald R. *Angry Voices; Left-of-Center Politics in the New Deal Era.* Lawrence, Kansas, 1958.

McGrath, John S., and Delmont, James J. *Floyd Bjornsterne Olson: Minnesota's Greatest Liberal Governor.* St. Paul, 1937.

McHenry, Dean E. *The Third Force in Canada: The Cooperative Commonwealth Federation, 1932-1948.* Berkeley, 1950.

Manahan, James. *Trials of a Lawyer.* Minneapolis, 1933.

Mayer, George H. *The Political Career of Floyd B. Olson.* Minneapolis, 1951.

Morlan, Robert L. *Political Prairie Fire; The Nonpartisan League, 1915-1922.* Minneapolis, 1955.

Naftalin, Arthur. "A History of the Farmer-Labor Party of Minnesota." Ph.D. dissertation, University of Minnesota, 1948.

Nye, Russell B. *Midwestern Progressive Politics: A Historical Study of Its Origins and Development, 1870-1958.* New York, 1965.

Pinard, Maurice. *The Rise of a Third Party: A Study in Crisis Politics.* Montreal and London, 1975.

Ross, Martin. *Shipstead of Minnesota.* Chicago, 1940.

Rude, Leslie Gene, "A Rhetorical Analysis of the Minnesota Farmer-Labor Movement." Ph.D. dissertation, University of Illinois, 1962.

Saloutos, Theodore, and Hicks, John D. *Agricultural Discontent in the Middle West, 1900-1939.* Madison, 1951.

Shideler, James H. *Farm Crisis: 1919-1968.* Berkeley, 1957.

Shover, John L. *Cornbelt Rebellion: The Farmers' Holiday Association.* Urbana, 1965.

Stephenson, George M. *John Lind of Minnesota.* Minneapolis, 1935.

Stuhler, Barbara. *Ten Men of Minnesota and American Foreign Policy, 1898-1968.* St. Paul, 1973.

Sundquist, James L. *Dynamics of the American Party System. Alighment and Realignment of Political Parties in the United States.* Washington, 1973.

Reference Sources

MANUSCRIPT COLLECTIONS IN
THE MINNESOTA HISTORICAL SOCIETY

Herman Aufderheide papers
Elmer A. Benson papers and interviews
John T. Bernard papers
Richard T. Buckler papers
Joseph A. A. Burnquist papers
Ray P. Chase papers
Citizens Alliance papers
Committee of 48 papers
Vincent Day papers
Democratic-Farmer-Labor party papers
Benjamin Drake papers
Duluth Federated Trades and Labor Assembly papers
Farmer-Labor Association papers
Walter M. Frank papers
Joseph Gilbert papers
Harold C. Hagen papers
E. George Hall papers
Clarence A. Hathaway papers
Oscar F. Hawkins papers
Hubert H. Humphrey papers
Iron Range Industrial Union Council papers
John M. Jacobsen papers
Jewish Community Relations Council of Minnesota papers
Magnus Johnson papers
Frank B. Kellogg papers
Stafford King papers
Ole J. Kvale papers
Richard Leekley papers
Arthur LeSueur papers
John Lind papers
Charles A. Lindbergh papers
George H. Lommen scrapbook

Clinton W. Lovely papers
John J. McDonough scrapbook
William Mahoney papers
James Manahan papers
John F. D. Meighen papers
Thomas J. Meighen papers
Minneapolis Central Labor Union Council papers
Minnesota Commission on Public Safety papers
National Nonpartisan League papers
Knute Nelson papers
Floyd B. Olson papers
Charles N. Orr papers
Hjalmar A. Petersen papers
Hjalmar O. Peterson papers
Victor L. Power papers
Jacob A. O. Preus papers
Prohibition party papers
Herman Roe papers
St. Paul Trades and Labor Assembly papers
Thomas D. Schall papers
Henrik Shipstead papers
Francis M. Smith papers
Socialist Workers party papers
Jean E. Spielman papers
Susie W. Stageberg papers
Irwin C. Strout papers
Henry G. Teigan papers
Arthur C. Townley interview
Andrew J. Volstead papers
Knud Wefald papers
Roy W. Wier papers
Howard Y. Williams papers

NEWSPAPERS

Anoka Herald
Appleton Press
Askov American
Bemidji Northland Times
Communist Daily Worker
Duluth Herald
Duluth Labor World
Duluth News Tribune
Fargo Daily Courier-News
Fargo Forum
Farmer-Labor Advocate
Farmer-Labor Leader
Hibbing Tribune
Mankato Free Press
Mesaba Miner
Midwest Labor
Minneapolis Journal
Minneapolis Labor Review
Minneapolis Star
Minneapolis Tribune
Minnesota Leader

Minnesota Star
Minnesota Union Advocate
Minot Daily News
Montevideo News
New York Times
Nonpartisan Leader
Park Region Echo
Rochester Post-Bulletin
Roseau Leader
Russell Anchor
St. Cloud Times
St. Paul Daily News
St. Paul Dispatch
St. Paul Pioneer Press
St. Paul Union Advocate
Swift County Monitor
Swift County News
Virginia Enterpirse
Ward County (North Dakota) Independent
Willmar Tribune
Worthington Globe

Index

Index

369